Virtuous War

Virtuous War is the first book to map the emergence and judge the consequences of a new military-industrial-media-entertainment network. James Der Derian takes the reader from a family history of war and genocide to new virtual battlespaces in the Mojave Desert, Silicon Valley, Hollywood, and American universities. He tracks the convergence of cyborg technologies, video games, media spectacles, war movies, and do-good ideologies that produced a chimera of high-tech, low-risk "virtuous wars."

In this newly updated edition, he reveals how a misguided faith in virtuous war to right the wrongs of the world instead paved the way for a flawed response to 9/11 and a disastrous war in Iraq. Blinded by virtue, emboldened by technological superiority, seized by a mimetic terror, the U.S. blundered from one foreign fiasco to the next.

Taking the long view as well as getting up close to the war machine, *Virtuous War* provides a compelling alternative to the partisan politics, instant analysis, and technical fixes that currently bedevil U.S. national security policy.

James Der Derian is Research Professor of International Studies at Brown University, where he directs the Innovating Global Security and Global Media Project at the Watson Institute for International Studies. He has produced numerous books, articles, and documentaries on diplomacy, war, media, and technology, including, most recently, *Critical Practices in International Theory* (Routledge, 2008)

Reviews for the first edition

"This eye-opening, entertaining and sobering study of the increasing 'virtualization' of American politics—and of war in particular—via media manipulation makes an important contribution to political, media and social studies ... this fascinating and important material will make a splash in academic circles."
Publishers Weekly

"The virtual wars that are being fought and planned are far from 'virtuous,' and the author is to be congratulated for bringing this simple reality to our attention."
Political Affairs

"Der Derian is successful in mapping out this newly digitized world."
New Political Science

"The first book to offer a 'virtual theory' for the military strategies, philosophical questions, ethical issues, and political controversies surrounding the future of war and peace."
TechDirections

"[*Virtuous War*] is an important book, and a relevant one, especially given the current administration's struggle to transform and finance a military suited to the 21st century."
Naval Proceedings

Reviews for the second edition

"*Virtuous War* was a seminal contribution to our understanding of war and international relations in the 21st century. The expanded, brilliantly realized 2nd edition makes indispensable reading. The world is catching up to Der Derian's vision of where we are and what we must do about these lethal linkages of war, media, entertainment."
Richard Falk, *Visiting Distinguished Professor of Global and International Studies, University of California, Santa Barbara.*

"There's a marvellous unmasking here of the modern military-media-entertainment fantasy, a disease that pretends to be the cure. There's a literary virtuosity, too, a kind of "magical realism" of global politics as we patrol the pre-9/11 and post-Iraq terrain and the neural pathways of the Pentagon in the company of Nietzsche, Borges, Virilio, the beloved Walter Benjamin, and the quirky, brave and brilliant James Der Derian. This is a book that brings theory and theorists to life, a book that horrifies and delights on virtually every page."
Christopher Lydon, *Open Source*

Virtuous War

Mapping the military-industrial-media-entertainment network

Second edition

James Der Derian

NEW YORK AND LONDON

All photographs are by James Der Derian unless otherwise noted

First edition published by Westview Press,
A Member of the Perseus Books Group 2001

Second edition, 2009 published by Routledge
270 Madison Avenue, New York, NY 10016

Simultaneously published in the UK
by Routledge
2 Park Square, Milton Park, Abingdon, Oxon OX14 4RN

*Routledge is an imprint of the Taylor & Francis Group,
an informa business*

Typeset in Times New Roman by
RefineCatch Limited, Bungay, Suffolk
Printed by Edwards Brothers Inc

British Library Cataloguing in Publication Data
A catalogue record for this book is available from the British Library

Library of Congress Cataloging in Publication Data
Virtuous war : mapping the military-industrial-media-entertainment-
network / James Der Derian.—2nd ed.
    p. cm.
  Includes bibliographical references and index.
  1. War—Simulation methods.   2. War games.   3. Imaginary wars
and battles.   4. War—Moral and ethical aspects.   5. United States—
Military policy.   6. Military-industrial complex—United States.
7. Mass media—United States.   8. War in mass media.   9. Mass
media and war—United States.   10. World politics—1989–   I. Title.
  U21.2.D347 2009
  355.02—dc22
  2008036921

ISBN 13: 978–0–415–77238–9 (hbk)
ISBN 13: 978–0–415–77239–6 (pbk)
ISBN 13: 978–0–203–88153–8 (ebk)

ISBN 10: 0–415–77238–9 (hbk)
ISBN 10: 0–415–77239–7 (pbk)
ISBN 10: 0–203–88153–2 (ebk)

Contents

Photographs

Acronyms

AAR	after-action reviews
AI	Artificial Intelligence
AOR	Area of Responsibility
ATF	Alcohol, Tobacco and Firearms
AWE	Advanced Warfighting Experiment
C4I	command, control, communication, computer, and intelligence
CAOC	Combined Air Operations Center
CCTT	Close Combat Tactical Trainer
CMTC	Combat and Maneuver Training Center
DARPA	Defense Advanced Research Projects Agency
DIS	Distributed Interactive Simulation
DOD	Department of Defense
DSS	Dismounted Soldier Simulation
GPS	global positioning satellite systems
HCA	Helsinki Citizen's Assembly
HLA	high level architecture
HMMWV	High Mobility Multipurpose Wheeled Vehicles, "Humvees"
I/ITSEC	Interservice/Industry Training Systems and Education Conference
ICANN	Internet Corporation for Assigned Names
ICT	Institute for Creative Technologies
IT21	Information Technology for the 21st Century
IVIS	Inter-Vehicular Information System
JSIMS	Joint Simulation System

JSTAR	Joint Surveillance and Target Attack Radar System
LOEs	limited objective experiments
LTAs	limited technical assessments
MILES	Multiple Integrated Laser Engagement Systems
MIME-NET	military-industrial-media-entertainment network
MIS	Manager of Information Systems
MODSAF SGI	Modulated Semi-Automated Forces, Silicon Graphics Images
MOOTW	Military Operations Other than War
NDP	National Defense Panel
NTC	National Training Center
NUPI	Norwegian Institute of International Affairs
OPFOR	Opposing Forces
OOTW	Operations Other than War
PRIO	Peace Research Institute
QDR	Quadrennial Defense Review
RMA	Revolution in Military Affairs
SAIC	Science Applications International Corporation
SETAF	Southern European Task Force headquarters
SFOR	Stability Forces
SHIRBRIG	Stand-by Forces High Readiness Brigade
SIMNET	simulation network
STOW	Synthetic Theaters of Wars
STRICOM	Simulation, Training, and Instrumentation Command
TOWS	Tube Launched Optically Tracked Wire Guided missiles
TRADOC	Training and Doctrine Command
USC	University of Southern California

Acknowledgments for the first edition

A generous group of institutions and individuals provided the money, sanctuary, and time to write this book. I would like to thank the Ford Foundation, the John D. and Catherine T. MacArthur Foundation, and the Social Science Research Council for supporting my research and writing. I am grateful to the editors at *Wired*, *The Nation*, *The Washington Quarterly*, and *21c* for underwriting and publishing segments of my travels in virtuality. I was fortunate to be able to think, write, just catch my breath at some wonderful academic way stations, and my gratitude goes to: Avi Shlaim and Andrew Hurrell at St. Antony's College at Oxford; Stanley Hoffmann and Charles Maier at the Center for European Studies at Harvard; Thomas Biersteker and Tom Gleason at the Watson Institute for International Studies at Brown; and Adam Ashforth at the School of Social Science at the Institute for Advanced Study at Princeton. None of this would have been possible without the beneficence of my colleagues in the Political Science Department at the University of Massachusetts in Amherst.

It is impossible to single out for appreciation the many individuals in the military who let me travel through their worlds, who generously shared their stories with me, who impressed me to no end. I owe them, and I hope this book gets it right by their account, and helps to set it right by mine. Where it doesn't, I take as much responsibility as one can in these matters.

I had some great traveling companions on this journey. I am indebted to my editor, Leo Wiegman, for making good on a pool game bet; to my agent, Joe Valley, for keeping the faith; to John

George Moyer and grandson.

Santos, for being there from the beginning; to Hannah Riley, for the roads well traveled; and to Catherine McGarty, for showing the way ahead.

This book is dedicated to Toros Der Derian and George Moyer, two virtuous men who taught me more than they could possibly have known.

Acknowledgments for the second edition

At either end of the publication of the first and second editions of *Virtuous War* there lurks the twin disasters of Wall Street. The first resulted from a kamikaze attack by Al Qaeda terrorists acting in the name of virtue; the second from a virtual cascade of bad sub-prime loans, bad computer models, bad credit derivatives—and some pretty bad leadership, too. The verdict is still out on which event will ultimately prove more devastating to the United States and to the world. This new edition was made necessary by what happened in the years between these two calamitous events: Afghanistan invaded, Iraq occupied, New Orleans devastated by Hurricane Katrina, and coterminously if not coincidentally, George Bush elected and then re-elected. Although I would like to believe that this revised and expanded version might provide some insights for how we got here, I am under no delusion that it will prevent even worse calumnies from befalling an already dire state of global affairs.

This grim appraisal should not diminish my deep gratitude, nor transfer even an iota of responsibility, to those who helped make this second edition possible. Some wonderful institutions and generous funders provided me with sanctuary and sustenance to continue the project, including the Watson Institute for International Studies at Brown University, Trinity College in Dublin, Ireland, Carnegie Corporation of New York, Ford Foundation, Rockefeller Foundation, and Richard B. Salomon Faculty Research Fund. However, as Ralph Waldo Emerson wrote, institutions are the lengthened shadows of individuals, so I wish to target my appreciation to: Craig Fowlie and Nicola Parkin of

Routledge Books, the best and coolest editors one could ever wish for; Thomas Biersteker who invited me to join the closest thing to academic nirvana; Stephen Del Rosso who provided the incentive to be innovative about global security; David and Michael Udris of Amedia Productions for expressing through documentary film what a book alone could not; Lizzie Goodfriend, Ellen Darling, and Christie Kilgus, master jugglers and managers of the Global Security Program; Lena Buell, Phil Gara, Marie-Claude Hamel, Claire Harlam, Christina Kim, Anne Krapu, and Joshua Sargent all fearless Brown students who followed the research no matter where it led (zombies be damned); Thomas Y. Levin and Franziska Nori, curators extraordinaire of the multiple media of modernity; John Phillip Santos, co-conspirator of the Global Media Project, fellow-traveler in subterranean politics, and practitioner of extraterrestrial poetics; and Marguerite White, who helped put the song and dance back into my life, along with her mother and my wife, Catherine McGarty, for painting me into her most perfect picture of a life.

Preface to the new edition

"If we only knew then what we know now." This refrain was used by many U.S. officials, several presidential aspirants, and not a few experts to answer critics who questioned their early support of the Iraq War and after the weapons of mass destruction failed to materialize, an insurgency rather than democracy broke out, and total costs edged towards the one trillion dollar mark. This excuse—they didn't know what they didn't know, to paraphrase a past Secretary of Defense (that would be of the United States, not the English language), until they knew what they knew—always struck me as absurd. If only those in the government, the media, and the academy had known that U.S. administrations had engaged in foreign fiascos before (Bay of Pigs and Vietnam); lied to the public (Watergate, Monicagate, and all the other lesser-gates); presented indisputable proof of new dangers (tapes in pumpkins, satellite photographs); trundled out false analogies (Munich redux); cited unpredictable and expansionist powers (the "Reds"); exaggerated an arms race (bomber and missile gaps); trampled on constitutional rights in the name of national interest (Alien and Sedition Act, McCarthyism, COINTELPRO); and elevated a distant danger into an imminent threat (duck and cover—now). How do we explain such a level of collective historical amnesia?

To be sure, the trauma of a major attack on the American mainland as well as the anxiety induced by the specter of future ones, made it easier to support or merely to acquiesce as the Bush administration constructed an ever-expanding universe of terror, against which, the argument went, a global war must be perpetually waged. And of course, disinformation campaigns were integral to the global war of and on terror. It is almost understandable why a compliant Congress, fearful public, and an intellectual "coalition of the willing" were ready to give President Bush the necessary authority and legitimacy to wage an unnecessary war. Understandable, but hardly explanatory and certainly not excusable. Why were so many unable or unwilling to know then what they know now? Why were those who did know unable to change the minds and actions of those who did not? How did ignorance and arrogance transform a containable conflict into a war of necessity?

This new edition of *Virtuous War* attempts to answer these questions, not always directly or explicitly, but by way of a decade-long travelogue through the military-industrial-media-entertainment network that traces the path to the Iraq War. This is not a revision of an earlier text. The original chapters, written between 1993 and 2000, are unaltered. Nor is it a revisionist history of the Iraq War, in which the past is reinterpreted to neatly add up to the present. I have corrected a few typos (including one that must have set my grandfather spinning in his grave, when somewhere between the final proofs and publication he became an "American" rather than "Armenian" guerilla fighting the Turks). And I did sacrifice one chapter: my original effort to elaborate a virtual theory for International Relations was just too much of a speed-bump for readers who prefer a travelogue to a "heterologue" (it was *de trop*, in that French kind of way). I have added four new chapters, written between 2000 and 2008, in an attempt to make what I salvaged of virtual theory worthy of the global events that preceded and followed 9/11. I left the original chapters untouched because I wanted to maintain the chronology of discovery, as well as occasional divagation, that came with my research travels; and, more importantly, because I wanted to make it quite clear that it was possible to know then (prior to 9/11) what many still seem reluctant to acknowledge now (after Iraq): the U.S. was on the path to a disastrous war, many years before President Bush became commander-in-chief or Osama Bin Laden became the living embodiment of evil.

The result is not a scholarly treatise on international relations. Nor is it an op-ed article padded into a foreign policy book.[1] This book draws from a twenty-year inquiry into the ethics, efficacy, and effects of, and ultimately the decision to choose between diplomacy and war. This entailed more granular investigations into challenges posed by new global forms of terrorism, espionage, and media to traditional practices of statecraft.[2] Targeting the most pressing dangers of the day, I never considered these investigations to be an academic exercise. From the start I sought to apply a critical attitude, developed outside (geographically, culturally, educationally) the mainstream of American politics and scholarship, to current foreign and defense policies. My skepticism towards official stories was bolstered by empirical work in the field, where I was able to witness firsthand the concerted efforts and mixed results of powerful public and private institutions, seeking to adapt to new global challenges within the exigencies and bounded power of sovereign states.

Nor does this book fit easily within a paradigm of International Relations. When the World Trade Center and the Pentagon were struck by kamikaze suicide bombers, my response differed from many of my colleagues in the field of International Relations, with a minority opposed and a majority supportive or acquiescent to a military response.[3] I supported the intervention into Afghanistan to quash Al Qaeda; but I was critical of the effort to expand a limited objective into the eradication of not just global terrorism but the "evil" behind it; this seemed to me an impossible goal that would inevitably produce high levels of collateral damage against the "good" as well. I was also hesitant, in spite of the erosion of civil liberties at home and a creeping militarization of American policies abroad, to lay the blame solely at the doorstep of the Bush administration. I wished to present a more complex back-story of the various ideological, technological, and military forces that were in play before the 2000 election. Earlier administrations (including Clinton's) planned, experimented, and sought to operationalize a "revolution in military affairs" (RMA) in a series of armed humanitarian interventions; the road to Iraq led through Grenada and Panama to Somalia and Haiti to Bosnia and Kosovo. To be sure, in the run-up to Iraq, Bush, Cheney, Rumsfeld, Powell, Tenet, and others abused intelligence, miscalculated risk, froze out the UN, and displayed all kinds of ideological blunders. They deployed an effective infowar to construct their own reality and to neutralize the few critics who might be living in what they deemed an unpatriotic worldview.[4] But they did not invent a new game: they effectively used 9/11 to radically up the ante, making *virtuous war* the only game worth playing.

Designed by the Pentagon, auditioned in the Balkans, and dress-rehearsed in Afghanistan, virtuous war took center stage in the invasion of Iraq. Virtuous war projects a technological and ethical superiority in which computer simulation, media dissimulation, global surveillance, and networked warfare combine to deter, discipline, and if need be, destroy the enemy. Ethically intentioned and virtually applied, drawing on the doctrines of just war when possible and holy war when necessary, virtuous war plays on its ambiguous status as a felicitous oxymoron. After September 11, as the United States chose coercion over diplomacy in its foreign policy, and extolled a rhetoric of total victory over absolute evil, virtuous war became the ultimate means by which the United States intended to re-secure its borders and assert its global suzerainty.

My other reason for bringing out a new edition of *Virtuous War* was to bridge a widening gap in International Relations, between the theory and practice of international relations.[5] Given our supposed expertise, could we not have done more to prevent this sorry state of affairs? In the run-up to the war, why did silence rather than dissent dominate the ranks of IR? A personal experience drove this question home. Several months before the war in Iraq had started I had been invited to present at a conference on "The American Media and Wartime Challenges," sponsored by Triangle International Security Studies (composed of North Carolina State, University of North Carolina, and Duke University). As luck would have it, the conference took place right at the start of Operation Iraqi Freedom. In spite of the gung-ho mood in the room (and America in general) I decided to stick to my original plan to present a paper that was highly critical of the wartime interpenetration of the military and the media.

The reaction was, to put it mildly, hostile. In the course of my career I have been attacked by some of the best (as well as the worst), and truth be told, I prefer a good fight to preaching to the choir. But the crowd was out for blood like I have not witnessed ever before. The questions (more in the category of shouted "comments") barely rose from the mud, and got personal very quickly. I could understand why the twenty or so mid-career officers from the nearby Fort Bragg Special Operations School attending the conference might be passionate about the topic. Indeed, one warned me to leave by the other door because his friend—whose idea of refutation was to demand whether I had ever been to boot camp—"wanted a piece of me." But probably the most worrying aspect of the encounter was the agreement or acquiescence of just about every other academic in the room. Many seemed to agree with the soldiers, some more obviously than others. One co-panelist pretty much jettisoned her talk to launch an attack on anyone (primarily me) who could possibly think that enemy or civilian casualties are legitimate issues for a wartime press or academic conference. The other panelist, an ex-general (one of the few I guess who didn't get the call to explain the war to us on CNN, Fox, ABC, or other networks), spent most his time extolling the necessity of strategic bombing regardless, again, of civilian casualties (based, I presumed, on his experience of flying over 200 missions in Vietnam). Several individuals in the room did come up to me afterwards to apologize for the behavior of the audience, including an instructor from Fort Bragg and the director of the Institute, Peter Feaver (who would later join the Bush administration and launch the ill-fated "Victory in Iraq" media blitz). A few said they actually agreed with me. However, my question to them was: where were you when I was under attack? Missing in action, I am afraid.[6]

The day that our television screens were filled with looped images of Saddam Hussein's statuesque fall from power, I wrote a critical essay on how this was really a game for a war that had yet to be fought.[7] I argued that no prior war ever had been so enabled by the attributes, defined by the language, and played by the rules of the game than the war in Iraq. As the velocity of strategic movement was being force-multiplied by the immediacy of the embedded journalism; as the virtuality of high technology warfare was enhanced by the reality of low battlefield casualties; as the military and the media as well as weapon-systems and sign-systems became mutually embedded; as the viewer became player, war and game were melding in realtime on primetime. I fully realized that to speak of war as a game was to invite attack, and so, in keeping with the spirit of the new U.S. national security strategy, I decided to launch a pre-emptive strike of my own. I wrote that war with Iraq was not simply a game—it was a stupid game. I believed and wrote that it would prove to be a waste of lives, resources and the world standing of the United States. Indeed, I thought it seemed like a waste of time and intelligence even to speak of this war as rational activity, as a Clausewitzian continuation of politics by other means. Between the September 11 attack and the first shot of the Iraq War, a mimetic war of fundamentalisms had set a predestined course, and in this regard, Bin Laden had succeeded.

This war made for strange bedfellows in IR. I remember the relative silence about the war at the March 2003 meeting of the International Studies Association meeting in Portland, Oregon. In response, a small group of us staged a silent (complete with duct-taped mouths) protest in the main lobby of the hotel convention center. Overwhelmingly, our ranks came from the critical, feminist, poststructuralist or (and often overlapping) "foreign" representatives of IR. It is worth noting that a past and a future president of the ISA, John Vasquez and Steve Smith, respectively, joined the protest, neither of whom fall within the liberal or realist paradigms that dominates IR in the U.S. Those most likely critics of foreign aggression, liberal institutionalists and humanitarian interventionists like Joseph Nye, Michael Ignatieff, and Anne Marie Slaughter, split hairs over the morality, legality, and legitimacy of the war but did not oppose it. However, the realist camp did resist. Following in the footsteps (if not to the barricades) of Hans Morgenthau during the Vietnam war, paleo-realist John Mersheimer and uber-realist Steve Walt published high-profile renunciations of the rush to war. I think it is important to recognize the superior diagnostic powers that realists displayed, especially in their general assessment of U.S. national interest in the Middle East, and in their particular advocacy for proportionality between means and ends in the war against global terrorism. Realists pride themselves as depicting things as they really are, rather than as idealists might wish them to be. And by idealists we must include, in a strange convergence, the born-again fundamentalists, true-believer neoconservatives, and ardent Straussians—sometimes one and the same—who in their advocacy of regime change and human rights found more allies from within the ranks of liberal institutionalists than from erstwhile allies in moderate national security circles.

But I do not think we should let realists off the hook so easily. Walter Benjamin said it best in *The Arcades Project*: "[T]he history that showed things 'as they really were' was the strongest narcotic of the century."[8] Contemporary realism is not without its own self-serving constructions, like the permanence of international anarchy, the immutability of human nature, the objectification of the state, and the reification of a balance of power. In spite of all the transformations of world politics after the Cold War and after 9/11, fatalistic realists long for the stability of a bipolar world while well-intentioned liberals perpetually wait for a multipolar world that cannot be born. This new edition of *Virtuous War* aims for the space between: a critical yet pragmatic pluralism for understanding and living in an increasingly heteropolar world.

[. . .] This conjunction of an immense military establishment and a large arms industry is new in the American experience. The total influence—economic, political, even spiritual—is felt in every city, every statehouse, every office of the federal government. . . . In the councils of government we must guard against the acquisition of unwarranted influence, whether sought or unsought, by the military-industrial complex. The potential for the disastrous rise of misplaced power exists and will persist . . . The prospect of domination of the nation's scholars by federal employment, project allocations, and the power of money is ever present and is gravely to be regarded. Yet, in holding scientific research and discovery in respect, as we should, we must also be alert to the equal and opposite danger that public policy could itself become the captive of a scientific-technological elite. . . . We want democracy to survive for all generations to come, not to become the insolvent phantom of tomorrow. Down the long lane of the history yet to be written, America knows that this world of ours, ever growing smaller, must avoid becoming a community of dreadful fear and hate, and be, instead, a proud confederation of mutual trust and respect. Such a confederation must be one of equals. The weakest must come to the conference table with the same confidence as do we, protected as we are by our moral, economic, and military strength. That table, though scarred by many past frustrations, cannot be abandoned for the certain agony of the battlefield. [. . .]

(President Eisenhower's farewell address)

(Radio and TV, January 17, 1961)

The virtuous

And others are proud of their modicum of righteousness, and for the sake of it do violence to all things: so that the world is drowned in their unrighteousness.

Ah! how ineptly cometh the word "virtue" out of their mouth! And when they say: "I am just," it always soundeth like: "I am just—revenged!"

With their virtues they want to scratch out the eyes of their enemies; and they elevate themselves only that they may lower others.

And again there are those who sit in their swamp, and speak thus from among the bullrushes: "Virtue—that is to sit quietly in the swamp.

We bite no one, and go out of the way of him who would bite; and in all matters we have the opinion that is given us."

And again there are those who love attitudes, and think that virtue is a sort of attitude.

Their knees continually adore, and their hands are eulogies of virtue, but their heart knoweth naught thereof.

And again there are those who regard it as virtue to say: "Virtue is necessary"; but after all they believe only that policemen are necessary.

(Friedrich Nietzsche,
Thus Spake Zarathustra)

Toros Der Derian.

George Moyer.

Prologue

> ***Virtual 1. a.*** Possessed of certain physical virtues or capacities; effective in respect of inherent natural qualities or powers; capable of exerting influence by means of such qualities. **g. Computers.** Not physically existing as such but made by software to appear to do so from the point of view of the program or the user; specifically applied to memory that appears to be internal although most of it is external, transfer between the two being made automatically as required.
>
> (*Oxford English Dictionary*)

Technology in the service of virtue has given rise to a global form of virtual violence, *virtuous war*. This book retraces my travels in virtuality, where made-for-TV wars and Hollywood war movies blur, military war games and computer video games blend, mock disasters and real accidents collide, producing on screen a new configuration of virtual power. Going on site to find the ghosts in the war machine, I map the emergence of a new virtual alliance, the *military-industrial-media-entertainment network*.

There are many reasons for undertaking such a journey, some obvious, and, as will become apparent, many not. I was driven by inner reasons, two virtual memories that converge and then disappear in my life, in this book, as tracks in the distance. The memories are of my grandfathers' wars. Toros Der Derian, an Armenian guerilla for the *Hunchak* ("Bell") revolutionary party, fought in one of the many lost nationalist causes of the First World War. Unlike other struggles of the war, this one earned the sorrowful title, after the Turks forcibly rid Anatolia of Armenians through political terror, massacres, and death marches through the desert, of the first modern genocide. Hitler, facing resistance at the cusp of the next one, infamously remarked, "Who after all remembers the Armenians?"

I, for one, was constantly reminded. My earliest memory of the massacres comes from a photograph my father showed me: two Turkish gendarmes stand to either side of a shelf that seems to bow under the weight of a row of severed heads. Pointing to one of the heads, my father said, "This was your cousin." Maybe it was my age at the time, or the more permanent fact of my semi-assimilated, mixed-blood heritage, but I think the intended message missed its mark. I was left wondering whether all my distant relatives were missing bodies.

During the same war, George Moyer, my mother's father, left his upstate New York farm to join the U.S. Army and become a machine-gunner in France. He was gassed but not permanently injured and came home with some funny-sounding French songs and a couple of medals that were kept in the attic along with his mothballed tunic, cartridge belt, gas mask, and rusting helmet. Neither of my grandfathers spoke of their foreign wars, and I learned from a young age not to ask.

Their work radically differed. For over forty years, Toros was a straw boss of the coke-ovens at the River Rouge plant, Ford Motor Company's enormous industrial complex in Dearborn, Michigan. In the Mohawk River valley, George kept bees in the summer and trapped fur animals in the winter. Toros forged his past into a manageable if not domestically acceptable level of violence, beating his wife and son on occasion and spending most of his spare time hunting, fishing, and—shouting in Armenian and swearing in Turkish—playing combative games of backgammon. Eager for the opportunity to fight, or perhaps to fight back, my father left home at the outset of the Second World War. He was underage when he joined the navy and eventually rose to the rank of lieutenant junior-grade. George, on the other hand, never showed any anger in private or public; he took his war violence elsewhere, reenacting the Civil War with fellow veterans all up and down the East Coast. War also forever changed the life of my mother: she left the farm to go work as a secretary for the

U.S. Army in occupied Germany. On one page of the family photo album she is standing in front of ruins in Frankfurt; on the next, skiing with American officers in St. Moritz.

These memories are etched by moments of trauma. During my first and only visit to "The Rouge," as Toros's workplace was called, I do not remember the famous Diego Rivera murals of the working man that my father had taken me to see. I don't even remember seeing a single car being made. What I see when I look back at that moment is my younger self, looking down from a great height above the metallic din, molten heat, and orange-red spray of sparks from the foundry, clinging in a paralytic terror to the catwalk railing as my father worked to pry my fingers free. Where Bible School had failed, Ford Motor Company succeeded: Hell truly did exist.

The other memory is of George in his blue and gray uniform of the Union Army, engaged in a mock battle at Frontier Land, one of America's earliest theme parks. Charging up the hill toward a fort full of Confederates, getting too old to go the full nine yards, he stopped halfway and discharged his muzzleloader in a spurt of yellow flame and blue smoke. Suddenly he threw back his arms in the classic gesture of the mortally wounded. It was too good, too convincing for a credulous grandson, who broke from the ranks of the roped-in crowd and ran onto the battlefield to comfort his dying grandfather. I did not hear, but I am told that bystanders laughed.

A few years later George really did die, in bed, of a pulmonary embolism. The bee-yards and the farmhouse were eventually sold. Shortly after a pilgrimage back to Armenia and the Holy Land, Toros was killed by a lymphatic cancer caused, said the lawyers, by leaking gases from the coke-ovens. Most of the Rouge went cold, untended by émigré progeny like me who grew up intent on keeping their distance from industry and war. I dodged one bullet when my birth date came up number one in the lottery for the draft, but it was January 1973, the month of the cease-fire and the year that the Treaty of Paris ended the Vietnam War—at least for the Americans. My luck held with scholarships, first to McGill University in Canada, and then to Oxford University in England. Staging high-school strikes against the Cambodian invasion, marching against nuclear weapons at the U.S. Air Force base outside Oxford, I would be the first son in the family who chose to protest rather than to go to war.

Since my grandfathers' wars, much has changed and yet remains the same. Technological innovations have transformed the battlefield. In the First World War, the telephone provided generals with the means and the arrogance to send hundreds of thousands of soldiers to their deaths from the relative safety of their chateau headquarters. In the Second World War, the radio, tank, airplane, and, as final punctuation, the atomic bomb, all radically altered the nature of warfare. Strategists, pundits, and politicians of one stripe or another have called various aspects of these changes a "revolution." Now the arrival on the battlefield of networked information technology is being heralded as a "Revolution in Military Affairs" (RMA). However, it takes more than technological innovation to make a revolution. A past defeat and the desire for a quick victory can give cause for one military, as it did the Germans, to take up new technologies and strategies, like the tank and blitzkrieg, while others, like the British and French, missed the boat. But the desire for a revolutionary, technological fix can also lead a country down the wrong path, as happened later in the war, when Hitler gave rocket science priority and resources over nuclear physics. Political and strategic doctrines as well as civilian and military values must mesh if new technologies are to constitute anything approaching a revolution. In the twenty-first century, we seem to be approaching at great speed just such a moment. It is a virtual revolution in military and diplomatic affairs.

Unlike other radically new developments in means of transportation, communication, and information, this virtual revolution is driven more by software than hardware, and enabled by networks rather than agents, which means adaptation (and mutation) is not only easier, but much more rapid. Moreover, this virtualization is taking place at a pivot-point in history. Post-Ford, postmodern, or just post-Cold War, the international system has entered a state of economic, cultural, and political flux. And when order and predictability decline, leaders reach for the technological fix.

On its own, virtualization does not embody a revolution in diplomatic or military, let alone human, affairs. However, deployed with the new ethical and economic imperatives for global democratic reform and neoliberal markets, it could well be. In spite and perhaps because of efforts to spread a democratic peace through globalization and humanitarian intervention, war is ascending to an even "higher" plane, from the virtual to the *virtuous*. At one time, the two words—and the two worlds they represent—were barely distinguishable. Both originated in the medieval notion of a power inherent in the supernatural, of a divine being endowed with natural virtue. And both carried a moral weight, from the Greek and Roman sense of virtue, of properties and qualities of right conduct. But their meanings diverged in modern usage, with "virtual" taking a morally neutral, more technical tone, while "virtuous" lost its sense of exerting influence by means of inherent qualities. Now they seem ready to be rejoined by current efforts to effect ethical change through technological and martial means.

The United States, as unilateral *deus ex machina* of global politics, is leading the way in this virtual revolution. Its diplomatic and military policies are increasingly based on technological and representational forms of discipline, deterrence, and compulsion that could best be described as "virtuous war." At the heart of virtuous war is the technical capability and ethical imperative to threaten and, if necessary, actualize violence from a distance— *with no or minimal casualties*. Using networked information and virtual technologies to bring "there" here in near-real time and with near-verisimilitude, virtuous war exercises a comparative as well as strategic advantage for the digitally advanced. Along with time (in the sense of tempo) as the fourth dimension, virtuality has become the "fifth dimension" of U.S. global hegemony.

On the surface, virtuous war cleans up the political discourse as well as the battlefield. Fought in the same manner as they are represented, by real-time surveillance and TV "live-feeds," virtuous wars promote a vision of bloodless, humanitarian, hygienic wars. We can rattle off casualty rates of prototypical virtuous conflicts like the Gulf War (270 Americans lost their lives—more than half in accidents), the Mogadishu raid (eighteen Americans killed), and the Kosovo air campaign (barring accidents, a remarkable zero casualty conflict for the NATO forces). Yet most of us would not know the casualty figures for the other side, of

Iraqis, Somalis, and Serbs. Post-Vietnam, the U.S. has made many digital advances; public announcement of enemy body counts is not one of them.

Unlike other forms of warfare, virtuous war has an unsurpassed power to commute death, to keep it out of sight, out of mind. Herein lies its most morally dubious danger. In simulated preparations and virtual executions of war, there is a high risk that one learns how to kill but not to take responsibility for it. One experiences "death" but not the tragic consequences of it. In virtuous war we now face not just the confusion but the pixilation of war and game on the same screen.

The U.S. leads the way, but other countries as well as international organizations are in hot pursuit of virtual solutions to long-running political conflicts. At the "Millennium Summit" of the UN in September 2000, the member nations endorsed a report for the establishment of a permanent peacekeeping structure and rapidly deployable multinational force (Stand-by Forces High Readiness Brigade or SHIRBRIG) with its own, albeit limited, command, control, communications, and intelligence capability. The same year, the European Union proposed a new European Rapid Reaction Force, or "Euro-Army," to undertake regional humanitarian interventions. At the height of the Israeli withdrawal from Lebanon in May 2000, the London *Daily Telegraph* pronounced from a safe distance on its "real" meaning for the future of warfare: "The Israeli dot-com generation seems not to have the stomach for mortal combat. They have started to ask why they should risk their lives when precision weapons can reduce war to a video game. For the pony-tailed youth of Tel Aviv's night spots, the war in Lebanon was becoming their Vietnam and they would rather their government fought it by remote control."[1]

However, the *Daily Telegraph* article conspicuously fails to note, and the subsequent "Days of Rage" in the West Bank and Gaza clearly demonstrate, that virtuous war is anything *but* less destructive, deadly, or bloody for those on the receiving end of the big technological stick. And the newspaper is not alone in this sometimes blithe but often intentional oversight. Bloody ethnic and religious conflicts involving land mines, small arms, terrorist bombings, and even machetes persist. In the chapters that follow,

I try to comprehend how the sanitization of violence that began with the Gulf War has come to overpower the mortification of the body that marks communal wars in Nagorno-Karabakh, Somalia, Bosnia, Rwanda, and elsewhere. Virtuous war is many things: a felicitous oxymoron, a form of deterrence, a growing paradox, an ominous sign of things to come. Yet in the final analysis that it seeks to evade, virtuous war is still about killing others.

Virtuous war is much more than a new form of organized violence. From the fifties' cybernetic notion of the "automation" to William Gibson's 1987 coining of "cyberspace" as a "consensual hallucination," the virtual has shared an isomorphic relationship to the unreal, surreal, the hyperreal. And like reality's most intimate counterpart, the dream, virtuous war requires a critical awakening if we are not to sleepwalk through the manifold travesties of war, whether between states or tribes, classes or castes, genders or generations. Call it a dream-state, a symbolic realm, or merely an illusion, virtuous war projects a mythos as well as an ethos, a kind of collective unconscious for an epoch's greatest aspirations and greatest insecurities. Indeed, it is heroic if not Homeric in its practice and promise: On one side, the face of Achilles, a tragic figure who represents the *virtù* (as well as hubris) of the great warrior, of honor, loyalty, and violence, willing to sacrifice his life for others in a strange land; and on the other, Odysseus, a man of many devices (*polymechanos*) and many contrivances (*polymetis*), who prefers *techné* to *virtù*, cunning (and punning) to warring and wandering, who just wants to come home. Observing similar tensions at work in interwar Germany, the literary critic Walter Benjamin said, "Only a thoughtless observer can deny that correspondences come into play between the world of modern technology and the archaic symbol-world of mythology."[2]

My grandfathers' wars gave me virtual cause for this book. But my personal motivations come with a perennial intellectual reservation: How to tell the story of war? How to convey its dangers and horrors without falling prey to the preferred contemporary formats of neutral documentary or Oprah exposé? Any portrayal of war presents dangers for the chronicler, many obvious, some not so obvious; but virtuous war in particular poses some serious obstacles. One tactic is to record war from the bunker and the beaches, so close that the word on the page, the image on the film, is imprinted by, practically drips with, the carnage of war. We might call this approach, *pace* Spielberg, "Saving the Reality Principle."

Another is to keep a distance, to extract the causes, structures, and patterns of war. Either way, the choice seems to be Hobbes or Hobson: the blood-drenched prose, the cinéma vérité, the permanent war-of-all-against-all of the realist; or the bloodless, value-free, hygienic wars of the social scientist. Some writers, like John Keegan and Stephen Ambrose, have managed to work effectively, even eloquently, the space between the trenches and the ivory tower. But the wars they wrote about, full of heroic figures caught in black-and-white representations, are not the wars that we face now and in the future. The new wars are fought in the same manner as they are represented, by military simulations and public dissimulations, by real-time surveillance and TV live-feeds. Virtuality collapses distance, between here and there, near and far, fact and fiction. It widens the distance between those who have and those who have not. Representing the most penetrating and sharpest (to the point of invisibility) edge of globalization, it disappears the local and the particular. It leaves little space for the detached observer.

The problem of representation is compounded by the erosion of war as the ultimate reality-check of international politics. Declared once, many times, dead, sovereignty remains the primary means by which the supreme power and legitimate violence of the state is territorially exercised in international politics. Now, however, the sovereign state seems to regain its vigor virtually, through media spasms about new threats from States-of-Concern-formerly-known-as-Rogues (to invoke the other Prince) that warrant a $60 billion ballistic missile defense, and new strains of killer diseases that make *X-Files* seem understated. The most ballyhooed virtual threat is "cyberterrorism," ominously mooted by the media and anticipated by the Pentagon as the "next Pearl Harbor"—which must amuse (and motivate) teenage hackers who make up the overwhelming bulk of such computer "attacks."[3] Notorious as they might be, infowar, netwar, and cyberwar do not constitute the most dangerous form of virtuous war.

Dwarfed by the seeming ubiquity of the cyberthreat, drowned

out by the white noise of media coverage of it, important questions about virtuous war go begging. Is virtualization, not globalization, turning the millennial tide? Are war and the sovereign state disappearing, soon to be relics for the museum of modernity? Or have they virtually become the undead, haunting international politics like specters? Is virtualization the continuation of war (as well as politics) by other means? Is it repudiating, reversing, or merely updating classical strategists like Carl von Clausewitz? Is virtuality replacing the reality of war? Will real or just a simulated peace result from "humanitarian intervention"? In short, is virtuous war the harbinger of a new world order, or a brave new world?

This book raises these questions by means of a travelogue. Rather than attempt a neutral, academic account of new forms of warfare and diplomacy, I have chosen to take the readers along: to put them virtually inside the war machine, to experience its power and seduction, to understand its inertial development, to try to plot its future path, and perhaps even to find the monkey wrench that might stop it dead in its tracks. The latter is unlikely, however, for I have come to accept Clausewitz's belief that although particular wars might not be necessary, war in general and for the foreseeable future is inevitable. Which is why the future of war—after the Cold War, uncivil wars in the Balkans, a genocidal war in Rwanda, a ratcheting war in the Middle East, a convulsion of nuclear tests on the subcontinent of Asia, and a brewing war of blood and oil on the Caucasus—remains a consuming issue. I do not find all the answers; but I end this book with the first steps toward a *virtual theory* for the military strategies, philosophical questions, ethical issues, and political controversies that surround the future of war and peace.

I begin my travels in virtuality on a hilltop in the Mojave Desert, watching the first digitized Advanced Warfighting Experiment (AWE) unfold at the Army's National Training Center. Historically, however, this book begins where general-turned-president Eisenhower left off in his famous (but little debated) 1961 farewell address, warning of the "danger that public policy could itself become the captive of a scientific-technological elite." But with the addition of the media and entertainment industries to the mix, a seductive captivation now augments the powers of what he had labeled the "military-industrial complex." When the simulations used to train fighter pilots show up in the special effects of Hollywood movies, four-person Marine fire-teams train with the video game *Doom*, and Disney's former head Imagineer, Bran Ferren, becomes an interior decorator for a naval command ship, reality becomes one more attraction at the Virtual Theme Park of War and Peace.[4]

With apologies to Eisenhower, this project travels to the cyborg heart of the "military-industrial-media-entertainment network," not only to investigate the role of "MIME-NET" in the production of war, but to study up close the mimetic power that travels along the hyphens. I am not claiming that this relationship is wholly new. The River Rouge plant in which my grandfather worked owed a great deal to Henry Ford's copying of the British Royal Navy's innovations in the mass-production of cannon and ships; and in turn, Ford's assembly line production and hierarchical system of manufacturing became a mimetic model for the new Hollywood studio system of vertically controlling actors, movies, and theaters.[5] The feedback loop between military and civilian technology, particularly during and after the Second World War, from the cracking of German codes at Bletchley Park (the computer), to the early development of radar (the television), to the first semiautomated air defense systems (networks), has also been well documented.[6] What is qualitatively new is the power of the MIME-NET to seamlessly merge the production, representation, and execution of war. The result is not merely the copy of a copy, or the creation of something new: It represents a convergence of the means by which we distinguish the original and the new, the real from the reproduced.

Where once the study and practice of war began and ended with the black box of the state, new modes of production and networks of information have created new demarcations of power and identity, reality and virtuality. My intention is to map how new technologies and media of simulation create a fidelity between the representation and the reality of war; the human mimetic faculty for entertainment and gaming join forces with new cyborg programs for killing and warring; and, as our desire for peace and order confronts an increasingly accelerated, highly contingent, uncertain future, virtuous war becomes the preferred means to secure the global interests of the United States.

In search of answers, and to separate the hype from the hyperreality of virtuous war, I decided early on to forgo the public affairs machine of the Pentagon, to avoid the vices of academic abstraction as well as secondhand journalism, and to go where doctrine confronts reality (or, as my military handlers liked to put it, "where the rubber meets the road"). I have spent the last seven years trying to get behind and beyond the images of modern warfare. My travels have taken me to places not usually visited by scholars or pundits. I journey in the chapters that follow to: Orlando, Florida, to see military officers and corporate leaders showcase their information technology at joint conferences on simulations; the East Mojave Desert to chase after the "Krasnovian Brigade" during digitized war games at the Army National Training Center; to Central Command in Tampa to learn how computer gamers were busy programming the lessons of the Gulf War for the next war; to Fort Knox, Kentucky, to observe a distributed SimNet tank exercise in action; to the Combat and Maneuvering Training Center in Hohenfels, Germany, to watch the First Armored Division "peacegame" their humanitarian intervention into Bosnia; to X-File territory at the Defense Advanced Research Projects Agency (DARPA) in Virginia, to learn how the Synthetic Theater of War (STOW) was being created to integrate virtual, live, and constructive simulations of war in real time; back again to Orlando, to visit STRI-COM (Simulation, Training, and Instrumentation Command), the newest, and probably the most unusual command post in the military; to the Bay Area to observe its occupation by the navy and marines in the "Urban Warrior" experiment; and then to Vicenza, Italy, to compare the claims and the outcome of the air campaign in Kosovo. I did eventually make the pilgrimage to the Pentagon, interviewing, among others, Andrew Marshall, director of the Office of Net Assessment, the Yoda of the Revolution in Military Affairs, and General Wesley Clark, former Supreme Allied Commander in Europe, on the day before his retirement from the army.

My travels end not far from where they started, in Los Angeles, where the Pentagon and Hollywood announced at the University of Southern California a new collaborative project. Over $40 million will be spent to establish an "Institute for Create Technologies," where the best military gamers, computer graphic artists, and entertainment executives can gather to prepare for the next war. From the desert to the laboratory to the studio, this book chronicles the successive stages—if not always successful staging—of virtuous warfare.

Inside and outside the military, and with the recent Republican presidential victory, the future of war is up for grabs. With lives and profits at stake, wars of position and maneuver are being fought on multiple fronts, within and among the military services, between Congress and the White House, in think tanks and defense industries, at home and abroad. In my travels, I come across many cases of open dissent and secret battles, where "mud soldiers" are fighting a rear-guard action against the "virtuous warriors." All are struggling with the uncertainties of the post-Cold War era. And many, while paying tribute to the virtual technologies as well as the virtues of humanitarian intervention, harbor great doubts whether they will bring us closer to or further from the intended goal of a more secure and just world order.

In the meantime and in most of the world, violence, fear, and terror persist and continue to resist both moral indictment and technological fixes—which is why I try to remain agnostic yet engaged in my travels, to avoid both neutral academic observation and simple moral condemnation. The argument of this book will not make for good sound bites, Powerpoint slides, or policy bullets. My goal is to intrigue rather than instruct the reader; in this sense, this book is as much a detective story as a cautionary tale. Scholars and journalists have been slow to cover the story of virtuous war, mainly because they can't find the smoking gun, let alone the increasingly virtualized body. I know where the bodies are, and, from my own family history, know too well the significance of when they go missing. I committed myself to wandering in deserts real and virtual because I believe most profoundly, as Walter Benjamin did in the waning days of the Weimar Republic, that "in times of terror, when everyone is something of a conspirator, everybody will be in a situation where he has to play detective."

1 The tank and the tortoise

Theorists soon found out how difficult the subject was and felt justified in evading the problem by again directing their principles and systems only to physical matters and unilateral activity. As in the science concerning *preparation for war*, they wanted to reach a set of sure and positive conclusions, and for that reason considered only factors that could be mathematically calculated.

(Carl von Clausewitz, *On War*)

When you emerge from the desert, your eyes go on trying to create emptiness all around; in every inhabited area, every landscape they see desert beneath, like a watermark.

(Jean Baudrillard, *America*)

In the high Mojave Desert, a pale imitation of trauma brought memories of my grandfathers' wars back to the surface. Except for the odd schoolyard fight, and getting beat up in a demonstration in Paris, I had managed to avoid anything remotely as violent as a battlefield. Yet on a desert hilltop, images of my grandfathers' wars rose and merged with the heat, noise, and immediacy of the approaching battle below.

I first heard of Fort Irwin at the beginning of the end of the Cold War, in a brief newspaper report about a visit made by the first President Bush. He had come by in February 1989 to observe a war game pitting the Third Armored Brigade of the Ninth Infantry Division against the Ninety-seventh Krasnovian Motorized Rifle Brigade. On the day of Bush's arrival, President Mikhail Gorbachev had done the unthinkable and announced an

Tank crossing.

Turtle crossing.

end to the Soviet Communist Party's monopoly on power. Outfitted in camouflage jacket, pinstripe trousers, and wing-tip shoes, Bush called a five-minute time-out to the war game to let the 2,689 soldiers below know the good news. By radio link he informed them from a ridge above that "we are pleased to see Chairman Gorbachev's proposal to expand steps toward pluralism." He pledged, however, "not to let down our guard against a worldwide threat." Inspired, the Krasnovians, as they are wont to do at the National Training Center (NTC), made borscht out of the Third Brigade. Bush didn't get to see the Soviet victory; he had already left for the Livermore Labs for a briefing on Star Wars, another system designed to defeat factual forces by fictitious ones.

Five years later I decided to make Fort Irwin the first stop of my virtual pilgrimage, to see how the future of warfare was being written in the desert sands of the Mojave. Created in 1981, Fort Irwin's purpose is to take American troops (and NATO allies) as close to the edge of war as the technology of simulation and the rigors of the environment will allow. My trip got off to a bad start. I was on a seemingly endless two-lane highway; it was too early, too dark, and, not wanting to give the public affairs officer another opportunity to explain what oh-five hundred meant, I was driving too fast to catch the first yellow warning sign. Fortunately I spotted the second one, just before the real thing crossed the road, of a black silhouette of a tank and underneath, TANK XING.

Digitally enhanced, computer-accessorized, and budgetarily gold-plated from the bottom of their combat boots to the top of their kevlar helmets, the 194th Separate Armored Brigade from Fort Knox, Kentucky, had come to Fort Irwin for Operation Desert Hammer VI. The first "Digital Rotation" of troops, this experimental war game was developed to show the top brass, a host of junketing congressmen, any potential enemies, and us— an odd mix of media—how, in the words of the press release, "digital technology can enhance lethality, operations tempo and survivability across the combined arms team in a tactically competitive training environment." In other words, the task force had come wired, to kill better, move faster, and live longer than the enemy.

In my mind, the pre-war game hype triggered all kinds of skeptical questions. Was digitization going to cut through the fog of war, or just add more layers of confusion? Could computers control the battlefield, or would the friction of war conquer the computers? Would the digital buzz drown out ethical questions? Would these new technologies further distance the killer from the business of killing?

These are hardly unfamiliar questions, even for the army. Back when messages traveled at the speed of a horse and overhead surveillance meant a hilltop, the Prussian strategist, Carl von Clausewitz, warned in *On War* against the arrogance of leaders who thought scripted battles would resemble the actual thing: "The general unreliability of all information presents a special problem in war: all action must, to a certain extent, be planned in a mere twilight, which in addition not infrequently—like the effect of fog or moonlight—gives to things exaggerated dimensions and an unnatural appearance."[1] Would digitization, the merging of the infospace with the battlespace, render Clausewitz's famous dictum obsolete? Understandably, Clausewitz didn't have much to say about infowar, netwar, cyberwar, and the like. He did, however, dismiss all contemporary attempts to use "positive theory" and technical knowledge to close the gap between planned and actual war. In his words, models, systems, and codes of war were finite syntheses, while war was inherently complex, open-ended, and interactive. To fight the digital hype and the illusion of a technological fix, I intended to follow his advice: apply, in his words, a "critical *inquiry*" that "poses the question to what are the peculiar effects of the means employed, and whether these effects conform to the intention with which they were used."

Operation Desert Hammer, however, was to turn Clausewitz on his head. Not only did the strategic effects of digitization prove to be very peculiar and to bear little conformity with the advertised intentions of the army; they seemed destined to replace an increasingly irrelevant nuclear balance of terror with a simulation of digitized superiority: call it the new *cyberdeterrent*.

By the end of the first day, after chasing the black-bereted Krasnovians through the Whale Gap and, lo, into the Valley of Death, watching them kick American khaki all the way to the John Wayne Hills, I was left with no better sense of whether the professed claims for the digitized army were true or not. One reason is that the use of digitization was not readily apparent—or even visible. So we largely had to rely on the claims of the glossy brochures and our voluble briefers and handlers. Since these claims often came in packaged phrases and punchy sound bites, my skepticism kicked in early. Many had the ring of a corporate advertising campaign. Top of the list, with budget cuts clearly on everyone's mind, was "Smaller is not better: better is better." Others sounded like a hybrid of Nick Machiavelli and Bill Gates— "Win the Battlefield Information War"—or of a New Army for the New Age—"Project and Sustain the Force." Analogies proliferated like mad: digitization is equivalent to the addition of the stirrup to the saddle, or the integration of helicopters into the army. By the second day I could fathom the meaning, but not test the truth of some statements, like "digitization will get us inside the enemy's decision-making cycle." And I could only think of a sky full of frogs with wings when one of the public affairs officers boldly declared that "If General Custer had digitization, he never would have had a last stand."

On paper, however, the combination of brute force and high tech did appear formidable. At the high end of the lethality spectrum there was the improved MIA2 Abrams main battle tank, carrying an IVIS (Inter-Vehicular Information System) which could collect real-time battlefield data from overhead JSTAR aircraft (Joint Surveillance and Target Attack Radar System), Pioneer unmanned aerial vehicles equipped with video cameras, and global positioning satellite systems (GPS) to display icons of friendlies and foes on a computer-generated map overlay. At the low end, there was the "21st Century Land Warrior" (also called "warfighter," but never "soldier" or "infantryman"), who came equipped with augmented day and night vision scopes mounted on his M-16, a GPS, 8 mm video camera, and one-inch ocular LED screen connected by a flexible arm to his kevlar, and an already-dated 486 Lightweight Computer Unit in his backpack, all wired for voice or digital-burst communication to a BattleSpace Command Vehicle with an All Source Analysis System that could collate the information and coordinate the attack through a customized Windows program. "Using the power of the computer microprocessor and digital electronics," digitization was designed to be a "force multiplier": the "horizontal integration of information nodes" and the "exchange of real-time information and data" were going "to establish friendly force dominance of enemy forces." In short, the army was creating a C4I bundle (command, control, communication, computers, and intelligence) of soft-, hard-, and wetware for the coming information war.

I wondered what Clausewitz, who warned that "a far more serious menace is the retinue of *jargon, technicalities, and meta-phors*,"[2] would have made of this press packet. Or what was handed out in the predawn along with it and our helmets: two sets of release forms with lots of fine print. I sensed the disdain of my media cohort, a reporter and photographer from the *Army Times*, because I insisted on reading the release before signing it. It wasn't the physical harm stuff that bothered me (that much); it was the clause about permissible photo-ops. It seemed to suggest that the army could refuse the taking of any staged photographs. Since I interpreted *all* of what we were about to see as staged, couldn't this amount to a blanket restriction? A higher-up was called over, who assured me that this meant only that I could not request a *rerun* of a battle scene in case I missed it the first time around. Dan Rather probably would have demanded rights to a director's cut, but I signed the thing before I used up my quota of goodwill.

When the motto miasma met the fog of war on the first day of battle, the fog seemed to win out—especially since it came amply supplemented by sand, dust, and smoke (the latter provided in copious amounts by M54 pulse-jet smoke dischargers). Our hand-ler, Major Childress, already introduced, did his best to explain what was going on around us. After leading our small convoy of three High Mobility Multipurpose Wheeled Vehicles (HMMWV), known as "Humvees," to that fine hillside perch to watch the dawn battle unfold, he provided a running commentary for what we could see—and also what we could hear as we eavesdropped on the radio traffic among the combatants, and heard those reports of fratricide or "friendly fire."

Nobody wanted to go on record to say how the battle started. I later learned from a defense industry rep squirreled away in a back room that it began out of sight (and out of the public eye) with the launch of a cruise missile off the Californian coast; it landed somewhere on the live-fire range (rather than, say, a Las Vegas casino). For us, the battle began with an array of Black Hawk and Apache helicopters coming in so close to the deck that we looked down from above as they flew by. My first thought was of the two U.S. helicopters mistakenly shot down by U.S. fighter planes over Iraq the week before the exercise, a deadly case of "friendly fire." The first Black Hawk, equipped with external fuel tanks, did bear a resemblance to a Soviet Hind. I filed away the question as an F-16 followed it, sweeping over our hill and dropping flares to confuse possible ground-to-air missiles. Had the pilots that shot down the helicopters ever trained against Black Hawks pretending to be Soviet Hinds?

The level of confusion rose as loud bangs joined the visuals. An M-22 simulator round, about the size of a fat shotgun shell, went off as a nearby Stinger crew fired at an F-16. Then came the white plumes of "Hoffmans," blanks that simulate the flash and bang of tank and artillery fire, spreading across the battlefield. The arrival of the main show was signaled by tracks of dust on the horizon. Tanks, Humvees with TOWS (Tube Launched Optically Tracked Wire Guided missiles), and armored personnel carriers came out of the wadis with a burst of speed. As the Opposing Forces (OPFOR) began to mix it up with the visiting Twenty-fourth Mechanized Division, vehicles bearing the orange flags of the war game observer/controllers darted in and out as they tallied up the kills. They depended on the MILES, or Multiple Integrated Laser Engagement Systems (first developed by Xerox Electro-Optical, now better known as laser tag), which were attached to every weapon from the M-16s to F-16s. Configured to match the range of each weapon system, the Gallium Arsenide laser, for example, on the M1A2 main battle tanks could reach out and touch someone at 3,000 meters. Hits and near misses were recorded by the sensors on the vests and belts that circled soldiers and vehicles alike, and transmitted by microwave relay transmitters back to computers in the "Star Wars" (also known in some circles by the more imperial-sounding "Dark Star") building from which the battle was run. From our hillside we could see the flashing yellow strobes of the MILES sensors spread across the battlefield as the OPFORS cut through the American forces. Simulation-hardened and terrain-savvy, the "Krasnovians," as they are, post-Cold War, nostalgically still called, rarely lose—even on the rare occasions when they must redial the threat and take on the garb and tactics of the "Sumarians" (Iraqis) or "Hamchuks" (North Koreans).

Suddenly we received a radio order to move: our position was about to be overrun. Events were moving more swiftly than commands: the Krasnovian tanks had already crested the ridge and were heading for us. Sensing a good photo-op, I brought my camera up to greet them. It wasn't until the tanks were within smelling distance that I realized everyone else had scurried, for good reason, to the other side of the hill. I found myself alone and in a very precarious position.

Synapses fired and hormones mixed into a high-octane cocktail, telling me to fight or take flight. I did neither. I froze, feeling that terrifying yet seductive rush that comes when the usual boundaries, between past and present, war and game, spectator and participant, break down. The catatonia was short; but caught in an extraordinary balance between real and pretend states of danger, I experienced a strange, dreamlike synchronicity. I was there, but not there. The threat was unreal, distanced by high technology and the simulation of war; and yet, with the approaching tank, all too real. I could imagine yet deny death, my own as well as others. Detached and yet connected to a dangerous situation by a kind of traumatic voyeurism, I watched myself watch the tanks bear down. In this moment elongated by terror, I entered the borderlands of simulation, where fear and fun, friend and foe, all blur together.

I was standing still and yet still traveling, from one grandfather's displaced experience to the other's, from the coke-oven hell to a theme-park Elysian Fields, from then to now, where soldiers died, got up, and lived to fight another day. In this virtual world, dying and killing become less plausible—and all the more possible.

Memory provided a way out of the trauma of the moment, not so much an escape but a way to reconnect the real and unreal, to put the present and past together, to put my cousin's head back on the body—to *re-member* who I was and why I was here. One might call what I experienced (but for fear of diminishing my grandfathers' wars) a poetic, even epiphanic moment. More precisely, since the event eventually transformed a jumble of thoughts and fears into these words, it represented a *poiesis*, the creative force that ancient Greeks derived from the staging of life's tragedies, many of them founded in deaths brought about by an excess of pride and violence. Fort Irwin might be a military base stuck in the middle of the Mojave Desert, but like not-too-distant Las Vegas, it was a perfect stage for the evocation of past and future, hopes and fears. I had entered the theater of war, not literally but *virtually*. And paradoxically, war became flesh.

In less poetic and more immediate technical terms, I witnessed the virtual continuation of war by other means. The means were technological; the continuation was one of distance foreshortened by speed of bytes and bits, missives and missiles. Distance was afforded by the F-16s and A-10s flying overhead; the simulated launch of precision munitions; the remote video cameras perched on the hilltops; the laser-sensor arrays on every soldier and every weapon; the computer networks that controlled the battle-space; and all the other digital technologies operating as "force-multipliers." To be sure, accident, friction, or miscalculation could, and at times did, collapse this virtual distancing. However, the ultimate measurement of distance in war, the difference between life and death, was nowhere in sight.

I eventually did manage to cut across the ridge, rejoin the group, and make my way back to civilization—if Barstow, California, qualifies. When I replayed the videotape of the battle in my Quality Inn room, a further shift in perspective took place, from a shared terror to a kind of personal voyeurism. In retrospect, out of the time-loopiness of the moment, where previews of the future merged with flashbacks to the past, my experience bore little resemblance to my grandfathers'. The reality of death had been twice removed, by video and by simulation. My grandfathers' wars disappeared into the multiple levels of virtuality inscribed on the blank desert slate of Fort Irwin. There the landscape was a five-dimensional "battlespace," with soldiers as "land warriors," and the enemy not as flesh and blood but as iconic symbol, a "target-of-opportunity" on a computer screen. At a purely tactical level, without the benefit of night-goggles, overhead drones, JSTAR aircraft, satellite reconnaissance, my grandfathers could not have even seen let alone recognized this virtualized enemy. Smart, brilliant, over-the-horizon weapons reached and killed far beyond their ken. Lasers attached to M-16s stood in for bullets, and when a sensor vest registered a hit, disappointment, not death, was the strongest reaction.

Nonetheless, in that moment of mimesis—what the Greek tragedians and many psychologists consider to be the most fundamental form of learning—a past trauma had been retriggered and newly comprehended. Trauma, Freud tells us, can be reenacted, even reexperienced, but cannot be understood at the moment of shock. This is what Michael Herr was getting at in *Dispatches*, when he wrote about his experiences in Vietnam:

> It took the war to teach it, that you were as responsible for everything you saw as you were for everything you did. The problem was that you didn't always know what you were seeing until later, maybe years later, that a lot of it never made it in at all, it just stayed stored there in your eyes.[3]

In a sense, then, war has always been a virtual reality, too traumatic for immediate comprehension. But now there is an added danger, a further barrier to understanding it. When compared to the real trauma of war, the pseudotrauma of simulation pales. But an insidious threat emerges from its shadowing of reality. In this high-tech rehearsal for war, one learns how to kill but not to take responsibility for it, one experiences "death" but not the tragic consequences of it. In the extreme case, with the predisposed pathologies of a Slobodan Milosevic in Serbia, a Timothy McVeigh in Oklahoma City, or an Eric Harris in Littleton, Colorado, this can lead to a kind of doubling or splitting of the self that psychologists Robert Jay Lifton and Erik Markusen see as a source of the "genocidal mentality." But what I witnessed was more a closing than an opening of a schism, between how we see and live, represent and experience, simulate and fight war. New technologies of imitation and simulation as well as surveillance and speed had collapsed the geographical distance, chronological duration, the gap itself between the reality and virtuality of war. As the confusion of one for the other grows, we face the danger of a new kind of trauma without sight, drama without tragedy, where television wars and video war games blur together. We witness this not only at the international level, from the Gulf War to the Kosovo campaign, but also on the domestic front, where two teenagers predisposed to violence confused the video game *Doom* for the high school classroom.

Of course at the time, all this was more of a psychobiological reaction than an intellectual insight. But I did sense at the moment a dirty secret of war-cum-game bubbling to the surface. I tasted for the first time that combination of fear and fun that allows the soldier to espy yet deny death, their own as well as others'.

As we rode back to the base that day, I wondered what effect digitization would have on this existential juice. Not quite sure how to pose the question to Major Childress—who already seemed to have some doubts about my take on things after I asked if they simulate accidents ("No, we have those for real here")—I decided to let it sit for awhile. Besides, bouncing around and eating dust in a Humvee at fifty miles per hour was an effective deterrent against long, philosophical conversations. Remarkably, the correspondent from the *Army Times* had fallen asleep, his kevlared head jerking around like a rag-doll version of G.I. Joe. I longed for the comfort of my motel, the coolness of the pool— or just a vehicle with a windshield. I could barely hack a day of simulated battle, let alone a real war. Judging from some of the thousand-mile stares I got from the Stinger teams, Abrams tankers, and Paladin howitzer crews that I had interviewed, I realized that Fort Irwin had effectively replicated at least one of the primary characteristics of modern, round-the-clock warfare: fatigue. Surprisingly often, to the extent that it almost appeared scripted, soldiers responded to my question about the reality factor of simulations with the claim that the Gulf War was much easier than this. Keeping up with machines is a dirty business.

Day Two began, as the first, in the dark and behind schedule. But this time I did catch the icon on the first yellow warning sign. It was a tortoise, not a tank. One more question for the major.

The main group had already left. A Humvee was waiting and ready to catch up to the media convoy. My new driver, however, failed to inspire much confidence. He was unable to make radio contact with the major and kept switching frequencies until I suggested that he put up the antenna. And finally acknowledging we were lost, he radioed for directions, only to get the message wrong. I thought the LAPD clearly had the digitized jump on the army in communications: with all the ambient noise of a mechanized battlefield, a screen readout would be vastly superior to the spoken word. But our next stop revealed that the army was actually preparing to leapfrog that generation of technology.

After a cross-country shortcut through a minefield (marked by round plastic bowls that looked like doggie dishes) and a couple more wrong turns, we caught up with the rest of the group at what appeared to be a desert rest stop for twenty-first century warfighters. I was directed to a medical unit, simulating the latest in "telemedicine." Each soldier in Operation Desert Hammer carried a 3.5 inch computer disk in their breast pocket, not to stop a bullet but to store a digitized image of their predestined wound. In a real war in the near-future a video camera would record the body damage. In this case the medic popped the disk into a portable Powerbook to discover that his victim had a sucking chest wound. The image was digitized and transferred via a radio link to a triage unit in the rear, where a doctor talked the medic through the treatment of the wounded soldier. It seemed to work: the soldier got up and walked away from the stretcher when I moved on to another way station of the digitized army.

My next stop was the *Next Generation*, or so it seemed, for a Borg was on display. Here was a warfighter in the flesh—and metal—just as he had been described in the brochures. His eyes shielded by wrap-around Terminator shades, he gave me a long rap about the capabilities of his gear in a flat monotone, Kansas or thereabouts.

"At the top of my kevlar is the Global Positioning antenna. It goes to the computer which fits in the radio compartment of the ruck. It gives me an eight-digit military grid, wherever we are in the world. On the right side of the kevlar we have the helmet-mounted display—or HMD as we like to call it. Through this we see our computer screen and our three digital visual devices. One, our Sony 8 mm camera on the left side of my kevlar, which is a daylight camera—what you see is what you get. The second device being a thermal sight which picks up heat off the battlefield and transfers it into an image we can see, through smoke, fog, anything that limits our visibility. The third being the image intensifier, or eye-squared as we like to call it. It takes available light and intensifies it to give us a picture. All three of these can take pictures which we send back to the rear through our 486 light-weight computer unit in my rucksuck, beside the PRC-139 which is a standard military radio modified to send digital messages over FM radio wave. This is only a prototype. The system right now weighs thirty pounds, including weapon, but in the future we plan to get it smaller and lighter."

After the warfighter finished I asked if he knew that it had all been done before, that he was a dead ringer for one of those tough, wired-to-the-max colonial marines in the film *Aliens*. His reply bordered on curt: "I don't know about that, sir" (all media reps enjoy an instant field promotion to officer); but it came in a tone that said he sure as shit did know about that. Never, never confuse an army grunt, especially a fully digitized one, with a marine no-neck, even if only a fictional one. It seemed that all the hype we were hearing about the new era of joint operations was slow in making its way down through the ranks.

Next I was led to the latest version of the Abrams tank, an M1A2. I took a few pictures and started to walk away but was stopped by the hovering major, who asked, as he might ask a child if they wanted a piece of candy, "Do you want to take a look inside?" He surely registered my surprise. During a preliminary visit to the NTC I had been told that I could take pictures of just about anything—but in no instance the inside of an M1 tank, which remained classified. Now I was being urged to videotape a state-of-the-art model of the same vehicle down to the last micro-chip. A gunner walked me through the cyberspaces of the IVIS computer targeting system: your position triangulated by satellite, here an enemy targeted by laser range-finding and thermal-imaging, and there a friendly identified by a relay from a JSTAR flying overhead.

At the end of this digital whirlwind I was left impressed—clearly the intent—and somewhat confused, not just by the untroubled faith in high technology but also by this untrammeled access to it. I had asked the stock questions: Would the friction of war overheat a cybernetic battle plan? Would the surge of information overload all these digitized systems, especially the primary informational node of the battle net, the warfighters? And I had received for the most part by-the-book responses: per-haps, but not so far, and besides this is all in the experimental stage. I remembered Clausewitz's critical approach, to match means and ends, to pair effects and intentions. Surely they could not be effectively tested here at Fort Irwin, for the simulation of digitized battle only further distanced the theory and planning from the violence and chaos of war, and reduced the ethical question of killing to a matter of maximizing efficiency. Perhaps I was asking the wrong set of questions.

Perhaps it was my preoccupation with the Gulf War, or rather, the quick victory for which the NTC training was being credited. The army prided itself on being grounded in reality, in the way that General Schwarzkopf during the war always referred to himself as nothing but a "mud soldier." Now, like the navy and the air force before, the army was leaping into a realm of hyperreality, where the enemy disappeared as flesh and blood and reappeared pixilated and digitized on computer screens in killing zones, as icons of opportunity. Was there a paradox operating here, that the closer the war game was able to technically reproduce the reality of war, the greater the dangers that might arise from confusing one for the other?

At the levels of tactical training as well as strategic planning, a growing body of evidence warrants a critical investigation. The case of the Black Hawk fratricide was perhaps still too fresh, but a similar case, the shoot-down of the Iranian Airbus by the *USS Vincennes* in 1988, does illustrate the problem. Both the radar operator and the tactical information coordinator of the Aegis missile system mistook a blip on a screen for an attacking F-14. Did nine months of prior training by computer simulation tapes undercut their own critical judgment and overpower the correct information on their radar screen, of a plane flying level at 12,000 feet?

At the strategic level there was a series of reported events leading up to Desert Shield that never seemed to have been followed up on. In a *U.S.A. Today* interview Schwarzkopf revealed that two years before the war U.S. intelligence had discovered that Iraq was running computer simulations and war games for the invasion of Kuwait. Indeed, Iraq had purchased a war game from the Washington military-consulting firm BDM International to use in its earlier war against Iran. Almost as an aside it was reported in September 1990 on *ABC Nightline* that the software for the

Kuwait invasion simulation was also purchased from a U.S. firm.[4] Moreover, during the Desert Shield conflict Schwarzkopf stated that he almost daily programmed possible conflicts with Iraq on computers. It should be noted that Schwarzkopf's mainland posting was commander in chief of Central Command at Tampa, Florida, which was an *administrative* headquarters in charge of the Middle East, Southwest Asia, and Northeast Africa: that is, a paper army without troops, tanks, or aircraft of its own. Hence, without real troops, his affinity for computer simulations is unsurprising.

It turns out that the mud soldier Schwarzkopf was the first cyberpunk general. Not well known is that Schwarzkopf sponsored a highly significant computer-simulated command post exercise that was played in 1990, July 23 to 28, under the code name of Exercise Internal Look '90. According to a news release from Central Command, approximately 350 high-ranking members from each of the military services gathered at Eglin Air Force Base to war game how "command and control elements from all branches of the military will be responding to real-world scenarios similar to those they might be expected to confront within the Central Command AOR [Area of Responsibility]."[5] The trigger for the real-world scenario? An Iraqi invasion of Kuwait. The resulting contingency plan was the size of a large telephone book, and spelled out everything from the number of divisions required, to the number of casualties expected, and the best way to handle the news media. Less than a week after the exercise was completed, the Iraqis actually invaded Kuwait. Schwarzkopf, according to his autobiography, found that his planners at Central Command kept mixing up the reports from Internal Look with the real thing (see Chapter 7, interview with Michael Macedonia).

Had the paradox of simulation moved from the surreal to the hyperreal? Was the Gulf War the product of a U.S. war game designed to fight a war game bought by Iraq from a U.S. company? To be sure, the given reasons of protecting the oil fields and deterring aggression were significant factors for rallying the coalition forces. But is it possible that new—let us say digitally improved—simulations can precede and engender the reality of war that they were intended to model and prepare for? To reinvoke and upend Clausewitz: can the strategic effects of digitized means predetermine policy intentions?

Clearly the army wasn't reading up on French critics like Jean Baudrillard or Paul Virilio who inspire such questions. But I was surprised to discover that they were reading—and reprinting—cyberpunk novelist and *Wired* writer Bruce Sterling on the same issues.[6] The day before my departure I had received from the NTC an air-express package from the office of the Secretary of the Army. Officially it was identified as the press kit for the Advanced Warfighting Experiment, or AWE for short. But this did not do it justice. Collected in a large three-ring binder with the triangle logo for "The Digital Battlefield" on the cover (satellite, helicopter, and tank in each corner, connected by lightning bolts to a warfighter in the middle) were over thirty press releases, brochures, and articles on the army of the future. In style and content they replicated the corporate publications that I had picked up at the annual Interservice/Industry Training Systems Conference in Orlando, where simulation industries like Loral, Silicon Graphics, and Evans and Sutherland paraded their wares to the military (see Chapter 4). Computer-generated images were mixed in with all kinds of fonts and graphics. Indeed, it all looked a bit like *Wired* magazine.

Leading the paper charge of the simulation brigade was a prolegomenon from the office of the Chief of Staff. It bears quotation, since it provides the best encapsulation of the rationale behind the twenty-first century army:

> Today, we are on the threshold of a new era, and we must proceed into it decisively. Today the Industrial Age is being superseded by the Information Age, the Third Wave, hard on the heels of the agrarian industrial eras. Our present Army is well-configured to fight and win in the late Industrial Age, and we can handle Agrarian-Age foes as well. We have begun to move into Third Wave Warfare, to evolve a new force for a new century—Force XXI.

A series of categorical imperatives for the Force XXI follow. They call for nothing short of a paradigm-shift:

Force XXI will represent a new way of thinking for a new wave of warfare. We must be strategically flexible and more lethal. We must leverage the power of the best soldiers in our history through the use of state-of-the-art simulations and realistic, simulator-enhanced training. We must accommodate the wide-range of operations being demanded of the U.S. Intellectual change leads physical change—the mental shift goes before the software and hardware.

One brochure, slicker than all the rest, maps out how the army was making the future present. It bears the short yet pretentious title "The Vision." It leads with the now common litany of the national security mandarins, that with the fall of the Berlin wall, the dissolution of the Soviet Union, the rise of regional powers, and the advent of MTV (reading between the lines here) no one can safely predict what is to come, nor who is to be the next enemy. The Chief of Staff, General Gordon Sullivan, asks, "What's next?" and answers, "No one knows." Therefore, "We are relatively safe in predicting, however, that the strategic environment in the next decade will be dynamic, uncertain, and unstable." Military jargon married to technospeak usually calls for high waders, so I was surprised to find a few pages later a box in the section on "Exploit Modeling and Simulation" that read, well, like a good cyberpunk novel:

The Distributed Simulation Internet, projected for the turn of the century, is to be a creature of another order entirely from SIMNET. Ten thousand linked simulators! Entire literal armies online, global realtime, broadband, fiber-optic, satellite-assisted, military simulation networking. And not just connected, not just simulated. Seamless.

It gets better, and for good reason: it was written by Bruce Sterling for *Wired*. What does it mean when *Wired* is appropriated for the army's "Vision"? Perhaps in the void of post-Cold War strategy, when "enlargement" of democracy and free markets is the first foreign-policy concept offered by the Clinton administration as a plausible replacement for "containment" of the Soviet threat, it is wholly understandable that the army's visionary reach should exceed its rhetorical grasp. Indeed, I had come across much stranger intertexts in the course of the visit to Fort Irwin. One briefer had described the intensity of Desert Hammer as somewhere between the Gulf War and *Red Storm Rising*. Not such a surprise, considering that former Vice President Quayle had once defended Star Wars (the antimissile system, not the movie—or the building on base) by citing the same Tom Clancy novel.

Or perhaps something else was going on, something I sensed in the M1A2, and again when I was granted video-taping privileges not once but twice in the Star Wars building, command central of the NTC. Was my presence at Fort Irwin, no less so than Bruce Sterling's in "The Vision," just one more tactical exercise in the army's much-vaunted Information War? As early as 1964, after reading a breathless promotional account of the "cyborg" under development by GE and the military (from the photographs it looked like a robotic elephant), Lewis Mumford warned of the coming of a new "technological exhibitionism."[7] Thirty years on, was I bearing witness to an even more powerful, possibly perverse hybrid? What happens when we combine media voyeurism, technological exhibitionism, and strategic simulations? News flash: In the twenty-first century army, we get the cyberdeterrent.

If this sounds far-fetched, consider the worst-case scenario that continues to dominate strategic thinking. With the fall of the Soviet Union, CIA director James Woolsey declared at his confirmation hearings that a "bewildering variety of poisonous snakes" has sprung forth from the slain dragon. With the dragon went the mighty if mainly illusory deterrence value of nuclear weapons. On a quest since Vietnam (to fight only quick, popular, winnable wars), and imbued by the spirit of Sun Tzu ("Those skilled in war subdue the enemy's army without battle"), the twenty-first century army has perhaps now found in the cyberdeterrent its Holy Grail. It is fast, digitized, and as spectacular in simulation as it is global in effect. As nuclear proliferation increases and the nuclear threshold declines, digitized warfare has the advantage of being out of reach of all but the richest states of concern (formerly known as rogues). And it makes a hell of a photo-op.

Moreover, the digitized deterrence machine bears an important similarity to its nuclear counterpart: it does not *necessarily* have to work in order to be effective. Its power lies in a symbolic exchange of metaphysical signs—give or take the odd reality-check in the desert to bring religion to the doubters. Hence spectacles like Desert Hammer IV, to render visible and plausible the cyberdeterrent for all those potential snakes that might not have sufficiently learned the lesson of the first (if prototypical) virtuous war, Desert Storm.

Once again the desert functions as backdrop for the melodrama of national security. With an assist from Disneyland, Hollywood, and Silicon Valley, the National Training Center, full of video cameras, computerized special effects, not to mention thrilling rides, has superseded Los Alamos and the Nevada Test Site to become the premier production set for the next generation of U.S. strategic superiority. Can the army go on to win the information war without firing another (real) shot? Of slightly lesser concern, can one conduct a critical inquiry of the information war without becoming, well, just another informant for it, a box in the army's sequel issue, "(Re)Vision"?

Biologist turned social critic Donna Haraway, more sanguine than Mumford about the technological turn, offers a possible escape pod from the dilemma. She seeks to avoid the disasters but does not forsake the advantages of technoscience. In her embryonic 1985 essay, "A Manifesto for Cyborgs," she troubles the binary opposition between Mother Nature and Father Science to imagine a friendlier model:

> From one perspective, a cyborg world is about the final imposition of a grid of control on the planet, about the final abstraction embodied in a Star War, apocalypse waged in the name of defense, about the final appropriation of women's bodies in a masculinist orgy of war. From another perspective, a cyborg world might be about lived social and bodily realities in which people are not afraid of their joint kinship with animals and machines, not afraid of permanently partial identities and contradictory standpoints. The political struggle is to see from both perspectives at once because each reveals both dominations and possibilities unimaginable from the other vantage point.[8]

On Day Three, at the finish line of the war game, I discovered a protocyborg that played by a different set of rules, one that might just offer another perspective and some of the alternative possibilities envisioned by Haraway.

The Army, it turns out, did not have the desert on its own. Heading back at the usual hell-bent speed from the battlefield on Day Two, I asked the major over the wind and noise about the strange warning sign that had caught my attention early in the morning. "Desert Tortoise," he shouted. "Fifty thousand dollars if you kill one." I had to wait until we returned to the base to find out whether that was the bountry or the penalty. I learned that the desert tortoise had been given emergency endangered species status back in 1990. And since the NTC encompassed some of its main breeding grounds, a clash of armored vehicles and reptilian counterpart seemed inevitable. What was the army to do? It decided to go Green—or at least a slightly muddy version of it—to protect a sign of life in the desert that predated it and could well outlast all the killing machines. Detecting some interest on my part, the major offered to set up a briefing the next day with Fort Irwin's environmental scientists who were in charge of protecting the tortoise, among other environmental concerns. Suffering from a bad case of simulation fatigue, I quickly accepted.

At a reasonable hour the following morning, they were ready and waiting for me. In the conference room there was a large table covered with photographs and plaques, wall charts and easels, coffee and donuts. And next to the slide projector stood three guys in ties armed with laser pointers—and yes, pocket protectors. Judging from their intensive prep and genuine enthusiasm, they didn't get many opportunities to sell their ecowares to the press. After all, how could a lumbering desert tortoise possibly match the media appeal of an attacking M1 tank? The slide show was informative ("Without our help, the survival rate of the tortoise is 1 percent"), moving ("To a raven, a freshly hatched tortoise looks like a walking ravioli"), and amusing ("Here we see several tortoises in parade formation after completing their training at Fort Irwin"). The scientists proudly showed off awards for their environmental work, including a controversial one from the Sierra Club ("Some members didn't think it was right to give one to the *Big* Green"). And they were matching the warfighters, chip for chip, in the information war. Tortoises were tagged with transmitters, tracked by radio telemetry, and graphed in grid locations by computers. Landsat satellites identify potential breeding areas, aerial mine detection technology locates nesting sites, and electronic sensors warn off intruders. By the end of the briefing I began to believe that I had just witnessed the telling of a postmodern fable. Perhaps, with a techno-ethical assist and a leap of faith, the tortoise might yet beat the tank.

I know that's a stretch—and not quite Aesop—but what more can we expect when machines take the place of animals in the imagining of the human race?

Krasnovians on attack.

"Star Wars" at Fort Irwin.

2 Between wars

> What follows here is an experiment in awakening. . . . The imminent awakening is poised, like the wooden horse of the Greeks, in the Troy of dreams.
>
> (Walter Benjamin, *The Arcades Project*)

At daybreak, hours before that elongated moment of terror and minor epiphany, I had surveyed from a hilltop the beginning of the simulated battle at Fort Irwin. Black Hawk and Apache helicopters flew so close to the deck they were below us, F-16s and A-10s roared overhead, and the dust and smoke trails of M1A1 tanks and Bradley armored personnel carriers cut across the desert floor. It was difficult to tell just what was going on, but our personable handler, Major Childress, former commander of an OPFOR unit and then head of public affairs at the National Training Center, did his best. He provided a running commentary for what we could see, but we learned more by eavesdropping on the radio traffic among the combatants. Accounts of confusion and in more than one instance, fratricide or "friendly fire," were overheard. It was, however, an aside from a member of the press that provided some much-needed perspective.

For the most part my media cohort had avoided me. I would like to think it was because of my intelligent questions and refusal to suck up to the brass; but it was more likely something less significant, like my failure to observe the press dress code. But at that moment, Austin Bay, ex-army, military historian, and co-author of *A Quick and Dirty Guide to War*, turned to me and said,

"It's just like Salisbury Plain." Without a clue, I knowingly nod-
ded, and wondered what TV dinners had to do with digital battlefields. I took the opportunity of the long ride back to the base
headquarters to ask Bay to explain further. Over the wind and
noise of the open Humvee, he filled me in. Salisbury Plain was the
British forerunner of the NTC, and it was there in the 1920s that
troops, tanks, and airplanes, aided by wireless, came together for
the first demonstration of mobile armored warfare. It was, Bay
shouted, a revolution.

About a year later, thanks to the grant gods, I had a chance to
check out his story at the Bodleian Library in Oxford. I began by
searching the microfiche roles of the *Daily Telegraph*, not so much
out of curiosity about the event as how it registered among the
military and politicians. Were the Salisbury Plain exercises recognized as a revolution at the time? Were they viewed as technological
solution, or dangerous innovation? Who learned what lessons?
I chose the *Telegraph* because I knew that Liddell Hart had been
its military correspondent—and much more.[1] Hart, a decorated
officer during the First World War, had made a name for himself as
an early proponent for mechanization, for a "New Model" army
based on "tank marines" ready to use "the indirect approach," to
fight highly mobile battles on land as the navy fought at sea. He
was not particularly well loved by the traditionalists, and his
legacy continues to be debated among modern strategists.[2]

Hart was writing at a time when Germany was disarming under
the agreements of the Treaty of Versailles, and the French, under
the direction of war minister Andre Maginot, were recasting trench
warfare and protecting falling birth rates by a defensive frontier
of concrete. The British, on the other hand, had the luxury (no
real enemy threat), the temperament (no desire to repeat the
slaughter of the previous war), and the technology (still the leader
in industrial innovation) to experiment. From August 1927 to
1931, Salisbury Plain became the premier laboratory of a new
form of warfare. Armored cars, light and medium tanks, motorized artillery, infantry in trucks and half-tracks, and even the odd
horse were on the move, first during the day, later even at night.
Hart's initial reports on the first exercises in 1927 were somewhat
disdainful: aircraft were simulated, colored flags stood in for antitank guns, and radios, when in evidence, rarely worked. But by the

"Armoured Force" exercise of 1928, the tone begins to change. In a display of networked warfare, 150 wireless sets were used for a strategic maneuver that left an assembled group of brass and members of Parliament highly impressed. Hart considered the exercises a success in 1931, when the First Brigade Royal Tank Regiment, taking orders by radio, managed to maneuver through the fog in concert to arrive on time before a gathering of the Army Council.

The first and last reports that he filed in the *Daily Telegraph*, during one seminal year of exercises on Salisbury Plain, 1927, provide a sense of their far-reaching significance for the future of warfare. On the front pages were stories about the naval conference in Geneva (most notably, friction between the U.S. and Great Britain—with Japanese support—on cruiser tonnage and gun size); death sentences for Nicola Sacco and Bartolomeo Vanzetti, the Italian anarchists; and my favorite headline: "Trotsky's Victory—Stalin's Move Checked—Surprise for Moscow." Hart's earliest articles were on page five or after, mixed in with pictures of military bands and tanks bogged down in the mud; gradually the articles moved up to page one. Entertainment is liberally mixed with education: the reports read like the bread and circuses of late empires—much like our own evening news. Here is an excerpt from his first report, "Tidworth Tattoo—Modern War Staged," dated Monday August 1, 1927:

Tidworth is the home of the mechanized force which is expected to play a great part in the future development of the Army. Therefore it is fitting that the star attraction of the Southern Command Tattoo, which commenced before many thousands of people in the arena in Tidworth on Saturday night, should be a "battle" in which the latest mechanized units take part. When an interesting programme was nearing its end, the searchlights flashed on to an Eastern fort, where picturesque Eastern marauders were taking rest. Almost immediately the battle began. A signal for assistance sent by the British commander brought a reconnaissance car to the spot, and, following quickly in its wake, came the mechanized machine guns, the latest swift-moving tankettes spitting fire, with a self-propelled gun giving protection to the British force, and in doing so adding to the din. The mobility of the new armoured units enhanced the realism of the episode, and undoubtedly this battle will prove one of the most attractive features of the performances.

There is plenty of variety in the programme, for following community singing and the fanfare of trumpets, massed bands of the 2nd Cavalry and 7th Infantry Brigades enter the arena in peace-time uniform, the cavalry bandsmen mounted, and all playing delightful music. . . . Lancer trick riders carry through amazing feats and some remarkable jumping, the obstacles including a donkey and cart, bed, fire hoop, and fire bar. . . . The concluding item before the reassembling of the soldier actors is a display by the Royal Air Force in illumin-ated aeroplanes. . . .

The tattoo was a huge success on its first night and will be continued during the week . . . the railway companies are running excursions from all over the South of England and buses are expected to bring many hundreds of spectators.

If the performative, spectacular, even exotic nature of the exercise is not obvious from this account, consider his last article on August 23, 1927, about the Salisbury "Tattoo" (so-named for the traditional bugle call or drum beat that would begin a battle). It was headlined, "Mechanical Gods of Modern Warfare—Tanks in Night Move—Driving Feat in the Dark":

I watched the column from a point close to Stonehenge, and in the apt and eerie setting of that dreary monolith-surmounted down, at midnight, little imagination was needed to picture it as the passage of a herd of primeval monsters or legendary dragons, with glassy eyes shining in the darkness, fiery breath, and scale-coated body. So irresistible was the impression that I pity any belated motorist who met them, unprepared on his homeward road. And the passage by Stonehenge had also a symbolical effect, for there the gods of the prehistoric past could be conceived as watching from their long-abandoned altars the procession of the mechanical gods of modern man—both equally the creation of man, but the one expressing the static mentality of the past, and the other the ever-changing, restless motion of the mind of to-day.

Impressed, but not convinced, the British general staff failed to learn the lessons of armored warfare war-gamed on Salisbury Plain. Defeated, and some might even say rendered desperate by disarmament and the fiscal restraints imposed by reparations, the German staff did not. They studied the writings of Hart, the 1929 booklet *Mechanized and Armoured Formations* by Colonel Charles Broad, and the controversial views of the other great advocate of armored warfare, J. F. C. Fuller, who was one of the first to conceive of the tank not as a support for infantry but as a fast-moving independent force that could create shock, chaos, and demoralization in enemy forces. In 1939, they applied those lessons—with some intent but more often through expediency—with spectacular results in the blitzkrieg into Poland.

One should also note that another revolution in technology was taking place. Although it did not receive equal billing, on the same day, on the same page of the *Daily Telegraph* that covered Hart's report, there was a headline, "Hearing a Face—Television Broadcast":

Giving a broadcast lecture at the British Empire Exhibition at Edinburgh on Saturday night, Mr. J. L. Baird, the inventor of television, said he had asked three chance acquaintances the meaning of the word "television." One said that it was an island off the Coast of Africa, the second that it was a form of telepathy, and the third that it was a kidney disease. Television meant actually seeing by wireless. The scene was first turned into a sound, which was then broadcast, and turned back into an image at the receiver. Every face had its own particular sound.

A phonograph record was then played on which the television sound of Mr. Baird's face had been recorded. It sounded something like the rasp of a file with a peculiar rhythmic whistle underlying it. This was broadcast by the BBC, so that listeners for the first time in history had the opportunity of hearing what a face sounded like. The lecturer went on to describe his discovery of television, and said that the first person ever seen by television was an office boy, who had to be bribed with 2s 6p to submit to the experiment. The latest development of television had rendered it possible to see in total darkness, invisible rays being used. Steady progress was being made in developing the invention to a commercial stage, and he hoped that television would very shortly be available to the general public.

One year after motorized and wireless transmissions were linked in simulated warfare on Salisbury Plain, similar breakthroughs in television were made by engineers at General Electric. From experimental station "W2AXAD" they broadcast the second-ever television image, about the size of an index card. What did they choose to broadcast? A simulation of a missile attack on New York City. The point of view was from the missile, a flight ending in an explosion, then nothing—an eerie foreshadowing of the last industrial and first virtuous war in the Gulf.[3]

The interwar returned with a vengeance when I made my pilgrimage to the Pentagon. From the beginning of my virtual travels I heard the same name, regardless of the stripes on the sleeve or the political colorings of the individual: go talk to Andrew Marshall, officially known as the director of the Office of Net Assessment, but unofficially, "St. Andrew," the Yoda of the so-called Revolution in Military Affairs (RMA); Marshall, brought in by President Nixon, helped set up the innocuous-sounding Office of Net Assessment, "to weigh the military balance in specific areas, determine what the important long-term trends are, and to highlight existing or emergent problem areas, or important opportunities that deserve top level management's attention to improve the future U.S. position in the continuing military-economic-political competition." His memoranda are legendary, and for the most part classified. They have ranged from broad politico-strategic issues like the decline of the Soviet Union, to no less important tactical debates about the advantages of sending Stinger antiaircraft missiles to Afghanistan. The one that created a serious ripple in several policy circles is only seven pages long and bears a simple title: "Some Thoughts on Military Revolutions." When it was first circulated on August 23, 1993, it was an idea in the wind; a year later, there were five task forces at the Pentagon alone, exploring the ramifications of the "Revolution in Military Affairs." I had learned the hard way that when it came to the RMA, the hype-to-reality ratio skewed as one went up the ranks. But here was a powerful bureaucracy headed by an individual with long-standing clout in the defense community, ready not only intellectually to defend but actually to implement an RMA. The disciples of "St. Andrews"—the better known include former secretary of defense William Perry and vice chairman of the Joint Chiefs of Staff Admiral William Owen—reach beyond the government and include top executives at defense industries.[4] His powers might have waned somewhat under the Clinton administration, but in our interview he provided some rare insights into just how an idea can be transformed into a policy—and the extent to which an interwar mimesis continues to shape, through technology, analogy, and allegory, our virtual constructions of the future.

The interview took place in his spacious, paper-filled, very unmilitary Pentagon office. What looked to be a small primitive rocket stood upright between us. If it was meant to disconcert, it did. During the interview, he told me about his past and the two major projects in progress. The first, predictably, was an assessment of threats that might emerge from Asia. The second caught my attention: the appearance of post-Cold War political and military parallels with the interwar. Here are some excerpts from our conversation:[5]

JD: Could you tell me who you are and what you do?
AM: Well I'll start with the history. I went to Rand at the beginning of '49 and I was there until the beginning of '72. Then I went and worked for Henry Kissinger at the National Security Council, and a couple of years later came here to set up this office. I've been here ever since. This is the Office of Net Assessment and fundamentally what it tries to do is assess military situations with the intent of surfacing for the very top managers issues that they should pay attention to. I mean, based on emerging problems or opportunities. Of course, when I was first here we focused very much on the Soviet Union, and the more intense military, political, economic competition. Now we really are working fundamentally on two things. One is exploring this idea of, you know, that the next twenty, thirty years may be another one of these periods where warfare changes in some very

significant ways. We've done some earlier analyses of that before but, about four years ago, we began a much more intensive effort. I suppose we really began in '89 or so, and put out a preliminary assessment in July of '92 and have been pursuing a variety of activities to try to understand the potential character of the change, to better understand the actual nature of what the change might be. So that is one thing we are doing. The other is trying to take a very long-term view of Asia and where it may go, again, over the next twenty or thirty years.

JD: Would you call it a revolution or not?

AM: Well, I mean, we have picked up this terminology of revolution and, I think, at one level, or in one way, that's appropriate. It turns out that tactically it gets you into a lot of arguments you don't really need to be in about whether it is a revolution, or what things can be called revolutions. Anything that can happen over a couple of decades can't be called a revolution, for some people . . .

JD: Would you call it a revolution?

AM: Yeah, I would . . .

JD: Why?

AM: Well I think, again if you look back, there is all this historical work that people have done on, way back to the fifteenth century, looking at periods where over the course of, you know, a couple of decades or so many new forms of warfare emerge that just dominate whatever was dominant before and that seem reasonable to call a revolution. It was the Russians that first brought it to my attention, in the writings that they began to put out in the late seventies and early eighties.

JD: You mean your counterparts in Russia were the first to talk about a military revolution?

AM: Well, yes, beginning in the seventies and on into the early eighties they began talking about the fact that we were entering, or that the world was entering, another period of what they initially called a "military technical revolution." And they cited two previous periods as exemplars. One was the twenties and thirties where you get the big change in many areas of warfare, because of, well, in some ways, the technologies of the internal combustion engine, radios, and so on. Then the second period, right after World War II, where it's a combination of nuclear weapons, ballistic missiles, and the beginnings of computers that leads to big changes. Their function, as military intellectuals, was to diagnose when there were these periods of big change. And so they began to say one of these periods of big change was coming, because of the microprocessor and other related technologies. It was triggered, I think, by a program to develop a system that they called the "assault-breaker," that conceptually was a reasonably long-ranged rocket with a smart front end coupled to long-range sensors.

JD: I was at the first digitized rotation at Fort Irwin when the Fort Knox brigade was out there, and did some interviews. I've been looking at this from the bottom up, from the field, and it seems there's a lot more skepticism about a revolution going on.

AM: Yeah, I would think so. I wouldn't particularly expect to see it down there. It's also spotty on the top, although growing, I would say. What I tend to argue with people is that we ought to see ourselves as in something like in the early twenties where we don't fully see what the outcome would be. But there is just enough, on the one hand, to see that the technologies are moving rapidly and it's plausible that there would be a big impact. We are about in a position, where people say, at the Naval War College, were about in '22 or '23, where we now have a bunch of war games that are being played, that are beginning to explore, in some sense, the logic of the situation that would exist if you had, let's say, twenty years from now, a number of new kinds of systems.

JD: Are you familiar with the exercises on the Salisbury Plain in the twenties—

AM: Yes, '27 and so on, oh yes . . .

JD: Last fall I checked out the back issues of the *Daily Telegraph*, where Liddell Hart wrote about them, and what struck me is that he didn't really call it a revolution, or understand it as such. When you are really in the middle of it, you are least aware of it.

AM: Yes, well I suppose to an extent there were people in the military in the twenties that thought of things as revolutions that were primarily associated with air. Even the Germans, who really boast of being a hell of a lot better than the British, were not consciously thinking in terms of a revolution. So, what would be unique this time, in a certain sense, I think, or more so, is that because of things that have happened since the twenties and thirties—both the historical literature that has been built up that looked at these kinds of periods and the Russians who began intellectualizing about it and raising it as one of the unique things about the next twenty or thirty years. If in fact we will go through such a thing, it will be almost the first time in which it is, in a widespread sort of way, self-consciously, you know, pursued or experienced as a revolution.

JD: Who do you see as our next enemy?

AM: Well, I'm interested in Asia mainly because of some general reasons. You look at long-range projections, that's the place where the most rapid economic growth is going to take place. Also, Asia has been dominated by the West for over 150 to 200 years and that's over. And so, exactly what Asia would be like, what kind of internal rivalry will be there is something that really needs to be looked at.

JD: Can you really compare our times to any other? When suddenly everything is wide open yet connected, do you think a global threat is going to emerge?

AM: No, I think not in my time. But if you look back into history I think you can see that the twenties was like that. The twenties turned out to be a period of illusion about what the world was going to be like. I think we are in the twenties. Both in terms of the beginning of technical change that is working out its implications, and in terms of, well, in the twenties the United States didn't really have any big immediate threat, and the forces were very small. Whether something like the thirties is before us, I don't know.

JD: But to what extent do we create our enemies? Do you think it is completely a unilateral action, or do you think it's more like the whole idea of the security dilemma?

AM: Well I don't see that right now. You have a little of that in

Asia with the growth of China and how we react against it, and to the extent that we get to be seen as, you know, the people who are intervening in this place and that place . . . to the extent that we have gotten ourselves in the position of being the leader of the interventions for the UN.

JD: In the way that the nuclear deterrence maintained a relative peace for some, do you think there is such a thing as a high-tech deterrent, in the way that people would see what happened in Desert Storm and then would not want to take on the U.S.?

AM: I think so, I mean it's a deterrent in a sense, but it also has these other effects. I mean it deters people from taking us on in this way. But it may substantially increase incentives to go after nuclear weapons, or look for other clever ways of using the technology.

JD: It's clearly part of your job here, but do you really think war is persistent, that we will always have wars to fight?

AM: I tend to be pessimistic about it, and not just because of my job. If you just look at history and human behavior you can't be very optimistic about it . . . .

JD: You don't want to think of war as obsolescent?

AM: I would tend towards that view, yes.

Austin Bay's historical analogy of the interwar and Andrew Marshall's sober take on the future helped to define the route of my journey ahead. In an era of high uncertainty mixed with high hopes, digitized war games and virtual simulations were becoming more and more important for U.S. defense and foreign policy. But no one seemed to be asking the critical questions. To what extent would virtual simulation become the foundation of virtuous war? To what extent would history, experience, intuition, and all those human traits that shape reality become secondary factors? Twice removed by scripted strategies and technological artifice from the bloody realities of war, were simulations taking warfare into another realm? Sold by their users as mere *preparations* for worst-case scenarios, did they in fact produce and delimit, through holistic training, hyperreal modeling, and potential negative synergy, the future they claim only to anticipate?

In the search for answers I would turn to many thinkers outside the beltway and beyond the MIME-NET. For a journey that would take me from complex issues of life and death to the banality of evil in service of the war machine, two German thinkers became essential companions: Friedrich Nietzsche and Walter Benjamin. I also came to rely upon three contemporary analysts of virtuality who have gone beyond—some might think one galaxy too far—the conventional approaches of international relations: Charles Perrow, Gilles Deleuze, and Paul Virilio. These five thinkers would be my counter-pentagon for assessing the power of virtuous war and constructing a virtual theory of war and peace.

Friedrich Nietzsche is the first guide one must consult for understanding virtual powers. Most people know this nineteenth-century German philosopher for his repudiation of God and his descent into madness, two events that always seem to be inextricably linked in the secondary literature. However, I believe that Nietzsche, seeing the coachman beat his horse at the Piazza Carlo Alberto, embraced the dying beast not out of madness but clairvoyance. Probably better than any other philosopher who preceded or followed him, he understood the virtual effects of the near-dead object on the not-yet-alive observer. He deeply, even tragically, understood the nihilistic as well as potentially affirmative relationship between the real and the virtual. And he understood, as only could a philosopher who placed the joker above the priest, beating an old horse is not the best way forward.

Given the persistent caricature of Nietzsche (as a nationalist, anti-Semite, proto-Nazi, corrupter of youth, and worst of all, the forefather of postmodernism), I suppose it is necessary to emphasize once again that Nietzsche was anticipating and responding to rather than endorsing a condition of nihilism that he witnessed at the turn of the century. As for the relativism of his perspectivist philosophy, it too was a response to what Nietzsche poetically described as "the breath of empty space," that void left by the death of gods. The historical relativity of values has always been with us, in spite of the diligent efforts of philosophers, priests, and politicians to keep it at bay with first principles, transcendental morals, and patriotic absolutes. The human task, and all too often a tragic one at that, is how to shape an ethical response in the face of relativism.

His argument goes something like this. Faced by the uncertainties of life, we seek a *virtual security* from the dead, incurring debts that can never be repaid:

> Within the original tribal community . . . the living generation always recognized a juridical duty toward earlier generations, and especially toward the earliest which founded the tribe. The conviction reigns that it is only through the sacrifices and accomplishments of the ancestors that the tribe *exists*—and that one has to *pay them back* with sacrifices and accomplishments: one thus recognizes a *debt* that constantly grows greater since these forebears never cease, in their continued existence, as powerful spirits, to accord the tribe new advantages and new strength.[6]

If the origins of sovereignty lie in an ancestral debt to the dead, how can we possibly surmise its end? Nietzsche neither disenchants nor flinches from the spectral effects of the state. Nietzsche links the obdurate violence of the state and the primal fear of death to a "moral prejudice" for security and sovereignty that has, literally and violently, outlived its lifetime. Nietzsche writes of the "idiosyncrasies of philosophers" who take any idea of becoming and "make a mummy" of it, hoping to find in a "gravedigger-mimicry" the certainty of being.[7] Nowhere is this more evident than in the philosophers' conflation—and resulting moral confusion—of the "good" with certainty, predictability, and rationality, and of the "evil" with fear, contingency, and the unknown.[8] The "good life" becomes synonymous with the ideal, and objectified into the legal concept of security against violence through sovereignty.[9] Fear, once the spur to overcoming and life, becomes repressed and identified with death. At one time this might have been a "natural" state of affairs, but Nietzsche exhorts the modern, "*Be grateful!*—The greatest accomplishment of past mankind is that we no longer have to live in continual fear of wild animals, of barbarians, of gods and of our own dreams."[10]

Herein lie buried the foundations of the modern states-system, "thought of as sovereign and universal, not as a means in the struggle between power complexes, but as a means of *preventing* all struggle in general."[11] In short, the sovereign state is an *unnatural* state. "Life is a consequence of war, society itself a means to war," writes Nietzsche; but once denied and repressed, fear comes to provoke hostility and resentment in the moderns: "they fear change, transitoriness: this expresses a straitened soul, full of mistrust and evil experiences."[12] Where lies the greatest certainty, the least change? Death, whose power is manifested in life as an unpayable debt to ancestors, remains the enforcer of sovereignty.[13]

Nietzsche works the graveyard shift to offer a penetrating critique of sovereignty, yet ... it lives, most demonstrably in the practice of war and diplomacy, as no less than the *realist* perspective in international relations. What do we mean by "realism"? It encompasses a worldview in which sovereign states, struggling for power under conditions of anarchy, do what they must to maintain and promote their own self-interests. But what do "we" mean by "realism"? Constituted by and representing disciplinary schools of thought, diplomatic corps, intelligence bureaucracies, we realists depict things as they really are, rather than as idealists might wish them to be. And what do "we" *mean* by "realism"? We mean what we say and say what we mean, in that transparent way of correspondence that provides the veridical, commonsensical, deadly discourses of realism, as "mutual assured destruction" assures our security, or "we had to destroy the village in order to save it."

But with the end of the Cold War, and *pace* Nietzsche, why beat a dead horse? *Because* realism does death so well, by refusing to acknowledge not only its ongoing complicity in the death of others but also the fact that it gave up the ghost a long time ago. How many times after "revolutionary" transitions have we heard that sovereignty is at bay, at an end, dead? That sovereignty is an "essentially contested concept" or a "convenient fiction"? The frequency of such remarks, from politicians, military strategists and pundits (as well as academicians) leads one to suspect that something other than funerary oration, philosophical speculation, or the allure of tenure is at work, that there is a darker, even gothic side to the sovereign state, a hidden power that resides in its recurrent morbidity.

Take a look at some of the principle necroses. Realism has built a life out of the transformation of fictions, like the immutability of human nature and the apodictic threat of anarchy, into facticity. With a little digging, realism comes to resemble nothing so much as the undead, a perverse mimesis of the living other, haunting international politics through the objectification of power, the fetishization of weaponry, the idealization of the state, the virtualization of violence, and the globalization of new media. Now the fact of its own death lives on as a powerful fiction, as the morbid customs, characteristics, and habits of the living dead. Realism has become virtual.

If this interpretation sounds more like Buffy the vampire slayer than Freddy the horse savior, so be it. But it does seem uncanny how, without fingering particular administrations or naming names, the undead of realism might temporarily retreat to universities, think tanks, consultancy firms, and media posts, but are always there in the wings, ready to come back and to take once again the reins of the national security apparatus. Perhaps it is not possible or even preferable to "interpret" realism into the closed coffin of history. Nietzsche himself recognizes the allure of realism by citing some exemplars in history:

> My recreation, my preference, my *cure* from all Platonism has always been *Thucydides*. Thucydides and, perhaps, Machiavelli's *Principe* are most closely related to myself by the unconditional will not to gull oneself and to see reason in *reality*—not in "reason," still less in "morality." . . . One must turn him over line by line and read this hidden thoughts. *Sophist culture*, by which I mean *realist culture*, attains in him its perfect expression. . . . *Courage* in face of reality ultimately distinguishes such natures as Thucydides and Plato: Plato is a coward in the face of reality—consequently he flees into the ideal; Thucydides has himself under control—consequently he retains control over things.[14]

Nietzsche helps us understand the obduracy of realism as we increasingly interact with a mimetic world that seems to be in the control of virtual "things" that imitate reality (from opinion polls, worst-case scenarios, and Star Wars to Sky TV, Microsoft, and Disney Inc.). In the realm of diplomatic and strategic theory, realism mirrors a fluctuation of appearances, at one moment fleeing into the ideal of a "democratic peace" underwritten by an expanding neoliberal global order, and at the next, retreating into a "fortress America" protected by a ballistic missile defense. It takes more than the courage of the Sophists to face the seemingly inexorable forces of such virtual realities. Perhaps Nietzsche is right: it takes a virtuous, even poetic willfulness, like Thucydides' or Machiavelli's, to confront the reality principle of realism, sovereignty, and its ultima ratio, war. It requires an expression of self-control, as antidote to the will, born out of resentment and fear, to control or to isolate the other.

Realism's long, intimate history with violence, whether in the guise of impartial observer or amoral reproducer, requires that if we are to have anything meaningful to say to realism, we too must get up close to the virtual representation, preparation, and execution of war. The social sciences, especially its dominant methodology of rational choice, have shown a reluctance to enter into proximity talks with violence. We are in need of an extra-disciplinary, intersubjective, ethical inquiry into the mimetic relationship of realism to organized violence, beginning with but not stopping at the state violence of political realism, the class violence of social realism, the global violence of nuclear realism, the technoviolence of hyperrealism. Again, as Nietzsche shows us, it is better to embrace than to beat an old horse.

Continental philosophers like Nietzsche, but also deeply American thinkers from transcendentalists like Henry David Thoreau and Ralph Emerson to pragmatists like Thomas Dewey and Richard Rorty, are valuable because they provide a philosophical perspective that links public space with responsive as well responsible private choices. They provide a philosophical basis to render realism more responsible for reproducing a world it claims only to record. They and others have not, however, out of historical circumstance or personal choice, kept up with the avant-garde of the war machine, which is continually at work to define the ethical and political through policies of state-sanctioned killing and patriotic dying. As much as I admire Nietzsche's transvaluation of realism and sovereignty we are still left with all-too-real effects of virtual violence: representations can kill. After the crown jurist for the Nazis, Carl Schmitt, exposed the illiberal exceptionalism of violence at the core of sovereignty, in which every friendship is dependent upon a common enemy, I think it is rather spurious to pretend that one can disenchant the violent if spectral power of sovereignty with a wave of the Weberian wand, or cure it with the stroke of the deconstructive scalpel. In spite of the call for new world orders, declarations of democratic peace, celebrations of globalization, even strenuous critical exorcisms, war continues to be the rule that proves the exceptionalism of sovereignty. By a recent UN estimate, in the recorded history of sovereign empires and states stretching over three millennia, humankind has enjoyed a total of twenty-nine years free of war.

Nietzsche offers a way into the core of the sovereignty problematic, but not a way out. Nietzsche's hope for the overman, always overly romantic, has been corrupted by history. When it comes to modern warfare, which remains the ultimate form of public bloodletting, the strategies of transvaluation and deconstruction are at best homeopathic. For the vampire heart of realism, we need a blunter tool, the political equivalent of a wooden stake. The problem is compounded when the heart of the state becomes a transplant, and a cyborg one at that. Think of Arnold Schwarzenegger in *The Terminator*, or worse, the "liquid metal" Terminator 1000 series he confronts in *T2*, that has no heart at all, that can morph at will into multiple forms: it is, according to Arnold in his imitable accent from repressive regimes past and future, "made of a mimetic polyalloy."

"Mimetic polyalloy" aptly captures the shape-shifting dangers of contemporary global politics that exceed Nietzsche's grasp. After Nietzsche, one thinker stands a head above the rest, for his understanding of the relationship of new technologies of representation to the transformation of political culture and warfare, the Jewish-German literary critic Walter Benjamin, who understood the power of mimesis in interwar in a way that no task force in the Pentagon possibly could. His concept of mimesis might not serve as the vaunted wooden stake, but it does act as a window into a future that is now upon us.

From its original conception as the reproduction of reality through dance, ritual, theater, image, and writing, mimesis thrived as an aesthetic concept, capturing the perceptual and representational powers of mimicry, imitation, and metaphor.[15] Its linguistic roots go back to fifth century Greece, to *mimos*, whose many derivatives convey a dramatic act of representation through imitation. At the outset, mimesis attracted philosophical criticism, as one would expect from any powerful form of representation that created whole worlds, that made one thing into something other, even if it was done through symbolic actions.[16] Perhaps we moderns know best (and appear to universally detest) the figure of the "mime"—one who depicts life "as it is," but with a satirical twist: he or she "fools" people (which is one of many reasons Plato came down hard on mimesis in *The Republic*).

This performative character of mimesis, ranging in effects from theatrical artifice to political deceit, came under renewed scrutiny in the period between the First and Second World Wars. When modes of violence took an aesthetic turn in the interwar period, the concept was revived by Walter Benjamin, Siegfried Kracauer, Theodor Adorno, and others from the Frankfurt School of critical theory, to comprehend the power of new mimetic mediations like radio, film, and the popular press. Considered by positivists as too vague, or worse, too much in vogue, the concept never caught on in the social sciences.[17] In our virtual moment of overmediated politics, I think a serious reconsideration of mimesis is overdue.

Benjamin was acutely aware that new technologies were changing the nature of politics, and that theory and ethics were not keeping pace. This was most apparent in the marrying of new technologies of killing with new technologies of representation. In his highly influential essay, "The Work of Art in the Age of its Technical Reproducibility," Benjamin warns of the evolution of warfare into an art form. War was becoming the deadliest exhibition of *l'art pour l'art*, in which self-alienated humans become "their own showpiece, enjoying their own self-destruction as an aesthetic pleasure of the highest order. This is the aestheticization of politics that fascism manufactures, which is answered by communism's politicization."[18]

In one form or another, mimesis shows up in Benjamin's most significant essays on the tumult of the interwar period, running as a common thread through his early essays on aesthetics and later ones on technology. As imitation and repetition, mimesis emerges as a fundamental force in human development. In a highly condensed, almost poetic fashion, Benjamin presents his case in the 1933 essay "On the Mimetic Faculty." Language and play, mystery and violence are evinced as mimetic manifestations. He opens the essay with a general statement:

> Nature creates similarities. One need only think of mimicry. The highest capacity for producing similarities, however, is man's. His gift of seeing resemblances is nothing other than a rudiment of the powerful compulsion in former time to become and behave like something else. Perhaps there is none of his higher functions in which his mimetic faculty does not play a decisive role.[19]

But the mimetic faculty "has a history" in the development of language and the self, or as Benjamin puts it, "in both the phylogenetic and the ontogenetic sense."[20] In self-development, "the school" for mimetic development is "play"; children imitate not only others but objects. In linguistic development, children learn through the mimetic faculty of onomatopoeia. Language, through script, becomes "an archive of non-sensuous similarities," the most important site where the semiotic (the play of signs) and the mimetic (the play of objects) fuse.[21] In a poetic passage, he tries to reinstill mystery into the mimetic activity of reading by tracing it back to the earliest mimesis, the reading of entrails and the stars by the ancients. But he ends on a melancholic note, acknowledging that modern forms of writing have reached "the point where they have liquidated those of magic."[22]

Benjamin further identifies a link between mimesis and violence that stretches from the earliest forms of inscription to the latest technical reproduction of art. In "On Aesthetics," a short piece dating from 1936, he paints a vivid image of a possibly originary relationship between the two:

> It would be more emphatic than it ever has been up until now, to make fruitful for the early history of the arts the recognition, that the first material to which the mimetic faculty applied itself is the human body. . . . Perhaps the human from the stone-age sketches the elk so incomparably, only because the hand which leads the crayon still recalls the bow with which it shot the animal.[23]

Language and violence, politics and aesthetics, technology and war: in the thirties, the mimetic faculty returns as the repressed. In his 1930 "Theories of German Fascism," a review of Ernst Junger's collection of essays *War and Warrior*, Benjamin attacks the "boyish rapture that leads to a cult, to an apotheosis of war."[24] He fully acknowledges the "significance of the economic causes of war," but adds that "one may say that the harshest, most disastrous aspects of imperialist war are in part the result of the gaping discrepancy between the gigantic power of technology and the minuscule moral illumination it affords." He concludes that "any future war will also be a slave revolt of technology." In a Berlin radio program for children from the same period, he speaks of the origins of toys in the artisan workshop as "miniature reproductions of everyday life."[25] With echoes of Freud, he elsewhere links the repetition of playing to the "domestication of trauma."[26] Toys, again, are key: "Toys, even when not imitative of adult utensils, are a coming to terms, and doubtless less of the child with adults than of adults with him."[27] Benjamin's message is deeper and certainly more complex than critics who would dismiss modern warfare as "boys with toys." But his study of mimesis does give considerable philosophical depth to the idea that we are prepped for war from an early age.[28] It is one that the literary theorist Rene Girard picks up, and in a more anthropological treatment, investigates how every desire is desire for the desire of the other, which, unmediated, inevitably leads to hatred, rivalry, violence.[29]

Benjamin challenges the hegemony of realism by revealing its dependence upon the mimetic faculty. At a time when Western leaders promote the virtues of democratic peace and pacifying globalism, it might seem strange to still speak of a hegemonic realism. But in the post-Cold War era, and with the Bush administration, a chasm has widened between the global rhetoric of peace and the continuation of particular practices of violence. This chasm is not unrelated to the ballyhooed digital divide, and is certainly a function of the inequality, exploitation, and internalized dominion—what Virilio calls endocolonization—that persists in regions kept distant by tropes like "the inner city," "the near abroad," "the third world," and, most generic of all, "the South." But it is also related to the philosophical deadening that realism feeds upon. In short, by breaking down the mimetic barrier to imagining otherwise, Benjamin traces potential pathways from the interwars of realism to the interzone of virtualism. Both are born out of war, but also of the hope that new ways of thinking, dreaming, and deciding will attenuate the forces aligned with violence. Quoting Karl Marx ("The reform of consciousness consists *solely* in the awakening of the world from its dream about itself"), Benjamin identifies two alternative steps—one virtuous, the other not—that one can take to escape modernity's most pernicious effects: "The genuine liberation from an epoch, that is, has the structure of awakening in this respect as well: is entirely ruled by cunning. Only with cunning, not without it, can we work free of the realm of dreams. But there is also a false liberation; its sign is violence."[30]

Benjamin provides a timely account of the dangerous consequences, unintended as well as intended, of a realism that purports to be realistic, yet takes no account of differing realities, whether they are culturally, historically, virtually produced. Realism assumes, and through mimesis, asserts a sameness of motives rooted in human nature and geopolitics. In contrast, Benjamin posits the importance of recognizing difference or alterity in humans, and confronting it with imagination in politics. He deals perceptively with the sources of recurrent dangers in world politics, like the interrelationships of sovereignty, violence, nationalism, technology, and war, without recourse to the realist conceit of parsimony, which reduces all actors to a single mimetic identity, the self-maximizing unit. While this "ideal" typology of human behavior might grant the parsimonious realist an advantage in explaining simple events in a disinterested way, it leaves them at a loss when it comes to complex social issues, transformative political moments, crimes against humanity, and virtual forms of representation—all of which have taken place in our own post-Cold War era, all of which have defied the realist imagination (to the extent there can be said to be one).

Benjamin pursues these hard questions of human relations with the kind of theological, existential, even metaphysical reflections that one rarely if ever finds in the social sciences. Paradoxically, he sounds and looks like a realist for it. For he is after the truth; not truth as a universal waiting to be deciphered or learned, but as the most powerful norm of the day, whose normalizing nature (to paraphrase Nietzsche[31]) has been hidden or forgotten—at potentially great peril for the politics of their era as well as ours. The truth is not to be found in some Aristotelian *via media*, or through a Weberian disenchantment: surrounded by ambiguity, contingency, and uncertainty, the truth is to be attacked from the periphery, discerned from all, even the most oblique angles. This is not an excuse for quietism. This is a politics of subjective perception and radical imagination based on *decisiveness*, by which Benjamin means a willingness to decide on a course of action when confronted by paradox, especially those that arise between religious or moral observance and political obligations:

> I am speaking here of an identity that manifests itself solely in the paradoxical reversal of the one into the other (in whichever direction) and only under the indispensable pre-condition that each observance be carried out ruthlessly enough and radically in its own sense. The task here, therefore, is to decide, not once and for all, but in every moment. But to *decide*. . . . To proceed always radically, never consistently in the most important matters.[32]

Finally, Benjamin warns us of the dangers that attend the mimetic fix for political problems. We witness such efforts in our own shape-shifting "phase transition" between order and disorder (so far, the best nonmathematical description physicists have come up with for "complexity"), when rationalist methods appear inadequate, and the temptation grows to use coercive interventions or technical fixes to seemingly intractable problems of alterity, like immigration, ethnic cleansing, and fundamentalist politics. In his own way, Benjamin helps us to understand (in ways that rationalist methods do not) how a "social problem," like the role of drugs or the refugee in society, can suddenly escalate into a life-and-death "security issue." By making ways of being and ways of knowing one and the same, Benjamin shows us how questions of violence are always already problems of identity. In the absence of alternative modes of knowing, when a whole people become a "problem," violent final solutions can result.

I invoke Benjamin's work, life, and times for more than heuristic reasons. Many of us come from safe or detraumatized zones of living and learning, where we are tempted, even trained, to ignore new dangers, for reasons that Zygmunt Bauman, a Polish social theorist with intimate knowledge of these dangers, locates in the rationalist myth of modernity:

> None of the things that happened in this century were, however, more unexpected than Auschwitz and the Gulag, and none could be more bewildering, shocking and traumatic to the people trained, as we all have been, to see their past as the relentless and exhilarating progression of the ages of reason, enlightenment and emancipatory, liberating revolutions. . . . What we learned in this century is that modernity is not only about producing more and traveling faster, getting richer and moving around more freely. *It is also about—it has been about—fast and efficient killing, scientifically designed and administered genocide.*[33]

It might seem tendentious to invoke thinkers and concepts drawn from a period of revolution, totalitarianism, and genocide. But after my visit to Fort Irwin and the Pentagon's Office of Net Assessment, and through my readings of Nietzsche and Benjamin, I came to realize that the interwar was as much an invocation of a dream, conveyed in the guise of a virtual and inevitable reality, as it was a demarcation of past history. "The history of the dream," writes Benjamin, "remains to be written, and opening up a perspective on this subject would mean decisively overcoming the superstitious belief in natural necessity by means of historical illumination."[34] Hence, the dream's long and intimate relationship to the ultimate "necessity," war:

> Dreaming has a share in history. The statistics on dreaming would stretch beyond the pleasures of the anecdotal landscape into the barrenness of a battlefield. Dreams have started wars, and wars, from the very earliest times, have determined the propriety and impropriety—indeed, the range—of dreams. No longer does the dream reveal a blue horizon. . . . Dreams are now a shortcut to banality. Technology consigns the outer image of things to a long farewell, like banknotes that are bound to lose their value.[35]

Benjamin sets the course for my travels ahead: to awaken a critical consciousness against the soporifics of the realist undead, the serial murder of the imagination by worst-case scenarios, the mimetic allure of the interwar.

3 Global swarming and the Bosnia question

The abstract humanitarian-moralistic way of looking at the process of history is the most barren of all. I know this very well. But the chaotic mass of material acquisitions, habits, customs and prejudices that we call civilization hypnotizes us all, inspiring the false confidence that the main thing in human progress has already been achieved—and then war comes, and reveals that we have not yet crept out on all fours from the barbaric period of our history. We have learned how to wear suspenders, to write clever leading articles, and to make milk chocolate, but when we need to reach a serious decision about how a few different tribes are to live together on a well-endowed European peninsula, we are incapable of finding any other method than mutual extermination on a mass scale.

(Leon Trotsky, *The Balkan Wars, 1912–13: The War Correspondence of Leon Trotsky*)

So wrote the out-of-work, in-exile revolutionary Leon Trotsky in 1912, killing time during the Balkan Wars as foreign correspondent for the *Kievan Thought*, seeking answers to the so-called "Eastern Question" of what next after the decline and fall of the Ottoman Empire.[1] History never repeats itself, yet with the information revolution it does seem at critical times to get caught in a feedback loop. Certainly the technical reproducibility of war, a.k.a. TV, has produced a kind of *global swarming*, where free electrons and voyeuristic viewers chase the queen bees of TV, "This is Christiane Amanpour reporting from yet another war-torn region of the world." We have neither the promised new

Mock mayor in mock town Übingsdorf.

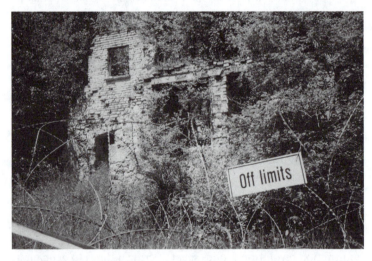

Real ruins are off limits in a mock war.

world order, or hoped-for global village of interdependence, but the angry global hive of real-time TV. In this virtual community, the victims get stung while the viewers enjoy the buzz.

But the information revolution also gave the successor to the Eastern Question an urgency and political proximity that the first and second Balkan wars never had. Campaign statements notwithstanding, what Western leader is willing to say (at least on TV) as did Bismarck, that "the whole Balkan Peninsula is not worth the bones of a single Pomeranian grenadier"? In the era of virtuous war, not many, if any.

The "Bosnia Question"—what to do with an ailing nation—was done to death. By bombs, artillery and mortars, sniper bullets, water, gas, and electric shortages, and bad, little, or just no food. But also by less tangible but no less deadly and condemnable forces, like ethnic terror, cartographic diplomacy, Machiavellian geopolitics; by over sixty United Nation resolutions and a UN Protection Force of over 25,000 that provided neither protection nor force in places like Sarajevo and Srebrenica; by a media that tried to make a difference—sometimes too much of one—and a public that seems now to have been image-shocked into indifference. And of course, by pundits like myself who drop in and drop out of the story with their new angle, that quickly proves obtuse whilst Bosnia—one day closer to peace, the next immersed in war—endured another year of suffering.

Bosnia is an unlikely place for virtuous war. Many would argue that this was not cyberwar, antiwar, postwar, or anything else remotely connected to the future. This war barely makes it into the present. This war was dirty and atavistic, with static trench lines, wetware-to-wetware combat, and a very intense—even if highly imaginary—ethno-confessional hatred going back to centuries-old holy wars between Christendom and the Anti-Christ Turk.

Yet like past holy wars, Bosnia was about the linking of virtuous intentions with new technologies of killing. After the Gulf War, it became the most televised, most real-time, most virtualized conflict of the nineties. The ubiquity of the image seems to have produced yet another simulation of war, dirtier than the Gulf War, yet just as simulated for the viewer as it is deadly real for the victims. "It is only television!" said French agent provocateur, Jean Baudrillard, of the Gulf War. "The United Nations has given the green light to a diluted kind of war—the right of war. It is a green light for all kinds of precautions and concessions, making a kind of extended contraceptive against the act of war. First safe sex, now safe war." Although hyperbolic, what he said then applies to Bosnia: "In our fear of the real, of anything that is too real, we have created a gigantic simulator. We prefer the virtual to the catastrophe of the real, of which television is the universal mirror. Indeed it is more than a mirror: today television and news have become the ground itself, television plays the same role as the card that is substituted for territory in the Borges fable."[2]

Baudrillard's allusion is to the story of Argentinean writer Jorge Luis Borges (see Chapter 4), about the emperor who sends out his royal cartographers to make the perfect map of his empire, only to have them return years later with a map that dwarfs the now-shrunken empire; the emperor naturally comes to prefer the model to reality. Like all Borges's stories, not an entirely fabulous tale. Did we not witness in Bosnia the effects of a similar decline of empires, a denial of reality, a retreat into virtuality? Does TV now play the role of the emperor's cartographers, electronically mapping an empire, a state, a history that no longer if ever existed? Now TV adds a human dimension—if not depth—to the fable, anthropology to cartography, and so provides a hologram of tales of ancient hatreds that brook comprehension by the "civilized" viewers. They come to recognize the former Yugoslavia as that region at the edge of the map where the sea monsters lurk: Do not go there. The Slovenian social theorist, Slovoj Žižek, believes this "evocation of the 'complexity of circumstances' serves to deliver us from the responsibility to act . . . that is, to avoid the bitter truth that, far from presenting the case of an eccentric ethnic conflict, the Bosnian War is a direct result of the West's failure to grasp the political dynamic of the disintegration of Yugoslavia, of the West's silent support of 'ethnic cleansing.'"[3]

So what were we left with? The dissimulations of Bosnian Serb leader Radovan Karadzic and Serbian president Slobodan Milosevic, first honed under the delegitimated deceit of communism, condoned as an acceptable conceit of nationalism, then used to conceal the revival of national socialism (that is, fascism). This was a national fascism enabled by the decadent simulations of Western rulers and their pundit-cartographers, who first waxed utopic about the new world order of self-determined polities, then rued nostalgically the lost stability of empire, only to be left with the pretense of TV to keep and video-bombs to make what is not peace. We, the viewer/reader, see the bleakest of bleak recombinants: Gibbons of imperial decline and fall meets Gibson's cyberspace as the last frontier in the Balkans: Bosnia as a looped sim/dissim war.

I decided to take the Bosnia Question on the road in Europe, to visit the people who were drawing an entirely different map of Bosnia with an array of new networks. In the course of one very intense month in 1995, I traveled to Hohenfels, Germany, to observe U.S. NATO forces simulating an answer to Bosnia as they shifted from war games to high-tech "peace games"; to Oslo, Norway, where researchers were busy rewriting the book on peacekeeping/making; to Paris for an interview with Paul Virilio, who was remapping the relationship of war, media, and technology; to the outer reaches of Aberystwyth, Wales, where a group of critical theorists met to redefine human rights and wrongs; and back to London, to witness the gathering of activists from Eastern and Central Europe as they plotted to protect and expand the multiethnic, multiconfessional communities of Bosnia under the umbrella of the Helsinki Citizen's Assembly, a pan-European peace, democracy, and human rights organization. By the end of the trip the grid of a new network of critical consciousness and civic action had begun to emerge around the elusive issues of Bosnia.

I found a wide variety of people who were combining new philosophies and new technologies to overcome the intractability and complexity of the issues. Some were more interested in redefining the problem than offering solutions; others were concerned less with the philosophical niceties and more with the pragmatic necessities of what the prevailing strategy—as often put, to clean up or to clear out of Bosnia—really meant for Europe. Some relied on the power of ideas, an alternative media, and a reconstructed civil society; others on the power of diplomacy backed by war, in this case the air power of NATO and the land power of the U.S. First Armored Division. The efforts ranged from laudable to laughable. But all deserve serious scrutiny, not least because the Balkans have a history of turning a local disease into a European pandemic.

But the metaquestion of Bosnia requires one more meta-theoretical aside, on the not trivial question of approach. This record started as a travelogue, of how words and images travel, sometimes reaching their intended destination, sometimes not. But travelogues usually move at steamship speed, represent the world in the sepia tones of old black and white postcards, and render the foreign exotic and sometimes erotic to escape the responsibilities and dullness of everyday life at home. This one moves at train-plane-automobile speed, with occasional shifts into Net overdrive, to bring those "alien" responsibilities back home. It does not, however, resort to the breathless heroics of war corre-spondence, where the "truth" is presented only in the form of live, flak-jacketed, stand-up reportage. I did not intend to "go" to Bosnia. I was more interested in how new intellectual, techno-logical, and activist networks were bringing Bosnia home to a European public consciousness. Was the Internet becoming a new territory for global political action? In search of answers, I dipped in and out of the virtual Bosnia represented on the Web, moving through bulletin boards, booklists, home pages, electronic archives, and even a "Bosnian Virtual Fieldtrip" on the Internet. In the spirit of Paul Virilio, the best guide for technologically induced states of consciousness, my account of these new efforts could be better described as a "dromologue": at once a sampling and a study of how networked words and deeds traveling at speed might penetrate the most resistant borders of the Bosnia Question.

Ever since Kraftwerk droned their Kerouacian ode to the "Bahn, Bahn, Autobahn," I've felt a strong urge to travel at hyperspeed encased in German steel. However, my Alamo rental proved too slow for the fast lane and I ended up stuck on the A3 motorway behind endless convoys of U.S. Army trucks and Humvee jeeps on their way, as I was, to the Hohenfels Combat and Maneuver Training Center (CMTC). Worse, Armed Forces Radio had Cher's latest hit, "Love Can Build a Bridge," on loop-play. The Cold War is over, the majority of the troops have gone home, but the U.S. occupation of Germany persists on air and on the road.

The U.S. Army owns, or more precisely, has "maneuver rights" over a significant piece of real estate in southern Germany, 178 square kilometers in Hohenfels alone. Spread out over the state of Bavaria like an isosceles triangle are the three major sites of the U.S. Seventh Army Training Command, through which the European-based U.S. troops, as well as some units from the British, Spanish, Canadian, and German armies and the Dutch marines, rotate through for some laser-simulated warfare and for live-fire exercises. The centers have an interesting heritage. Grafenwoehr, the oldest, was set up by the Royal Bavarian Army in 1907 to "play" some of the earliest Kriegspiele, or war games. It served as the southern tactical arm of the northern Prussian head, most infamously represented by Count von Schlieffen, chief of the General Staff, who in 1905 designed the famous Schlieffen Plan that was supposed to anticipate the next European conflict. Instead, its ironclad "war by timetable" helped to precipitate the First World War as one mobilization triggered a cascade of others throughout Europe. The two other training centers owe their origins to Hitler's rejection of the Treaty of Versailles, the peace of the victors of the First World War, which included the humiliating 100,000-troop limitation for Germany. Rapidly filling up the ranks with new conscripts, the Wehrmacht found itself short on training space. Grafenwoehr was expanded, and two new sites were created: Wildflecken in 1937 for the IX German Corps, and Hohenfels in 1938 for the VII German Corps.

The morning I drove past the front gate and into the Hohenfels Combat Maneuver Training Center, I learned a lesser-known part of its history. The tank-crossing sign, resembling First World War lead toys more than the M1 behemoths that skidded up the hill ahead of me, momentarily caught my attention. But it was a more conventional warning sign that seemed out of place—Cobblestones: Slippery When Wet. I later asked my handler, the very knowledgeable, very affable Colonel Wallace, why the short strip of quaint cobblestone interrupted the modern asphalt road into the base. He thought it had been left intact as a tribute to the Polish construction workers. Later I filled in the blanks: Hohenfels, begun in 1938 and finished in 1940, had evidently been built by Polish *sklavenarbeiter*, slave laborers. "Slippery when wet" was to become something of a coda for me during my visit to Hohenfels. Wars, when gamed, tend to lose their history of blood and deception.

The reason I was there had taken on a special urgency. Just before my arrival at Hohenfels, NATO air strikes on Bosnian Serb ammunition dumps triggered the hostage taking of over 300 UN peacekeepers. The cold peace flared hot when French soldiers in Sarajevo fought back after Bosnian Serbs disguised in French uniforms and UN blue helmets tried to take the Vrbanja Bridge. Britain and France announced plans to send a rapid reaction force: debate ensued whether it would be under UN command— and whether the new artillery, armored vehicles, and helicopters would be painted UN white or sovereign camouflage. President Clinton, breaking with the stated policy of only providing U.S. troops in the event of best- and worst-case scenarios—to monitor a peace accord or to cover a UN withdrawal—suddenly announced that he was ready to "temporarily" send troops in support of the British and French forces. But morning-after polls and the shoot-down of an F-16 U.S. pilot by the Serbs quickly reversed that readiness. In fact, as I drove through Hohenfels for my morning briefing I spied in the *Stars and Stripes* newspaper box in front of the PX Burger King a tall headline and a big photo: "A Hero's Welcome ... Air Force Pilot Capt. Scott F. O'Grady looks mighty glad to be back—alive—at Aviano AB." It seemed like the right time to come to Hohenfels to observe that most virtuous form of military conflict, "Operations Other than War."

Just what that meant was supposed to be the subject of the morning brief. But confusion reigned, not least because sometime between my first fax-barrage requesting a visit to the base and my arrival, a name-change had taken place. The more anodyne "Stability Operations" had replaced "Operations Other than War." Word hadn't quite gotten through the ranks, and people kept shifting back and forth between the two. The confusion mounted as I sat in a darkened theater with my two handlers, Captain Fisher and Colonel Wallace, on either side, and listened to the opening to Major Demike's multimedia, name-negating "brief." The major clearly had a take-no-prisoners attitude toward the English language: "Army units from U.S.AREUR (troops in Europe) rotate through the CMTC (I got that one) at least once a year for 21 days of Force-on-Opfor training" (good guys versus bad guys), "situational training with MILES in the Box" (dial-a-scenario field exercises using lasers rather than bullets), "BBS training" (not bulletin-board systems, but networked computer battle simulations with units based elsewhere), and "after-action reviews" (video presentations of what went wrong on the battlefield).

It was all very impressive, but with Clausewitz's warnings about military jargon in mind, I had just about reached my tolerance level. I had gone one brief too far and, short on sleep, I started to fade and daydream about some desk jockey sitting somewhere in an inner-ring, windowless office of the Pentagon, whose sole mission was to regularly abbreviate and if necessary change the name of anything in the military that becomes decipherable to the layman before its shelf life of usefulness is expired.

But once the briefer hit the simulation hotkey, my attention returned. Major Demike got into it with vigor: "We have at CMTC the most realistic battlefield. The instrumentation system is state of the art. It is the best in the world." He skipped through technology like the MILES (Multiple Integrated Laser Engagement System) for firing and recording laser hits; the microwave relays that allowed for near real-time production of the video after-action reviews; and the simulated mortar and artillery capability. To punctuate the point, Colonel Wallace stepped in: "Once a unit goes into the Box, with the exception that they're shooting laser bullets, and that a guy, instead of falling down with a gunshot wound, will read from a card he's carrying in his pocket how badly hurt he is, virtually everything we do is real. There's nothing simulated in the Box."

The major became more animated when he moved into the details of the technological capability of the CMTC. Instrumentation systems gather and process battlefield data that observer/controllers use to provide instant feedback for both sides of the operation. There is a seamless web of command and control between Building 100 (like its Fort Irwin counterpart, called "Star Wars") from which the battles are run and the troops out on maneuvers in the Box. For instance, simulated artillery attacks are launched via Silicon Graphics workstations, and hits are assessed according to probability software, which calculates trajectories, terrain, and the grid locations of vehicles and troops, which are constantly updated by Global Positioning Systems. Hits are then transmitted to each vehicle, as a "commo kill" (communications knocked out), "near miss," or "catastrophically destroyed." News of a simulated death comes in a female voice: the tone evidently better captures the attention of the adrenalized or battle-fatigued soldier. My query about what happens when women eventually join combat simulations was met with a blank stare by the major, but the colonel picked up on it: he assured me that the female voice will always stand out from the background of male ones. My stock question about the realism of the simulated battlefield received the stock answer, but with a raising of the technological ante: the National Training Center, CMTC's better-known stateside rival in the Mojave Desert, was still using the first generation of MILES to simulate weapons' effects, while they had the interactive MILES 2 with data communication interface ($9,000 a unit). "*Everything* is wired," said the major, who clearly had an enthusiasm for hackneyed sound bites.

After a long slog through computer graphics on the organization and function of the CMTC, we finally got to the geopolitical gist of tomorrow's "Stability Operation." Up came a map of "Danubia," trisected into "Sowenia," "Vilslakia," "Juraland," and, looking very much like a small fiefdom among them, the CMTC. The major's pointer started to fly: "Three separate countries have split off from Danubia—Sowenia and Vilslakia are at odds with each other. When we want to transition into high-intensity conflict, we have Juraland, which has heavy forces, come in on the side of one or other of the parties." Prodded to just once utter the word "Bosnia," he would go no further, except to say that the scenario was based on intelligence sources, CNN reports, and the "threat books." For my benefit he did add, "You don't have to be a rocket scientist to figure out what this is modeled on."

No rocket scientist, I resorted to a kind of semiotics to sort out the countries. The new countries of the disintegrating Danubia bore some obvious similarities to the region of Yugoslavia: to the former republic, now independent state of Slovenia, or more probably, the western enclave of Slavonia contested by the Croats and Serbs; and, of course, to the Jural mountain range. "Vilslakia" remained a mystery. The countries surrounding Danubia were familiar enough that I accessed my own laptop intelligence source, Microsoft's CD-ROM version of *Cinemania '95*. It was

not needed for the country to the northwest: "Teutonia" referred
back to the early Germanic tribes. However, "Freedonia" to the
northeast of Danubia was clearly taken from the 1933 war satire
Duck Soup, in which Groucho Marx so effectively played the
power-hungry dictator of said country that the real dictator Mus-
solini banned the film from Italy. And below Danubia was "Ruritania," the country in the clouds that provided the surreal setting
for W. C. Field's 1941 classic, *Never Give a Sucker an Even Break*.
What should one make of the army's strange choice of simulated
countries? Probably nothing much, except that some war gamer
had a sense of humor as well as of history—and, perhaps, also
something for Margaret Dumont, who plays in both comedies the
great dame (or Great Dane, as Fields might have drolled). But I
was left wondering: play by the intertext, die by the intertext?

The briefing ended with a short video of a Stability Operation.
By way of introduction, Colonel Wallace informs me that "none
of this stuff is staged, it's all from live footage taken by the Viper
video teams in the Box." Before I can fully enjoy the colonel's
knack for paradox, the lights dim, the screen flickers, and Graham
Nash is singing about "soldiers of peace just playing the game."
The first clip is of a confrontation between partisans and soliders
that escalates into heated words; the last is in the same tent, with
handshakes and professions of friendship being exchanged. In
between UN convoys are stopped by civilians, soldiers go down,
wounded or dead, a body-bagged corpse is spat upon by a partisan, food supplies are hijacked by townspeople, a female member
of the media gets shoved around, an explosion and panic in the
town streets, a sniper fires on a Humvee, dogs sniff for explosives,
infiltrators are caught in a nightscope, a UN flag waves defiantly,
and an old man drops to his knees in the mud in front of a
Humvee, begging for food. More in the sentimental aesthetic of
an AT&T advert than a hyperreal MTV clip, it is strangely moving. I am disarmed by it.

But the mood shifts quickly when the major concludes the
briefing by handing me a four-inch thick pile of documents. The
rest of the day was a whirlwind of briefs-to-go. First stop was
the Warlord Simulation Center, full of desktops and Sun Graphic
computers for planning, preparing, and running simulations in
the Box, out of the Box, or through the cyber-Box, that is,

simulation networking (SIMNET), "remoting via satellite in and out of the Box to anywhere in the world." Next stop was a cavernous warehouse, full of MILES gear under the watchful eye of Sergeant Kraus, who probably gave the best brief of the day. A man who clearly loves his job—or is just eager for some human company—he was as articulate as his lasers ("instead of a bullet it sends out 120 words on a laser beam, in the center are eight kill words, anything else is a wound or near miss"), as he made his way through the various shapes, types, and generations of laser and sensors, all set up on a variety of weapons and menacing mannequins. He was only temporarily stumped once, when I asked what would happen if a Danubian snuck up and hit one of his dummies on the head. Would any bells and lights go off? He replied with considerable sarcasm: "Excuse me? ROE?" Colonel Wallace translated: "Against the Rules of Engagement. One-meter rule. No physical contact in the Box." It seems that one conveys body-to-body harm with real words, not laser words, for example, "I am butt-stroking you now, so fall down." I would later find out that in Operations Other than War, the Rules of Engagement were there to be broken.

The day ended with an interview with the pugnacious commander of the base, Colonel Lenz, who made a persuasive case for Stability Operations as essential training for the increasing number of missions in that "gray area between war and peace." He would not, however, be drawn out on the significance of the euphemistic downgrading of "Military Operations Other than War (MOOTW) to "Operations Other than War" (OTW) to "Stability Operations" (too new to have an acronym?), especially when I queried him about the possibility that some might find the notion of stability based on the status quo to be offensive, in both senses of the word, when stabilization is perceived to be an enemy of justice, or simply just deserts. "That's above my pay-grade," was the colonel's reply. At the end of the interview he kindly suggested a debrief after my visit to the Box: "I've got people upstairs who can suck a guy's brain dry."

That was sufficient incentive to stay up that night and wade through the stack of papers that I had been given. The bulk of it was a 400-page document called the "Coordinating Draft of the 7th Army Training Command White Paper of Mission Training

Plan for Military Operations Other than War."[4] A substantial part of it breaks down the "Critical Tasks of the Task Force," like the establishment of a quick reaction force, checkpoints, lodgments; conduct liaison with local authorities and convoy escort operations; provide command and control and protect the force; and of no lesser importance, plan for media. Specific scenarios for battalions, company, and platoons are spelled out. The philosophy of operations other than war is conveyed in the introduction, and after wading through all the acronymic muck and bureaucratese ("Traditional MTP crosswalk matrixes for references and collective tasks are also included in this MTP") the final paragraph emerges as a reasonably clear summary of the purpose of the plan:

> As we continue to maintain our proficiency in traditional wartime operations, our forces must also be ready to operate effectively in non-traditional roles. Units involved in conflicts anywhere within the full spectrum of operations will always face some elements of a complex battlefield. These elements include civilians in the area of operations, the press, local authorities, and private organizations. This White Paper is designed to assist leaders at all levels to more fully understand and prepare for these new challenges.[5]

In other words, the "White Paper" was this year's model for the high-tech, post-Cold War simulations and training exercises that would prepare U.S. Armed Forces for pre-peacekeeping non-interventions into those postimperial spaces where once- and wannabe-states were engaged in postwar warring. In terms of past experiences rather than future threats, Somalia, Haiti, Rwanda, and—judging from the many references to the *British Wider Peacekeeping Manual*—Northern Ireland lurked between the lines. But in this simulated shadowland between military combat, police action, and relief aid, other ghosts could be discerned: Bosnia, yes, but why not, as the next operation other than war, a counternarcotics operation in Colombia? Or a quarantine of a paramilitary survivalist camp in Idaho? Or checkpoints and convoy escort through a riotous Los Angeles? This week, however, the enemy at Hohenfels reflected the headlines.

Very early the next day, I was heading for the Box, where the warring ethnic groups of a disintegrating "Danubia" were about to make life very hard for the visiting First Armored Division. The morning began with a low fog—confirmed by the weather report at yet another brief, the "Battle Update for Rotation 95–10." The mission: "To provide humanitarian assistance and separate belligerent factions." It was broken down from the level of UNDANFOR (United Nations Danubian Force) commander to squadron tasks, and equipment lists, tactical rules of engagement, task-force organization, and maps with vehicle and troop positions were presented through a series of computer graphics. A schedule of major events followed, some of which required translation from the briefer, like "1100—Scud Ambush of Convoy" (not the missile, but the "Sowenian Communist Urban Defenders"), or "2230—Jerk Raid versus Care Facility in Raversdorf (again, not Steve Martin, but the "Jurische Ethnic Rights Korps," guerrilla forces operating in the south sector). By the end of the brief I was badly in need of a scorecard.

Finally we were on our way to the Box. There was a bit of delay as I struggled with the camouflaged ensemble of Gore-Tex jacket, pants, and boots (for the mud). My faith in our Humvee was tested when the door handle came off in my hand. But Colonel Wallace proved to be as good a handle-fixer as he was a handler, and we were soon off. During the short ride through a gently sloping open terrain with trees on most of the hilltops, Colonel Wallace did the eco-army routine—"there are more trees and grass growing now than when we got here"—and as if on cue, a substantial herd of deer dashed across the road in front of us. The valleys and hillsides looked pretty chewed up by all the maneuvers, portaloos dotted the landscape, but the fauna seemed to appreciate the fact that the U.S. Army—unlike the Bavarian hunters outside the Box—were shooting blanks.

The first stop was a UN checkpoint, one of many where civilians were stopped and forced to do a kind of "self-search" for weapons or explosives. No hands-on policing here. Most of the M1 tanks and Bradleys had their turrets reversed, the universal symbol of nonaggression (or surrender). We arrived with a UN food convoy that was supposed to pass through the mock town of Übingsdorf. The town came complete with the steep-roofed houses of Bavaria, a church with a steeple (no sniper in sight), a cemetery (no names on the gravestones), a mix of Vilslakian and Sowenian townspeople (dressed by a retired psy-ops sergeant in what he described as "the eastern European grunge look," accessorized with the requisite MILES vest), and a mayor in a green felt fedora, who was insisting that the food be off-loaded for his hungry people.

Language differences, a belligerent crowd, an aggressive reporter with an intrusive cameraman, all jacked up the tension level. "Lt. Colonel Vladimir," commander of the local Vilslakian garrison, was refusing to bring the rabble to order. Chants for food in a kind of pidgin German—"Essen, Essen"—made voice communication difficult. Suddenly the crowd began to move towards the trucks, and a few rocks were thrown. The U.S. troops began to retreat back to the trucks, but already some of the townspeople were clambering up onto them. It was then that the first rule of engagement, right up there with the Prime Directive of no-no's, was broken by one of the soldiers when he grabbed a civilian to toss him off. "One-meter rule, one-meter rule!" was shouted by the observer/controllers on the scene. Some tanks and Bradleys, probably called up by the besieged sergeant in charge of negotiating with the mayor, came roaring up to join the convoy. When I turned to capture their arrival with my Hi-8 camera, a soldier suddenly knocked it—and me—backwards. As I stumbled, an observer/controller jumped out again to reprimand the soldier. Besides breaking the one-meter rule, he had failed to tell the real media from the pretend ones.

The situation eventually died down when the townspeople were rounded up and put under guard. Negotiations resumed, resulting in something of a compromise: the food would be unloaded at the local UN headquarters. But after the troops pulled out, I watched as some of the townspeople pulled off the most realistic maneuver of the day: they scampered off with some of the large crates of food. Colonel Wallace later told me this was not in the script. I had witnessed some Box improv.

The scriptwriters clearly had it in for this convoy. At just about every checkpoint, food had to be traded for safe passage. And now, as we roared ahead in the colonel's Humvee for high ground, I noticed an observer/controller crouched in the ruins of a building probably dating back to the Wehrmacht days. A bad sign. As the convoy descended down the hill all hell broke loose—machine-gun fire from the hills, smoke bombs marking hits, and the light-and-sound show of MILES sensors going off. The M1 tanks and Bradleys reacted sluggishly to the ambush, not moving, and worse, keeping their turrets reversed in the defensive posture, making it impossible to identify the enemy with thermal sights. Instead, someone from the convoy called in for a Cobra helicopter gunship, breaking another rule of engagement: only "minimum" or proportional force should be used in a counterattack, to prevent a needless escalation of violence. From the last two engagements, it seemed apparent that the shift from war/sim to peace/sim was not going to be an easy one.

Two nonstop days of high-tech peace-mongering had left me ready to demilitarize, decompress, and—with a little help from some deep thinkers—reconstruct what I had witnessed in Hohenfels. I headed north for Oslo, Norway, where peacekeeping was enjoying something of a philosophical renaissance at NUPI (Norwegian Institute of International Affairs) and PRIO (Peace Research Institute). Working the margins of peace studies all through the Cold War, these institutions, along with the Stockholm Peace Research Institute in Sweden and the Center for Peace and Conflict Research in Copenhagen, were now at the center of the debate of what was next for Europe. They had written the book from which the U.S. Army had cribbed their stability operations. But through conversations with Iver Neumann and Age Eknes at NUPI, Dan Smith and Ola Tunander at PRIO, and e-mail with Ole Wæver from the Copenhagen School of International Relations, it became clear that they had moved on to broader, deeper issues than peacekeeping. They were busy redefining the question of European security, not through the conventional concerns of national interest, international trade, and high diplomacy, but through a new pragmatic mix of identity politics, environmental issues, and cultural policy. They had come up against the limits of geopolitics and game theory as well as structuralism and marxism for understanding, let alone constructing, a European community where flows of capital, information, technology, drugs, and refugees were supplanting and in some cases subverting the powers of the European community and the sovereign states within it. What happens when the center—whether it is the sovereign state, the sovereign self, or a suprasovereign European Union—no longer holds? Has its self-identity become dependent upon a non-European other? In other words, does Europe actually *need* Bosnia, the danger it represents, the otherness it embodies, for its own identity formation? Is Bosnia the dumping ground for the West's violence?

These Scandinavian scholars were looking to the works of continental thinkers, like Michel Foucault, Emmanuel Levinas, Jacques Derrida, Julia Kristeva, Gilles Deleuze, and Paul Virilio, not so much for answers as for their challenge to the Cold War narratives that no longer made any sense but seemed to persist out of a fear of uncertainty and ambiguity. After the Cold War, what? Postmodernity? A neomedievalism of overlapping political, religious, and economic authorities and wars? Or, more frighteningly, the new world order in real time on CNN? These were dangerous flux times for Europe, when fragile identities get squeezed into a fearful sameness, and petty differences get split up into a hostile otherness. In this broader context these Nordic think-tankers were working hard on the Bosnia Question, not with the pretense that there was *an* answer, but that in the very networking of it Europe might rewrite its future.

At my next stop in Paris I met with a man who seemed intent on exploding the Bosnia Question into a hundred fractals of perceptual fields. Urban architect, social theorist, museum curator, bunker photographer, cinematist, teacher, researcher into the relationship of war, perception, and technology, author of over a dozen books, Paul Virilio was ready to talk about Bosnia—and just about any other topic that we could fit in between courses at La Coupole.

JD: Why do you write?

PV: War. I am, I would say, a "war baby." I was born in 1932 with the advent of fascism. During the Second World War, I was a child. I lived in a terrible way. I lived under the reign of technological as well as under an absolute terror. I lived in a town, Nantes, which was destroyed by the Americans, the English, the Allies. When people tell me about speed, I say I lived at this incredible moment: we could hear on the French radio that the Germans were in Orleans. I was in Nantes, and ten minutes later, I could hear noise in the street. We were already occupied. It was blitzkrieg. After, I lived through the air battles and bombings. It's extraordinary how a town can vanish in one bombing. For a child, a town is like the Alps, a town is eternal like mountains. One bombing and everything is destroyed. These are the traumatizing events that shaped my thought. War was my university: everything came out of that.

JD: In *War and Cinema* and in much of your more recent work you draw a direct link between war and, as you put it, the "logistic of perception."

PV: Of course. The logistic of perception started by including immediate perception, that of the high sites, that of the tower and then that of the telescope. War started with high spots. So the logistic of perception was, in first place, the geographical logistic of the domination of a high site. . . . One can notice the way in which the field of perception of war and the battlefield developed, simultaneously, at the same time. At first, the battlefield was local, then it became worldwide and finally became global, which means satellized with the invention of video and of the spy satellites of observation of the battlefield. So at present, the development of the battlefield corresponds to the field of perception enabled by the telescope and the wave optics, the electro-optics, video, and of course for infography, in short all the medias. From now on, the battlefield is a global one. It is not worldwide anymore in the sense of the First or Second World War. It is global in the sense of the planet, the geosphere.

JD: Did the Gulf War not take place, as Baudrillard claims?

PV: Baudrillard's sentence is negationist, and I reproached him for it. The Gulf War was a reduced world war, in the sense that control through satellites was needed. One could say that it was a fractal war. Just as I said before, that with modern techniques and new logistics of perception, the battlefield of the Gulf War also developed within the field of perception. It appeared to be a local war, in the sense that its battlefield was very small compared with the Second World War. However, considering its representation, it was a worldwide war. It was worldwide at the media level, thanks to the technology of object-acquisition with satellites, and thanks to the remote control of war. I am thinking about the Patriot antimissiles that were directed from the Pentagon and from a satellite situated over the Gulf countries. So, on one hand, there was a local war of small interest, with very little human loss on one side, with very little consequences, but on the other hand, there was a unique field of perception operating. Unlike the Vietnam War, it was a worldwide war, live, with all the special effects, of course, the data processing supervised by the Pentagon, and by the censorship of the military staff. So, yes, this war happened, more on a screen than on the ground. It happened more on the TV screen than in the reality of the battlefield. To that extent, one can say that real time defeated real space.

JD: And how does cinematic space fit in?

PV: Cinema really interested me because of its roots. I would like to remind you that the totality of my work is about speed, my work is dromologic. Unavoidably, after dealing with metabolic speed, the role of cavalry in history, the role of speed in the human body, the athlete's body, I became interested in technological speed. Just after technological speed, after railways and aircraft, comes absolute speed and the passage to electromagnetic waves. Cinema interested me as a step leading to the speed of electromagnetic waves. Cinema interested me because of cinematism, the way in which images move, their acceleration. But today with video and television, this speed is absolute. We are at the foot of the wall of speed. We are confronted by this wall of the speed of light, we have reached the limit of acceleration, according to relativity. It is a great historical event. The cybercult is a cult to the absolute speed of electromagnetic waves, which convey information.

JD: What about Bosnia?

PV: It's very different. The Gulf War and the Bosnian one share nothing in common. First, because their territories are so different. Iraq is a desert, an ideal territory for experimenting with new weapons, whereas Bosnia is a complex territory because of the topography. The conditions in which the Bosnians are fighting are those of a guerrilla. So these wars can't be compared. Once we have said that, it is possible to compare the role of the media in both wars. I mean that without the media, without television, the Lebanese war or the Yugoslavian war wouldn't have happened. The trigger of the operations of the civil war was linked to the medias, to their crime-inducing role, to their war appeal. The geostrategic and also the geopolitic dimension are related to the war powers of those who control television, to their ability to provoke and start a war. I am not the one who says it, many people in Sarajevo say so. The photographic and televisual coverage is not of the same nature. So each war has its own personality. Each time a war starts it has to be learned. It is unique in itself even if the armaments aren't quite the same.

JD: What is the difference between geostrategy and geopolitics? In Bosnia?

PV: Geopolitics relies mainly on geography. Geopolitics is older than geostrategy. I would say that in order to have geostrategy, there has to be a very developed technological means such as an air force, or naval fleet. Naval geostrategy existed before the aircraft one and before the global one with the satellites, the conquest of space. So, geopolitics goes back to Julius Caesar, the conquest of the Gauls, or the war of the Peloponnese with Thucydides. It is a war of land, a conquest of sites and towns. The domination of the territory is a determinant element in the battle. So, war in Yugoslavia is still linked to the territory. It is a determinant element in the battle. This is why the Western countries are afraid of it; they are afraid of an Afghanistan or a Vietnam in Europe, of something inextricable. Yugoslavia was the first one to start a strategy of popular defense, the famous defense-in-depth. Yugoslavians have a co-managed society that co-manages defense. War has been able to develop in Yugoslavia because defense and armaments were shared out on the whole territory—except for the tanks that were kept in the barracks of the big towns. So, the structure is very particular: it is a guerrilla and a civil war structure that is linked to territory. For example, a civil war wasn't possible in the desert of Iraq. Geography doesn't allow a very developed geopolitical war. On the other hand it allows a very developed geostrategy, because the territory is like a billiards table, like the sea, a naval strategy.

JD: Taking into account both the geopolitical and geostrategic factors, what should the West do in Bosnia?

PV: Police. When it's impossible to make war, police. At present, the NATO forces and the UN are a police army. And in such a situation, a situation that is not unlike that of some towns in America and the suburbs in France, a situation on the verge of civil war, the only possible thing to do is police.

JD: Is there a technological solution for such a national crisis?

PV: A terrible question, in philosophical terms. One is forced to speak about the unequal development of the nations. The national identity is linked to the industrial or technological development of a country. And in our world, technical development of the means of production is inseparable from the development from the means of destruction. We are talking of armaments. I would say that the proliferation of the conflict in Bosnia was encouraged because the countries that owned the means of destruction sold their technology of destruction. They did so for market reasons and for the arms race. So the unequal development between the nations remains technologically unbalanced. The worst example is that of nuclear proliferation. Whether we want it or not, the unequal development nowadays is unequal because of the armament race and because of the dealers. . . . You must go to Le Bourget [the Paris Air Show] and see for yourself.

JD: Which will be more important in the future: software, hardware, or wetware?

PV: I have a theory that I have developed in my book. There are three industrial or technologic revolutions. The first important one, at a technological level, is that of transport, which will encourage the development of territory with railways, airports, motorways, airports of all kinds, electric wires, cables, etc. It's a geopolitical element. The second revolution is nearly simultaneous: it is that of transmissions. It is Marconi, Edison, radio and television; and from then on, technology detaches itself from the territory. It becomes immaterial, electromagnetic. The third revolution, which is preparing itself, is of a revolution of transplantation. All these technologies of communication, the capacity of grafts—which have been used in aircrafts and missiles—encourage nanotechnology, the possibility to reduce technology up to the point of introducing it into the human body, to the point of introducing what Marinetti and some others wished for: the possibility of feeding the human body not only with chemicals but with technique. So, in the future, we will have the possibility of a technological colonization of the human body just as the geographical world was colonized by transports, communication, equipment. It is an incredible event. What enabled the development of territories, towns and also the urban development will be applied to the human body just as if we had the town in the body and not only around the body. The town at home: *in vitro, in vivo*, the town in oneself. There is here a return of the anthropomorphic dimension of technology in the human body. We see it with additional technologies on eyes, with heart stimulators, the possibilities of adding electronic memories to the brain as Marvin Minski suggested. So three revolutions: transport, transmission, transplantation. Technique is introduced in the body. Biomachine is on its way.

JD: This sounds familiar. Everyone in the United States seems to be reading Toffler—

PV: Personally, that does not reassure me. I criticize it, man overexcited by technique, the machine man. But I don't think it's progress.

JD: What are the ethical implications of these new technological developments?

PV: First, I think that the three revolutions we have just talked about lead to a technical integrism. I think that the power of technique will lead to its religion, a technocult, a kind of cybercult. Just as there is in Islamic, a Christian, a Jewish integrism, there is a technical integrism in power, which is made possible with the technologies of information.

Fundamentalism, in the field of technology, is just as dangerous as the religious one. Modern man killed the God of transcendence, the God of Judeo-Christianity, and he invented a machine god, a deus ex machina. One should be an atheist of technique. I try to be an atheist of technique. I am in love with technique. My image is that of the fight between Jacob and the angel. He meets God's angel but in order to remain a man, he must fight. This is the great image.

JD: What comes next?

PV: I think that the infosphere, the information sphere, will impose itself on the geosphere. We will live in a reduced world. The capacity of interaction, interactivity will reduce the world, the real space, to next to nothing. So, soon, in the future men will have a feeling of being shut up in a very small world, a narrow world. As I said, there is a speed pollution that reduces the world to nothing. I think that, just as Foucault talked about this feeling of being shut up in prison, the future generation will have this feeling of being shut up in the world, of incarceration which will certainly be on the verge of the unbearable. The last image: interactivity is to real space what radioactivity is to atmosphere. It's destructive.

JD: It's pessimistic.

PV: It's critical. Criticism is Jacob's fight against the angel. It's not negative. We mustn't abandon technique. We have to fight it without denying it. It's the angel. O.K., we can have lunch now.

Twenty years ago Virilio wrote that airports had become the *ur*-model of future cities: with their highly mobile populations, increased surveillance, fear of the other, recurrent violation of basic rights in the name of security, tracked movement, and mise-en-scène for the metaphysical collapse of arrival and departure. These proved to be home truths as I left for Charles-de-Gaulle Airport, with, on Virilio's recommendation, a planned stop-over at Le Bourget airport where the annual Paris Air Show was in full swing. This had become the high-tech arms bazaar for the twenty-first century: the French Dassault Rafale fighter, Eurofighter 2000, Eurocopter Tiger, Swedish Gripen fighter,

Russian Sukhoi-32 bomber, even a European Space Agency Ariane 5 booster were on display. But all this Euro-hardware was blown out of the sky by the first public outing in Europe of the U.S. B-2 Stealth Bomber, the so-called "flying wing" that was to fly nonstop to Paris after a simulated bombing run over the Netherlands.

But the real insight came as I killed some time on the metro platform, talking with a couple of midlevel arms dealers on their way back from the show. Tom, from New York and in cowboy boots, filled me in. "What do you want to know? The reason why everyone is here? For everybody to see just how proficient we have become at killing people. One manufacturer will tell you that his machine can kill 5,000 people, the next guy is selling 5,050. That's a sad commentary, believe me. . . . Unfortunately, I make a living at it." I asked him the Bosnia Question. "We're getting into a political thing now. I'd just like to give them the arms and let them fight . . . let them defend themselves." I had a plane to catch to England, but at Charles-de-Gaulle Airport I got to watch my Airbus pull away without me as passport control held everybody up to shake down a Colombian woman. Virilio was right: you're either on the plane or off the plane.

While at Oxford to research the interwar, I met with Timothy Garton Ash at Gee's, a glass conservatory turned into a restaurant, a fitting venue for the pellucid historian to throw stones at the conventional wisdom on Bosnia. He believes the violence of the Bosnia Question can only be understood in the context of the more peaceful transformations in Poland, Germany, Hungary, and Czechoslovakia, which he had artfully chronicled as an eyewitness in his book *The Magic Lantern: The Revolution of '89.*[6] "There is no such thing as 'postcommunism.' It differs as radically as the Czech Republic—probably a more stable democracy than Greece—and Bosnia." The differences can be traced to their particular mixes of history, geography, and leadership, with the "most obvious" being the Western inheritance of Central Europe, "from the Renaissance through the Reformation to the Enlightenment and the Industrial Revolution, and the experience of democracy in the twentieth century." But less obvious factors play a great if not greater role in the outcome: "Central Europe had liberal, postcommunist elites who were determined to steer their countries to the West, which was just next door, whereas the key to what happened in Bosnia is that you had communist elites who were prepared to manipulate, to exploit nationalist sentiments to remain in power, and this is the crucial feature—'the Milosevic phenomenon'—a manipulative, postcommunist nationalism, that is the key to the descent of the former Yugoslavia into civil war."

With less hyperbole but equal passion, Ash believes like Virilio that the media contributed to the unique, almost viral character of the transformation, an accelerated blend of networked reform and peaceful revolution that he calls "refolution." It was Vaclav Havel quoting Tim Garton Ash on the *samizdat* TV program *Videojournal* who said it best: "Ten years in Poland, ten months in Hungary, ten weeks in East Germany, ten days in Czechoslovakia." Ash wrote as an eyewitness of a "telerevolution," in which Hungarian oppositionists led their first major demonstration to the television station, and of Czechs, after seeing Germans demonstrate in Leipzig, come out in the tens of thousands to Wenceslas Square, chanting as one, "Do it like the Germans," and later, "Live transmission!" Now he wants to take the idea further, playing with the concept of a "virtual revolution." "The Czech revolution was a fairy tale, revolution as opera, no violence whatsoever. And then comes the Romanian revolution—shell-pitted building, blood-soaked flags, Central Committee in flames—and everyone in the West says to themselves, ah, this is a real revolution, we know what a revolution looks like—when in fact it was the Czechs who had the revolution, not the Romanians."

Garton Ash is underwhelmed by current academic efforts to understand the region. "Just as SS-20s have been turned into tractors, sovietologists have been turned into 'transitologists' . . . that is to say, a political scientist trying to interpret postcommunist Europe according to one dominant paradigm. For the whole Soviet period it was one of stasis, there was no fundamental change, what was unthinkable was the end of communism, only intrasystem change was thinkable. Now it's the opposite paradigm, namely the paradigm of permanent change and the teleological paradigm of transition to democracy—which is almost equally inappropriate." Over coffee I asked him for his best- and worst-case scenarios for Bosnia. At first he begged off, saying that he preferred description to prescription. He would go only so far as to invoke the insight that comes from historical knowledge, chief among them that all empires eventually come to an end. "The realistic best case now is that some sort of a crude balance of power, a mutual terror, is created between all three partners in the conflict, rather than the current two, and on that basis you have a partition and probably a transfer of populations as with Greece and Turkey after the First World War. Then in twenty years time you might have a *modus vivendi*." His worst case? The third world war. "I can absolutely see, if it is not controlled or exhausted, a knock-on effect to Hungary and Slovakia. If you start pushing up into Eastern and Central Europe, if that's the direction that the fire spreads, then it becomes less likely that German interests will remain unaffected. I mean, then, that the cliché that the E.U. has made war in Europe an impossibility is just that—a piety."

From Oxford I left for Aberystwyth, a seaside town in Wales that sells postcards on the boardwalk almost as faded as its heyday as the last stop for Victorian holiday-makers. My favorite was captioned "Mixed Bathing at Aberystwyth," with a turn-of-the-century crowd gathered on the shore to watch two elephants cavort in the water. This weekend, however, center ring was at the University of Wales, where leading international thinkers on human rights had gathered to ask the Big Questions. What good is the legal pretense of human rights when the fact of human wrongs is so in evidence? Are there universal human rights or are rights culturally relative? Does citizenship exhaust our obligations as human beings?

The presentations were marked by critical and ethical attempts to trouble the simple truths as well as cynical dismissals that often surround the discourse of human rights. One speaker stood out from the crowd, as much for his long service in the trenches of human rights struggles as for the measured hopefulness that he had managed to maintain throughout it all. Richard Falk, Milbank Professor of International Law and Practice at Princeton University, true to form, was opposed to intervention in Bosnia. He sees something of a scissors effect operating, between public pressure "to do something," produced by media exposure to human wrongs, and the dominant realist predilection of states to keep out unless vital interests are at stake. The result is that "you get shallow intervention and a 'politics of gesture' rather than any intervention of a transformative nature. This politics of gesture means that you do something, but you do something that doesn't involve big risks. Sanctions are a perfect example of that, which has a very cruel impact, as in Iraq and Bosnia, where the impact is not on the supposed wrong-doers but on the civilian population that is caught in between." This leads to the so-called "Mogadishu syndrome," where "world leaders become extremely wary of any kind of exposure to indigenous resistance, which is likely to occur in Bosnia." Falk is not ready to take liberal professions for human rights at face value. "One has to remember that genocide has never been opposed in international society on its own; it has only been opposed when it has been incidental to some other kind of enterprise. The liberal democracies were willing to live with fascism and Nazism so long as it stayed within its own borders." So too will it be with Bosnia.

Not one to end on such a pessimistic note, he asked as I was putting away the recording gear to clarify something said earlier. "The language of humanitarian intervention creates the illusion that states and their international organizations really serve to promote humanitarian goals. I think one needs to look elsewhere, to the energies of civilian society, to find out how humanitarian projects are promoted and realized, and I think maybe the experience of Eastern Europe in the late 1980s, South Africa's struggle against apartheid, and the civil rights in the United States is the place to look. I'm skeptical of intervention from above, as distinct from what might be called intervention from below, facilitated by transnational civil forces."

It was my good luck that the person who wrote the book on "détente from below"—and was now applying those lessons to human rights issues from the Baltic to the Balkans—was also in Aberystwyth for the conference. In her writings and political activism, Mary Kaldor, program director of the Centre for the Study of Global Governance at the London School of Economics, has provided one of the clearest and most persuasive replies to the Bosnia Question. She spoke to me of Bosnia as a new type of disintegrative violence. "The disintegration of state structures involves the disintegration of the state's monopoly of violence and the state's legitimacy, and with it the sense people once had that the state can protect them and that it deserves their respect. A second characteristic is the prevalence of identity politics that you belong to a particular group for no other reason than a label. You are a Catholic fighting against an orthodox Christian, but unlike the Catholic of the seventeenth century who was born a Catholic and would die one, these identities are really only labels, and as such, reflect a kind of moral vacuum. A third characteristic is the economic consequences that are very much linked to globalization and to the disintegration of productive structures like the prevalence of unemployment, or trade-related activities, particularly black market activities."

All important characteristics, but her last remarks impart a virtuous character to new wars, as she calls them. "Just as crucial is the way in which these wars are fought, in what people say are low-tech ways, but I don't think it's true to say they're low-tech. They're small scale, they're dispersed, maybe nonhierarchical; nevertheless, they use very advanced technology, very advanced communications technology, which is very effective for mobilizing large numbers of people. For instance, in Rwanda even if the people use machetes, radios are very important to mobilize the people to do it." And for those politicians and pundits, from Jesse Helms in Washington to our arms dealers in Paris who would like to pull out and "let them slug it out," Mary Kaldor responds that these are already and always were "transnational forms of violence, and in all of these areas, they have become dependent on humanitarian assistance and income from abroad." Not least, she says, is "the long reach and the deep pockets of the diaspora populations."

Unlike many other analysts, Mary Kaldor is quick to respond to the question of what to do, and without resort to the usual clichés. "Absolute key is building an alternative form of legitimacy, based on a substantially forward-looking project—not looking backward to some probably imaginary time when Serbs were Serbs, and Croats were Croats. This must be undertaken by people in the area but also by international institutions, which haven't understood the importance of this. They see it as something nice or utopian, but they don't see it as something absolutely central to establishing order in these areas. You can argue that force is necessary, but unless force carries with it the consent of the people in the area, and is capable of mobilizing people, then the international institution will be no more than another party to this disintegrative violence." She strongly believes that less media attention on the violence, and more on the nonviolent action of civic groups—and to treat them as legitimate actors—is essential to any long-lasting remedy.

A week later I saw Mary Kaldor's words put into action. At her urging I went to London, where European Dialogue—Britain's section of the Helsinki Citizen's Assembly (HCA), which Kaldor cofounded—was putting on a "State of Europe" conference at the National Liberal Club. In this elite watering hole, upstairs in the ballroom above the members-only Savage Club, a transnational group of representatives from civic groups in Latvia, Romania, Hungary, Russia, Czech Republic, and Bosnia-Herzegovina were gathering to provide a perspective from below, for a new civil society in Eastern/Central Europe and the Balkans. On the agenda was a report for the upcoming European Union Intergovernmental Conference. But there was more urgent business: preparation for the Fourth Assembly of the Helsinki Citizen's group which is to be held in October on the fiftieth anniversary of the founding of the United Nations. Where it was to be held is as important as when: in the "safe haven" of Tuzla, Bosnia. TV kept our focus on Sarajevo, but it is Tuzla that managed throughout the conflict to preserve its multiethnic, multiconfessional, democratic community in defiance of Serbian aggression and pressure for Muslim consolidation. It became a model for the Balkans. By declaring it an "open city"—open to all nationalities and religions—and bringing in all their representatives and supporters, the HCA were going to stage their own peace simulation for Bosnia.

I arrived just as a "reverse question time" was about to begin, with Jon Snow of *Channel 4 News* moderating a long table full of Central and Eastern European representatives, and taking questions from an audience that included then-shadow, soon-to-be Foreign Minister Robin Cook, Shirley Williams, Robert Skidelsky, and a wide mix of émigrés, activists, journalists, and others. The Q and A produced a remarkable dialogue. To be sure, many of the questions were critical, centered on the failure of the

European Union and the United Nations to go beyond state-centric solutions, its inability to reach out to the multicultural, multiethnic groups represented in the room. But much discussion was on the pragmatics of getting the E.U. and the United Nations to truly implement their resolutions. To a person, everyone agreed that the battle was to be won or lost on television. I asked Jon Snow about the responsibility of media to counter the dissimulations by all parties to the conflict. He readily admitted that the international press had an abysmal record, all too often hiding behind the pretense of objectivity and neutrality that always gave the upper hand to the dissimulator. There clearly was a willingness on his part to take sides. Interestingly, during an interview that night on *Channel 4 News*, Jon Snow went after a Serb diplomat who kept referring to the "crimes of Muslim terrorists" with tenacity and temerity that would leave Dan Rather wondering what the frequency was.

Is Bosnia, after Kosovo, still too fresh, too unresolved, to draw any lessons? In the face of dangerous new relationships of technology to violence, media to war, us to them, I was most impressed by the efforts of the army, the academy, the average citizen to respond by constructing an array of new networks. But how could they match the most powerful forces in the Balkans, what Edmund Burke called the "empire of circumstance"? In spite of the baying of the Western triumphalists, the empire of circumstance was the only empire to emerge victorious from the end of the Cold War. The peace that followed, cold or hot, became an especially bad war for peoples in the borderlands like the Balkans who emerged from the thaw of once-rigid bipolar powers and truths into a traumatized condition of ethnic as well as ethical insecurity. All kinds of politicians, pundits, and soldiers-as-diplomats rushed into this geopolitical flux and moral void with electoral promises (from Clinton to Chirac) and nationalist propaganda (from Karadzic's hard cop to Milosevic's soft cop). Others created a parallel universe of computerized simulations (Operations Other than War) and dissimulations (genocide as ethnic cleansing). And the majority, I would say, have hung back and avoided the void; whether they, like the new, more isolationist President Bush, will be able to maintain their angelic status is another question.

The Bosnia Question, simulated, televised, smart-bombed, and finally negotiated at Dayton, would be superannuated by its Kosovo sequel (see Chapter 8). Both were conducted as much on networks—prime time, computer, and civic—as in real space. Both triggered technological fixes and ethical responses in diplomatic, military, and nongovernmental circles. They were virtuous wars, yet unfinished by a virtuous peace.

As I decelerated from this dromologue, an unexpected invitation took me to Chicago for the National Strategy forum on "The Information Revolution and National Security." The setting, the First Division Museum, was eerily apt: it had been founded by the former editor and publisher of the *Chicago Tribune*, Colonel Robert McCormick, who had fought at the battle of Cantigny in the First World War with the same First Division that I had just seen fight a simulated peace in Hohenfels. The doughboys' first victory in Europe marked America's rise to great power status. The walls of the conference room were filled with propaganda poster art from the period. One in dark sepia tones stood out from the rest: Save Serbia, Our Ally. The gathering was remarkably eclectic: a Harvard academic followed by a UN representative followed by a Bruce Sterling scenario for a twenty-first century conflict. The epaulets of general and admiral trying to figure out how to deal with threats from the information revolution were rubbing up against the shoulders of longhairs from the Electronic Frontier Foundation and Sun Microsystems, warning of the civil liberties at risk if the military tried to regiment the elusive, fungible nature of information flows.

The proceedings were strictly off-the-record, but that evening, in a generous mood after dinner and brandy had been served, the former director of Central Intelligence, James Woolsey, waived the rule for me so I could quote from his keynote dinner address, "The Impact of New Information and Communications Technologies on National Security." The opening to his talk was pure cyberpunk, drawing from Neal Stephenson's *Snow Crash* to claim that people were coming to prefer the cyberspatial order of the "Metaverse" to the chaos and instability of the real world. He punched the message home with a line that drew the most laughs: "The Internet may be anarchic—but then we look at Bosnia." Woolsey, who probably gave the end of the Cold War its best if bleakest sound bite—"The dragon has been slain but the jungle is filled with a bewildering variety of poisonous snakes"—captured a paradox by mixing his metaphors. Perhaps he even helped to produce one, for how we represent the world helps to construct— as well as deconstruct—it. In this case, the simulated swords of the dragon-slayers and the cartographic pens of the diplomats failed, abysmally, in Bosnia. Is it not possible that the new virtuous networks, in all their anarchy and disorder, might provide a better, more *realistic* answer for the Bosnia question and the inevitable nationalist conflicts to follow?

4   The simulation triangle

On Rigor in Science

In that Empire, the Art of Cartography reached such Perfection that the map of one Province alone took up the whole of a City, and the map of the empire, the whole of a province. In time, those Unconscionable Maps did not satisfy and the Colleges of Cartographers set up a Map of the Empire which had the size of the Empire itself and coincided with it point by point. Less Addicted to the Study of Cartography, Succeeding Generations understood that this Widespread Map was Useless and not without Impiety they abandoned it to the Inclemencie's of the Sun and of the Winters. In the deserts of the West some mangled Ruins of the Map lasted on, inhabited by Animals and beggars; in the whole Country there are no other relics of the Discipline of Geography.
(Jorge Luis Borges, "Viajes de Varones Prudentes," *Dreamtigers*)

As a society, we're leaving the landscape and moving onto the map, without paying much attention to the process or the destination.

(John Perry Barlow, *Wired*)

The evidence lies, as it were, in the images. Flash back once more to the Berlin Wall taking its first hammer blows, President Bush and Secretary of State Baker at a hastily organized press conference, pointing to a map on the table in front of them, assuring the global viewing community that all frontiers—sovereignty indelibly inscribed on paper—would survive such an historic event. They sought in cartography what they could no longer

All but war is simulation.

Northrop Grumman's simulated casualty.

locate in reality: the fixity of former borders and former times. In their minds, paper would take stone taken down by hammer. In contrast, the atlases of Rand-McNally, more market-oriented than governments to the flux of post-Cold War times, began to sprout peel-away labels offering discounted replacements should there be any more border changes.

In the allegorical writings of Borges and Baudrillard, by the rearguard actions of Bush and Baker, we see how the map provides a more appealing, more plausible landscape when a familiar world spins out of control. After the End of History has been remaindered, The Coming Anarchy is the name of a retropunk band, the *X-Files* are under subpoena by a special prosecutor, and machines rather than humans determine the outcome of elections, what maps will we call home? In search of the source code for the virtual environments of the future, I undertook a trip to the Simulation Triangle.

I chose to ignore all cautionary road signs on this leg of the journey. No matter if the medium is paper and ink or software and code, we have seen how the mapper, in seeking to get it right, is structurally and graphically inclined to colonize the status quo, reduce the other to the same, even confuse the map for the "real thing." Whether it is in the name of abstraction, parsimony, or tradition, there is a scientific predilection in mapping that favors the global reach over the grasp of the local, the thin over the thick description, the revisionist over the visionary perspective. This is why the traveler must go where the signs say not to: the edge of the map. There we might find the dangerous complexities, banal evils, or even absurd circumstances that the mapped world avoids or effaces. The most interesting monsters lurk there, and we confront the dark allure of the edge that draws us on.

"All but war is simulation": this is the slogan that took me over the edge. I first heard it at the annual Interservice/Industry Training Systems and Education Conference in Orlando (I/ITSEC), where it kept popping up like a bad mantra. I had ambushed a colonel for a hallway interview after he finished a briefing on the virtues of virtual simulations to a packed room. At the end of the interview, he handed me a standard-issue business card with the slogan as its banderole. When I asked him what it meant, he gave me a quick history of his current base, STRICOM.

The slogan originated in 1992 with the activation of STRI-COM (Simulation, Training, and Instrumentation Command), the newest and—as I was to find out—the most unusual command post in the military. Tasked to provide the United States Army's "vision for the future," STRICOM chose a bold motto to go with the command post logo of a "land warrior" bisected by a lightning bolt in the middle of a bull's-eye. In the tone of instruction, he told me what the phrase means: "Everything short of war is simulation." But he then hastily added, "We don't *really* look at it that way, because you can't manage that properly." Sensing my confusion, he offered an analogical assist: "When you think about it, well, it's kind of like your love life: everything short of it is simulation."

An officer of lesser rank, someone who knew a dodgy sound bite when he heard one, cut in to remind the colonel that he had a plane to catch. I was left standing in the hallway, next to the potted palm with a frozen half-grin. What did he mean by "love life"? Did this mean war was to simulation as "love" was to stimulation? Was STRICOM into some kind of William Gibson *Neuromancer*, "sim/stim" thing?

These were not the kind of questions that had originally brought me to I/ITSEC. I came to Florida to bear witness to an auspicious alignment of the military, new media, and Mickey. In one corner of Orlando, I/ITSEC was occupying the Marriot World Center for three days, with over 60 panels, 180 exhibition booths, and enough uniforms and suits to gridlock the Beltway. Gathering under one cavernous convention roof for this year's theme, "Information Technologies: The World Tomorrow," the conference included an impressive list of special events, keynote speakers, and a who's who of industry CEOs, Defense Department higher-ups, and officers from all branches of the military. And truth be told, I was drawn to the prospect of hearing Tom Clancy as the banquet speaker (a no-show, as it turned out). At the other corner of Orlando, forty minutes up the Central Florida Greeneway, STRICOM was setting the stage for an award ceremony for the $69 million "JSIMS" contract. According to the press release, JSIMS (Joint Simulation System) was "a distributed computerized warfare simulation system that provides a joint synthetic battlespace ... to support the 21st century warfighter's preparation for real world contingencies." And making up the third leg, a few miles down International Drive through the pink arches and under a pair of mouse ears, Disney World was celebrating its twenty-fifth anniversary with a paroxysm of Imagineered (copyrighted) fun.

I entered the Simulation Triangle as one might enter a dangerous paradox, where slogans like "everything but war is simulation," "prepare for war if you want peace," and "the land where the fun always shines" quickly enhance the appeal of tour guides who don't rely on linear reasoning and conventional cartography. My intent was to ask a few questions, make some observations, and get in, get out quick. However, after several interviews I quickly came to see the wisdom of Liddell Hart's indirect approach:

> This idea of the indirect approach is closely related to all problems of the influence of mind upon mind—the most influential factor in human history. Yet it is hard to reconcile with another lesson: that true conclusions can only be reached, or approached, by pursuing the truth without regard to where it may lead or what its effect may be—on different interests. . . . In strategy, the longest way round is often the shortest way home.[1]

For the tighter, tactical navigations of the military-industrial-media-entertainment network (MIME-NET) on display, I drew from some thinkers who well understood the seductive powers of simulations, who consider hyperbole to be a *pragmatic* response to the hyperreal. To jump the monorails of spectacle where "everything that was directly lived has moved away into a representation," I borrowed from Guy Debord the subversive power of the "psychogeographic drift," the preferred situationist method for studying the psychological effects of a geographical environment on inhabitants as well as the transient observer.[2] To counter the hazards of simulacra, I relied on the hype of Jean Baudrillard, who anticipated the MIME-NET when he warned of "a group which dreams of a miraculous correspondence of the real to their models, and therefore of an absolute manipulation."[3] And to avoid becoming one more casualty of "the war of images," I planned to take seriously Paul Virilio's advice that "winning today, whether it's a market or a fight, is merely not losing sight of yourself."[4]

Hart's indirect approach was prompted by my first pilgrimage to I/ITSEC, five years earlier in the wake of the Gulf War, where the long way around yielded a victory in 100 hours. Back then there was a real Patriot missile in the Marriot lobby, flanked by two looped videos extolling its virtues through a series of blatantly phallic images. Many of the military present still seemed to be shaking the sand out of their boots. At this year's conference, however, with the kill-ratio of the Patriot dramatically downgraded, Kurds in refugee camps in the no-fly zone, and Saddam Hussein still playing the rogue, the victorious aura of the Gulf War had somewhat faded. Moreover, the poisonous snakes that emerged from the belly of the dead dragon (the post-Cold War metaphor and prophesy of former CIA director Woolsey) had since morphed into multiheaded hydras, in the former Yugoslavia, Somalia, Chechnya, Rwanda, and in other expanding pockets of the new chaos.

The pride and patriotism of the earlier I/ITSEC still flared on occasion into imperial hubris and technological hype, but this year's model was more a meld of corporate steel and glass with infotainment show-and-tell. Envisioning the future was still the goal, but enriching yourself and entertaining the stockholders en route made for a burgeoning of concessions on the way to Tomorrowland. Nowhere was this more apparent than in the war of signs itself, with the self-help vocabulary of management consultants giving the acronymic, ritualized language of the military a run for its fiscal allocations. "Synergy" was the conference buzzword. Synergy between the high-flyers in the military and top players in defense industries, to make those thinner and thinner slices of the budgetary pie go that much further. Synergy in the form of alliances or outright mergers among the major defense industries. But also synergy at the advanced technological level, to imagine and engineer a new form of virtual warfare out of networked computer simulation (SIMNET) and Distributed Interactive Simulation (DIS), a command, control, communication, computer, and intelligence system of systems (C4I), and complete interoperability through a common high level architecture (HLA). Perched at the top of this synergy pyramid was the endgame of all war games, JSIMS, the macro-mega-meta-simulation of the twenty-first century. Or so they said.

When I arrived at the convention the synergy wave was making its way through the Grand Ballroom, where the Flag and General Officer Panel was in full session. On a podium at one end of the vast room, against a projected backdrop of the American flag, multiplied and magnified by two oversized video screens, the top brass and officials from the Department of Defense presented their views on the role of information technologies for the military. Deputy Undersecretary of Defense Louis Finch warned of a return to a post-Vietnam "hollow army" if new information technologies were not harnessed "to manage a massive transition." Vice Admiral Mazach called for a post-Cold War strategy that could deal with more complex, multiple threats in a time of military downsizing, declaring that "We must walk down the information highway—or be run down." Vice Admiral Patricia Tracey endorsed the use of "infomercials" in boot camp to train our troops in issues like drug and alcohol abuse as well as in new sensitive areas like gender relations: "Disney has used it for years, we're ready to use it now." Major General Thomas Chase of the Air Force, citing the displacement of traditional battlefields by a digitized "battlespace," endorsed a global linking up of "synthetic environments."

Not everyone was so eager to jump on the cyberwagon. Wearing battle ribbons from two tours in Vietnam, unaccompanied by snappy graphics or intricate flow charts, Major General Ray Smith of the Marine Corps took a more cautious approach to simulations. No Luddite, he acknowledged the need for new skills and training techniques for the soldier, offering the story of a lance corporal abroad, who in a single day might rehydrate a starving child, mediate between members of warring clans, handle the media, and use a global positioning system with a satellite linkup to call in a gunship attack. Simulations, while useful, are not sufficient to train such a range of complex and compressed duties: only experience in the field would do. When asked from the floor what industry can do to help, he paused, then bluntly said: "Make it cheap." After the panel I probed him for the source of his guarded skepticism. "In war you fight people not machines.

We're training to beat computers, instead of training to beat the enemy. You cannot model the effects of confusion and surprise, the friction and fog of war." Paul Virilio puts it less bluntly, if more grandly:

> This makes the decisive new importance of the "logistics of perception" clearer, as well as accounting for the secrecy that continues to surround it. It is a war of images and sounds, rather than objects and things, in which winning is simply a matter of not losing sight of the opposition. The will to see all, to know all, at every moment, everywhere, the will to universalised illumination: a scientific permutation on the eye of God which would forever rule out the surprise, the accident, the irruption of the unforeseen.[5]

Smith's view ran against the grain of an emergent technological imperative to manage uncertainty, unpredictability, and worst-case scenarios of chaos through superior simulation power and global surveillance. All the major corporate players were making the pitch in force—Lockheed Martin, McDonnell Douglas, Boeing, Hughes, Evans and Sutherland, Raytheon, and Northrop—along with the rising stars of the simulation business, like SAIC, Silicon Graphics, Reflectone, and Viewpoint DataLabs. They had come to sell the hardware and software of the future. Human wetware was more problematical. Indulged as a consumer, it otherwise took on the look of an expensive add-on, or a plug-in with compatibility problems. In most instances the human component added a bizarro effect to the synergy mix. Consider an excerpt from one of the papers presented in the "Modeling and Simulation" section, called "Human Immersion into the DIS Battlefield":

> Recent advances in human motion capture and head mounted display technologies, coupled with Distributed Interactive Simulation capabilities, now allow for the implementation of an untethered, fully immersable, DIS-compliant, real-time Dismounted Soldier Simulation (DSS) System. The untethered soldier, outfitted with a set of optical markers and a wireless helmet-mounted display, can move about freely

within a real-world motion capture area, while position and orientation data are gathered and sent onto a DIS network via tracking cameras and image processing computers.

Fortunately, for those of us who couldn't tell DIS from DAT, there was a demonstration on hand to cut through the techno-babble. Occupying some prime real estate at the entrance to the exhibition hall, the STRICOM booth was running a looped version of the "dismounted soldier"—the "dis" saying it all about the level of respect for a grunt without wheels.

Tracy Jones, lead engineer of individual combatant simulations at STRICOM, gave me the blow-by-blow. "We are trying to prove the principle of immersing the individual soldier in a virtual environment and having him interact with other entities in real time. What we've got is a wireless optical-reflective marker system developed by the entertainment industry about ten years ago in movies like *Batman* and *Aliens*. It consists of a series of four camera systems with spotlights, sixteen markers on the soldier's body and three on his M-16. These markers will pick up exactly where he is in real time and render it into a 3-D model for a virtual database. He's wearing a wireless virtual head display so he can see where he is in the virtual environment."

She directed me to the back of the display. Lifting an edge of the camouflage netting, she revealed the *deus ex machina* of DSS. "This is a MODSAF SGI station." She translated for me: "Modulated Semi-Automated Forces, Silicon Graphics Images." It was a program developed by the army to construct computer-generated forces, because, as she put it, "you're never going to have enough men—uh, *people*—in the loop to populate a simulated battlefield, so we have computer-generated forces that are smart and intelligent, that can fight against our men in the loop." When I asked why "*semi*automated," she admitted that "they're not completely smart, you can't just push a button and let them go." I was going to ask her if she knew about SKYNET and the semiautomated sentinels in *Terminator* that synergized into a very nasty Arnold Schwarzenegger. But I feared she might find that condescending.

I asked the wired soldier instead, a big guy in camouflage who looked more like Sly with a mustache than Arnold in shades.

"Isn't this getting close to the *Terminator*? Aren't you afraid of the machines getting smarter than the soldiers and taking over?" He gave me the narrow-eyed Clint look—or maybe it was just the camera lights: "Uh . . ." Tracy intervened, "they're not that smart yet." Not sure who wasn't that smart, I asked who usually wins in the simulations. No hesitation from Sly this time: "I do." Is that programmed in? "Well, they can't kill me. Otherwise we'd have to stop and restart the program." So you're immortal? "No, I'm Rambo." Before I can get him to elaborate on this distinction, Tracy announces that it is time to start the demonstration.

At the front of the booth I recognized the new commander of STRICOM, Brigadier General Geis, from the front cover of the recently launched magazine, *Military Training and Technology*. He's surrounded by some VIPs but he amicably agrees to a quick interview. What I get is a verbal version of a press release on the cost-effectiveness of simulations in a period of military draw-down—which is understandable, given his short tenure on the job. But there is a payoff: after I confess to continued confusion about JSIMS, he invites me to come out to the base the next day to witness the signing ceremony of the contract award. There I could get a firsthand account from the architects and builders of JSIMS.

> The spectacle is the map of this new world, a map which exactly covers its territory. The very powers which escaped us show themselves to us in all their force.[6]

Guy Debord's words should have graced the entrance of the exhibition hall, as I left the STRICOM booth and plunged into the belly of the beast. The hall was vast, full of simulated gunfire, flashing computer monitors, and reps who varied in style from barkers at a freak show to the Zen haiku of a Nissan ad. There were simulated cockpits of jets and helicopters, tanks and space-ships. You could fire a simulated M-16 at "terrorists" (all looking like cousins of Yasser Arafat), throw simulated grenades (you could smell the posttraumatic stress with each flash-bang), tear up some turf in a simulated M1A2 tank (no German farmer to complain), take out a bad guy in a simulated drug raid (in a curious fashion-lag, the *Miami Vice* look prevails), or blow up a building with a simulated truck bomb (essential viewing for every militia member). In this electromagnetic maelstrom of simulation, patriotism, and profit, I thought a seizure was more likely than synergy. I drift, heading nowhere, searching everywhere for a psychogeography that might provide a map of meaning for the sound and light show.

But meaning, as Baudrillard tells, is illusive when fearsome objects rule the roost: "The problem of security, as we know, haunts our societies and long ago replaced the problem of liberty. This is not as much a moral or philosophical change as an evolution in the objective state of systems."[7] I found a familiar landmark immediately behind the STRICOM booth, where a small group of marines was using the synergy to make simulation fun. Compared to the surroundings, theirs was a low-tech operation: cordoned off by black curtain, there were four monitors with keyboards, a projection screen, and a sound system all hooked up to a minicomputer. I had stumbled upon *Marine Doom*. On a tight budget, and always looking for off-the-shelf technology, the Marine Corps Modeling and Simulation Office had decided to appropriate rather than innovate, to simulate what marines do best: to fight independently in squads with small arms. There wasn't a smart weapon in sight, just a computer-generated four-man fire team in a retooled game of *Doom*. The monsters had been replaced by distant, barely visible forces that kept popping up out of foxholes and from around bunker walls to lay down some lethal fire.

After giving a history and description of *Marine Doom*—"a mental exercise in command and control in a situation of chaos"—the lieutenant wanted to know if I was ready to walk the walk. Having spent some time in the video arcade, I thought it couldn't be too tough, especially since I would be playing with the lieutenant and two kids barely in their teens, who seemed to have acquired squatter rights. That was my first mistake. The plan was simple enough: with mouse and keyboard strokes controlling speed and direction, we were to head out of our foxhole, traverse the road, go around some bunkers, and clear a building of bad guys. In eight attempts, I was killed seven times. The single time I made it all the way to the building, I killed the lieutenant in a burst of "friendly fire." I wasn't sure if you had to say you're sorry in simulations, but I apologized nonetheless. The high quality graphics, sounds of gunfire and heavy breathing, and the sight of rounds kicking up in your face, as well as the constant patter of the lieutenant ("Save your ammo. Point man, take that bunker. You're taking rounds. I'm going up, cover me. Ahh, I'm down), gave the "game" a pretty high dose of realism, especially if accelerated heartbeat is any measure.

The appropriation of *Doom* by the Marine Corps was significant for another reason. Usually the technology transfer goes in the other direction, with military applications leading the way in research and development, from the earliest incarnations of the computer in simulation projects like "Whirlwind" at MIT's Servomechanisms Laboratory during the Second World War, to "SAGE," the first centralized air defense system of the Cold War. We could say there has been from the very first a close "Link" between military simulations, the development of the computer, and the entertainment industry. In 1931 the navy purchased the first aircraft simulator from its designer, Edward Link. By 1932, the military still had only one Link Trainer; the amusement parks had bought close to fifty. Now the developmental lag between the real thing and its simulation has just about disappeared. From the F-16 to the F-117A, the M1A2 tank to the Bradley armored vehicle, the Aegis cruiser to the latest nuclear aircraft carrier, the video-game version arrives on the shelves almost as soon as the weapon system first appears. Indeed, a Pentium chip and a joystick will get you into the Comanche helicopter, the F-22, and the newest *Seawolf* SSN-21 submarine—which is more than a real pilot or sailor could claim as these projects suffer delays and budget cuts.

> For it is with the same Imperialism that present-day simulators try to make the real, all the real, coincide with their simulation models. But it is no longer a question of either maps or territory. Something has disappeared: the sovereign difference between them that was the abstraction's charm.[8]

My drift through the exhibition hall with Virilio, Debord, and Baudrillard was interrupted by an invitation to attend a lunch laid on by Lockheed Martin. Over a catered meal in a hotel suite,

Stephen Buzzard, vice president for Business Development at Lockheed Martin walked a group of journalists—mainly from the military and defense industry journals—through a series of organization flow charts that seemed to be in constant need of verbal revisions. Merger-mania had outstripped the capabilities of the graphics and public relations departments. Lockheed, having barely digested Martin Marietta, added Loral in July, Quinitron in August, and have since reorganized forty subsidiary companies into "virtual organizations" to "create a mix of cultures." And just in case the assembled press missed the point, Buzzard concluded by stating in the sovereign voice usually reserved by statesmen, "We have alliances with various other companies."

The first-name basis of the journalists and the corporate executives, the inside jokes, and the closest thing to investigative reporting appearing to be a vying for stock tips, all combined to make "synergy" a continuation of monopoly capitalism by other means—only this time the highest stage was not Lenin's vaunted imperialism but Baudrillard's hyperbolized simulation. This suspicion was supported the following week by Boeing's announcement of a $13 billion takeover of McDonnell Douglas, creating one more aerospace colossus.

But the smaller industries weren't waving any white flags. Silicon Graphics, for some time the David among the simulation Goliaths, had developed the most powerful slingshot yet, the Onyx2, with a memory capacity of 256 GB, memory bandwidth of 800MB/sec/CPU, and, most importantly for simulation graphics, the capability to generate 20K polygons at 60HZ/pipeline. Watching one of these generate a simulation of a helicopter on the deck, down to the details of its reflections in the water and cows stopping in midrumination as it passes overhead, was a reality-check that everyone seemed eager to cash. A hierarchy of booths could be drawn from those that did and those that did not have one (or even two or more) of the sleek, black Onyx2; obvious from their placement that they were there not just to run displays but *to be* the display of the simulation edge. Other firms were compensating by making synergy work at the organizational level. Highly visible—and offering the best food and drink at its reception—was "The Solution Group," a consortium of close to twenty industries formed by Paradigm Simulation in 1994 to integrate product, services, and support for the simulation consumer. Judging from current trends, one could imagine two, maybe three enormous booths filling the hall at I/ITSEC 2001: if you're not part of the Solution, you're part of Lockheed Martin Raytheon or Boeing Northrop Grumman. And even if there are no more enemies in sight by the year 2001, one could surmise that there would still be a Solution in search of a problem.

Niche synergy was another way to go. One member of the Solution Group was leading the way, infiltrating the military-industrial-entertainment nexus by creating an ever-expanding database of hyperreal, real-time 3-D simulations. Viewpoint DataLabs might not have high name recognition, but anyone who has viewed over the last few years a commercial, a television show, a hit film, or a video game with computer-generated graphics has probably sampled Viewpoint's product. Their booth's promo video was riveting and revealing, for the eclecticism of the content as well as the monotony of the style. It opens with the memorable scene of the alien footfighters swarming the F-18s in *Independence Day*, which buzz-cuts into a pair of attacking mosquitoes in a Cutter Insect repellent commercial, then to spaceships attacking in *Star Trek Voyager*, followed by some requisite mega-explosions, a simulation of a missile launch from two helicopters, the dropping of a fuel-air dispersal bomb from *Outbreak*, and a trio of Eurofighter 2000s doing maneuvers that are aerodynamically impossible (a case of wishful flying, since the problem-plagued real Eurofighter had yet to make it into full service). Interspersed is a whimsical scene of a museum-bound T-Rex doing a little chiropractic for a McDonald's ad and, to my émigré eye, an offensive ad of Lady Liberty plucking an Oldsmobile Aurora off the Staten Island Ferry Lady (give her your riches, your muddled mind, and she'll make the right car choice for you—that's freedom). Big Bang backed by Bang-Bang, especially when it comes in 3-D with a technorave sound track, is a big seller.

That night I made the rounds of the receptions hosted mainly by the larger defense industries. I learned a lot about the field from ex-fighter jocks turned corporate VPs, ex-artists turned graphic designers, ex-hackers turned software developers. After a few drinks, nearly everyone was eager to let me know about their former lives. I suppose making a living making the machines that help stop others from living doesn't make for easy cocktail chatter. Nonetheless it was there, in all the stories about what they once did. I didn't dwell on it, for fear of sounding sanctimonious, but also because I too was in the triangle, collecting data to entertain/train others in the ways of war, making war fun for the consumer/reader. I took some notes on what was being said, but I lost the cocktail napkin on which they were written. A final imprecation from Virilio would have to suffice:

> An idol capable of realizing exactly what men's faith has been unable to accomplish. . . . A utopia of *technical fundamentalism* that has nothing at all to do with the religious variety that still requires virtues of men instead of advantages to "machines"?[9]

The previous night was not the only reason I was late the next morning for the awards ceremony at STRICOM. I could not find the place. When you drive up to most military bases, there's a perimeter, guard booth, at the very least a recognizable headquarters with flags flying out front. Here there were just row after row of sleek steel and glass buildings, interrupted by nicely landscaped parking lots. This was military base as corporate research park, with all of the major defense industries represented on the base. I finally located the right building and room, and joined a circle of dark suits and a mix of army khaki, air force blue, and navy white, standing around a large conference table. At the front, Naval Captain Drew Beasley, program manager of JSIMs, was just getting into the background of the program. It began with a memorandum of agreement among the leadership of the armed forces and the Department of Defense, signed in 1994, to develop "an interoperable training simulation capable of combing warfighting doctrine, command, Control, Communication, Computer and Intelligence (C4I), and logistics into a team event." It would replace, said Beasley, older war games devised "for the dreaded threat of the great Russian hordes coming over the tundra." Thirty-two military operations since the end of the Cold War, ranging from famine relief to armed conflict, have demonstrated that "we need a different paradigm that allows us to work cooperatively and jointly."

JSIMS would make it possible to combine and distribute three forms of simulations: *live simulations* (conducted with soldiers and equipment in "real" environments), *virtual simulations* (conducted with electronic and mechanical replications of weapons systems in computer-generated scenarios), and *constructive simulations* (the highest level of abstraction where computer-modeled war games play multiple scenarios of conflict). Advances in microprocessor speed, interactive communication, and real-time, high-resolution video mean that military exercises will be able to mix and match live, virtual, and constructive simulations not only in Synthetic Theaters of Wars (STOW) but also on commercially available computers and networks. Experiments have already been conducted where a group of colonels at Fort Leavenworth in Kansas introduce an electronic OPFOR (enemy or "opposing forces") battalion into an actual training exercise at the National Training Center in the Mojave Desert, while soldiers in Martin Marietta tank simulators at Fort Knox "ride along" in real time with either side as part of a distributed Battle Lab simulation. But by the year 2003, JSIMS would make it possible for "all the services to play together" with "just-in-time" mission rehearsal, and "a worldwide terrain database."

With the flash of cameras and a round of applause, Captain Beasley and Lane Arbuthnot, program manager of "JSIMS Enterprises" at the Fortune 500 global technology firm, TRW, put pen to the $69 million contract. A very efficient public affairs officer had arranged an interview for me with Beasley, Arbuthnot, and Kurt Simon, also from TRW, who was actually in charge of the technical aspect of building the simulation. The captain once more deployed his demise of the Russian hordes metaphor to emphasize the external motivation for a new macrosimulation, but spent most of the time going over the internal factors, like the need to standardize the disparate models of the different services (some based on hex-systems, others on Cartesian coordinates) and to globalize our preparation for future threats. Sounding like a modern-day Francis Bacon ("knowledge is power"), he made JSIMS appear as glorious as the founding of the library of Alexandria: "We are building a synthetic environment that can be used to pull down objects and representations out of our electronic libraries, objects that other services have placed there . . . as part of an overall streamlining process to bring a joint focus, commonality, and collaboration within government and with industry." The captain moved to a white marker board to draw a series of circles representing live and constructive simulations, which increasingly overlap as JSIMS goes through its stages of development: in his schema, the constructive had engulfed the live by the year 2003.

"The Disneyland imaginary," says Baudrillard, "is neither true nor false; it is a deterrence machine set up in order to rejuvenate in reverse the fiction of the real."[10] Compared to Disney World, the military and industry were open laptops when it came to the role of simulations. My efforts to set up interviews with the architects of Imagineering and Audio-Animatronics (always with super-scripted trademarks affixed), or better yet, to get a glimpse behind the technology of simulators like "Star Tours" or "Body Wars," were met by some very polite, very efficient stonewalling. People were in meetings, on vacation, in California. Getting into STRI-COM was a piece of cake compared to the obstacles I faced at Team Disney's postmodern headquarters. A series of abstracted mouse-ear arches, a formidable defense-in-depth of receptionists, multiple mazes of cubicles, and a sun-dial atrium that looked like a nuclear cooling tower did not invoke a sense that this was a place where the fun always shines. When I finally reached the right cubicle, I was told that my designated handler was at a meeting. Further efforts produced meager results. After a couple of phone calls, clearance was finally reached from higher up: I was given a copy of the "25th Anniversary Press Book and Media Guide" and sent on my way.

The guide was full of noteworthy information, like the fact that Eddie Fisher and Debbie Reynolds had a flat tire and showed up late for the 1955 opening of Disneyland (but no mention that film star Ronald Reagan emceed the event), and that Walt Disney did not live to see the opening of Disney World (but no mention that his vision of the future as a frozen past included a cryogenic funeral for himself). The chronology provided for the opening year of Disney World is even stranger. In the Disney version, in 1971 astronauts take the lunar buggy for a spin, George C. Scott wins an Oscar for *Patton*, eighteen-year-olds get the right to vote, and President Nixon fights inflation. And just about saying it all,

"Everyone was wearing smile buttons," and, "Charles Manson was convicted of murder." Others might have different memories, like President Nixon setting up the "Plumbers," eighteen-year-olds drafted to fight in Vietnam, the Pentagon Papers leaked to the *New York Times*, and thirty-one prisoners and nine hostages killed at Attica State Prison. Simulations of the future sometimes require a re-imagineering of the past.

My trip to the Simulation Triangle left me with a heightened sense of danger. When military forces and entertainment industries join in mimesis, when war games and language games become practically indistinguishable ("All but war is simulation"), when the imitative, repetitive, and regressive powers of simulation negate any sense of original meaning, more than just peace is at risk. I felt as if reality itself, like light being sucked into a black hole, was disappearing in the Simulation Triangle (a sentiment that was to return with a vengeance after the 2000 Florida presidential vote). Indeed, with increasing orders of verisimilitude, the simulations displayed a capability to precede and replace reality itself: Borges's nightmare again. Digital design and human desire partially explain the proliferation of simulation. But one must also acknowledge that, at the abstracted level of deterrence, simulations can and have "worked" for positive purposes. Total transparency through surveillance (at the airport or by satellites) combined with the occasional direct application of simulations (*COPS* or the Gulf War) are powerful, if not always democratic, cyberdeterrents. It is understandable why some might desire the virtual security of simulation (STRICOM's JSIMS or Disney's Main Street U.S.A) to the risks of the real (conflict overseas and crime in the cities)—even if it puts liberty as well as the reality principle at risk.

But there remains an irony if not a danger lurking at the edge of the map, where it comes up hard against the contingencies of life. As superior computing power and networking increase in representational power and global reach, simulation leaves little room to imagine the unpredictable, the unforeseeable, the unknowable *except* as accident. Will God's will, nature's caprice, human error seem puny in effect as simulation becomes more interactive, more complex, more *synergistic*? In the context

of industrial accidents, organizational theorists have already identified a "negative synergism" in complex systems that can produce
unpredictable, worst-case failures. In the technological drive to
map the future—to deter known threats through their simulation—are we unknowingly constructing new, more catastrophic
dangers? Conversely, will the "new" only be construed, and
feared, as the unmapped event? Or, worse, if the map does become
truly, hyperreally global, without the edge beyond which lies the
unmappable, where will the monsters go?

In spite of my three days adrift in the Simulation Triangle, and
the feeling that a bad case of postsimulation stress lay ahead, I
still had hope for humanity. But it was badly tested when I went to
catch my flight home at the Orlando airport and saw the sign
above the Delta curbside check-in: "Toy weapons must be
checked at the counter."

The CNN effect.

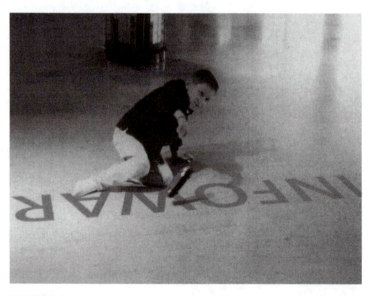

INFOWAR expo.

5 The virtual enemy

All names of good and evil are images; they do not speak out, they only hint. He is a fool who seeks knowledge from them . . . It is power, this new virtue; it is a ruling idea, and around it a subtle soul: a golden sun, and around it the serpent of knowledge.

(Friedrich Nietzsche, "Of the Bestowing Virtue," *Thus Spake Zarathustra*)

I'm running out of demons. I'm down to Kim Il-sung and Castro.

(Colin Powell, then Chairman of the Joint Chiefs of Staff)

The toughest part of my journey was finding the enemy. There was no shortage of "Blue," "Red," and "Brown" teams, or "opposing forces," "regional powers," even a "reemergent global threat" to contend with. But actual names and faces were hard to come by. To be sure, the Pentagon reached deep into its archive of historical, film, comic-book, and free-floating enemies to come up with menacing, foreign threats, like the "Krasnovians," "Sumarians," and "Hamchuks" who roamed the Mojave Desert in green jumpsuits and black berets; the unkempt "Sowenians," "Vilslakians," and "Juralandians" who clashed in the hills of Hohenfels that bordered on the countries of "Fredonia" and "Ruritania"; and the grungy Boolean and Furzian refugees who stirred up trouble in the "Country of Orange," located somewhere in the San Francisco Bay area. But without fail, whenever I asked for a real name, a real country, I got the party line: this is just a scenario, an exercise, an experiment. We don't do countries, as one air force spokesman put it when queried during a recent space war game.

Civilian officials, especially bureaucratically entrenched ones like Andrew Marshall, were usually less reluctant to name names (see the interview with Marshall in Chapter 2). But even the State Department, which once provided a list of "rogue states," is now gun-shy. On June 19, 2000, rogue states received their death notice. After being asked on a public radio news program if Kim Jong-il of North Korea, who had just summitted with South Korean leader Kim Daejung, was still a "rogue leader," then Secretary of State Madeleine Albright let it be known that "we are now calling these states 'states of concern' because we are concerned about their support for terrorist activity, their development of missiles, their desire to disrupt the international system."[1] Judging from that day's briefing transcript, some sympathy should be extended to the State Department spokesman who dealt with the aftermath:

QUESTION: Is "rogue state" then out of the lexicon as of today?

MR. BOUCHER: I haven't used it for a while.

QUESTION: Is it possible that some states will still be referred to as "rogue states" if they—

MR. BOUCHER: If they want to be rogues, they can be rogues, but generally we have not been using the term for a while, I think.

QUESTION: So it's not a matter of some countries continuing to be "rogue states" and others having progressed to "states of concern"; all of them henceforth are "states of concern"?

MR. BOUCHER: Yes . . .

QUESTION: Can you tell us how many there are?

MR. BOUCHER: No.

QUESTION: Has anybody actually done a rough list?

MR. BOUCHER: We have found the opportunity to express our concerns about different states at different times in different ways. We try to deal with each one on its behavior, on its actions, on its merits.

QUESTION: So there would be many, in fact, because you have often expressed concern about various aspects of countries?

QUESTION: Is Pakistan a "state of concern"?

MR. BOUCHER: I'm not trying to create new categories. The essence of this is not trying to categorize people. The essence of this is trying to describe our relationships with individual nations in terms of the issues that are most important to the United States and our ability to make progress on those issues.

QUESTION: So just coming out and saying that we're concerned about an event in a country, whichever country, does not necessarily mean that it's a "state of concern"?

MR. BOUCHER: I'm not trying to categorize or recategorize anybody. I'm trying to say that we're going to deal with each country based on the situation and the merits.

QUESTION: So are the same seven countries—or however many countries it was that were considered "rogue states" before— are they all now considered "states of concern"?

MR. BOUCHER: Yes, they would be. But I have to say the point is not to categorize them; the point is to deal with each country on the basis of what we can accomplish in terms of what we care about.

QUESTION: But when you change the category, that is necessarily a categorization.

MR. BOUCHER: We'll discuss that over lunch sometime. I think that's too philosophical for me to deal with from the podium.[2]

Right about the time rogue states disappeared, individual global villains started to show up. The State Department website, taking a cue from the FBI, began to sport wanted posters for a "Rewards for Justice" program that offered $5 million for information "leading to the transfer to, or conviction by, the International Criminal Tribunal of Slobodan Milosevic, Radovan Karadzic, and Ratko Mladic."[3] Perhaps this is a new characteristic of virtuous warfare: that as states dematerialize and deconstruct, as national identities become more fluid, as simulations and scenarios reach for a credible threat, the public image of the foreign enemy is (only) reducible to a wanted poster. This is the conundrum of virtuous war: the more virtuous the intention, the more we must virtualize the enemy, until all that is left as the last man is the criminalized demon.

Faces without states, states without faces: these are "virtual states of concern," requiring a deeper probe of the structures and processes that seek to define the enemy in uncertain times. For me, it meant taking the shuttle to D.C., then the Metro Blue Line into the Virginia fringe of the Beltway, a.k.a. "Spook Alley," where the marble, granite, and limestone architecture of public authority blurs into the steel and glass of corporate power: the home of the Defense Advanced Research Projects Agency (DARPA).

Officially, DARPA is tasked to go outside the box, to look over the horizon, to peer deep into the shadows—and then to come up with the right technology for the job. Or in its own words:

> The Defense Advanced Research Projects Agency (DARPA) is the central research and development organization for the Department of Defense (DOD). It manages and directs selected basic and applied research and development projects for DOD, and pursues research and technology where risk and payoff are both very high and where success may provide dramatic advances for traditional military roles and missions and dual-use applications.[4]

Perhaps the most famous dual-use application to emerge from DARPA was "ARPA-NET," the precursor and enabler (in spite of Al Gore's claims) of the Internet. But DARPA is also very much in the future-threat business. In recent testimony before the Senate Subcommittee on Emerging Threats and Capabilities, DARPA director Frank Fernandez opened his remarks with the rote post-Cold War warning about the threat of uncertainty:

> In today's world, change has become the norm, not the exception. The threats facing the U.S. are much different than those of the Cold War. We are faced, not with a peer competitor who is well known and well understood, but, instead, with adversaries whose location and capabilities are highly variable. As a result, our forces are being called to fight in places where the terrain and the preexisting infrastructure vary greatly. Our forces must interoperate and coordinate with an ever-changing mix of allied and coalition forces. And they must be prepared to perform a wide spectrum of missions—from

peacekeeping and humanitarian activities to full-scale, traditional warfare, with the resulting rapidly shifting rules of engagement.[5]

Judging by the rest of his statement, Fernandez unabashedly is ready to enlist DARPA for virtuous war. The primary task of DARPA is to "help the DOD find technical solutions to national-level problems"; and the secondary goal "is to be the technical enabler for the revolutionary innovation required for our warfighters to achieve dominance across the range of military operations—Operational Dominance."

To reach these goals, DARPA is fully diversified in information technology. Its multiple programs, including the Offices of Information Systems, Information Technology, and Microsystems Technology, seek to invent, develop, and then leverage into military superiority new networking, computing, and software technologies. DARPA's overarching Advanced Technology Office is more geared towards practical applications of the new technologies: "The ultimate goal is superior cost-effective systems that the military can use to respond to new and emerging threats."[6] For the army, this entails a Future Combat Systems program to "develop network-centric concepts for a multi-mission combat system"; for the navy, a "Netted Search," which can provide real-time target localization and tracking for torpedo guidance; for the marines, a semiautonomous robot that can "penetrate into denied areas"; and for the air force, an Airborne Communications Node with high-altitude unmanned aerial vehicles for "an autonomous communications infrastructure." And DARPA is also involved in "Operations Other than War" (OOTW) and humanitarian work, like the "electronic dog's nose" program that seeks to technologically replicate the canine's remarkable capability to sniff out land mines. Dual-use dogs (DUDs?), to be sure, but virtuous nonetheless.

My host at DARPA was Ryan Henry, a graduate of the naval academy and a former carrier pilot. We had met at one of the National Security and Information Technology conferences held at the Cantigny estate of Colonel McCormick (see Chapter 3). My talk had been on "Speed Bumps for the Information Revolution," and my concerns about the impact of two powerful forces of the information revolution—simulation and speed—had resonated with some of Henry's interests in simulation and training at DARPA. I doubt whether he thought I'd take up his invitation to stop by sometime, but I had an interest in the work DARPA was doing at the time on the Synthetic Theater of War (STOW), a prototype of immersive virtual environments that could use overhead reconnaissance, satellite communications, and massive parallel computing to integrate virtual, live, and constructive simulations of war in real time. Besides, I was eager to get a look from the inside of an organization that was shrouded in mystery.

A visit to DARPA did raise some personal questions for me, ones that I'd dodged for most of my journey, but now found difficult to avoid. I learned after the fact that I was a second-draft (or perhaps even further down) pick for the Cantigny conference on national security and information technology. My invitation evidently came after the first *Wired* writer, the much better-known digital-media maverick, Jon Katz, turned down the invitation on moral grounds. In an online article that drew a lot of attention, Katz wrote that journalists "shouldn't socialize with the muckety-mucks they write about or criticize, or go off on private retreats to yak about who's going to run the world."[7] I'm not a journalist, and I've never felt very comfortable on high horses, but I could see his point. I've felt the allure of power, especially when it comes with access, status, and perhaps even a ride in a Humvee. And as much as I might try to practice Vaclav Havel's injunction, to speak truth to power, it's highly unlikely that any of my interventions at such events altered the course of the state one iota—not least because my version of the truth usually comes too qualified for the powers involved. I've always advocated keeping an intellectual distance from power, and that for every trip scholars make through the revolving door of policymaking, the less of a claim they have on objectivity.

Not that I came close to ethnographical standards in my research of the MIME tribe, but I did try to uphold the balance between personal values and vocational ethics that anthropologist Clifford Geertz has best articulated:

> The outstanding characteristic of anthropological fieldwork as a form of conduct is that it does not permit any significant

separation of the occupational and extra-occupational spheres of one's life. On the contrary, it forces this fusion. One must find one's friends among one's informants and one's informants among one's friends; one must regard ideas, attitudes, and values as so many cultural facts and continue to act in terms of those which define one's own commitments, one must see society as an object and experience it as a subject.[8]

The ethical imperative that Katz invokes, laudable as it may be as abstract principle, starts to break down when confronted with the pragmatic task of investigating a virtual power enshrouded in classification and bureaucratic obfuscation. How can we find out how new technology works, if it even works, or whether it is accountable or truthful, unless we are willing and able to get up close, perhaps even get a little dirty? Getting the goods on the national security state is difficult if we never leave the ivory tower or the virtuous circle of journalism. If we stick to a moral position that precludes even the possibility of a dialogue with those most unlike us, isn't that what leads to war in the first place? To reinvoke Walter Benjamin, we must be ready to play the role of detective in times of crisis—which is pretty much the permanent and generally preferred state of affairs in national security circles. Besides, it takes more than a few free dinners and good port afterwards to change my—or most people's—convictions.

But my conscience was sufficiently armed for me to enter the lion's den one more time, in this case, the dramatic glass obelisk encased in a brown-and-black ziggurat that's the home of DARPA. My host, Ryan Henry, resembles Bill Pullman, the actor who saves the world—but not before they got the White House—from the aliens in *Independence Day*. Or perhaps it's just the subliminal power of advertising, since all of D.C. was blanketed with ads for the movie: "Whatever you do, don't look up." His office was government-issue, except for a large oil painting of an aircraft carrier at twilight that hovered over his desk. From his opening list of job descriptions to his choice of metaphors, his past carrier life peppered the interview.[9]

JD: Tell me about your life, pre-DARPA.

RH: I'm a former naval aviator, 20 years in the cockpit, about 6,000 flight hours, and 850 landings on aircraft carriers, 88 combat missions during Desert Storm, and three tours as an engineering experimental test pilot at Patuxent River [Naval Test Pilot School].

JD: What was your most memorable moment as a pilot?

RH: My first night landing in the flight simulator. Night landing on an aircraft carrier is the real test of pilots. I had made it through flight school, no problem, aced the night landing on a blacked-out island off San Francisco. I was feeling pretty cocky getting ready for my ship landing—I thought I owned the world. Two nights prior to going to the ship, they put us through the simulator, it had the body flow, the kinesthetic effect that you were actually flying, with hydraulics and wraparound vision systems: very, very realistic. I went to land on the simulator—and I didn't make it. My plane developed a high sink rate, and I put the simulator into the back of the aircraft carrier. The screen went totally dark, then flashes of white, red, and white again. It's like you jumped into the twilight zone. I sat there: I was breathing shallow and fast, my heart rate had doubled, and I could feel a cold sweat on my face. I was so caught up, for a brief moment in time I thought I had killed myself in the airplane. For the next 850 landings, I had that piece of experience to take with me.

JD: You make it sound like a religious experience.

RH: A religious experience? I would say a Pentecostal experience, probably.

JD: Did you ever lose faith in simulation?

RH: Yes. You could not fly a simulator within twenty-four hours of going out to the aircraft, and the training slope, the fall-off of expertise meant—

At this point, barely fifteen minutes into the interview, the Hi-8 videotape went completely blank, and stayed blank for the remaining two-hour interview and tour of DARPA. This had never happened in over 400 hours of tapings. But I always carry backup, my rugged Pioneer All-Weather tape recorder, which has survived desert sand, Bavarian rains, and a spilt beer at the Casa Castillo bar in Killeen, Texas. When I went to retrieve the tape from the shoebox stashed in the pantry, I discovered that it was missing. No videotape, no audiotape. At this point, I was starting to get spooked. I dug up my notebook from the interview and found just two pages of hastily scribbled notes under the heading of "Conversation with Christopher 'Ryan' Henry, 21 June 1996." There were some notes about "Robo-cruiser" and "negative learning from simulators": references, I seem to remember, to the aggressive reputation of the Aegis missile cruiser, USS *Vincennes* during the "first" Gulf War between Iraq and Iran, and its reliance on training simulations without civilian aircraft in them—both factors that probably contributed to its shooting down of an Iraqi Airbus. More meaningless scribbles, and a final note, which I assumed to be a quote from Henry: "I'm not here to problem-solve or to predict but to see what dangers lurk in the shadow." And that's the extent of a record of my visit to DARPA.

I subsequently learned that Henry left DARPA to become vice president for advanced planning and strategy at Science Applications International Corporation (SAIC)—another one of those innocuous corporate titles that conceals some very heavy lifting for the American defense community. Not widely known outside governmental circles, SAIC was founded by a small group of scientists in 1969; it is now the largest employee-owned research and engineering company in the United States, with over $5.5 billion in revenues last year alone. SAIC claims technical credits for the cleanup of Three Mile Island, the success of Desert Storm, the fixing of the Hubble Space Telescope. Recently it built the Egyptian armed forces its own Fort Irwin, a Combat Training Center for battalion-sized war games with full electronic instrumentation. And without too much more hyperbole, SAIC could also have claimed to control the dot in dot-com websites, since SAIC owned Network Solutions, which, until ICANN (Internet Corporation for Assigned Names and Numbers) stepped into the picture in 1999, had a highly lucrative monopoly over the registration of global domain names on the Web.

SAIC's National Security program is a leader in modeling, simulation, and gaming, providing prototypes of systems that form the operational core of virtuous war. For instance, it is developing a "virtual gateway" that can seamlessly merge virtual simulations and command and control systems (i.e., you can game and fight on the same systems, at the same time), as well as designing the software for semiautomated forces. Its "Centers of Excellence," numbering close to a dozen, offer seminars, workshops, and consulting in issue areas that range from information warfare and counterterrorism to humanitarian demining and arms control verification.

Before I even had a clue that SAIC existed, I had received a "personal invitation" from Andrew Marshall, director of the DOD's Office of Net Assessment, to participate in a two-day workshop on "Future War," to be held at the McLean, Virginia, Strategic Assessment Center of, yes, SAIC. The workshop featured an interesting combination of straight and very far-out folks, including an ex-CIA futurist, a biogeneticist, an anthropologist, a science fiction writer, a computer scientist, a bunch of military war gamers, and, of course, a very gnomic Andrew Marshall, who evidently provided the money as well as the topic of the seminar. He sat throughout the proceedings at the far end of the room, not uttering a word except for a few closing remarks, that made us feel, I thought, that we had under-impressed him. I do remember that all the figures of authority at SAIC looked and sounded ex-army or ex-navy; except for one or two guys wearing bow ties (ex-CIA?), they had that slightly-gone-to-seed, big voice mien of former jocks and lieutenant colonels. Moreover, and most sinister, there seemed to be an inordinate number of left-handed people working at the place.

Ever since that seminar I'd kept an eye out for SAIC, and it seems like they would show up at just about every conference or workshop with "security" in the title or theme. At a seminar on cyberspace and outer space at Le Chateau Montebello in Québec, the conference on national security and information technology at Cantigny, a CIA workshop on the future of global media at the Meridian Center in D.C.: SAIC would be there. A short time ago I was sharing some duty-free on the beach at Caesarea, Israel, winding down with some fellow participants from a conference called "Martial Ecologies." Since the conference featured the poststructuralist ideas of Virilio, Deleuze, and Foucault, I was somewhat surprised when I asked my left-handed scotch-drinker where he was from in the real world: "SAIC—bunch of us guys here."

Why concern ourselves with DARPA, SAIC, and the like? Because the truth is out *there*—sometimes *way* out there. If this sounds too much like *X-Files* (spelling SAIC backwards gets you not one but several reasons to believe Agent Mulder), consider what one member of the Syndicate—the white power elite who hang out in smoke-filled rooms somewhere on the East coast—told Agent Scully: "Our job is to predict the future—and the best way to predict the future is to invent it." One does not need to believe that there are extraterrestrial spacecraft in Area 51 to concur: how we prepare for future enemies might just help to invent them.

How, then, to approach a figure supposedly so ubiquitous yet so elusive as the "enemy"? How to challenge something that is considered a perennial threat not only to national security but also to corporate, environmental, family, and personal security? How to offer a plausible alternative to the powerful premise of sovereignty, that we live in a world at risk from alien threats, and that our ability to foresee, perhaps even to forestall danger, requires vast expenditures on technologies of surveillance, simulation, and speed which can oversee everything and everybody?

A good place to start is the Quadrennial Defense Review (QDR). If DARPA is the laboratory of virtuous war, then the QDR is the DNA, the bureaucratically designed code for the identification, preparation, and, if necessary, eradication of the virtual enemy. It effectively maps, in both the digital and cartographic senses of the word, the operational requirements and global contours of virtuous war. At one time the enemy was easy to identify; but with the end of the Soviet Union, the QDR is chasing a virtual enemy, our elusive "peer competitor." And this, going back to Nietzsche on definitions, is the virtue of the new enemy: undefinable by history—*for they do not yet exist*—they are delimited by the code of the QDR, the laboratories of DARPA, the simulations of STRICOM, the war games of the NTC, and their various, virtual equivalents in the other services. However, a threat without tangible limitations has vices as well as virtues for the policymaker. Warning of the practical consequences, one military expert, probably unintentionally, highlighted the special requirements posed by a virtual enemy: "The manpower commitments—coupled with manpower cutbacks—have placed our peacetime military on virtually a wartime mobilization schedule."[10] And we cannot rely on our friends to make it easier: according to a leaked report from the National Defense University working group, which is preparing the draft report of the QDR for 2001, "There are no potential cost and force structure savings evident through greater reliance on allies in major theater wars."[11]

The QDR is the latest in the checkered history of constructing a joint military strategy that matches means and ends for the defense of the United States.[12] After the major reforms enacted by the 1947 National Security Act, close to forty years passed before a second effort was made to systematically evaluate or structurally reform the armed forces. Some might attribute the stasis to a successful Cold War strategy of nuclear deterrence, notwithstanding regional failures like Vietnam, others to bureaucratic inertia and the particular interests of the military-industrial complex. But beginning with the 1986 Goldwater-Nichols Act, we witness an accumulation—and acceleration—of reviews for a major reorganization of the armed forces: the Defense Management Review in 1989, Base Force in 1991, Bottom-Up Review in 1993, and from 1997, the first QDR, a perennial four-year review mandated by Congress of defense strategy, force structure, modernization, readiness, infrastructure, human resources, and information operations and intelligence. And, to review the review, the National Defense Panel (NDP): an independent panel consisting of academics, industrialists, and retired flag and general officers created by Congress to assess the force recommendations of the QDR. Since it looks like the QDR has become and will remain for some time the major mechanism for defining the enemy and structuring U.S. forces, its origins and first applications warrant critical scrutiny.

We need to go back to just before the November election of 1998, when President Clinton and the United States Congress barely avoided another shutdown of the federal government by hammering out an agreement for a $1.7 trillion national budget. Lost in the white noise of sex scandals, threats of impeachment, and financial panics in Asia and Russia was the not insignificant fact that a hefty part of the agreement included the largest increase in military spending since Ronald Reagan was president in 1985. Topical (i.e., political) issues like the deployment of troops in Bosnia ($1.9 billion), military operational readiness ($1.1 billion), the Y2K computer bug ($1.1 billion), the drug war ($700 million), and embassy security abroad ($385 million)—as well as a last-minute deal that gave Republicans roughly the same amount for missile defense development as Democrats wanted for hiring 100,000 new teachers ($1 billion)—helped push the military budget to $280 billion for the fiscal year of 1999.

In a top ten list for 2000, the next nine countries' defense budgets do not *add up* to the United States'. As remarkable as the sheer size of the military budget might be, it begs a larger question, which in the rush to reach a budget agreement went mostly undebated: just where is this enemy who justifies such expenditure? This, of course, was the question that the QDR was mandated by the Congress to have answered the previous year. It too failed in this regard. The QDR represents the most recent effort of the United States's Department of Defense to square the global circle—to make order, security, and perhaps even peace possible in a time of great transformations and increased uncertainty. Or in the opening words of the Review document, to create a model of "potential threats, strategy, force structure, readiness posture, military modernization programs, defense infrastructure, and other elements of the defense program" for the "new and constantly changing security environment" and "the rapid rate of change in the world."[13] The professed aim of the QDR is "to provide a blueprint for a strategy-based, balanced, and affordable defense program." But this blueprint is so out of whack with the world that one begins to suspect that the Pentagon has come to prefer their models, simulations, and war games of old to the realities of the new, leading to virtuous circles of good intentions coming up hard against the always vicious circles of limited economic means.

At a time when the U.S. has been deprived of enemies of equal capabilities and will, all this security seems to come at a disproportionately high, perhaps dangerously high, cost. Can these new weapon systems, especially the high expenditure in smart and brilliant technology, information warfare, and next-generation

avionics, keep us safe? Make the world more peaceful? Even, perhaps, bring more justice to international relations? Unfortunately,
the QDR never makes the link between the new strategic con-
siderations, technological capabilities, and ethical implications of
a post-Cold War world. It operates with assumptions from the
past, especially the premises of the bottom-up review, that the
most important need is to be ready to fight and defeat at least two
major enemies practically simultaneously. Critics have questioned
whether this is a rational defense strategy. It certainly is not if we
conceive of rationality or strategy in the traditional sense, as some
level of proportionality between means and ends. Great gaps have
opened up between the laymen's and the DOD's perceptions of
global threats, as well as between the budgetary requirements and
the warfighting strategies of the QDR.

But critics of the QDR must at least consider whether there
is some method to this madness, as in the days when the DOD
claimed that the model of nuclear deterrence required the ability
to obliterate an enemy not once, not twice, but many times over.
We need to read the QDR between the lines and *behind the lines*.
Critics of defense policies, like generals, often fight the last war. A
criticism that focuses on the disjunction between the plan and the
reality it models is possibly missing the point. What if the plan is,
intentionally or not, irrational? If, by accident or by design, it
overdetermines outcomes and overrepresents enemies in the way
of previous theories of deterrence and compulsion? Are virtuous,
rather than purely temporal imperatives, at work?

Perhaps, then, it would be better to interpret the QDR not
as rational planning but as a virtual *theater of war*. Granted, this
virtual spectacle is not as immediately bloody as the "real" theater
of war, and in its pure excess, it often appears more comedic
than tragic. But in an age of live-feeds, photo-opportunities, and
infowar, the battlefield has gone through all kinds of displace-
ments and spillovers into other arenas. What this requires of us is
to treat seriously the plotting of distant threats, the staging of
military forces, the character development of rogue states, and
the rhetorical skills of the QDR craftsmen, from the secretary
of defense down to the lowest public affairs officer. Criticisms
based on the model of a one-to-one correspondence to reality
begin to seem out of date. New critical questions and possible

counterstrategies are suggested. What image of the world is the Quadrennial Review trying to represent? To what dramatic ends? Are these ends compatible with democratic, pluralistic values? And if not, what kind of counter-rhetorics, counterstaging, counterplots must the critic try to produce?

Past and future Quadrennial Reviews deserve close public scrutiny. To the extent that they are "blueprints," they will, intentionally or not, shape the future. The military is well equipped, in the sense of being more proficient with technologies of speed and surveillance, simulation and stealth, to understand the transformative forces of our times. But it is also fixed on worst-case scenarios, not best-possible outcomes. Other blueprints, especially civic visions, are needed, to test and to counter the military ones.

Back around the time of the Bottom-Up Review, a story broke that there were rats—real ones—in the basement of the Pentagon. At the time, I suspected yet another public relations ploy, one more way to garner taxpayer sympathy. But now I see the irony of the situation. For decades we have followed the piper's tune, worrying that security, prestige, jobs, and, given the higher cost of the volunteer armed services, perhaps even our children, would disappear if we did not give the pipers of the Pentagon what they asked for. Now, especially as once again the military budget becomes fodder for presidential politicking, it is time to write a different fable. To be sure, there are still rats out there, real and potential. But while they might have grown in numbers (again, as much a matter of staging as of reality), they have shrunk enormously in size and strength. Moreover, there seem to be more rats at home than overseas. Surely we can build better, less expensive rattraps than, say, the air force's F-22 Raptor (a gold-plated $125 million fighter plane, $24 billion already spent in development), the Marine's V-22 Osprey (the problem-plagued tilt aircraft, $40 billion spent), the army's Crusader (a howitzer too heavy for most roads and bridges, $5 billion spent), or the Navy's DD-21 (a stealthy destroyer, over $1 billion per ship).

It took another visit to the desert—not mine but then Secretary of Defense William Cohen's—to bring these lessons home. Nearly a decade after Bush's stopover (see Chapter 1)—and with the QDR already months overdue—Cohen undertook an expedition to Fort Irwin, to witness and to testify on the challenges facing America in the next millennium. The occasion was another Advanced Warfighting Experiment, pitting a brigade from Fort Hood, Texas, "digitized" with portable computers, satellite linkups, and networked sensors, against the tireless "Krasnovians," the local, lower-tech troops still playing the role of the last of the Soviet military tribe. Cohen's remarks about the exercise were less than articulate, but his message for the future came through loud and clear:

> Today, we all have seen the future of warfare. . . . I think what you're seeing here is a revolution in military warfare. We've had the age-old expression that knowledge is power, and absolute knowledge is absolute power. What we're witnessing now is the transformation of the level of information as broad and as absolute as one can conceive of it today. So, the actual domination of the information world will put us in a position to maintain superiority over any other force for the foreseeable future. . . . So, I think we talk about the future, the future is the United States as far as this capability is concerned. I'm not aware of any other country that has this capability, or even has this opportunity to examine in this kind of experimental basis the kind of technology that will give us this edge. So, we look to the future. The future is, as Toffler says, that unless you tame technology, you will encounter future shock. We're not only taming technology, we are turning technology into not future shock, but future security.[14]

Not quite the kind of prose you might expect from a former senator, one-time novelist, and published poet. But this media spasm of mixed aphorisms and pop-futurism yields rich material for the interpreters of national security discourse. At one level, perhaps the most transparent one, the message is a slightly more sophisticated (and definitely less satirical) version of Hilaire Belloc's infamous nineteenth-century ditty about the imperial benefits of technological superiority: "We've got the Maxim gun—and they've not." Translation: don't mess with us. However, behind this hubristic nose-thumbing lies a more rational purpose. In the bygone days of the Cold War, it would have been recognized as the language of deterrence or even compulsion: a willful, transparent threat of unacceptable punishment for any nuclear misdeed. But with bipolarity gone, or worse, internalized by the U.S. into a purely psychological state of manic highs of liberal interventionism and melancholic lows of neoisolationism, the sobering, neutralizing effects of reciprocity have been lost. Internally, the cyberdeterrent is to be taken like Prozac: a technopharmacological fix for all the organic anxieties that attend uncertain times and new configurations of power. Externally, it produces reality effects for a world in flux through a one-sided gaze—from the omniscience of the orbital geostationary platform to the beady eye of the hovering unmanned aerial vehicle—that aspires not only to oversee but to *foresee* all threats, rooting out potential as well as real dangers with an anticipatory, normalizing panoptic. For the putative and subsequently renamed "rogue states," Cohen offers a garden-variety *roguing:* "to remove (diseased or abnormal specimens) from a group of plants of the same family."[15]

Cohen's riff on the intimate relationship of knowledge and power should sound familiar to all readers of late modernity. But Cohen's anxiety of influence is much closer to Francis Bacon than Michel Foucault, with a *soupçon* of Lord Acton thrown in— albeit without the "corruption" that usually accompanies the "absolute." Most people know Bacon, the seventeenth-century English philosopher, courtier, and statesman, for his pithy aphorisms. But behind his declarative statement that "Knowledge is Power" lies a whole body of work dedicated to linking the power of the sovereign state to the furthering of modernism and science. This is, after all, the man who lived for the promulgation of the scientific method—and literally died for it, after catching pneumonia when he tried to prove that chickens could be frozen and kept for extended periods of time by stuffing them with snow.

Fowl aside, Bacon wished to bring together methods of inductive reasoning with a "realist" approach to politics. Indeed, Bacon was a great fan of Machiavelli, asking the reader to "thank God for Machiavelli and his kind of writer, who tell us not what men ought to do but what they in fact do."[16] For Bacon, the concept of the interwar was natural: since men seem to find good reason to war with great regularity, peace should be treated as merely an interlude between and a laboratory for war. By pretending that this is simply the way things are—*different, uncertain, and dangerous*—he maintains the pose of an empirical realist. But his prescription for the sameness of sovereign states and the certainty of pure science reveals him for what he is: a closet idealist. Hence, it is not surprising how quickly the pretense of inductive logic drops when Bacon begins to find all kinds of normative benefits from war. In his essay "Of the True Greatness of Kingdoms," Bacon locates the very well-being of the state in war:

> Nobody can be healthful without exercise, neither natural body nor politic; and certainly, to a kingdom or estate, a just and honorable war is the true exercise. A civil war, indeed, is like the heat of a fever; but a foreign war is like the heat of exercise, and serveth to keep the body in health; for in a slothful peace, both courages will effeminate and manners corrupt. But howsoever it be for happiness, without all question for greatness it maketh to be still for the most part in arms.[17]

In Cohen's pronouncements we find a comparable affinity for inducing from observation and experimentation the obvious: information plus technology equals security. Nor do we need to read between the lines to find yet another realist poseur. Cohen's conceit—that the maintenance of a sovereignty's well-being (under the unhealthy conditions of international anarchy and alterity) requires regular joint exercises of knowledge and power—echoes Bacon. However, he goes only so far as to apply the prescription to the *simulation* of war, the war game: post-Auschwitz, post-Hiroshima, post-Vietnam, the therapeutic effects of war are increasingly difficult to prescribe. Here again, it is useful to return to the originary moment of scientific realism, to find a frank appreciation of war and simulation. In "Of Simulation and Dissimulation," in his *Essays*, Bacon enumerates the positive powers of simulations:

> The great advantages of simulation and dissimulation are three. First to lay asleep opposition and to surprise. For

where a man's intentions are published, it is an alarum to call up all that are against them. The second is to reserve a man's self a fair retreat: for if a man engage himself, by a manifest declaration, he must go through, or take a fall. The third is, the better to discover the mind of another. For to him that opens himself, men will hardly show themselves adverse; but will fair let him go on, and turn their freedom of speech to freedom of thought.[18]

There lurks a similar Baconian pseudologic behind Cohen's exaltation of simulation. Through artful if not artificial stage-management, simulations can be used to project supposed capabilities and cloak real weaknesses, as well as to reveal the "mind of another," in this case, the intentions and capabilities of the OPFOR plug-ins that the U.S. will confront in the future. However, digitized war games, twice removed by scripted strategies and technological artifice from the bloody reality of war, take simulation into another realm. They take us from Bacon's world of strategic levels of deception to, once again, Baudrillard's fractal turf of the hyperreal, where distinctions between the simulated and the real begin to break down. We saw how the virtual theory of Baudrillard complements the Baconian distinctions: "To dissimulate is to feign not to have what one has. To simulate is to feign to have what one hasn't. One implies a presence, the other an absence."[19] "But," he says, "the matter is more complicated, since to simulate is not simply to feign."[20] Simulations produce real symptoms, hyperreal effects: "Thus, feigning or dissimulating leaves the reality principle intact: the difference is always clear, it is only masked; whereas simulation threatens the difference between 'true' and 'false,' between 'real' and 'imaginary.' "[21] Things get further complicated when "the real is no longer what it used to be"[22]—not an apposite description of post-Cold War attitudes— and the power of simulation, magnified by a fear of the future or a nostalgia for a mythical past, comes to dominate all other forms of representation. Baudrillard's conclusions bear repeating: simulation becomes "a strategy of the real, neo-real, and hyperreal, whose universal double is the strategy of deterrence."[23]

Have Cohen and crowd similarly left behind the reality principle that would allow them to distinguish the feigned from the real? Have they constructed, are they leading us into, the realm of the hyperreal, where cyberdeterrence takes on a highly fungible value for current symbolic exchanges of security—but leaves behind checks and balances, like historical experience and political choice? If a qualitative leap in technologies of destruction once produced a new balance of terror between nuclear states, and gave W.T.R. Fox cause to coin the concept of "Superpower," perhaps the rise of a new unipolarity based on cyberwar and cyberdeterrence has produced one more neologistic anxiety for International Relations: the "*Cyberpower*." Perhaps not.

It is not quite fair to load this all onto one sound bite from Cohen. But it is emblematic of a debate that began with the Gulf War and has been rejoined with the arrival of the Bush team at the Pentagon. Was the Gulf War the last, second-wave, industrial war, with the victory predetermined as much by the logistical might of the coalition—its ability to get x-amount of matériel in y-amount of time—as by the strategic doctrine or actual warfighting? Or was it the first of the third wave, information-based wars, showcasing the technological superiority of smart bombs, near real-time C4I (Command, Control, Communication, Computers and Information) and stage-managed media coverage? In other words, networked, multilinked, click-on-the-icon, hypertextual war? *Hyperwar*?[24]

The school of thought represented by Cohen and the cyberwarriors has for the most part continued to escape theoretical scrutiny. One sound bite from a press briefing cannot possibly capture the value of a phenomenon that goes by many more names than hyperwar. Trolling the Net yields a wide variety: cyberwar, infowar, netwar, technowar, antiwar, pure war, postmodern war. Conventional definitions emerging from the armed forces usually zero in on the role of information, going so far as to lump together all the related forms of conflict in the foreshortening rubric of "information war," infowar, "I-war." For operations other than or short of war, "Information Operations" has become the catch-all phrase. The military journals highlight the role of communications, intelligence, overhead surveillance, from aerial drones to space platforms, high precision, high lethality smart weapons, multispectral sensors, real-time battlefield data about the battlefield, networked commands, near real-time decision loops, just-in-time simulations. Less conventional definitions focus on deterritorialized forms of conflict, which use and target discourses of power—sign systems of belief, knowledge, representation—embedded in technologies of information.

Broadly conceived, infowar is as old as Sun Tzu's "strategic factors" and as new as the armed forces' Joint Vision 2010's "full spectrum dominance." However, the new infowar is significantly different from past forms in the proliferation of networked computing and the use of high-resolution video. This makes possible new forms of control and governance, which is why, dating back to the outbreak of the Gulf War, I preferred to use "cyberwar," that is, the computer as new "helmsman" or kyberion, over the umbrella term of "infowar."[25] The speed of interconnectivity that the computer enables has, more than any other innovation in warfare from the stirrup to gunpowder to radar to nukes, shifted the battlefield away from the geopolitical to the electromagnetic. Less obviously, the power of cyberwar comes from its ability to reproduce as well as to deconstruct reality with a real-time verisimilitude that will make future war more a contest of signs than of soldiers. This kind of language might still grate on the ear of a mud soldier or a mainstream security specialist. But new phenomena require new languages. Take, as just one example from many, a single phrase from an early article in *Airpower* on infowar, in which the author extols technologies that allow the pilot to "use multiple phenomenology to discriminate live targets from dead targets with exquisite resolution."[26] Even a cursory skimming of the armed services journals, war college articles, DOD white papers, and Beltway think-tank reports suggests that the so-called "Revolution in Military Affairs" (RMA) wrought by new technologies is about much more than how the U.S. will fight the next war. The same article in *Airpower*, "Information warfare: Principles of third-wave war," makes the case for an epistemological leap:

We all know that change is accelerating in every aspect in both our individual and collective lives. In such a world, standing still long enough to mass-produce anything is foolish. A long production run (or force buildup) will result in obsolescence before it achieves full rate. Our only alternative is to seek more perfect knowledge of events as they change, to select those events that we must force to change for our own self-interest, and to focus our energy on specific change strategies. Tomorrow's enemy may not even be a nation-state. It may be a radical fundamentalist or extremist ethnic group. Tomorrow's ally might be a corporation instead of a United Nations task force. Hopefully, the principles outlined in this article will start us thinking about how we can deal with such events.[27]

Where one experiences myopia in the academic study of International Relations, one finds flashes of oxyopia in the armed forces. Struggling to understand the transformative effects of new technologies of speed and simulation, surveillance, and stealth, many in the military are willing to step outside the box and into virtual theory.

Paul Virilio, more so than any other contemporary thinker, caught this development early. He provides us with a better understanding of why Cohen and Bacon, confronting radical ruptures between how we represent and how we experience the world, might not be such an incongruous pairing:

> As I see it, we've passed from the extended time of centuries and from the chronology of history to a time that will continue to grow ever more intensive . . . and this passage from an extensive to an intensive time will have considerable impact on all the various aspects of the conditions of our society: it leads to a radical reorganization both of our social mores and of our images of the world. This is the source of the feeling that we're faced with an epoch in many ways comparable to the Renaissance: it's an epoch in which the real world and our image of the world no long coincide.[28]

In the twenty-first century, as the rift between knowledge and power widens, players like Cohen become doubly concerned to close the gap, to make them seamless components of the national interest, that is, "force-multipliers" for the United States. However, as Virilio warns, dangers lie ahead when the military is leading the way into an uncertain future where speed, vision, and substitution dominate:

Since I am an urbanist as well as a war specialist, the things I take seriously are phases rather than objects. And perhaps because the military question has long since come to terms with the problem of the simulacrum: those demonstrative war threats that so often slip over into tragic replacements of themselves with the real thing. This is to say that reality is never simply given and is always generated by the technology and modes of development of a society at any given moment of its history. And in this respect, speed is an element of representation: it serves functions of vision and not of forward motion.[29]

What does it mean when we move from what Virilio calls an "aesthetics of appearances" to an "aesthetics of disappearances"? In the political realm, we lose the agency, the rights, and the obligations of the subject-citizen. Everywhere and nowhere at once, the citizen has been "disappeared" by all this high-speed interconnectivity. In the military realm—where spectacular technologies and ample funding assure a spillover into all other public and private spaces—it marks the passage from material to immaterial forms of war. At the strategic level, simulations and substitutions proliferate with plug-and-play worst-case scenarios; on the battlefield, the enemy soldier becomes an electronically signified "target of opportunity"—again, that much easier to disappear. In short, with the virtualization of violence comes the disappearance of war as we have known it.

Of course, this does not mean the end of physical violence and bloody wars. Violent conflict will undergo further virtual cleansing, from the shifting acronyms of Military Operations Other than War (MOOTW to OOTW), to euphemisms like Stability Operations (which gave us SFOR—Stability Forces—in Bosnia), and outright oxymorons like "bombing for peace" (Holbrooke's less than felicitous phrase for the Bosnia air campaign). And violence will continue to "go south," in the geographical as well as functional sense, of paramilitary, intrastate conflicts played out as terrorism, ethnic cleansing, and genocide in the "near abroad" and on the margins of the "civilized world." But while the enemy, to paraphrase Secretary Cohen, gets "future shock," we get virtual security.

Urban Warrior games invade San Francisco.

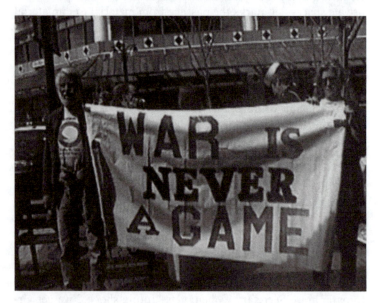

War is never a game.

6   Virtuous war comes home

We are running on borrowed time. I think it is just a matter of time before we have an event in this country that will be absolutely the most stressful thing to confront the country since the War of 1812.

(John J. Hamre, former Deputy Secretary of Defense, speaking at the U.S. Army War College's 11th Annual Strategy Conference on Homeland Defense, April 2000)

In March 1999, as the Rambouillet peace talks went critical, Serbian troops massed on the Kosovo border, and NATO prepared a final target list for "message strikes" of cruise missiles and smart bombs on Belgrade, the west coast of the United States came under attack. Although an earthquake, a terrorist attack, and a civil uprising took place, and several thousand military personnel were engaged, few people outside the Bay area took note. It is understandable why the largest military invasion of an American city since the War of 1812 failed to attract much attention.[1] It was, after all, virtual.

Called "Urban Warrior" on land, "Fleet Battle Experiment Echo" at sea, and "Littoral Lightning" everywhere in between, the week-long military experiment of "Kernel Blitz 99" played out on the beaches of Monterey, the academic setting of Stanford's Business School, an abandoned naval base in Oakland, and the "urban canyons" of San Francisco. The experiment envisioned a future war of stateless criminals armed with computers, "Orange Country" terrorists with weapons of mass destruction, and

"Boolean" and "Furzian" refugees in need of humanitarian assistance, all operating in the burgeoning global polity of the urban littoral—"what we," said one navy briefer, "perceive to be the battlespace of the twenty-first century." Californians, all too familiar with natural and unnatural disasters, might be expected to take such events in stride. But when it involves 6,000 sailors and marines from the U.S. Navy's Third Fleet and the First Marine Expeditionary Force joining forces with 300 civilian role-players and a veritable army of defense contractors, the locals take notice.

National press coverage, fixed on breaking events in Kosovo, was spotty and tended toward the whimsical (the *Washington Post* sported a headline, "Exercise in Futurity"). The Web was another story. From Left to Right, websites erupted in protest. The progressive "Coalition against Urban Warrior" called for a series of nonviolent protests against the "military invasion." Right-wing militia sites declared Urban Warrior a trampling of the century-old principle of posse comitatus, by which the military was excluded from domestic policing, and warned all vigilant citizens to keep an eye out for "black helicopters." At the demonstrations and events I witnessed, pretend protestors (easily identified by the laser-sensitive vests they wore over their slacker-anarchist garb) usually outnumbered real protestors by about ten to one (keeping in mind that the role-players were paid $55 to make a marine's day).

Urban Warrior was the last of a series of domestic exercises that have taken place in five U.S. cities over the last couple of years. But this was the Big One. Marines sprouted ultraportable Ericsson, Motorola, and Kenmore radios, integrated GPS receivers with two-meter accuracy, souped-up Toshiba Librettos with wireless LAN, as well as the new MILES 2000, a smarter version of the laser-tag vest that flashes and beeps when a hit leaves you dead, maimed, or merely the walking-wounded. They also carried low-tech *Mad Max* gear for the close quarters of urban warfare: axes, sledgehammers, gloves, and lots of padding on knees, elbows, and shoulders. One of the more bizarre weapon prototypes was a .50 caliber machine gun, a "Boom Gun," not to be confused with a "boom box." Perched atop a telescoping crane, the gun was remotely controlled by an operator in the cab below who could use a mounted video camera to shoot over and around buildings. Playing the "bad guys," and bearing an uncanny resemblance to Darth Vadar's command ship, the black stealth catamaran *Sea Shadow* plied the Bay waters. And lighting up everything, the glow from a thousand networked computer screens.

In spite of the best efforts of the military to "civilize" the experiment by including humanitarian assistance, environmental issues, and disaster relief, home-grown opposition refused to be placated. The National Park Service nixed the originally planned landing at the Presidio as too much of a "public disturbance." Even though the World Wildlife Fund designated Camp Pendleton as one of the "The 10 Coolest Places You've Never Seen," the California Coastal Commission curtailed the Monterey Bay amphibious landing for fear of endangering gray whales, snowy plovers, and sea otters. And throughout Urban Warrior, street demonstrations took place at the key sites, with the biggest headlines captured by the thirty real protestors who broke from the script and penetrated the Zen force field of Oakland Mayor Jerry Brown's office for a brief occupation. Uncharacteristically, Brown responded with the obvious: "This wasn't about the marines, this wasn't about the schools. It was political theater."[2]

With all the hoopla and protests, futurist rants and conventional throwbacks, Urban Warrior was a strange beast, a chimera of *Matrix* chips-and-code and *Private Ryan* blood-and-guts. Amidst the razzle-dazzle of new weapons, simulated scenarios, street and cyberdemonstrations, open ship tours, aerial acrobats, academic seminars, defense industry information booths, and stealth catamarans, an old threat to the domestic order was uncloaked in new form. For one week, on spectacular display, the mother matrix of war spread her wings, revealing the military-industrial-media-entertainment network in all its glory.

Unlike the fifties version presaged by President Eisenhower's farewell address, with its computers the size of boxcars, clunky tele-type machines, centralized command systems, and glowing vacuum tubes, the new MIME-NET runs on video-game imagery, twenty-four-hour news cycles, multiple nodes of military, corporate, university, and media power, and microchips, embedded in everything but human flesh (so far). It was in full form off as well as on the battlefield, when executives from Silicon Valley, navy admirals, and marine generals gathered at Stanford's Business School "to leapfrog to the next generation of technology" in a "Commercial Off-the-Shelf Strategic Planning War Game."[3] After the "hostilities" everyone from the Bay area was invited to visit the aircraft carrier USS *Hornet*, where the navy, marines, and defense industries set up over a hundred booths on the hanger deck to showcase the latest technologies of "network-centric warfare." It throbbed like a video-game arcade on acid. It was jammed.

My first stop was the USS *Coronado*'s command center (which, after its makeover by former Disney Imagineering executive, Bran Ferren, was called the "Disney Room"). The briefing for Kernel Blitz '99 started simply but quickly deteriorated into the military's preferred defense against civilian scrutiny: a mix of abbreviations, acronyms, and new concepts, all imaginatively arrayed on PowerPoint slides, leaving even a semiotician like myself in a state of slightly bewildered awe. The hammer-point of the brief was: "This is not an exercise. This is an experiment." The background scenario was easy to follow. "We've got Country Orange who are the bad guys, Green which are the good guys. Green has suffered some natural disasters, such as an earthquake, and the Orange folks are fomenting insurgency in Green. [A significant pause] There's no direct correlation with anything or anyone overseas." Which of course immediately got most of us wondering which rogue fits the bill.

Slides with logos, bulleted themes, maps, and images of ships, missiles, aircraft, and satellites followed. Out of about twenty slides and about eighty images, I counted just two shots with humans in them: a dripping navy Seal and some happy refugees getting off a helicopter. Each slide came with a short burst of information from the briefer. "This might be hard to follow, it's about network-centric warfare, it's about synergy." "This is about flow of information and leveraging technology." "Our Joint Chiefs of Staff came up with a road map for the future, Joint Vision 2010." "Our navy is unparalleled on the open ocean, but the next threat is going to be closer to the shore, coastal areas." The message was stark: home for roughly 70 percent of the global population by 2020, site of intense competition for scarce resources, staging area for tribal, ethnic, and religious conflicts, the urban littoral would be the most likely battlespace of the future. Moreover, a dense infrastructure and high number of civilian noncombatants put new constraints on the military. The briefing's most virtuous statement was haunted by the specter of Vietnam as well as by the present-day horrors of Chechnya: "American forces cannot and will not level cities to save them."

Acronyms and neologisms started to proliferate at a rate that made me reach for my weapons of mass deconstruction. "LOEs" (limited objective experiments), "AWEs" (advanced warfighting experiments), "LTAs" (limited technical assessments) were all tossed out as the key technologically driven scenarios; but the centerpiece of the presentation was clearly network-centric warfare. It opened with a "Command and Control Matrix" slide linking up in near-real-time "Sensors" and "Shooters" in information and decision grids for a "Dominant Maneuver" against "Asymmetric Threats." At this point I had to ask: do these asymmetric threats have names? The briefer took his first evasive action: they were "terrorists," who would be operating from pleasure boats, jet skis, underwater scuba gear, executing "swarming" tactics on individual naval vessels throughout the experiment. Back on track, he traced the passage from the end of the Cold War, in which the navy developed great open-ocean capabilities, to present day, when the goal was "to put all that synergy onto a small platform that can operate close to shore." Technology would be leveraged in a "Precision Engagement"—"it's all about targeting efficiency." A Wagnerian Ring of titles followed, designed to strike terror in the hearts of . . . terrorists, I guess: "Vicious Blaze"—"a deliberate process of collecting information of targets in enemy territory, most of it imagery that can be shared, just like a Home page, around the world on our classified Internet"; "Rings of Fire"—"once a decisionmaker decides to blow up a target we need to pick the right weapon and get the right information out to the right platform"; and "Silent Fury"— "we're going to launch real live weapons against targets on shore—but we obviously can't do that in San Francisco, so we're going to do that on ranges in Southern California." And, to add a rare dose of realism to the slide show, the briefer wrapped up the show with "Casualty Management"—"it's all about linking and collaborating with facilities on shore." Conspicuously, no actual bodies—unless one counts an X-ray of a broken fibula—were to be found in the slide show.

One big war net renders the enemy transparent and destroys it. With speed as the killer variable, network-centric warfare is the model for the next millennium. Live by the net, die by the net.

I hung in there for the rest of the brief, taking notes, asking for clarification of the odd acronym or name. But towards the end, when the briefer strayed from the PowerPoint presentation and put in a plug for antimissile defense, I started to lose what little grip I had on reality. He made the seemingly innocent remark that the Aegis-equipped surface ships with the upgraded "Linebacker" system spent the day practicing shooting down simulated ballistic missile attacks from unknown targets. He made it sound as easy as hitting a couple of clay pigeons. I couldn't let it pass, so I asked if he knew the attack's country of origin. "They're not out of any specific country." I pressed him: but if they have a trajectory, it must be a simple matter to track them back to the point of origin. "We gave them coordinates to inject into their computers, and they responded. The TANV cell can bring that up on the screen and will show where that was."

He'd used the oldest dodge, obfuscation, but I could feel others around the conference table shifting uncomfortably in their seats, eager to let it rest, and head out for the tour of the ship. Just then, from the back of the room a higher-up (judging from the briefer's response of "Sir?") asked if he could respond to my question. "Some of these asymmetrical threats are very difficult to identify. This is an experiment." Fair enough, I said, but doesn't this kind of generic simulation work to disconnect the model from reality? Or is it just not politically correct to name names? "We don't need to get specific. We need to look at the combination of off-the-shelf technology and new ways of doing things. Someone in a small watercraft is someone in a small watercraft. It doesn't matter where they came from. There's no need to simulate specific places, we can find that kind of threat virtually anywhere. Does that make sense?" I shelved what I really wanted to say—if the threat's "virtually anywhere" then it's virtually nowhere—and stuck to my point. Not to beat this one to death, but if you're going to try to knock down a ballistic missile, you have to know the trajectory from the original country. I realize this is a sensitive issue in Congress, but how can you run an exercise in ballistic missile defense (BMD) without picking out a real country, a real threat? "We are not simulating any specific country, because this is not an exercise: it is an experiment." I decided to give him the semantic victory. This was clearly not the time or place to go deep into the hard-wiring of network-centric warfare (a year later, the terrorist attack on the USS *Cole* in Yemen did give me cause to return to our conversation).

Before joining the rest of the group for the ship tour, I used my interlocutor's posting at the Naval War College as an opportunity to set up an interview with one of the primary architects of Fleet Battle Experiment Echo and president of the Naval War College, Vice Admiral Arthur Cebrowski. Judging from the briefing packet, his name was most directly linked to the concept of network-centric warfare. He considered speed to be everything in war, and whoever has the fastest networks wins. Nations make war as they make wealth, and networked information technology has become the enabler of both. Information, sensor, and engagement grids produce graphic-rich environments that increase battlespace awareness and combat power.

Several faxes and a couple of months later, I met with Vice Admiral Cebrowski at the Naval War College, where he mapped out the revolutionary implications of a networked global politics better than anyone else I'd heard on the topic. Cebrowski was not unlike many of the flag and general officers that I interviewed— articulate, ambitious, worldly—but his fires burned much more brightly. Trained as a mathematician and computer scientist, deeply religious, and always wanting to fly airplanes, he seemed to will these potentially contradictory elements of his personality into a very successful career in the navy. Cebrowski served as director of the Navy Space and Information Warfare Command, was deployed in UN operations in Iraq, Somalia, and Bosnia, and, during the Gulf War, commanded the aircraft carrier USS *Midway*. When I interviewed him, he had just completed his second year as the forty-seventh president of the Naval War College.[4]

JD: Could you first tell me a little bit about yourself? How you got here, why you went into the navy?

VADM: I suppose that one way to look at it is from seventh grade, when my teacher asked me what I wanted to be when I grew up. I said I either wanted to be a navy fighter pilot, a high school principal, or a Catholic priest.

JD: Is there a connecting link here?

VADM: I am generally doing those things in order. (laughter) I was very much the navy fighter pilot, here I am an education administrator, and at the same time very much involved in the Church and faith. So it's very consistent. All these things string together. They are related to disciplines, to philosophy, and to ordered thinking. The social psychologist would say I am the classic second son of an Eastern European family— does not enter his father's work, goes off, and either joins the military or the Church.

JD: What assignments have you had in the navy?

VADM: In my military career I have really never had an assignment more than twenty-four months long. When I've gone to sea, it is focused expressly on warfare. And when I've been ashore, there's been great variation ranging from graduate education in computer systems to a fellowship in foreign affairs, to a sabbatical in strategic studies, then a tour as an exchange student in the U.S. Air Force, and staff assignments in Washington.

JD: What were you doing in Washington?

VADM: One tour was in systems analysis, another as director of electronic warfare for the navy, and then I was in charge of customer service for navy communications. I served later with the Joint Staff as director for command, control communications, and computer systems, then on the navy staff as director for space information warfare command and control. So while this seems to be very broad, there is an underlying thread of an appreciation of technologies, interdisciplinary approaches to problem-solving, and an inclination to mix quantitative methods with intuition.

JD: I've brought along a quote: "We are in the midst of a revolution in military affairs, unlike any seen since the Napoleonic age." As I'd say to my students: "Discuss."

VADM: Well it's an absolutely outlandish statement—of the type I like to make (laughter). I made that statement a year and a half ago in print, longer than that from various other podiums, and I still believe it, maybe even more so now. We had Bran Ferren from Disney's Imagineering here [Naval War College] not too long ago, and he argued that the advent of interconnectivity is comparable to the advent of fire.

JD: Why did you choose the Napoleonic era?

VADM: Because that was a major societal change. It's the changes in society that lead to the changes in the military. I do believe that to a considerable extent the nation makes war the way it makes wealth. What you're seeing is a restructuring of society with the information age.

JD: What do you say to the people who say we're not in the midst of a revolution, that the RMA is comparable at best to the invention of the stirrup or the helicopter?

VADM: I don't think that the stirrup ever changed the way people bank, the way commodities move. I don't think the stirrup or the machine gun was ever directly linked to the creation and distribution of power and wealth in a society. It's a whole different class. You have to reach for those kinds of things before you come up with something comparable.

JD: Some people like Andrew Marshall are comparing it to the twenties and thirties, where for the first time you combine innovations like the wireless radio, tanks, and airplanes in exercises on the Salisbury Plain. Do you think there are any parallels?

VADM: When Andy Marshall and I first talked on this subject, I disagreed with him because he was talking about a gradual change, in terms of several decades, twenty-five, thirty years. I acknowledged that, yes, it's true that these things had taken so long in the past, but this is, after all, the information age. There is an acceleration, and we should expect to see acceleration in the adoption of revolutionary concepts. I think there is ample evidence that Andy is nearer the truth than I am on that, but it's still an open question. We may in fact go somewhat faster, but it's not clear yet. We may be lacking the catalyst to a profound acceleration; but it will come, I think there is little doubt.

JD: During the Forbes national security seminar at Harvard, you got into speed as the key variable, getting inside decisionmaking loops, the speed of maneuver, the speed of information flows. It almost sounded as though you were saying that speed is more important than the event itself. Is there an endpoint where you can accelerate no further? You seem to have this idea of an infinite progress to speed where you can just keep shrinking down decisionmaking, shrinking down response time. Isn't there eventually a diminishing return, where it even becomes detrimental to strategy?

VADM: Within any model there is an endpoint. You do things better or faster, then they become asymptotic with something, and things seem to stop. However, the history is that when we encounter these asymptotes, we move to a different curve. We essentially create a new model. And I think that's what happens here. I don't think this is so much an issue of making a faster hula hoop. In terms of business decisions, I think rather it's the speed with which you jump to a new mental model, a model with which a competitor is unable to deal, so you are in a whole different form, frame of measurement. One of the older examples of that, I believe, is the blitzkrieg. The French had a mental model for a semi-autonomous force operating at their rear. Which is different from saying these armored columns move very fast—or the front moved at a greater speed. That's not the phenomenon that happened. It's not that someone was causing events to happen faster than my hula hoop could tolerate. It's also who jumped out of the mental model.

JD: Wasn't blitzkrieg a notorious case of improvisation? The Germans, having been defeated, learned some lessons the British and French could not, or did not want to, apply. But the Germans didn't really have a concept of the blitzkrieg until after the fact, when they put all the technologies together and suddenly saw the advantages on the battlefield. The term itself wasn't even coined by the military—I think it first shows up in German in the newsreels about the invasion of Poland.

VADM: But I think the point you are trying to draw me toward is that one has to recognize all of the elements of the whole to make it a revolution in military affairs.

JD: I guess what I'm trying to get at is whether it is the technology or people thinking about technology that actually drives the revolution?

VADM: I think we are in a chicken and egg problem here. The technology can be simultaneously the catalyst and enabler. It's not just catalyzed certain developments but also new ways of thinking.

JD: If your revolution is always about being faster than the next guy, and it's the technology driving speed and acceleration, doesn't machine time begin to replace human-response time, because machines are ultimately faster than humans, right? Do you really want machine time to dictate your strategies and your tactics?

VADM: As soon as you can. Because what we try to do is move the human mind to successively higher levels of thinking and of problem-solving, if you will, so as soon as you can relieve humanity of a lower-level decisionmaking process, you should do that. That's laudable. Because then you can move on.

JD: What happens to deliberation time? For instance, in the Cuban missile crisis, Kennedy had thirteen days. In the Haitian crisis, Clinton had, with CNN real-time coverage, perhaps thirteen minutes to decide what to do. What happens to deliberation? Don't checks and balances go out the window? I know this is probably more an issue for civilians, but what do you say to that?

VADM: The decisionmaker is confronted by making his decision in certain contexts, within an environment. We might wish to change that, but that doesn't always mean you have the means to do so. The strategic questions are those questions which resolve issues of controlling the scope, pace, and intensity of conflict. But this is a two-sided undertaking. Merely because you decide you'd like to move more slowly doesn't mean that the people on the other side of the conflict will provide you that opportunity. Why does one leader have thirteen days and the other thirteen minutes? It's because that's what the circumstances allowed him to have. And those circumstances were created not just by him, but by the opponents and by perhaps any number of neutral, seemingly uninvolved players. It is difficult to see how the ability to increase speed can be bad. It becomes a choice, a strategic choice. So, if one rejects the ability to increase the pace, then you have narrowed your strategic options. Just because one has the option doesn't mean one has to take it.

JD: Do you ever worry about something like a blitzkrieg law of combined development, that it won't be the United States that gets there first, but some other power that learns from our mistakes?

VADM: Absolutely, that is a major concern. This is a very open society and this openness isn't new. We did after all have American officers present in the field with German commanders when they invaded Poland. We had ample opportunity to observe this force in action. We had many years to study their writings. So this kind of openness is not new. If you carry this to its logical conclusion, if there were infinite speed of technology proliferation and infinite speed of information proliferation, what kind of attributes would I have to have to maintain a competitive advantage? Because if you look toward the trajectory, and it's toward increasing speed of technical proliferation and information dissemin-ation, you're not going to stop that trajectory. Bending to that effort would be a folly. Therefore, the thing to do is to go ahead, leap ahead, and you start finding those things that would decrease your agility, decrease your speed of response, and those get revalued downward.

JD: Can you give some real-life examples of that?

VADM: In command and control of fire support. We have troops engaged, they call for supporting fire. There are three elements of the problem. Sense the target, decide to engage, and weapon delivery. Of those, the long pole in the tent is the pairing of weapon with that particular call for fire.

JD: What if you have to use an ATT calling card on a payphone to call in fire support, like that U.S. soldier in the Grenada invasion?

VADM: No one's been able to tell me exactly how true that story is.

JD: Is there a point where automation leads to the abrogation of control? You know, the worst-case scenario, like Skynet taking over?

VADM: People fail to realize that it's the human who controls the rule set for the automation. People say if you automate this, you're giving up control. You're not.

JD: So AI [Artificial Intelligence] is never going to figure that out?

VADM: Even if you allow AI to take over that choice of rule set, someone will have to make up the rule set that governs the AI (laughter). The human cannot avoid responsibility for the consequences of human choices.

JD: Which science fiction book or film do you think gets it right about the future?

VADM: I haven't read any. That bears some explaining. There are millions of things to see as well as to read. And I rely on people to bring me things. The people who come in this office are incredible people of considerable accomplishment. And this one search engine isn't adequate to me. Like Kevin Kelly says, the rule about a well-nurtured network is the first thing you need for innovation.[5] It's the same thing here. Three hours watching someone else's rumination in science fiction doesn't do much for me. You'll walk in here and give me a couple of thoughts, which I'll then marry them up with some of his, and then I'll go ruminate on my own, based on this variety of things that I see. But I try to do just a few simple things, find dots that other people aren't seeing, and then find useful ways to connect them that other people don't see. Very simple, not original, but that's largely what I find myself doing.

JD: I'd like to know if you agree or disagree with Kevin Kelly's definition of a network as "organic behavior in a techno-logical matrix."

VADM: First, network-centric warfare is behavioral-based. Many folks miss that. They go to the "network," which is the adjective; warfare is the noun. Warfare is based on human behavior. We are looking at self-synchronization as what we talk about in network-centric warfare. That is, what happens to the military when it becomes well informed, and has the opportunity to behave according to a certain rule set based on that level of information, that level of knowledge. And that's what you have in the marketplace. Advertising, for example, informs the marketplace. And then the marketplace synchronizes itself according to some very basic rule sets. You get marketplace behavior which is extraordinarily powerful and that's what we look for in network-centric warfare. To the extent that you use technologies to inform the actors, then yes, you can talk about a technical matrix.

JD: That works for me on the strategic level, but I'm not sure that the military can or should function like the marketplace. I was thinking about this on the drive down, when I heard a talk about horse races, in particular, why claiming races works so well. In a way the marketplace is like a claiming race: you don't have horses with incredibly different skills because in a claiming race you can buy that horse after the race for a given amount. So if you put a $30,000 horse in a $60,000 race, you're not going to make any prize money. And if you put a $60,000 horse in a $30,000 race, that horse could then be bought and you'd be out of any future winnings. But we don't really fight wars that way. We now fight wars where we put in a $100,000 horse in a $10,000 claiming race, and win the race, then take over the track, and change the rule set. We're making the rules, so it's not reciprocal action, and it's not multilateral, it's incredibly unilateral. It's sort of like Weinberger's [former Secretary of Defense] or Powell's [formerly National Security Advisor and Chairman of the Joint Chiefs of Staff, currently Secretary of State] warfighting doctrine, that we go in with everything we've got, no matter the level of opposition.

VADM: It's the American way of war. That's why we love Super Bowls. The Super Bowls are absolute blowouts. We want to see the opposition swept off the field of play (laughter).

JD: So you agree that the marketplace might be good for innovation, but not for rational warfighting?

VADM: No, I think it's excellent for warfighting. But when I'm talking about marketplace behavior, I'm talking about the ability of our own well-informed force to synchronize and to organize itself according to a basic rule set. Because if you have a well-trained force, which is then well informed and knowledgeable in its rule set, that is, it has very good unity of effort, then there is an excellent chance that you will prevail over someone at a lower level of knowledge, who lacks the discipline to respond to the organizing rule set. Or does not have a coherent rule set which would develop coherent behavior. Which is one of the reasons why you now start the war against an opponent by fighting over information superiority. Because what you want to do is to remove from him the ability to have organized behavior. One of the key principles of the organization is his ability to be well informed. So you seek to deny him that. You don't necessarily have much control over his organizing rule set, which is more a function of the quality of his leadership, his rules of engagement, his unity of effort.

JD: Say you were asked by the president to advise whether to intervene in some place like Kosovo, where you're not sure if you can go in with overwhelming force because of humanitarian restraints. What does that mean for network-centric warfare? Can network-centric warfare be applied in such a context?

VADM: Absolutely. There are many who think that NCW only talks to top-end, intensive violent warfare. Hardly the case. How could it be the case, when all of its principles really come from peace? Really come from the marketplace? Really come from individual behavioral activity? Furthermore, one of our existence proofs is in the decreasing crime rate. As police forces change their basic rule sets—their organizing principles—as they change the information flows, this allows various precincts to organize dynamically along a much shorter time line than before. That's what's responsible for the change in the crime rate. You might say that's a very low level of conflict—still quite violent, but the principles are still there. But to put it another way, because the level of conflict is somewhat lower, would I want to be less well informed? Certainly not. Not only that, to the unit that is actually engaged, at risk to their life, that is not low-level conflict. The scope of the engagement might be less, but the intensity for that engaged unit is high.

JD: That scenario seemed to be played out in Urban Warrior—what kind of lessons did the navy draw from Fleet Battle Experiment Echo?

VADM: We are still pulling data out of that. I'd rather not get into it. . . .

JD: On a tour of one of your Aegis missile cruisers at the experiment, I was struck by the number of computers everywhere, how everyone was staring at screens, and not much else. I had this flashback to the USS *Vincennes*, where they had trained for months with computer simulations, and nowhere in the training had there been an Iranian Airbus in the skies overhead. Even when their screens told them there was something that did not correspond to the track of an F-14, they didn't believe their eyes. They believed their computer simulations and training, and shot it down.

VADM: Well, they had other, or they thought they had, other information that indicated a descending plane, and consequently they were conflicted. And this calls to question what the future warrior will have to be able to do. I'm not necessarily talking about a rifleman in the field, but such people as Captain Rogers [commander of the USS *Vincennes*] in that case. It's not so much a question of how well supported he was by the technology, or the people, but rather by the whole decisionmaking environment. Of which he of course was a part—and he helped shape that environment as well as become the victim of it. I believe that people in such command centers in the future will have to have certain interdisciplinary skills in at least three major sectors. First, warfare discipline, which is critically important; secondly, information discipline, including display technology, not just pipes; and then third, from the behavioral sciences, knowing how people make decisions, what are the cognitive processes. It's a different view of epistemology. This then becomes the power of education versus training.

JD: How would you distinguish the two?

VADM: Training has to do with repeatable skills, repeatable format situations; education has to do with being able to reason from principles to a useful conclusion in a situation which you've never seen before.

JD: How do you see this playing out among the services? Is there a lag? Do you find resistance in joint operations?

VADM: Resistance is large, it is probable, it is systemic: it is just like any other major firm with a long track record of success. We have a very robust ideologic system, and different parts of different services have more or less robust ideologic systems; and, therefore, advance is uneven. That was one of the reasons why this command was reshaped the way it was last summer. The Naval War College never had a subordinate command before; now it does—the naval warfare development command. People sometimes say, you know, "Work in your lane." I don't have a lane. That's the ground rule.

JD: Is this more like the army's TRADOC [Training and Doctrine Command] at Fort Leavenworth, where teaching and doctrine are combined?

VADM: These things are meant to work back and forth against each other. Over on the teaching side, because we are very much into education, we talk about a critical understanding of the principles. On the other hand doctrine is meant to be forward-going. It's not meant to chronicle the past. So we expect that doctrine is a pull on the institution. We're already doing that for example in network-centric warfare. So you take all these principles, these case studies, and revalue them through the lens of network-centric warfare, in other words: get into the information age. You know, with a two hundred-year history of industrial-age warfare, we now have the opportunity to ask ourselves questions from an information-age perspective.

JD: Is this what you'll be doing at this year's global warfare games?

VADM: Yes, as a matter of fact, last year's games were billed as network-centric warfare games, and we were just beginning. I thought it was at one point frustrating and at another point fascinating. The frustration it took so long for people to come to grips with things and move on to the big issues that I really wanted to have them address. They only barely began that process because they wanted to start with, "Well, what's the definition of network-centric warfare?" I said, "Well, here's a working definition." Then they said, "Well, I don't believe that." I said what do you mean you don't believe a definition? It's a working definition. You know, God did not hand down on tablets the definition of network-centric warfare. Here's a working definition, just use it and move on.

JD: My students are like that—they want every lecture to start with definitions. I come back at them with Nietzsche's famous line, that only that which has no history can be defined. You know as soon as you apply a concept, the definition mutates. They usually buy that. But how far down does the network go? If you wire up everybody and each individual soldier becomes part of the network, when does that become part of a communication breakdown, just noise?

VADM: You don't know. You don't know until you do it. When we upgraded the information capability on the ships, we had no idea what the first level of impact was going to be of IT21 ("Information Technology for the 21st Century"). The first impact wasn't in terms of combat direction: it was improved retention rate, lower stress, greater productivity on the part of sailors. This is a delightfully unintended consequence. They are now no longer detached from family, things that they value. Morale stays up, sense of purpose stays up, they now feel coupled with the rest of the world. So that helps reinforce the sense of purpose. Why? Because suddenly a sailor can make a phone call, send an e-mail. Two years ago, when the first battle group with the new information technology came home, I was able to report with delight to the flags that in six months they had sent 54,000 e-mails. The last battle group that came home said we stopped counting when we passed 5 million (laughter).

JD: You know the old line that with interdependence comes vulnerability. What new vulnerabilities do you see coming from the spread of information technology?

VADM: Anytime you determine something's valuable on the battlefield it becomes a target to the enemy. There is no difference. It's just a feature of the landscape. Airplanes became important, so what did you do? You started fighting for air superiority, and blowing up airfields, surface-to-air missile sites. This is no different.

JD: Is the information network more difficult to defend than an airfield or carrier?

VADM: Actually it's far easier to defend, if you make the right architectural choices at the beginning. Part of the overhang of the industrial age is to highly integrate and optimize systems and subsystems and in doing so you create striking systemic vulnerabilities. In the information age, you have the opportunity to move toward structures that are networked and are characterized by dynamic fitness, in which case your vulnerabilities or risks tend to be localized. These are choices that we have. One of the issues for us in the military, indeed for any firm, is that if you reach to the industrial-age rule set, you will not make the correct architectural choices. And so this is now what we are chafing against, and what I believe many firms are chafing against, is the value is now different. Optimization is not what's of value. What are Kevin Kelly's rules? Increasing performance at decreasing returns on investment. And it's particularly problematic when you are dealing with information-based technologies. Every time you decide to upgrade, maintain that software, you introduce complexifiers, you make it harder to do, so cost-per-unit performance goes up. Failures go up; it should come as no surprise that in the marketplace now you find large amounts of shrink-wrapped failures as you continue to pursue the paradigm of optimization in software as opposed to pursuing dynamic fitness and modularity in network structure.

JD: So you're not too worried about hackers working for rogue states?

VADM: That's a concern, but it's just part of the landscape. It is not a showstopper.

JD: What's your worst-case scenario?

VADM: You asked about science fiction. This is what I think is the worst-case scenario. We have something like a major Y2K problem. Not necessarily major technically but it becomes major in the way society chooses to respond to it. And it cascades by virtue of increased globalization. And this is not like natural disasters where you can take things from more recent geography and use these things to help out; the geography of the information domain is not amenable to that kind of reallocation of resources. And when people say, as they increasingly do, "Fix this now because so much of our quality of life depends on it," someone says back, "We can fix this.

This can be fixed. There are, however, some elements of convention we have to suspend to do that. Certain privacy rights, the tort codes, liabilities, indemnification." Soon we are talking about things that today would upset a whole lot of people because they seem to attack the rule of law. And then people start to say, "I can accept that to reestablish order and my quality of life." That is the doomsday scenario.

JD: What's the role of the navy in this scenario?

VADM: The way ahead for the navy is becoming increasingly clear. We are increasingly committed to NCW as our organizing principle. We think it reflects the bedrock principles of the information age as they are emerging, and it has within it the resiliency or adaptivity to take on the properties of the information age as it continues to change. Because we cannot look at where we are today and say, "Ah-ha this is it, this is the next age." Because we are far from bumping up against the asymptotes. So there is going to be considerable movement and you need an organizing principle that is capable of accommodating change. Network-centric warfare is such an organizing principle. Secondly, assured battlespace access will be a principle-shaping force for the navy. I'm not talking about infrastructure, access, overseas basing and things like that, because the navy doesn't worry much about things like that compared to other forces. But rather we see the principle operating in domains such as the sea, space, and cyberspace.

Vice Admiral Cebrowski laid out the future of networks like a grid. However, back at Urban Warrior, when the plan for network-centric war hit the less linear pavements of San Francisco and Oakland, the net often seemed more hay- than hard-wired. The experiment got off to a bad start, at least in the smoke-filled eyes of the reporters aboard a Navy Sea Knight helicopter that caught fire and had to return quickly to the USS *Bonhomme Richard*. I was safely on land, with Marine Bravo Company while they waited for the order to assault the abandoned Alameda Naval Hospital in Oakland, which according to intelligence reports had been occupied by a group of defectors from "Country Green." Communications were spotty because both commercial brands of the new portable radios kept going down, victims of either jamming, or just too much ferro-concrete in the area. "This is not," said one general at the scene, "a computer-friendly environment." So far, the assembled military forces and civilian support were running out of bandwidth faster than bullets.

Suddenly there was the flat crack of sniper fire, followed by machine guns, which sent the refugee crowd scurrying. It wasn't clear to the marines in nearby Humvees whether the refugees were heading for cover or for them. Coordinates were sent to the off-shore command ship, USS *Coronado*, where, we were told, officers pinpointed and redirected fire with the use of overhead satellite imagery and a circling Predator unmanned aerial vehicle (which I later discovered to in fact be a Cessna installed with a Predator sensor packet—the UAV was deemed too risky by the FAA for an urban flyover). Coordinates and commands were transmitted directly to an "autonomous/minimally manned" 120 mm mortar known as Dragon Fire. Just as Bravo Company geared up to storm the naval hospital occupied by the rogue militia, the bespec-tacled corporal next to me (who resembled too much for comfort the character "Joker" in *Full Metal Jacket*) looked up from his End User Terminal—the chest-mounted Toshiba Libretto 100CT equipped with integrated GPS and wireless modem—and told us we're all dead. "Friendly fire," he said.

Fortunately for us—a cluster of defense contractors baby-sitting their new battle toys and me as tagalong—reality is the first casualty of simulated warfare. However, as a warwise gunnery sergeant told me, this is why they call it an experiment. Things go wrong and you work it out now rather than later, before mistakes end up as body bags. But the spectacle of it all seemed to have another goal in mind: to deter both real and potential enemies. Now if you mix it up with marines, you're going to mess with a war machine as smart as it is mean. Yet in the weeks that followed the experiment, Slobodan Milosevic appeared to have missed the deterrent intentions of Urban Warrior and similar displays of might.

At another level, the simulation seemed to rehearse if not antici-pate the reality of Somalia, Bosnia, and Kosovo. For instance, just prior to the marines' arrival in Somalia, Admiral David Jeremiah, then vice chairman of the Joint Chiefs of Staff, remarked that

"The last thing I want to do is kill people we're trying to feed." Urban Warrior had several moments when events that began as "humanitarian assistance" deteriorated into body-on-body conflict. And it wasn't only the U.S. Marines. Among the French and British foreign participants of Urban Warrior, the Dutch marines were known to get physical at the drop of a kevlar. One U.S. Marine told me, with no small amount of admiration, that the Dutch "kicked ass." I filed it away as compensatory behavior after the Dutch shame of the massacre at Srebrenica. A degree of escalation was preprogrammed into the exercise: better to learn your lessons here than in less forgiving environments. But it didn't take much aggravation from a refugee to get the marines to violate not only the rules of engagement (deadly force permitted only in life-threatening situations) but also the rules of the game (no physical contact whatsoever). The lesson I observed is that you shouldn't expect combat soldiers, especially marines, to make good peacekeepers. Here the hardwiring of boot camp seemed to overpower one of the prime directives of Urban Warrior, "to provide disaster assistance and simulate civil-military relations."

It took a couple of particularly eccentric events to deconstruct the net-centric intentions of the experiment. One happened as I followed the marines in their most intense force-on-force operation, the retaking of the abandoned naval hospital at Oak Knoll from opposing forces played by the Twenty-third Marines out of San Bruno. The sound of gunfire from the stairway ahead dropped the Bravo company into firing positions, M-16s ready. Just then, a young African-American woman descended the staircase, stepped over the prone marines, and walked out the door. She was dressed in the refugee-slacker look of enemy "Country Orange," but her red jacket and the freeze-frame quality of the moment evoked the girl walking through the grayness of the Jewish ghetto in *Schindler's List*. After a long pause and an exchange of befuddled looks, an order was shouted out, and three marines scrambled to their feet to grab her as she left the building. Was she a terrorist, a hostage, or just lost? Adding to the tension—and absurdity—two observer/controllers in colonial pith helmets kept a careful watch from a short distance away. The marines couldn't tell who or what the young woman was: using some kind of sign language, she appeared to be either deaf, or foreign. Literally dumb-founded, the marines finally let her go. Later, after the battle was over, I spotted her chatting among a group of fellow refugees in the hospital parking lot. I asked her what had happened in the hospital. She laughed, and said that she had been bored and decided on the spot to do some improv.

In another of those hurry-up-and-wait moments before the storming of the abandoned hospital, I got into a rambling conversation with the biggest and baddest-looking NCO on the scene. I had seen a mock-up to the "Marine 2010," with a heads-up display, adjustable lethality weapon, reactive body armor, adjustable camouflage pattern, medical monitors, heel compression generator, and situational awareness control panel. I asked him whether it wasn't getting too much like a Nintendo game. He gave me a look and let the question hang. Finally, with some weariness, he said, "Yeah, all this technology around, everyone with their own computers and cameras, they run you here and there—it's all starting to look like aliens." I traveled back to the first digitized rotation at Fort Irwin. You mean little green men, or the colonial marines in *Aliens*? "Yeah, the movie." But didn't Ripley [Sigourney Weaver] have to take over when the officers screwed up? "Dang right, commander sat in his vehicle, wasn't out with his men, you always need a warrior somewhere, someone not afraid to get dirty." I told him how I had unintentionally offended the cyborg soldier at Fort Irwin by likening him to the colonial marines. "Yeah, they think we're no-necks, we think they're derelicts. But the worst are the air force—they're fourth-level cub scouts." I suspect he would not be the only marine to score Ripley higher than both officers and soldiers from the other armed services.

From Mogadishu to Kosovo, players stray from the script. No plan survives first contact with the enemy—a hard lesson recounted in detail by Clausewitz that always seems to get lost with each new wave of technology. Experiments, exercises, and war games might diminish the uncertainty and risk of future battlefield encounters. And networks, including the MIME-NET, might well be a force-multiplier for American foreign policy. They might even act, especially with the help of CNN and other prime-time networks, as a kind of cyberdeterrent against potential foes.

Judging from the aftermath of the experiment, when simulated battles gave way to a public carnival, Urban Warrior was also a good way to muster domestic support. Publicity releases from the military emphasized the benefits to the Bay area, including over $4.5 million in direct spending, disaster relief training, and tourist attractions galore. Naval ships were opened to the public, AV-8B Harrier jump jets hovered overhead, the stealth catamaran uncloaked and tied up on the pier, crowds danced to a military rock band (yes, an oxymoron) in Jack London Square, booths full of new weaponry and defense industry products lined the hanger deck of the aircraft carrier USS *Hornet*, and local news anchors jockeyed to get it all on the six o'clock. Occupying one corner of the square, holding a white-sheet banner that read "War Is Never a Game," the handful of protesters from the "Coalition Against Urban Warrior" were clearly outmanned and outgunned.

Spectacle aside, as the dependency on networked technologies increases, as the way we fight and report wars converge onto a single screen of electronic representation, one cannot help wonder if something fundamentally human is being lost. In Iraq, Bosnia, and Kosovo, networked weapon systems attack other networked weapon systems, like air defense systems. But they also hit vital life-support systems like electrical grids, oil pipelines, and water supplies. Virtuous becomes notorious, like the case of the air strikes on Belgrade's bridges. Most Americans supported them, because it was argued that they disrupted the dispatch of military vehicles. Aside from the specious narrowness of the argument, few took into account that electrical and communications lines that ran along the bridges were also destroyed, with consequences for the well-being of many citizens. Collateral damage might be minimized but human suffering is not avoided. It is just deferred, as is any immediate ethical accountability for deaths later recorded as higher rates of infant mortality, untreatable diseases, and malnutrition. This is the darker side of virtuous war that goes largely unreported, or is belatedly revealed, long after the first images of technological wizardry yielding political success have been burned into the public consciousness.

On legal, military, and purely practical grounds, foreign inter-vention is never an easy issue. Debate will and should continue about the efficacy as well as the ethics of "bombing for peace," one of Ambassador Holbrooke's less salubrious phrases. But in the context of a future Kosovo, Urban Warrior highlights the potential danger of choosing quick military fixes over the more deliberative process of diplomacy. Through the MIME-NET, the enemy can be reduced to an icon in a target-rich environment, perhaps even efficiently vilified and destroyed at a distance. Aboard the AEGIS cruiser *Port Royal*, I was shown with great fanfare how its phased-array radar system could take on forty targets at once and destroy them with surface-to-air, antiship, and cruise missiles, and, as a last resort, the Phalanx Gatling guns. Many of these systems and strategies were originally planned and designed for open-water operations and a single preponderant threat, the Soviet Union. Further systemwide upgrades were in the works to create a whole new class of AEGIS-class "Smart Ships" that would have automatic cruise control, new control and surveillance systems, and an integrated bridge: in other words, more computers, fewer sailors. With more computers running the ships, fewer sailors were needed, a boon in times of falling recruitment rates. Amidst all the enthusiasm for techno-solutions, no one seemed to be looking at the endpoint of the trajectory: a battlefield in which networks, systems, robots, and smart weapons target each other, and *all* damage measured in flesh and blood becomes "collateral."

In many ways, Urban Warrior confirmed a worry I had first felt on a trip to Fort Hood two months earlier. Fort Hood, the largest military installation in the United States, is located in the Bible Belt of Texas, just outside of Killeen, which probably has the highest ratios in the United States of churches (and pawn shops) to bars (it's dry). Home base of the Third Corps, it also has the largest collection of armor, simulated and real, in the world. Driving up Tank Battalion Avenue, I came upon row after row of Abrams, Bradleys, Humvees, and just about every other kind of wheeled and tracked vehicle, perfectly arrayed behind chain-link and razor-wire fence, as far as the eye can see—which in the flat, dusty terrain of central Texas seemed like miles. There was enough heavy metal here to give a headbanger whiplash and a compass serious magnetic deviation. After a few miles of this, I began to wonder: warehouse, or cemetery?

I had come for the virtual armor, to check out the formation of the "First Digitized Division." Once more I had to sit through the initiation ritual of the brief; at least this one had some great 3-D Silicon Graphics visuals, featuring the centerpiece of Fort Hood, the Close Combat Tactical Trainer (CCTT). There's not much to impress when you first enter the cavernous gymlike home of the CCTT. Full of stacked containers, it looks like a trailer park set up in a very large and very clean gymnasium. But inside each container is a replica, complete with screen, controls, sound, and electronics, of the interior of an armored vehicle, mainly mock-ups of M1A1 and M1A2 Abram tanks, M2/M3 Bradley Armored Personnel Carriers, and Humvees. Each is networked to an oper-ation center and computer workstation; and like an electronic beehive, each forms a node of a distributed interactive simulation network. The aim is to create for the operator a combination of live (field exercises), constructive (interactive training), and virtual simulations (computer-generated scenarios), or, in the words of the brief, "to interoperate on a virtual battlefield" where a CCTV operator in a Fort Hood constructive simulation could link up in real time with a Fort Irwin tank crew in a live simulation out in the desert and a Fort Leavenworth virtual simulation in training and doctrine. The entire CCTV system consists of the manned simulators; high-fidelity semiautomated opposing forces that are projected on each of the simulator's screens that stand in for windows; a virtual terrain database that encompasses 100 by 150 kilometers with a variety of weather conditions; and separate areas for after-action reviews where the soldiers learn, one hopes, from their mistakes. The video briefing ended with the image of an Abrams going flat out, and a pitch that sounded right out of an ad for Ginzu knives: "And because all but war is simulation, you need the support of the world's most efficient and effective training systems. You need CCTT."

My immediate conclusion was that I needed to get out of there. But after the briefing, I had been handed a plastic bag and then sealed into one of the simulators for a test run in the semiprone position of the Abrams tank driver. Although I did not experi-ence what's known as simulation sickness—a cue conflict between the brain and the body over what's real and what's not that can cause disorientation, even nausea—I did feel an intense claustrophobia. It was like being trapped inside a cell of a vast metallic beehive; one is surrounded by the canned soundtrack of armored warfare, all clanking, banging, and the loud *whumpf* of a direct hit. I wondered what my grandfather the apiarist and Civil War reenactor would have made of this strange brood, and once again, the strange slogan, "All but war is simulation."

In search of a simulation antidote, and intrigued by a chance remark from one of my Fort Hood handlers, I decided to leave Fort Hood a day early and to make the pilgrimage to Waco, fifty miles to the east. After April 19, 1993, and the FBI assault on the Branch Davidian compound, Waco is no longer known as the birthplace of Dr Pepper. After getting very lost, I finally spotted the landmark blue water towers. It was a desolate place, no one there, a rusted-out, bullet-ridden bus the only sign of what had taken place. Four Alcohol, Tobacco, and Firearms (ATF) agents had been killed in the initial raid, and more than eighty Branch Davidians died in the fiery aftermath of the April FBI assault. Many controversies surrounded the tragedy: why didn't the ATF arrest David Koresh when he was making one of his frequent trips to town? Who fired the first shot during the ATF raid? What started the fires? Were flammable tear gas canisters used? Why no fire engines on the scene?

One question received little public scrutiny: what was the military role? The Posse Comitatus Act forbids the military to engage in domestic law enforcement. But clearly the military, in person and by choice of strategies, was very much on the scene. The ATF was supposed to execute an arrest and search warrant against Koresh. Instead they arrived in full battle gear, "hidden" in cattle trucks. Two "unidentified military experts" from Fort Hood provided operational advice to the Justice Department, and Delta Force soldiers were involved in the planning and execution of the FBI assault.[6] And although press accounts routinely referred to "FBI tanks," "FBI Bradleys," and even "FBI combat engineering vehicles" (the armored tanklike vehicles that were modified to pump tear gas into the compound), one of my handlers told me most of the armor came from Fort Hood (a fact confirmed by a subsequent interview I did with General Wesley Clark, who was at the time commander of the First Cavalry at Fort Hood).[7]

Two weeks after my return from Fort Hood and Waco, President Clinton announced plans to boost military spending for a new program called "Homeland Defense." A task force would be set up to consider whether a new national command should be established to defend America against chemical and biological weapons attack, cybersabotage, and yes, missile attack from rogue states. On the last day of Urban Warrior, the Senate approved in a lopsided 97–3 vote a bill committing the Pentagon to build a limited ballistic missile attack, "as soon as technologically possible." By the first days of the Bush administration, it was not a question of building "Fortress America"; it was just a matter of taking up the drawbridge.

My trips to Fort Hood, Waco, and Urban Warrior only confirmed my belief that we must be ever vigilant against those who would wish to bring the military and technological fix home. Do we really want the military to be in the business of planning and executing military operations in the domestic United States? Are there hidden costs to the military training city police, fire, and medical personnel to cope with biological and chemical terrorism? Should "homeland defense," as Deputy Defense Secretary Hamre asserted, "be the defense mission of the next century"?[8] In the absence of viable enemies abroad, are we too eager to find new ones at home?

Leaving Urban Warrior, the in-flight movie on my trip back east was *Enemy of the State*, a full-blown conspiracy thriller that makes Oliver Stone's most paranoid vision look like a state-of-the-union address. At the end of the movie, after a rogue faction of the National Security Agency is reined in by the heroics of lawyer Will Smith and ex-government agent Gene Hackman, and domestic order is semirestored (i.e., lots of people get killed and buildings blown up—this is after all a Jerry Bruckheimer production—but Smith goes back to the wife and his Mercedes Benz), one of the National Security Agency computer geeks is asked why he went along with the criminal machinations of his superior, played by the quintessential embodiment of bureaucratic evil, Jon Voight. He whines, "They told us it was a STO—Standard Training Op." And in a last-ditch effort to mix some *virtù* in with the *vérité*, Larry King gets the last words of the film: "We must draw the line between national security and civil liberties—you have no right to come into my home." Unlike in real life, there was no cut to commercial, only a fade-out.

7 Virtuous war goes to Hollywood

War is the continuation of politics by other means. Clausewitz said that. Politics is the continuation of show business by other means. I said that, but it might just as well have been said by Julius Caesar or Napoleon or F.D.R. or even my former boss, Richard M. Nixon. You have to keep that in mind when you ponder why the G.O.P. is meeting in, of all places, gritty urban, old-fashioned Philadelphia, while the Democrats gather two weeks later in glamorous Los Angeles, center of the universe of sybaritic fantasy-making.

> (Ben Stein, on the Republican and Democratic Party Conventions in 2000, "On Location in Philadelphia")

Thus the Convention could evolve literally in a space and a time of its own; thanks to perfect manipulation, it became not so much a spontaneous demonstration as a gigantic extravaganza with nothing left to improvisation. This stage show, which channeled the psychic energies of hundreds of thousands of people, differed from the average monster spectacle only in that it pretended to be an expression of the people's real existence.

> (Siegfried Kracauer, on the Nuremberg Party Convention in 1934, *From Caligari to Hitler*)

Y2K will be remembered not for a bug in the computer, but for the ghost in the voting machine. In the U.S. presidential elections of 2000, candidates won and lost, more than once, by the triumph of the virtual (exit polls, networked media, and voting machines) over the real (fallible voters, subjective counters, and actual results).

ICT convention display.

Computer generated civilian encounter.

In retrospect, this virtual shift in the relationship of politics, war, and the media can be traced back to the 2000 National Party Conventions. Somewhat disingenuously, as if they had no influence on the matter, the major networks and newspapers declared the Republican convention in Philadelphia a "non-news circus," an "infomercial," and, amidst the poorest ratings ever for a national convention, "soporific." They offered spotty coverage, most of it at the level of metamedia, out-equivocating Hamlet on whether it is better to see or not to see just how illusory our national politics have become. In turn, upset Republican officials demanded that the three major television networks devote "not a minute more" to the Democratic convention in Los Angeles.[1] If the Republican convention was an infomercial, said one pundit, "the Democratic convention is a minefield," an unpredictable mix of L.A. celebrities, potentially violent anarchists, and a narcissistic president reluctant to leave the stage.[2] While the Republicans relied on the simulacrum of military might and warrior virtues, the Democrats went Silliwood, basking in the reflected light glow of 56 iMac computers on the convention floor and a parade of Hollywood stars and directors. We witnessed the morphing of the body politic into a virtuous entity, a new amalgam of brass, silicon, and silicone.

The prime-time networks, so fixed on the old reality principle of politics, where parties represent the people as words represent the truth, missed the story: the convention, the party, national politics, the media itself had been absorbed by its own simulacrum, a copy of a copy in search of an original. Where the majors feared to focus, cable network news and a variety of web-based services rushed in, but none so foolishly as C-SPAN, which gave us an unblinking, relatively unmediated look at what American politics has become: ever so virtuous.

The virtual dwarfed the real from the moment the lights went up at the Republican convention, to reveal a stage full of little people standing under gargantuan video screens that were perched on two squat white edifices, each bisected by a black row of what appeared to be mirrored windows. The whole structure bore a startling resemblance to the slit-bunkers that once graced the beaches of Normandy. What would architect and philosopher Paul Virilio have made of this stage? Virilio, who first stumbled upon Rommel's Atlantic Wall as a "war child," and who in 1975 in his first book and museum exhibition, *Bunker Archeology*, wrote of the bunker as now "a myth . . . present as an object of disgust instead of a transparent and open civilian architecture, absent insofar as the essence of the new fortress is elsewhere, underfoot, invisible from here on in."[3] Were the Republicans uncloaking America as a virtual fortress?

The answer came on the first day as past and future wars jostled on the same stage at the Republican convention. The assembled national security experts, Condoleezza Rice notwithstanding, had a distinctly Cold-War pallor to them. On hand from the Reagan-Bush years were the old guard, Henry Kissinger, George Shultz, and Brent Scowcroft, as well as the old-before-their-time crowd, Paul Wolfowitz, Richard Armitage, and of course, Dick Cheney. On one panel, when former secretary of state Lawrence Eagleburger was asked about the threat of private encryption to national security, he requested an explanation of the question. But virtuosity was irrepressible. Whether wielded as scalpel by William Bennett, or as sledgehammer by Dick Cheney, "virtue"—particularly of the martial and marital variety—was the weapon of choice against the Clinton administration and all those who might wish to forgive or at least forget the president's shortcomings in these areas.

Adding some bang to the banality of the convention, Republicans repeatedly evoked the honor and sacrifice of past wars as well as scenarios and forebodings of future wars. Heroes from Second World War to the Persian Gulf War were on parade for "National Security Night." Prime-time slots included, on stage, Bob Dole, John McCain, and General Colin Powell; by live-feed, General Norman Schwarzkopf on the deck of the USS *New Jersey*; and in memoriam, a video tribute to the living and dead Second World War veterans. But this should not be confused with old-fashioned militarism. "When the real is no longer what it was," says Jean Baudrillard, "nostalgia assumes its full meaning. There is a proliferation of myths of origin and of signs of reality."[4] On stage, controversial issues of the day receded as past glories and future hopes merged in scripts of nostalgia, a political version of Tomorrowland, once Disney's vision of the future ("The future that never was in finally here") but now more of a virtual NeverLand (where, in fact, the "Bug's Life" exhibition has been replaced by a Virtual Reality Studio).

Repeating the nostalgia mantra of the convention, presidential nominee George W. Bush offered a paean to the "greatest generation in history" (not the X'ers but the guys, in George W.'s inimitable intonation, from "dubya-dubya-2"). He did take a stab in his acceptance speech at a substantive defense issue, the "decline in military readiness" (a shibboleth among Republicans), declaiming "two entire divisions of the army" unfit to fight. In the days that followed, his charge was rebutted by several administration officials as well as the chairman of the Joint Chiefs of Staff, General Henry H. Shelton.[5] But military readiness, national missile defense, and preparation against weapons of mass destruction, all platform highlights on National Security Night, were not facts to be disputed; they are in their own right simulations to deter enemies abroad and political opponents at home who might try to offer an alternative reality for international relations. "This is how simulation appears," says Baudrillard, "a strategy of the real, of the neoreal and the hyperreal that everywhere is the double of a strategy of deterrence."[6]

Outside the Philadelphia convention hall, some conflicts did flare up, only to be virtualized by the media into irrelevant sideshows. Several newspapers seized on a preconvention controversy, about the Pentagon setting up—at taxpayers' expense—a three-day exhibition of the latest military hardware at the former Naval Shipyard. The *New York Times* reported that the marines sent the "V-22 Osprey, which has crashed three times in the past decade"; the air force "plans to include an unmanned surveillance aircraft, the Predator, as well as missiles and bombs and storyboards promoting its newest fighter, the F-22"; the army, "not [to] be outdone, has mobilized a virtual armory of equipment, including an Apache attack helicopter, its own unmanned aircraft and its troubled theater missile defense system"; and "by contrast, the Navy is sending only an aging Sea Sprite helicopter, two surveillance vehicles, and a small riverine boat."[7] As scandal, it was a news flop: nobody seemed to really care, and, according to the air force, fewer than twenty-five delegates showed up at the exhibition.

Network-centric warfare made a brief appearance in the streets, if not in the mainstream media. The two major umbrella protest organizations, bearing the web-signs of "R2K Network" and "D2K Network," used e-mail to mobilize the troops, cell phones and radios to keep street tactics fluid, and linked networks to spin their story.[8] Hypersensitive to post-Seattle advances in the art of networked protest, Philadelphia authorities early on designated a 40 by 190 foot area as a "Free Speech Zone," in which each group of preapproved protesters were allowed fifty minutes to state their piece and move on. In effect, the first amendment was suspended outside the zone, and the Philadelphia police used intelligence, infiltration, surveillance, and extralegal raids of the protester headquarters with blanket arrests—followed by prohibitively high bail amounts (set at a half-million dollars to a million dollars for "ringleaders")—to effectively preempt the asymmetrical, networked tactics of the protesters. The Los Angeles Police Department made a similar effort to curtail protests by establishing a "security zone" around the Staples Center—effectively sealing off a 186-acre area around the convention site—but was quashed in a successful lawsuit brought by the American Civil Liberties Union (ACLU). U.S. District Court Judge Gary Feess ordered the LAPD to create a constitutional alternative to their original plan, stating that "You can always theorize some awful scenario [but] you can't shut down the First Amendment about what might happen."[9]

On a Sunday that fell between the conventions—and somewhere between fact and fiction—the cable channel *TNT* ran the made-for-TV movie *Running Mates* while HBO showed Warren Beatty's *Bulworth*. Starring a slicked-back Tom Selleck, *Running Mates* is about a presidential nominee on his way to his "virtual coronation" at the Democratic convention (at yes, the Staples Center in Los Angeles), surrounded by ex- and present lovers (all professionally promoted from campaign worker or intern to a veritable matriarchy of campaign manager, media magnate, and beltway power broker, the last played boozily and wonderfully by Faye Dunaway). That is, until a bomb goes off in an abortion clinic, and candidate James Pryce, after the swelling music signals the coming epiphany, says screw-the-damn-polls, turn-off-the-damn-television-cameras, and becomes a virtuous politician. Declaring "America's Not for Sale" to big money, he becomes, in the words of the ad for the movie, "the candidate of your dreams." *Running Mates*, in spite of its remarkable first hour of refreshingly cynical candor, never gets the mix right, of right-eousness and realism that proves so effective for Martin Sheen as President Bartlet on the NBC series *The West Wing*, or, for that matter, the idealism and satire that makes Warren Beatty's *Bulworth* such a malicious treat. But one detects in the rash of movies and TV series centered on political figures a backlash as well as a paradox in operation. As voter turnouts decline and convention ratings drop, "real" politics is increasingly played out by virtuous means: we seek to find in Hollywood—to paraphrase what philosopher Ludwig Feuerbach saw as the human origin of heaven—what we can no longer find in Washington.[10]

Perhaps no event better captured this parallel universe that exists between Hollywood and Washington than Warren Beatty's quixotic nonrun for the presidency. Fascinated by *Bulworth* (his 1998 film, which he wrote, directed, and starred in), I decided a year before the elections to invite Warren Beatty to be a keynote speaker at a conference I was organizing at Brown University, called VIRTUALY2K (a.k.a. VY2K). This was at the height of speculation about whether Beatty might run for high office. What some saw as a media-created campaign (triggered by, of all people, the suggestion of Ariana Huffington—who plays "as herself" in *Running Mates*), others as a flirtation by a man who craved public attention (think back to the song of Carly Simon—for whom Bill Clinton played his sax at a preconvention party), I saw Beatty's candidacy flirtation as one more sign of the virtualization of poli-tics. After many faxes, the disappointment of several hit-and-miss phone calls—offset the couple of times a sympathetic Annette Bening answered—I finally got him on the phone and made my pitch about the political significance of the "virtual president." He kept interrupting, to ask, "but what does it all mean?"—which I thought I had just explained. After a long back-and-forth about the peculiar state of American politics and where he fit in it, he abruptly said he simply couldn't decide right now and would get back to me. Evidently he couldn't, and he didn't; I did, however, receive an invitation a few weeks later to hear him speak at Harvard's Kennedy School, where he proved in front of a standing-room-only crowd to be, as one might expect, an exceptionally good actor playing a smart and very entertaining politician. Which is, I must admit, much more and, sadly, so much less than I can say about the two presidential nominees who eventually did make it to the conventions.

If the Republican convention stage groaned under the weight of so much martial history and military brass, the Democratic convention was practically levitated by the lightness of L.A.-being. The virtual nature of the Republican convention was at the top of the hit list for Democrats, Jesse Jackson, as ever, getting the best licks in, saying the Republicans only provided the "illusion of inclusion," while the Democrats were "the real deal." But the money-dealing behind the scenes is what got the headlines. Before getting booted out of L.A. by the Gore team, President Clinton and Senate-candidate Hillary Clinton got first shot at the Hollywood cash cow; no longer called fundraising, they engaged in some very lucrative "donor-servicing" and "donor-maintenance." On Saturday night, Paramount Studios and Stan Lee, creator of Spiderman, hosted a concert with Stevie Wonder, Cher, and Patti LaBelle, among others, performing; Hillary's take was $4 million. After gushing his thanks to the audience, Clinton remarked that he finally understood "what Franklin Delano Roosevelt meant when [he] said that the president must be the greatest actor in America." On Sunday, an appreciative president joined sixty donors for a Sunday brunch held by Barbra Streisand ("the greatest artist of all time"): the take was $10 million for the presidential library. That afternoon, Warner Brothers threw a "West Wing" party, complete with facsimile of the Oval Office (where, evidently, Chelsea Clinton spent most of the party). On Monday night, after Clinton's convention speech—which featured, amidst many rhetorical flourishes, a warning to all potential enemies that it would be a mistake to underestimate America's military strength—the party moved to Paramount Studios, where Clinton giddily waved overhead an Oscar that had been given to him by California Governor Gray Davis. On Thursday night, Barbra Streisand once again stepped into the role of hostess for the Gore/Lieberman fete at the Shrine Auditorium, home of the Oscars ($150 to $20,000 was the ticket price). After original host Hugh Hefner was diss'ed by the family-values faction of the DNC, Universal Studios graciously offered to hold Representative Loretta Sanchez's fund-raising party to get out the Hispanic vote. In the middle of all this Hollywood weirdness, there was no sight more incongrous than Al Gore's "real" running mate, Joe Lieberman, a man chosen for his virtuous reputation, in particular his criticism of President Clinton during the Lewinsky scandal, not missing any opportunity to castigate the values of the music, video game, and entertainment industries. The pundits liked him all the more for it; "what chutzpah," they said. Meanwhile demonstrators, surrounded by cops, held daily rallies at their designated site, the John J. Pershing Square, named in honor of the First World War general.

An inversion of Clausewitz was in full evidence at both conventions—politics as the continuation of war by other means. In fact, politics was even further attenuated: as we travel from past to present wars (of Clausewitz and Cebrowski), from foreign to domestic policy (from Kracauer to Stein), and back again, we witness both a reversal and virtualization of the war continuum. If we do—or rather *should* (to follow the Clausewitzian imperative for the rational use of violence)—conduct war as we conduct politics as we conduct business, the question hangs: which business? Network-centric war, with speed as its killer app/op, can hardly model itself on GM, the business that was once the business of America, or even IBM, "the network solution." They and their postindustrial ilk are too slow, too "old economy." Much attention has been put on the rapid rise of Internet companies, from Netscape to Amazon.com to eBay, the birth of a new economy, and with it, a new politics. On the Sunday between the conventions, the *New York Times Magazine* featured an article on "PAC.com," a group of Internet start-ups that is set to donate stock rather than hard cash to congressional candidates: "All politics is virtual" reads the caption for the photograph (after the NASDAQ crash a few months later, the caption might better be, "the new economy is virtual").[11]

But there is another virtuality out there, a much bigger, more powerful one. The dominant networks of virtuous war continue to be prime-time, real-time, all-the-time hyphenated hydras like Time-Warner-CNN-WB-AOL (and, with World Championship Wrestling, combined value at $225 billion), ABC-Disney-Go, GE-NBC-MSNBC-Snap, and Viacom-CBS-MTV-Paramount-Blockbuster-Iwon. These networks merge, break up, form new alliances, create "virtual corporations," spy on one another ("A civic duty," said the chairman of Oracle, Lawrence Ellison, after acknowledging that a detective agency they'd hired got caught trying to buy Microsoft's trash[12]), and sometimes they even go to war. After negotiations broke down between cable carrier Time Warner and the ABC network on April 30, 2000—and ABC vanished in several major cities—the president of Disney, Robert Iger, said he was "reminded of the 1983 movie *The Day After*, in which Kansas City is hit by a nuclear missile."[13]

The airwave absence of ABC barely lasted twenty-four hours, but on current networks, downtime is measured in seconds. As we move from geopolitics to chronopolitics, power is as much a function of time as space. "60/60/24/7/365" are the key coordinates of the new networks, numbers that I first saw stretched across the double-spread of an Intel advertisement in *Fortune* magazine, projected on a room-sized eye, hovering over row after row of flat-screened computers and transfixed operators, bathed in a blue light, offset by a smaller caption: "Finally, human beings as relentless as the web."[14] Is this the face—and the guts—of a virtual future? Is this what we want, humans as relentless as computers in business, politics, and war?

It would seem so, judging from my experience a year earlier, when I traveled to L.A. to get the first look at the beta-networks of virtuous war. The occasion was the opening of a new Institute for Creative Technologies (ICT) at the University of Southern California (USC). The innocuous title and placid setting concealed a remarkable joint project: to pool expertise, financial resources, and tools of virtual reality for the production of state-of-the-art military simulations. Prominent political leaders, military officers, and representatives from the computer and entertainment industries had gathered for the event. On hand for the signing ceremony and press conference were Steven Sample, the president of USC; Louis Caldera, secretary of the U.S. Army; "Rocky" Delgadillo, deputy mayor of Los Angeles; Rick Belluzzo, then CEO of Silicon Graphics; and Jack Valenti, perpetual president and CEO of the Motion Picture Association of America. Even Governor Gray Davis was to make an unannounced appearance, virtual and gargantuan on screen via satellite link from the Capitol in Sacramento.

We were prepped before the press conference with a variety of exhibits that had been set up to showcase the wizardry that would be the basis for the collaboration between the entertainment industry, the armed forces, and the university. Artificial intelligence was getting a hard sell (as ever), but not proving to be very artificial or intelligent (as usual). "Virtual Helicopters" offered a 3-D mission rehearsal in a desert terrain with intelligent agents in tanks and Apache helicopters. USC's Center for Advanced Technology, Research and Education had "Steve" on display, an "intelligent pedagogical agent" engineered to operate in simulation-based training environments. Steve looked like Hans from *Saturday Night Live* and sounded like HAL from *2001*. A less intelligent dummy was lying down on a stretcher, with white-coated figures around him who spoke in such heavily accented (Russian?) English that I couldn't quite tell what was going on.

Things took an even stranger turn when CNN reporter Jennifer Auther attempted to conduct a stand-up interview with Air Force Lt. General Bob Springer, now retired and president of Nova-Logic, an entertainment company that brought us *Iron Fist* and the highly popular *F-16* and *F-22* simulations. As Springer was telling Auther what NovaLogic had to offer the army, I was distracted by a monotone voice in the background. Standing in front of the USC booth, I suddenly realized Steve was trying to join the conversation; but with such an unscripted interlocutor, he was only managing to come up with a string of non sequiturs. General Springer declared that, "Most of the young men and women joining the military have been brought up on the computer and the Internet and are readily adaptable to the technology of simulation." Steve responded: "OK, I would press the function test button on the temperature monitor." Springer: "The mean age of our customers is twenty-seven years old, so they know the difference between war and games." Steve: "We need to trigger the switches on the alarm sensors." Saying "We seem to have some competition," Auther stopped the interview and asked the USC booth operator to shut down the program. Before the screen went dark, I wondered if Steve took it personally that his Boolean algorithms and database capacity were not up to CNN talking-head standards.

The press conference was much more conventional. The front

rows of the auditorium were sprinkled with uniforms and suits, the military's top computer war gamers swapping stories with executives from the entertainment industry. Towards the back of the room the major network and print media, including CNN, set up to broadcast this new alliance to the world. After some opening remarks, USC President Sample introduced the featured speaker, the Honorable Louis Caldera. Caldera mapped out the purpose and potential of a "very exciting partnership" that seemed to include just about every major L.A. player in high-tech, higher education, and high- as well as low-brow entertainment. "This 45 million dollar contract will fund joint modeling and simulation research and has high-value applications for the army as well as for the entertainment, media, video game, film, destination theme park, and information technology industries that are such a key part of the California economy. . . . This partnership will leverage the U.S. national defense and the enormous talent and creativity of the entertainment industry and their tremendous investment in cutting-edge applications of new technology." Having stroked the local powers, Caldera addressed the needs of his own constituency, in the now-common military language that makes *Neuromancer* sound like an out-of-date army field manual. "The ICT will significantly enhance complex interactive simulations for large-scale warfighting exercises and allow us to test new doctrines in synthetic environments that are populated with intelligent agents in future threat challenges." The speakers that followed parroted the press releases in simpler language. "Synergy" and "verisimilitude" popped up with cue-card frequency; everyone was keen to dance on the "cutting edge."

While the soldiers and politicians vied for media attention, the guy who made it all happen hugged the auditorium wall. The only evidence of his affiliation was a government pay-scale suit, a loud hawhawing at the speakers' jokes, and a slight rolling of the eyes at questions asked by the press. The ICT was the brainchild of Mike Macedonia, son of one of the army's best war gamers, graduate of West Point, and now chief scientist and technical director at STRICOM (Simulation, Training, and Instrumentation Command), the new military base that I had visited a year before in Orlando (see Chapter 4). Steel and glass corporate buildings, owned by Lockheed Martin, Silicon

Graphics, Westinghouse, SAIC, and other defense industries, encircle the various headquarters of the army, navy, Marine Corps, and the air force. Tasked to provide the U.S. military with a "vision for the future," STRICOM leads a combined military and industry effort to create "a distributed computerized warfare simulation system," and to support "the twenty-first century warfighter's preparation for real world contingencies." It is the *ur*-site of the motto that kept popping up in my travels, "All But War Is Simulation."

Under the auspices of his boss, Michael Andrews, deputy assistant secretary of the army for research and technology, Macedonia had brought STRICOM to L.A. after he realized that the commercial sector, in particular the film, computer, and video-game industries, was outstripping the military in technological innovation. Where trickle-down from military research on main-frame computers once fueled progress in the field, civilian pro-grammers working on PCs could now design video games and virtual environments that put military simulations to shame. Macedonia had come to Hollywood to find the tools and skills for simulating and, if necessary, fighting the wars of the future. As the blood and iron of traditional war gave way to the bits and bytes of infowar, netwar, and cyberwar, he saw the ICT as a vehicle for integrating the simulation and entertainment indus-tries into the much-heralded "Revolution in Military Affairs." Having sold the ICT to the Pentagon, Hollywood, and now the university, he was presenting it for the first time to the public— with some anxiety.

Judging from the Q and A that followed the signing ceremony, he need not have worried. The closest thing to criticism arose from the recent shootings at Columbine High School, with several questions fixing on the theme of video-game violence. I broke ranks to ask whether there wasn't a danger of repeating what happened during the Second World War, when the pairing of Hollywood and the Pentagon produced films that mixed training documentaries and actual footage, blurring entertainment and propaganda? Would there be any ethical checks and balances to assure that military simulations would not become a tool for public dissimulation? That something like *Wag the Dog* won't be coming out of the ICT? President Sample hesitated, dead-panned a nervous look to the other side of the stage, and replied: "As Jack is coming up to respond to that." Earlier Sample had said that the ICT would develop "synthetic experiences so compelling that people will react as though they were real—a virtual reality of sensations and sights." He responded to my question by making a deft analogy to Plato's poor opinion of the poets, not actually using the word mimesis, but suggesting as much was going on at the ICT: by performing the classical function of poetry and theater—artistically and dramatically mimicking reality for a higher purpose—it could not help but arouse anxieties about whose version of reality was the true one.

Valenti took this as his cue. He had opened his earlier presentation by correcting a remark by L.A.'s deputy mayor: "Los Angeles is not the 'entertainment capital of the world' (pause). Washington, D.C., is the entertainment capital of the world (laughter)." He now politely but pugnaciously informed me of another of their similarities. "I would like to illuminate a central truth to the gentleman—everything leaks, in Hollywood *and* in Washington. There's no way you can keep a secret. You can't fool the people for very long, the truth will come out." He paused, then declared that I needed to correct my "Copernican complex." Executing his trademark overkill, he contrasted my view to the decision to drop the atomic bomb on the Japanese. Some might have seen that as a "heartless and terrible thing to do . . . but not the 150,000 young American boys whose lives would have been lost if we had invaded Japan. This is a lesson in Philosophy 101 that I am giving to you right now."

Although I came away with a different lesson from his playing of the Hiroshima card, I did take Valenti's point: what separates and elevates war above lesser ("Copernican") conceits is its intimate relationship to death. The dead body—on the battlefield, in the tomb of the unknown soldier, in the collective memory, even on the movie screen—is what gives war its special status, what trumps any lesser issues, such as those expressed in my question. This fact, the material facticity of the dead soldier, can be censored, hidden in a body bag, air-brushed away, but it provides, even in its erasure, the corporal gravitas of war.

But Valenti and his cohort at the ICT seemed unaware of their own potential role in the disappearance of the body, the aestheticizing of violence, the sanitization of war. Some history might prove more illuminating than Valenti's "Philosophy 101." The link between film and war goes back further than the Second World War, at least to the nineteenth century, when chemists experimenting with the same nitrocelluloids found in explosives created new emulsions that could fix images on film. Ever since, the military and the movie industry have been in a technological relay race for seeing and killing the enemy while securing and seducing the citizen. Strategy and commerce merged in their goals to shrink distances, increase accuracy, accelerate delivery.

The historical convergence of modes of representation and destruction has been vividly plotted by Paul Virilio. In *War and Cinema*, he tracks the dual development of weapons and cameras from the American Civil War to the First World War, revealing how the first hand-cranked machine gun and multichambered revolver inspired the "chrono-photographic rifle" and the moving picture camera.[15] In later works Virilio plots the modern necessities of war that gave rise to peacetime industries, from the development of radar (and television), to targeting systems (and mechanical computers), to encryption machines (and software codes). In these dual economies of sight and might, Virilio locates the very origins of modernity, a "logistics of perception" where images war with one another, becoming a substitute for reality itself.[16]

War has served as the aesthetic as well as the technological laboratory of modern films. Here again, the parallels with the interwar are striking. From Siegfried Kracauer to Friedrich Kittler, German social critics, especially sensitive to the political use of film, have noted how the earliest filmmakers, moving between the backlot and the battlefield, learned to give their films and propaganda a dose of verisimilitude by mixing the real and the fictional.[17] The practice dates back to the origins of filmmaking. Consider one "father" of modern cinema, D. W. Griffith. Already famous for his 1915 *Birth of a Nation*, a war-at-home film, he went to work for Lord Beaverbrook's War Office Cinematograph Committee in the First World War. His 1918 *Hearts of the World* spliced together a love story with war footage, including scenes of Griffith actually (as opposed to *Gump*-ly) shaking hands with British Prime Minister Lloyd George. His highly creative cameraman Billy Bitzer applied techniques mastered while filming the

Spanish-American War for the American Mutoscope Company, like attaching a camera to a moving train—and staging naval battles with toy boats in tubs of water.

Hollywood might have been the first but not the last cinema to rely on the storyline of war. War movies, especially post-Vietnam, have been as likely to challenge as to promote military values, often conveying in the same film the glory and honor as well as the agony and futility of war (think Tom Cruise in *Top Gun*—and *Born on the Fourth of July*). But from the earliest war movies a Hollywood template emerged which persists today. In war movies like Griffith's *Hearts of the World* (1918) or King Vidor's *The Big Parade* (1925), ordinary men leave the girl behind; undergo a trial by combat; overcome deep fears and insecurities; bond with fellow soldiers through acts of heroic, stoic, or sometimes just senseless self-sacrifice; wander in no-man's-land or some commensurable moral wasteland; seek and find private redemption: all of which provides a public catharsis. This soldier's story, recycled with great success through the genres of cowboy, cop, and cyborg, became the metaplot for Hollywood.

Gun and camera took on a single calibration with the mobilization of Hollywood in the Second World War. At the start of the war, military-preparedness documentaries were quickly reedited to produce quick-and-dirty propaganda movies like *To the Shores of Tripoli*. However, famous Hollywood directors soon joined the cause, contributing feature and training films like Howard Hawks's *Air Force* (1943), John Huston's *The Battle of San Pietro* (1945), and Frank Capra's series "Why We Fight." The war also proved to be something of a fillip to flagging careers, like that of Ronald Reagan, who starred in several army air force training and reenlistment films—and, based on his subsequent political career, suffered permanent damage to his reality principle for it. The War Department supplied manpower, equipment, and funding, and Hollywood provided actors, directors, and, for the most part, the talent. Between 1939 and 1945, close to 2,500 films were made.

If war is the mother of all things, Hollywood has become its most notorious offspring. After such extensive collaboration, the opening of the Institute for Creative Technologies might appear to be a minor case of incest, just further proof that L.A. has never had much of a purchase on reality, rather than a cause for alarm.

But there is a difference. By its very task and potential power to create totally immersive environments—where one can see, hear, perhaps even touch and emotionally interact with digitally created agents—the ICT is leading the way into a brave new world that threatens to breach the last fire walls between reality and virtuality. Set against the larger technostrategic scheme of things, ICT matters—very much. It could well be the first joint avant garde—or at least first since the futurists joined ranks with the Italian fascists—of both filmmaking and warmaking.

Never one to underestimate the reaction provoked by any reference to fascism, I wish to make clear that I am *not* citing the futurists and the fascists—as well as quoting Kracauer at the beginning of this chapter—to make the claim that Nuremberg and Philadelphia and Los Angeles are one and the same. Rather, it is an attempt to better understand virtuous war in all its contemporary trappings by going back to its historical beginnings, when technologies of representation first developed in the interwar displayed a remarkable capacity to upstage and in some cases displace democratic politics. In the rush to vilify, we might fail to understand how fascism is more than a historically fixed event. It is also a symptom of a dormant malaise that can be triggered by the failure of democracies to understand and harness the powers of new technologies.

In for a penny, in for a critical pounding, let's return to the 1934 Nuremberg Party Convention. Staged as much for the cameras of Leni Riefenstahl as for the party faithful (she had 30 cameras and a staff of 120 at her disposal), the convention featured a speech by Nazi Minister of Propaganda Joseph Goebbels, in which he endorsed a creative and popular propaganda:

> May the shining flame of our enthusiasm never be extinguished. This flame alone gives light and warmth to the creative art of modern political propaganda. Rising from the depths of the people, this art must always descend back to it and find its power there. Power based on guns may be a good thing; it is, however, better and more gratifying to win the heart of a people and to keep it.

Siegfried Kracauer, perhaps the most acute observer of the interwar alliance between film and politics, considered Goebbels's "genius" to be his ability to stage a popular enthusiasm, where "Reality was put to work faking itself, and exhausted minds were not even permitted to dream any longer."[18] This, says Kracauer, is why the newsreel figured so largely in the process:

> To keep the totalitarian system in power, they had to annex to it all real life. And since, in the medium of the film, the authentic representation of unstaged reality is reserved to newsreel shots, the Nazis not only could not afford to set them aside, but were forced to compose from them their fictitious war pictures.[19]

Walter Benjamin also warned of a new and incestuous relationship between mass politics and mass means of reproduction. In the final footnote to his essay "The Work of Art in the Age of Mechanical Reproduction," he focuses on how new technologies of representation and perception produce political effects:

> One technical feature is significant here, especially with regard to newsreels, the propagandist importance of which can hardly be overestimated. Mass reproduction is aided especially by the reproduction of masses. In big parades and monster rallies, in sports events, and in war, all of which nowadays are captured by camera and sound recording, the masses are brought face to face with themselves. This process, whose significance need not be stressed, is intimately connected with the development of the techniques of reproduction and photography. Mass movements are usually discerned more clearly by a camera than by the naked eye. A bird's-eye view best captures gatherings of hundreds of thousands. And even though such a view may be as accessible to the human eye as it is to the camera, the image received by the eye cannot be enlarged the way a negative is enlarged. This means that mass movements, including war, constitute a form of human behavior which particularly favors mechanical equipment.[20]

If this rings familiar, think back to Vice Admiral Cebrowski's interview comment, on why the American public like the Super Bowl and U.S. warfighting doctrine so much (see Chapter 6), and consider present-day methods of technically updating bread and circuses:

> The Colosseum as recreated for Ridley Scott's *Gladiator*—a sword-and-sandal epic of the kind they didn't make anymore until he did—appears to be three massive stories high, but only the first story actually existed. . . . The rest was painstakingly added with computer-generated effects, one byte at a time. The gladiator sequences, which are at the heart of Mr. Scott's film, were shot to mimic the way modern-day sporting events are shown on television . . . to subliminally make them more real to today's audiences. There is, for example, the "blimp shot," a favorite at the Super Bowl, in which the camera seems to float over the top of the massive Colosseum.[21]

If this all seems to be too much of a historical reach, consider a more recent event, Super Bowl XXXII, where, after the singing of the national anthem, a global audience of 800 million viewers was treated to a low-level flyover of Tampa's Qualcomm Stadium by a B-2A Spirit stealth bomber, prompting one of the announcers to remark that he was sure glad it missed the Budweiser blimp. The interwar was not, is not, predestined: It is, among other things, a failure of democratic politics to understand the mimetic appeal of primal, emotive sources of identity in times of great uncertainty.

In a remarkable 1935 essay for *Harper's* Magazine, "The Revival of Feudalism," political theorist and theologian Reinhold Niebuhr interpreted the rise of Hitler as a reaction to a misguided effort by liberalism to suppress "the organic character of society" that is expressed, sometimes excessively, in displays of tradition, community, and ethnic loyalty. "Fascism," says Niebuhr, "is this outraged truth avenging itself." He concludes that Nazism "could not have achieved such monstrous proportions if our culture had not foolishly dreamed and hoped for the development of 'universal' men, who were bereft of all loyalties to family, race, and nation."[22]

In a strange and disturbing way, Niebuhr's theoretical speculations from the interwar find an echo in a recent study undertaken by the Triangle Institute for Security Studies in North Carolina.[23] The first part of their extensive project involved a survey of military and civilian leaders, to determine whether there "is a gap between civilian society and the military, and if so whether differing values, opinions, perspectives, and experience, harm military effectiveness and civil-military cooperation." The survey is a complex document, and cannot be reduced to a sound bite. But three conclusions, which underpin the basic assumptions of virtuous war, leap from the page: 1) elite military officers today "express great pessimism about the moral health of civilian society and strongly believe that the military could help society become more moral and that civilian society would be better off if it adopted more of the military's values and behaviors"; 2) "Contrary to a traditional understanding of civilian control, elite military officers believe that it is their role to insist and advocate rather than merely advise on key elements of decisions concerning the use of force, for instance: "setting rules of engagement" (83 percent), developing an "exit strategy" (80 percent), and "deciding what kinds of military units (air versus naval, heavy versus light) will be used to accomplish all tasks" (89 percent); and 3) "On non-traditional missions, elite military officers are twice to four-times as casualty averse as American civilians (mass or elite). Casualty aversion may be more a function of a zero-defect mentality among senior officers, in which casualties are viewed as indications the mission will be perceived to be a failure."[24] During the interwar, at the conventions, in the movies, and yes, even at the Super Bowl, this gap between military virtues and civilian values was on spectacular display, representing a democratic void that all kinds of virtuous solutions appeared ready to fill. Was the Institute for Creative Technology leading the way?

At the closed luncheon that followed the ICT press conference, the featured speaker, writer and director John Milius (*Apocalypse Now, Red Dawn*), told war stories to an audience dining on chicken breasts and "whipped goat cheese yukons." He spoke, half-jokingly, of how he wanted to put an end to the alienation between the military and the movie industry by setting up a production team for the army that would make *Wag the Dog* look tame. Things got even stranger when I left the lunch. Students in prep-school outfits lounged in front of the scenically old (for California) administration building. A closer look revealed cameras, lights, and a sign: "Notice—Filming Today. Columbia

Tristar Television will be filming at USC today. By entering this location, you hereby irrevocably consent to and authorize Columbia Tristar Television to photograph you and/or make sound recordings of you and to use same worldwide, for any purpose whatsoever in perpetuity."

As I waited for the setup of the next shot, I leafed through the press releases from the USC News Service. One virtuous statement stood out from all the rest: "Maintaining a strong military is, and has been, national policy since the birth of our nation. It is entirely appropriate that USC do all that it can to assist the U.S. Army in fulfilling its mission, which is the defense of our nation and its citizens."[25] It sent me back once again to general-turned-president Eisenhower's neglected 1961 farewell address, when he warned of the "danger that public policy could itself become the captive of a scientific-technological elite." What would he have made of this addition of universities, new media, and entertainment industries to his "military-industrial complex"? Of new technologies of simulation being built at universities to create a high fidelity between the representation and the reality of war? Of the human mimetic faculty for entertainment and gaming joining forces with new cyborg programs for killing and warring? He'd probably not have let it get in the way of his golf game. But by the end of the day, I was left wondering, *pace* Eisenhower, if the military-industrial-media-entertainment network had just gone online.

That night, in pursuit of an insider's perspective, I interviewed Mike Macedonia. I brought several German beers with me to his room at the Beverly Hilton—not exactly a hardship billet—because I knew he had spent a considerable chunk of his time in the army with the mechanized infantry in Germany. Macedonia wore the oversized ring of West Point, from which he had graduated in 1979 as a political science major with a concentration in electrical engineering. He'd gone through infantry school, airborne rangers, and training at Fort Leavenworth. He was eight years in before he saw the electronic fonts on the wall.

JD: How did you first get interested in computers and simulations? Was it in the genes? The environment?

MM: I was always interested because my dad was [Ray

Macedonia, one of the first to introduce computer war games to the Pentagon] but it really wasn't until 1986, when a colonel from DARPA showed up at our base in Germany, and said he was going to give us a computer to use for battlefield operations—for all the message traffic, tactical maneuvers, the complete battlefield situation, in real time. And we said, oh really? And he said, yeah really. Needless to say, it never happened.

JD: AI before its time.

MM: Way before its time. But we started experimenting with computerized war games on these big green boxes—we're talking four hundred pounds, with archaic displays, designed to survive nuclear blast ten feet under water. So you can imagine these things weren't too portable on the battlefield. But it gave us a taste of things to come. You have to remember, when I first got to Germany in 1985, we didn't even have crypto, and we were only thirty miles from East Germany, so they could hear everything we were saying on the radio during these war games—

JD: Did you hear about "Able Archer" around that time? The NATO war game that the KGB thought was the real thing? They sent flash messages to Moscow and started burning documents in their Western embassies.[26]

MM: I can believe it. Anyway, the army decided I should go back to school, to do information science at the University of Pittsburgh. While I'm there I'm hearing all about this thing called ARPANET, and I'd seen in Germany how data networks were the biggest issue. This was right around the time of the first internet worm by Morris. So I learned everything I could about networks, starting with telephones. From there I went to the Joint Electronic Warfare Center in San Antonio, became a MIS (Manager of Information Systems), bought the first Silicon Graphics, thirty of them, to do information warfare simulations. We took them operational to support counternarcotics in Panama, mainly to transmit and collate data from aerostat radar balloons on the borders.

JD: What was your job during the Gulf War?

MM: The day Saddam Hussein invaded Kuwait I was underneath a panel of a Sun computer in the Pentagon war room, trying to install cables for the drug war. Then they flew me down to CentCom [Central Command] in Tampa. Everybody was in shell shock—they'd just come off a command-post exercise, "Internal Look," which simulated an Iraqi invasion of Kuwait, and suddenly they were faced with the real thing.

JD: I read about that in Schwarzkopf's memoirs, where he talks about how he had to rubber-stamp incoming communications—

MM: "Not exercise," that's right. I came into CentCom and what do they have on the boards? Exercise maps. What are they using as orders? Basically stuff taken right from the exercise and sent out to the field. But the computers weren't up to it. The Unix was falling apart, these old Honeywell computers were overloaded, the message queue was three days old, full of backed-up "flash" messages. One scene I'll never forget was watching Schwarzkopf in the CentCom war room, radio in one hand, talking to the captain on the bridge of a navy ship trailing an Iraqi tanker, phone in the other, talking to Powell—who's talking to Bush—and they're all trying to decide whether to blow it out of the water or not.

JD: Bob Woodward in *The Commanders* talks about Schwarzkopf showing up at the White House with all his spreadsheets from "Internal Look," listing all the assets that were needed, and that his briefing tipped the balance for intervention.

MM: That sounds right. Central Command brought all the gaming computers and everything else with them to Saudi Arabia, in effect constructed a private virtual land between the United States and Saudi Arabia. You couldn't tell on your screens whether the computers were operating in Tampa or the Saudi Ministry of Defense. This is a big transition, we had never done anything like this in war before.

JD: The irony is, according to ABC News, that Hussein used a war game bought from a U.S. firm, BDM I think, for the invasion of Kuwait, something that was customized from the Iraq-Iran war.

MM: I've never heard that before. Really?

JD: Yeah, but I can't get anybody to go on record. Schwarz-kopf made a big thing out of the fact that he could game battles throughout the war on his portable computer—

MM: Exactly, in fact, all the CINC's had war-gaming cells, something my dad started. War starts, and say you need the Nineteenth Dog Patrol from someplace in Mississippi. Just so happens you have this big spreadsheet that you did for the exercises already loaded in the computer, so you can start transmitting orders. I carried during the whole Gulf War a Dell portable and crypto-phone, and we could plug in anywhere, and see what was going on.

JD: What happened after Desert Storm?

MM: I flew back the day the war ended, a bizarre set of circumstances that I will only reveal in my memoir. I'll never forget one scene. They put me in a plane, we stop at the air base in Sicily, planes from every nationality, and the bar looks like it's right out of *Star Wars*—all these pilots from every coalition country, and what are they all doing? Watching the war end on CNN. The war left us with this feeling, exhilarated, but the stakes had been impossibly raised. How could we possibly replicate this, to win with so few casualties?

JD: To bring us up to date, before our tape and beer run out, where does the ICT fit in this?

MM: Our job is to imagine the worst, the burden we have to bear, the curse of the paranoid. If you're not paranoid, you're doing a disservice to the people we're going to have to send to war. They pay us to be that way. We're going to need to take more technological risks, not risks with people. If we don't want to bring back body bags, we need to think outside the box, to be unconventional. Everyone thinks it's so easy, but fate will catch up to us. Forty-five million dollars is cheap compared to the potential costs in lives. It might not work; but if we don't take risks like this, we will pay for it later. This is a great experiment. We're going to do strange and wonderful things.

At this point, Macedonia reaches over to the coffee table to get one of his favorite quotes, "from Trotsky," he says. It turns out to be from Leo Tolstoy, writing in 1910 on the significance of the moving picture camera: "This little clinking contraption with the revolving handle will make a revolution in our life, in the life of writers. It is a direct attack on the old methods of literary art. This swift change of scene, the blending of emotion and experience, is much better than the heavy long-drawn-out kind of writing to which we are accustomed. It is closer to life." The rest of the interview, probably suffering from going a beer too far, rambled through mutual appreciations of *The Matrix*, the yin-yang of technology, and the machiavellism of the university. The tape runs out just as he declares himself "a technological determinist who can only be optimistic because I have children."

A year after the interview, I was still wondering if the ICT, like other elements of virtuous war, was more deus ex machina than war machine. My effort to find out just what was in the works at ICT produced more promissory notes than any actual project developments: contra Valenti, if not outright secrecy, "I'd-rather-not-say-at-the-moment" was the most common response to my queries. The reasons given for not going on record were ongoing negotiations and imminent signings, with one of the "best-known directors in Hollywood" and some of the "best computer graphics guys on the planet." But the only names dropped were Randal Klieser (director of *Blue Lagoon* and *Honey I Blew Up the Kids*) and 3D Realms, makers of the video game *Duke Nukem* (motto: "The only good alien bastard is a dead alien bastard").

One person who had more to say was Mike Zyda, chair of Modeling, Virtual Environments & Simulation at the Naval Post-graduate School, chair of the original 1997 National Research Council report that gave cause and code for the establishment of the ICT,[27] and, not coincidentally, chair of Michael Macedonia's 1995 Ph.D. dissertation in Computer Science. He originally envisioned the Institute as a place that would act as coordinator and broker for the most imaginative and technically advanced modelers and simulators. ICT shouldn't be chasing Hollywood: it should target off-the-shelf video-games technology that is leaving computer-graphic industries like Silicon Graphics in the dust. "The Defense Department has spent millions," says Zyda, "and it still can't match SimCity." Commercial video games could be redesigned to test the intellectual aptitude and psychological attitudes of potential recruits. Spin-off technology would be used to help kids at risk to explore potential career paths.

Richard Lindheim, who was eventually appointed director of ICT, has a different vision. After a long career at NBC, Lindheim went on to become executive vice president of the Paramount Television Group, producing *The Equalizer* and taking charge of the later Star Trek series, *The Next Generation, Deep Space Nine*, and *Voyager*. I caught up with him at STRICOM where he was preparing for a series of Washington briefings. His previous employment probably best explains why the Holodeck kept popping up in our conversation (as well as how Herbert Zimmerman, the art director of *Star Trek*, was procured to design the ICT's office space). "The ICT is on a quest to envision and prepare for the future," and, says Lindheim, "Our Holy Grail is the Holodeck." Lindheim invoked writers like Jules Verne, who invented the idea of the modern submarine and inspired scientists to turn unreality into reality; *Voyager* could do the same for ICT. By the end of our conversation, I realized the Holodeck was not just a metaphor: it was the endgame for ICT.

The Holodeck and the Holy Grail notwithstanding, the Institute for Creative Technology is unlikely to save (or destroy) the world. It is not yet evident that it can run a project, a battlefield simulation, let alone an intergalactic war. However, cutting edge or opening wedge, the Institute for Creative Technology does look to be Hollywood's—and the Pentagon's—premier laboratory for virtuous war. Will this new alchemy of brass, celluloid, and silicon produce a kinder, gentler, sexier cyborg, like *Voyager*'s Seven of Nine? Or will the simulations of Creative Technology turn on their creators, like Frankenstein's monster? Either way, the ICT warrants public scrutiny.[28]

One last coda: In the lead-up to the Democratic convention, and then at the hearings in Washington on Hollywood violence, I become convinced that Jack Valenti, as he seemed to appear on every news show, live and simultaneously, had been cloned. His sound bite mantra evoked the power of the MIME-NET: "Glamour and politics, it's a marriage made in heaven and let no man tear it asunder."

8   Kosovo and the virtuous thereafter

> And even when one has all the virtues, there is still one to remember: to send even these virtues to sleep at the proper time.
> (Friedrich Nietzsche, "Of the Chairs of Virtue,"
> *Thus Spake Zarathustra*)

Security was tight at the main gate of the U.S. Army Southern European Task Force headquarters in Vicenza, Italy. SETAF is the only base in Europe tasked to provide rapid deployment airborne and assault forces to hot spots from southern Africa to the northern reaches of Norway. Capable of "forced entry" within seventy-two hours, SETAF has been the leading edge of the ever-increasing "Operations Other than War" (OOTW). In August 1994, its airborne troops deployed to Rwanda on Operation Support Hope; in December 1995, SETAF was the lead element of the peace implementation forces into Bosnia-Herzegovina; in April 1996, a company from SETAF went to Monrovia, Liberia, with special operations forces to facilitate noncombatant evacuation operations; in November 1996, it was back in Africa, to lead Joint Task Force Guardian Assistance for Rwandan refugees in Zaire; in March 1997, it again led a Joint Task Force in the Congo as part of Operation Guardian Retrieval for potential evacuation of Zaire. And from March to July 1999, SETAF was the major staging area for Task Force Hawk during Operation Allied Force in Kosovo.

For these reasons I had come to Vicenza two weeks after the Kosovo air campaign ended. The other two reasons were close by,

General Wesley Clark.

General Clark's retirement review.

the Aviano Air Base, 100 kilometers to the north and launch point for most of the combat missions, and, just up the road, the lesser known command and control hub of the conflict, the Combined Air Operations Center (CAOC). SETAF, the largest base in Italy, had taken the brunt of regular anti-NATO demonstrations—largely unreported by the American press—culminating in a big one that drew several thousand people and ended with eggs and bottles thrown as well as a bunch of cars trashed. After much checking of car, faxes, and passport, the guards directed me to the base hotel, the Ederle Inn.

Like most of the base, with its Burger King, bowling alley, and movie theater, the Ederle could have passed for anywhere in America—including the two cases of empty beer bottles and the detritus of junk food that somebody had left behind in my room. However, judging from the fine selection of German beers in the fridge (my lucky day), I'd say the previous occupants had been officers in transit, probably from the First Armored Division in Bad Kreuznach or First Infantry in Wuerzburg, redeployed sooner than they expected. They'd also left an interesting document on the nightstand, a small government-issue pamphlet, titled "Individual Protective Measures for Personal Security." The Foreword contained a frank appraisal of some unfriendly global attitudes: "Department of Army personnel and their families are the symbols of the power and prestige of America. Americans are particularly vulnerable to terrorist attack. We are stationed on seven continents; we are generally highly visible; and our work is deeply despised by militants and extremists the world over." The advice on how "To Combat Terrorism" was broken down into four sections: "Keep a Low Profile"; "Be Unpredictable"; "Be Very Alert"; and "Be Suspicious."[1] In the course of the three days I spent at Vicenza, it seemed like just about everyone I met, talked to, interviewed, had taken this pamphlet to heart.

It probably didn't help matters that the base had been on full alert throughout the Kosovo campaign, and that my visit coincided with their first real break in months, the Fourth of July weekend. Understandably, most of the personnel preferred to spend their time at the barbecue and country western concert than with some part-time journalist. My public affairs handler was getting a kick out of telling people how he had thought I was from *Weird* magazine, supposedly because of a phone message written by some dyslexic secretary. I tried to roll with the joke, admitting that ever since Condé Nast bought *Wired* it was getting harder to tell them apart—which got me a response of "Connie who?"

It soon became clear that I wasn't getting much out of the visit. Kosovo was just too fresh. Nobody wanted to get into the air power versus ground troops debate, let alone the real versus virtuous war question. The NATO air survey was not yet completed, and there were conflicting reports about the actual bomb damage. The few people who weren't hanging out at the Fourth of July festivities were gearing up for another "Partnership for Peace" war game, this one in the Ukraine. The mood among the gamers was that Russia had thrown down the gauntlet: first, two weeks ago by "taking" Pristina airport without the prior consent of NATO; and now this week, by staging "West '99" in the Baltic region and North Atlantic, the largest war game on air, sea, and land since the end of the Cold War. The day I arrived at the base, the *International Herald Tribune* carried a scare headline: Russian Jets Flew Within U.S. Range in Exercise. In fact, the two TU-95 Bear strategic bombers only got as close as Iceland before being intercepted by U.S. F-15 fighters.[2] In response, Russian officials declared in one breath that NATO was, of course, not the intended enemy of the exercise; and in the other, that Kosovo had put to rest the idea that NATO was a defensive alliance.

I gave up early on the official interviews, and went to see what I could get out of the growing crowd at the country western concert, featuring the long-running Bellamy Brothers. Young local Italians in cowboy boots and hats mingled with tattooed, flat-topped soldiers. Two songs got the crowd whooping and hollering: "My Wife Left Me for My Girlfriend" and "Old Hippie." After the show I talked to a couple of roadies; from here the "Bro's" were going on to play for the troops in Tusla and Sarajevo. I bought an "Old Hippie" bandana for some friends back home and headed back to the Inn. The house selection of videotapes for the VCR was limited, but I found a beat-up copy of *The Russians Are Coming, The Russians Are Coming*, which I enjoyed much more than my first viewing, which I think was as a kid from the back of a Country Squire station wagon at a local drive-in. Nostalgia, always a cheap and powerful emotion, seems to visit more often when I am overseas. After that I watched Italy play Yugoslavia for the European basketball championship in a very close, very physical game, with an announcer who called it like a soccer match and unshaven players who all looked like Vlade Divac, (formerly) of the Los Angeles Lakers—then I realized one of them *was* Vlade Divac.

The next day got off to a bad start. My intention had been to see up close how NATO executed a virtuous war; as soon as the air campaign started I had been negotiating by fax, e-mail, and telephone to visit its epicenter, the Fifth Allied Tactical Air Force's Combined Air Operations Center. CAOC (pronounced kay-auk) was established in 1993 to plan and direct all NATO air operations in the Balkans. Over 400 personnel from fourteen coalition countries reported directly to Lt. General Michael Short, commander of Allied Air Forces Southern Europe, in Naples, Italy, who, in turn, answered to General Wesley Clark, the Supreme Allied Commander in Europe, in Mons, Belgium. Before the Kosovo campaign, CAOC's primary duties were to protect the Stabilization Forces (SFOR) in Bosnia as well as provide intelligence, surveillance and reconnaissance, treaty compliance with the 1995 Dayton Peace Accords, and long-range planning for NATO force requirements. All that changed on March 24, 1999.

All through 1997 and 1998, the tensions and violence between Serbian security forces and the Kosovars had been escalating. In September 1998, the UN Security Council adopted Resolution 1199, which demanded an end to all hostilities and the establishment of a cease-fire and cooperation with war crimes investigations. From that moment on, the combined strategies of virtuous war went into action: diplomatic negotiations, the threat of limited force, a public display of military exercises, intermittent signaling through the media, and the selective use of international normative prescriptions. The chess moves of Kosovo form the first leaves of the virtuous war playbook: on October 13, the North Atlantic Council, NATO's highest decision-making body, authorizes "Operation Deliberate Force" and gives the activation order for "limited air strikes" in ninety-six hours; October 14, NATO's Standing Naval Force Mediterranean heads for the Adriatic; after nine days of negotiation, Ambassador Holbrooke gets an agreement from President Milosevic to comply with UNSCR 1199 and to allow air verification missions in Kosovo; on January 20, with no evidence of withdrawal by Serbian military and security forces, NATO announces an increase in military readiness that would make it possible to strike in forty-eight hours; on February 19, as the Contact Group negotiates with the Serbs, NATO reaffirms that if no agreement is reached it will undertake whatever measures necessary to avert a humanitarian disaster; on March 15 the Serbian withdrawal deadline passes; the Rambouillet negotiations end with no agreement after the Yugoslav delegation refuse to sign a proposed peace plan that violates their sovereign rights; on March 24, NATO air operations are initiated in the Federal Republic of Yugoslavia under the code name "Operation Allied Force"; on June 9, NATO signs an agreement with the Yugoslav military authorities for their withdrawal from Kosovo; June 10, air operations end. After seventy-eight days of intensive bombing and cruise missile attacks (by comparison Desert Storm's lasted forty-three days), the combined allied forces of thirteen NATO countries suffered zero casualties, aside from accidental injuries. The number of Yugoslavian deaths is still moot.

Others have well documented the dance of diplomacy and force in Kosovo.[3] To understand the strategy and beliefs behind it, one must take a closer look at the two partners who first worked out the steps of virtuous war at the Dayton Peace negotiations: Ambassador Richard Holbrooke and General Welsey Clark. By their will and capability to put violence in the service of virtue, both men sanctified the conversion of coercive diplomacy into virtuous war.

Before Holbrooke and Clark took over, the dogs of war littered the Balkan conflict. "We don't have a dog in this fight," declared Secretary of State James Baker as the former Yugoslavia was engulfed by war in the summer of 1992. Three years and close to 300,000 deaths later—just a few days before his tragic death on Mount Igman—Robert Frasure, a deputy assistant secretary of state, passed a note to Richard Holbrooke during a critical negotiation with Croatian president Tudjman: "We 'hired' these guys to be our junkyard dogs because we were desperate—this is no time to get squeamish." In the pivotal month of August 1995, Secretary of Defense William Perry, trying to win over a reluctant congressional committee for the deployment of NATO forces in Bosnia, offered a guarantee that the American troops would be "the biggest and the toughest and the meanest dog in town." Richard Holbrooke took it upon himself to charm as well as to collar the curs of the Balkan conflict. With his preference for diplomacy backed by force, Holbrooke practiced power politics while preaching moral responsibility. He was, par excellence, a virtuous diplomat.

Holbrooke's apprenticeship in virtuous diplomacy began early, and draws from the experiences of the interwar and Vietnam. He first visited Sarajevo as a nineteen-year-old hitchhiking across Europe. He has remarked on the impression left when he came across the cement footsteps in the sidewalk that mark the spot where Gavrilo Princip stood when he assassinated Archduke Franz Ferdinand. It's clear that the interwar informs much of his historical reasoning. In his book, *To End a War*, he liberally quotes from two interwar British writers, the poet W. H. Auden and the diplomatist-turned-historian Harold Nicolson, to drive the point home: great power entails great responsibility. In the struggle against fascism in Spain, Britain and France sat on the sidelines, while "the poets," wrote Auden, "exploded like bombs." It wasn't enough then, and it would not be enough against the fascist thugs of Bosnia. America could not afford a righteous isolation from Bosnia. From day one of his involvement, Holbrooke, without irony or a trace of poetic license, advocated a program of "bombing for peace."

Holbrooke proved to be adept at negotiations not only with the belligerents, but with bureaucrats from the United Nations, the European Union, Congress, and the Pentagon, nearly all of whom displayed a great reluctance to use bombs—dumb, smart, or poetic—against the Serbs. However, Holbrooke's relationship with the military over Bosnia was not always a happy one. He was particularly critical of euphemisms such as "mission creep," "body bags," and "exit strategy." He thought the purpose of such rhetoric was to evoke the memory of Vietnam and preempt any consideration of troop deployments. Holbrooke would have none of it. As a State Department aide in Saigon and the Mekong Delta in 1962 (where paths—some say swords—first crossed with former national security adviser Anthony Lake), and as a junior member of the negotiating team at the Paris peace talks in 1968, Holbrooke's understanding of the Vietnam War was personal— and he was loathe to make it a political straitjacket for American foreign policy. There would be no talk on his watch of a "Balkan Vietnam."

However, Holbrooke was slow to comprehend how the military, whose lives and reputations were on the line in Bosnia, managed to take such different messages away from Vietnam. For much of the higher ranks, the most notable lessons—reinforced by the success in the Gulf War and the disaster of Somalia—were to use overwhelming force, to get in and get out quickly, and to have full public support. This came to be called the "Powell Doctrine," after National Security Advisor and then Chairman of the Joint Chiefs of Staff Colin Powell (who as Secretary of State in the Bush administration might very well seek to amend it). For the military planners, including Powell, Bosnia just did not present such a scenario.

From the outset of his involvement, Holbrooke insisted that the Serbs were bullies and thugs who would back down when confronted by the right mix of force and diplomacy. Ironically, it was a simulation, a worst-case scenario, that provided him with the bureaucratic leverage to shift administration policy. In June 1995, Holbrooke discovered a little-known, highly classified Pentagon document known as "OpPlan 40-104," which called for the immediate deployment of 20,000 American troops should the UN need to withdraw from Bosnia. Approved by the NATO Council the plan was, in effect, a standing operational order. Yet according to Holbrooke, neither Secretary of State Warren Christopher nor President Clinton had been briefed on OpPlan 40-104. It had all the ingredients of a military and political disaster: using American troops to cover a UN retreat at a time when most Republican congressmen were showing a distinct preference for bashing rather than saving UN assets.

Timing is everything in diplomacy, and Holbrooke chose well his moment to inform the president of the planning document. At a White House dinner for French president Jacques Chirac, Holbrooke approached Clinton after his last dance with the First Lady. Giving his regrets to have to ruin a wonderful evening, he told the president of the NATO plans that committed the United States to send troops to Bosnia if the UN decided to withdraw. After Christopher confirmed the significance of the plan, the president gave Holbrooke the green light to ratchet up the negotiations.

Over the next two months, Holbrooke combined diplomacy with coercion, using NATO air strikes and troops not to cover a retreat, but, as the title of his memoir states, "to end a war." After Serbian forces, with the acquiescence of UN peacekeepers, massacred thousands of Muslim Bosnians at Srebrenica in July, public support began to shift towards military intervention. In early August, the Croatians launched a successful offensive against the Krajina Serbs and altered the balance of power on the ground.

Holbrooke's memoir version of the twenty-one-day negotiations in Dayton is a strangely comic denouement after his harrowing accounts of the funerals for his State Department comrades (killed in a tragic road accident), the "bombs for peace" of Operation Deliberate Force, and the intense drama of arranging a cease-fire.[4] Sequestered at the Wright-Patterson Air Force Base, far from the prying media and the distractions of Washington, all the negotiating parties became slightly squirrelly. The "special weirdness" of Dayton, Holbrooke writes, included Slobodan Milosevic singing along to "Boogie Woogie Bugle Boy" with a black Andrew Sisters act; unnamed members of the delegation sneaking into the map room to use a computer-generated, three-dimensional map of Bosnia as a video game (the PowerScene program that helped convince Milosevic to accept a wider Gorazde corridor)[5]; and, watching the giant television screens of the base's sports bar, the Croats cheering Toni Kukoc of the Chicago Bulls one night, while the Serbs rooted for Vlade Divac of the Los Angeles Lakers the next. It might have been, as Holbrooke claimed, "a highwire act without the net," but at times it sounded more like a sitcom without a script. Holbrooke's style of choice for virtuous diplomacy was always more jazz improv than classical waltz.

Was Dayton a precursor of the virtuous war to come? Kradzic and Mladic, two of the worst ethnic cleansers, remained on the loose, in spite of the State Department's wanted posters. And excluding the Kosovars from Dayton came back to haunt Holbrooke. Second time around, Milosevic did not take the bluff, and it would take eleven weeks of "bombing for peace" and the threat of a ground war before the Serbian security forces would leave Kosovo. However, Holbrooke did find a kindred spirit in his military liaison at Dayton: General Wesley Clark, who in Kosovo would act on the hard lessons of Bosnia.

I had come to Vicenza to see the cyborg fist in the glove, the new force behind the diplomacy, which meant going the next day to the headquarters of the Combined Air Operations Center. CAOC was the electronic hub of the Kosovo air campaign, where all the electronic data from EC-130 (airborne command, control, and communications) and JSTARS (Joint Surveillance Target Attack Radar System) planes, satellites, and ground-spotters provided the fullest picture for the command and control of the air operation. CAOC is located on the outskirts of Vicenza at a small Italian military airport, Tomaso Dal Molin. In a warren of country roads surrounded by high hedges, I got very lost trying to find it. No one, even people living less than a kilometer from it, seemed to be aware of its existence. Or perhaps they took me as one of those Serbian spies who supposedly compromised NATO air operations during the campaign. After passing the same shrine to some fallen saint for the third time, I spotted an array of antennae up on a hillside; from there I could see the concertina wire surrounding the base. When I got to the gate, my American liaison officer was nowhere to be found. Probably he, like every other American serviceman, had left for the SETAF Fourth of July celebrations. At the small gatehouse, I met a less-than-cooperative Italian officer. After staring for a very long time at a fax that must have come from SETAF, he asked, "What is a weird magazine?" I never made it past the main gate.

Once I got back to the U.S., I decided that to get to the bottom of Kosovo, I needed to go to the top. If there is one man who could understand it and its significance for the future of warfare, it had to be General Wesley K. Clark, the man who ran the show. Born in Little Rock, Arkansas, first in his class at West Point, a Rhodes Scholar, he comes with an impressive résumé. Clark came out of Armor: he commanded a mechanized infantry company in Vietnam, commanded and completely revamped the National Training Center at Fort Irwin, and led the First Cavalry Division at Fort Hood, Texas. Before he became the Supreme Allied Commander Europe in July 1997, he was commander in chief of the Southern Command in Panama.

Clark clearly has no trouble leading, which is perhaps why he ran into trouble during the Kosovo campaign. The irony lacks much sweetness: after leading NATO forces to victory, the only blood spilled on the allied side was his. He was relieved of this command at NATO months before scheduled, so that his replacement, Air Force General Joseph Ralston, could step in and avoid his own retirement, as dictated by law if he did not have a new command by April. That's the official story. All kinds of other ones were circulating: that Clark, the loner warrior, was no match for Ralston, the consummate insider; that Clark's insistent push for more aggressive bombing and the use of ground troops rubbed too many people the wrong way; that Clark's last "shot from the hip," trying to send NATO troops to intercept the Russian sprint to Pristina airport, had terribly ricocheted. Not a few NATO allies viewed the replacement of Clark by an air force general, only the second to hold the position, as further proof of U.S. reluctance to risk American troops in combat. In private, Clark let it be known that he thought the administration had become too risk-averse. In public, Clark remained stoically tight-lipped, determined, it seemed, to go out the good soldier and to save the best for his memoirs. To get a better sense of the man and the circumstances under which a virtuous war was waged, I requested an interview. I timed it to coincide with his retirement ceremony, hoping that I might catch him in a more open and reflective mood. I met with him in the SACEUR office at the Pentagon, on June 22, 2000.

JD: What question do you get asked the most?
WC: Everyone's asking me what I think about what happened to me—that's not the question. That's the most *commonly* asked question, and I always say I won't answer it. I'm going to stick with that policy.
JD: OK. What's the next question?
WC: The next question is what do you think about being controlled by politicians? I always answer the same way: *of course* we're controlled by politicians. Who else would you want to be controlled by? You certainly don't give responsibility of war and peace to the military.
JD: How would you describe civilian-military relations at the moment?
WC: Well, as far as I was concerned, on Kosovo, they were good. I wouldn't want to characterize them on a whole range of issues.

JD: Would you answer that question any differently the day after tomorrow?

WC: No, I don't think so. [long pause]

JD: OK, let's get the last question over with: What are you going to do after this?

WC: I'm going to do a lot of writing, get into the business community. Somewhere down the line I'd like to have another opportunity at public service.

Clark was clearly not about to go into any political thickets. I thought he might be more forthcoming about the distant rather than recent past, so I asked what if any epiphany he ever had as a soldier. It turned out there was more than one, and they all seemed to involve perseverance, ingenuity, and some kind of breakthrough in the face of a collective, usually bureaucratic, resistance. The first came when he was a major, during a war game in Germany in 1977. In an early application of electronic disinformation, he figured out a way to jam the radios and deceive the opposing forces (not yet called that in Hohenfels), and execute an unorthodox yet successful attack. The higher-ups accused him of cheating—until he repeated the success. When I asked what lessons he had taken from his command at the National Training Center, it was short and simple—you "plan-backwards": work back from your objective, use all your available combat force multipliers, take risks, and make bold decisions—that's what he did. He pushed hard for instrumented after-action reviews (AAR), but more importantly, expanded the use of AARs all the way down to the platoon level. They have since become a model of learning in the armed forces: they were certainly some of the most impressive exercises in pedagogy I had ever witnessed. When I asked him about the impact of digitization at NTC, he said it didn't go far enough: you needed to get the information to "the point of the spear." The topic got him animated; he said now he was going to give away his best stuff. I promised him copyright.

WC: What you needed was integration, of the digitized images from the unmanned aerial vehicle flying overhead, your map coordinates, and the geolocations of the enemy from the GPS, and to project it all on the thermal viewer, to use it as a computer, so the driver and the gunner know when they get to the top of that hill, they'll know that the son-of-a-bitch is going to be right there. Not even the M1A2 does that. Instead, what you got at NTC was precision at the wrong level.

JD: You'll have to explain that.

WC: The higher the rank, the less you need to know. If you're a general, you only have to be in the right country; if you're a colonel, you have to be in the right valley; if you're a tank commander you have to know *precisely* what's over the hill; if you're a soldier, you have to know *exactly* what's on the other side of that building. It's turned upside down. The air force command, the national command authority believe *they* must have the precise information, and then it somehow trickles down to the pilots. But it's all a misperception. If you want the machine to work right, you should just be able to wave your hand from back here, and the people from the bottom have all the necessary information to get it done.

JD: Doesn't that kind of network technology lend itself to that kind of micromanagement from the top down?

WC: Well, no, it really doesn't, it lends itself to micromanagement *delusion*. During the Kosovo air campaign there was never any control on what Serb targets we were hitting. Of *all* the targets, all of the discussions were about *fixed* targets. Early in the war I exempted all mobile targets, by pleading the case that we could not go back to Washington to hit mobile forces, like tanks and ground forces. None of that was micromanaged, none of it.

JD: Would you have liked to have more of a say about the targeting?

WC: It was OK. It wasn't practical. But what it leads to is political leaders having to take responsibility for their decisions, and that's real important.

JD: Was Kosovo a war?

WC: No. It's coercive diplomacy. But I call it a war because the American public doesn't understand it.

JD: Would it have been a war if there had been ground troops?

WC: Well, we had a basic strategy: discuss an air threat, make an air threat, use an air threat; discuss a ground threat, make a ground threat, then invade. Each one built up to a greater coercive pressure.

JD: But isn't it true that the very act of making contingency plans produces a kind of coercion? Isn't this why you were prevented from planning a ground attack?

WC: We already had ground force plans. We were doing ground contingency plans in the summer of '98. Milosevic doesn't care about signaling; he looks at what's on the ground.

JD: You got to know Milosevic at Dayton?

WC: A lot. And I was in the shuttle diplomacy one hundred days before Dayton.

JD: Holbrooke mentions how the military plan for the retreat from Bosnia—

WC: 40-104, or something like that . . .

JD: —prompted Clinton to reassess his policy. Have you ever seen that kind of tail wagging the dog, where the military plans change civilian policy?

WC: All the time, that's why in February '99 the Joint Chiefs of Staff wanted to do ground force planning for Kosovo.

JD: And?

WC: They were blocked from doing so.

JD: That was a bad thing?

WC: I'm not saying it was a bad thing, I think it was a good thing. The reason they were blocked [was] because the intent behind the ground force planning was to show all the costs and the risk, and the most skillful planning would have taken four months, six months, eight months. And once committed down this path, it would have gone like this: "Mr. President you realize if you go forward with this, your talking about a 517,000 manned ground force, and our estimate of casualties are 117,000, counting sick, lame, and lazy. Mr. President, the cost will be $62.7 billion, we will have to call up the reserves, and the net impact on the economy will be such and such, and this is foolish. You don't want to drop the first bomb, Mr. President."

JD: So planning was actually a domestic deterrent against war?

WC: The basic strategy for opposing the use of air power was from the joint staff. Their strategy in opposition was to say, what if the air threat doesn't work? And I said, it will work.

And what if that doesn't work? Then we bomb. And what if that doesn't work? Then we invade, we'll overrun Belgrade. It is in the nature of military science not to want to get into anything unless you know the ending of it, the full bill. This inhibits you from taking the initiative. This drives you into Pearl Harbor situations: yes, they have invaded China, and they are moving into Southeast Asia, but if you start a war with Japan, it will cost millions of lives and billions of dollars. It becomes a three-cornered game in this town, between the Hill and the White House, the State Department, and the Pentagon. The Pentagon has prepared a national military strategy that's interested in fighting in certain areas, designed to justify keeping a cold-war force, while the State Department has taken a much more flexible view on the uses of military power. The Pentagon then buttresses its argument against using forces by demanding a $60 billion investment-target to replenish the cold-war forces. It didn't start out that way. Kosovo was the crucial test case.

JD: Some people talk about the Gulf War as the last industrial war, and Kosovo as the first postmodern war. Do you think Kosovo represents the end of classical war, the beginning of something entirely new?

WC: No. It's just one of a range of things. We said in Joint Vision 2010 that you should have "full spectrum dominance." What that means is that everything from the highest intensity conflict down to shows of force and peacekeeping, you should have dominance at every level, to excel at whatever level.

JD: Will Kosovo shift the spectrum, weight it towards one end?

WC: Not really. I don't think you can. We do have to be careful that we don't overtask ourselves with the peacekeeping scenario. One of the problems is that we take the NTC experience and we make a sordid virtue out of preparation.

JD: Can you explain that a bit more?

WC: You normally think that preparation is a good thing, but when you prepare to such an extent that you have driven out all other efforts and it becomes an event-oriented training rather than a skill-, knowledge-oriented training, then it's a bad thing *per se*. When you transpose that model into combat you get an alert, then train, then deploy model. You get: "Sir, we can't possibly go to Kosovo." "Sir, I'll go if you take risk." "Sir, what about mines, what about the SA-7s?" "These are mountains here, sir, and we don't do mountains, sir." I've heard all these arguments. I know these arguments.

An interview with Clark is also an engagement in full spectrum dominance: he could go from animated to agitated and back to ruminative within a single response. The intensity was barely suppressible—which perhaps was a reason why Clark preferred to avoid the political questions and stick to the guts of military training. He was especially critical of the attitude in the army that "anything worth doing is worth overdoing." We've got great people in the army, he said, but there's an increase in operational rigidities and a loss of flexibility. There were too many bored people in the army. He compared his own career, a rapid succession of different jobs and postings, each with a new challenge, to the stasis that current officers face—including the example of his son's army career (who according to one press release is no longer in the army but in L.A., working as a screen-writer). His objective had always been to attract and retain the highest quality people. Now he was hearing from young army captains that they're getting out because there are more opportunities for Chinese army captains to go to American graduate schools than there are for American ones. It wasn't easy, but I got him back to Kosovo.

JD: What happened with the Apaches, that took so long to get to Albania, and then so long to become operational?

WC: They overrated the risk. People would say, "What if Serbs invade Albania?" Do you think the Serbs are going eight miles into Albania to get your twenty-four Apaches? I don't think so. But the press got it wrong. The Apaches were always more than Apaches. I *liked* having the tanks, the artillery, and the radar all there. That *was* the ground threat.

JD: So you did manage to smuggle in a ground threat?

WC: Damn right.

JD: Would sending helicopters to the Pristina airport have "started World War III" [in reference to a statement made by General Mike Jackson, the British commander on the ground in Kosovo, on refusing to carry out Clark's request for an airborne assault]?

WC: No. Do *you* think it would have?

JD: Just wanted to get that one out of the way. Looking back on it, what would you have done differently in Kosovo?

WC: I don't look back. I can't answer that in any kind of an effective way. I had a strategy and I followed it. When you're dealing with the political world you can't *not* take the first step because the last step is incalculable. You *can't*.

JD: So exit strategies are really just a hidden way to veto military action?

WC: Exit strategies are a way to avoid military action. I mean, what was the exit strategy for World War II? It's absurd, it's a buzzword. Your foreign policy doesn't make sense, they say, show us an exit strategy. You have to find a *success* strategy—and then work backwards to see what it takes to get you to that objective. What was the exit strategy for Kosovo? Implement the Dayton agreement—*and* get rid of Milosevic. A simple, clear, exit strategy.

JD: Don't we have a national security directive against that, going after a country's leader? Did you intend to get rid of Milosevic during the air campaign?

WC: I would have liked to—but I had no intention of doing it.

JD: This raises an ethical question. Do you think air power, in particular, the use of precision munitions, is fundamentally more or less ethical than other forms of warfare?

WC: I have a problem with that. One has to obey the laws of warfare and follow the rules of engagement. But having said that, it is hard to make an ethical distinction between indiscriminate and discriminate weapons. We always try to use the most discriminate weapon, we always try to use the smallest weapon. It's always preferable to use a BB-gun rather than tear a hole in you, if that's what it takes. But then, there are these quirky things: like we don't mind decapitating you, tearing your legs off, but please don't blind people with lasers—that's too horrible.

JD: Do you think just war doctrine is out of date?

WC: No, it's a body of thought in flux; it's trying to adapt to changing circumstances, changing technology. The circumstances are important because we're going from a period when there were strong ethnic-based, cultural norms, into a period in which there is an effort of increased universalism, to see people as people, not as the "enemy." The Serbs were not the enemy. I mean, we didn't even want to kill Serb soldiers in the beginning. I know they probably deserved it; by conventional war theory, they were part of this killing machine. Three weeks later, when we couldn't get this thing stopped, we started bombing barracks. Maybe we could have stopped it earlier, if we had just started killing them earlier. You see, one of the things we tried to do in this operation was to execute the diplomacy with the minimum use of force and minimum number of casualties. In that sense, it is a highly principled and ethical strategy. Whether it is the most efficacious strategy is what's at issue. Would it be better to kill five hundred people on the first night? Or is it better to kill them slowly, and ultimately have them give up? I think all things being equal, it's better to get it over sooner rather than later. Therefore, I'm in favor in the most decisive use of force once you cross the threshold. I'm not in favor, as a matter of *theory*, of demonstrative use of forces, of signaling, of showing them what we can do, let's take out some stuff and show him what he's got to lose in the future. Mechanically it doesn't work that way: he reads your method of operation, looks at your vulnerabilities. Eventually you make a mistake and public opinion says, "*Come on*, you're a big country, this guy's a pipsqueak, how *long* is this going to take to do this? I mean there were people saying last summer, let's just keep the bombing going, we can't make a decision on the ground forces, so let's just keep it going until next spring. It would be just like northern Iraq. One target a day, you fly aircraft over, shout down: "Anybody alive down there? Anybody home?" The difference, of course, is that in Iraq we're dealing with a foreign culture that won't allow any press in. In Serbia, we're dealing with what the French call "our European brothers."

JD: So you're talking about the CNN-effect?

WC: Absolutely. And air campaigns have a sort of radioactive half-life. They decay. They start out with the best intentions, best laid plans and so forth. Then, after you shoot up their easy targets up front, you start to make mistakes; you start to lose aircraft, you run low on your preferred munitions, and you get pilot fatigue—pilots do get tired, even when they shouldn't, compared to army guys—and the result of all that is you get to a period when it is difficult to sustain an air operation. My concern is that in the future the sustainability of an air operation is going to be even shorter than it is today, because having seen it before, people will react against it even stronger the second time around.

JD: What about remote warfare? Just using precision munitions, no risk of losing pilots—

WC: Sure, let's do it. "We can put a sensor suite on this thing, you can buzz that target at 15 Gs, we'll have a TV camera in the back, it will be phenomenal." Meanwhile, you've got some guy on the ground, saying I can't follow this. There's a long way between promise and performance, like in this case, perhaps thirty to fifty years.

At this point, on the subject of precision munitions, I brought up the accidental bombing of the Chinese embassy; he told me I had five minutes left. Taking that to mean I should find a better exit strategy for the interview, I asked him what he had gained from his time at Oxford as a Rhodes Scholar: logical thought, nondogmatic approaches, and a life-long aversion to grenade-sized brussels sprouts picked in November and boiled into mush. I asked him about the role of the media in warfare: you can no longer do something on the battlefield and expect someone not to see it; Chechnya was the last war like that. And what was the next objective? "I don't make predictions," he said, "but we've got to finish the job with Milosevic." I decided as a final question to ask him about all the conspiracy theories on the Web that made him out to be the guy who supplied the tanks from Fort Hood for the assault on the Branch Davidians. "All ridiculous stuff," he said— but he did show some remarkable recall about what went down:

WC: They did come to my division, and they tasked my division to give up some equipment—"they" being my corps commander, and my assistant to that commander was a guy named Pete Schoomaker who was the former Delta Force commander. So he was well known, and the corps commander called him directly—he did not go through me—and he said, go see Ann Richards; so he went to see the governor. But Pete didn't really have much to do with it; it was the FBI, as far as I know. I didn't have anything to do with it, so I'm sorry for all those conspiracy theorists.

As he put on his tie for a meeting with Senator Warner, we talked about coercive diplomacy. He told me about a 1975 thesis that he wrote while he was at Fort Leavenworth. It was about contingency operations, from Berlin to Lebanon to Laos to Vietnam. But now he realizes it was really about coercive diplomacy: what worked, what didn't. The lesson he drew from his historical cases? The military is usually too timid, and politicians too constrained, to make coercive diplomacy work. With that, he was out the door, heading for one more courtesy call on his way to retirement.

I was glad to make it to General Clark's retirement review the next day, held on the vast Summerall Field of Fort Myers, just at the edge of Arlington Cemetery. It not only gave me the chance to see the army honor one of its own, but it also gave me the opportunity to use the word "resplendent": the weather, the four military bands, the cannon salutes, the polished medals on dress uniforms, the food, and the eagle—especially the ice-carved eagle on the banquet table—were all resplendent. The speeches were—less so. In the audience there were secretaries (Cohen and Caldera), undersecretaries (Talbot), distinguished members of Congress, and many foreign dignitaries and military officers.

The Army Chief of Staff, General Shinseki, led off the speeches. In spite of all the standard tropes—turning-in-your-spurs, colors-dancing-in-the-breeze, riding-off-into-the-the sunset—it was moving. Some phrases stuck, others just left me wondering. Did "a warrior scarred in battle" refer to Clark's tours in Vietnam—or Washington? When Shinseki mentioned the most important lesson Clark learned from "one of his great heroes, General

Dwight Eisenhower," it wasn't watch your back when the military-industrial complex comes to town: it was "Clark understood what it took to keep a delicate alliance together." He ended with a list of Clark's virtues—"incomparable toughness, drive, stamina"—and a legacy that I'm not sure would place him in the pantheon of great generals: "Perhaps more clearly than anyone he has articulated a vision of the future operational environment."

Clark opened his speech with personal stories about West Point and the close friends he made and kept, in spite of their strange musical tastes, like the Rolling Stones's "Satisfaction"; this was not to be Clark's last musical reference from the sixties. The speech had a grateful tone. He was proud of the achievements of the "post-Vietnam army." He was especially proud of what had been achieved in Kosovo: "I believe we got a glimpse of the future in Kosovo where NATO succeeded in righting a great wrong." In spite of an unfamiliar battlefield—one "not shown in the manual on the revolution in military affairs"—"we fought our campaign in the public, fully within internationally accepted and recognized legal standards, and we were held accountable on a daily basis." Kosovo was not "about oil, sea lanes, conventional cross-border invasions." It was about "fighting for our beliefs and values, for human rights and respects, for the freedoms of our own American dreams." At this point the speech took a turn for the strange: Clark invoked Bob Dylan to justify the air campaign.

> I think it maybe was Bob Dylan who said it best in his song "Blowin' in the Wind," when he asked, "How many roads must a man walk down before you can call him a man? How many years can some people exist before they're allowed to be free? How many times can a man turn his head and pretend he just doesn't see? And how many deaths will it take before he knows too many have died?" Bob Dylan said the answer was "blowing in the wind." But I think the answer in the Balkans was falling from the skies, and coming across the borders. It was NATO and the United States and our European allies in Operation Allied Force, and the skillful use of coercive diplomacy. This time we had seen enough people die, and we acted in time.

"Blowin' in the Wind" as "Bombin' for Peace"? Better, I thought, "A Hard Rain's Gonna Fall."

Clark finished on a philosophical note. I believe he was also getting in a last shot at the growing cult of casualty avoidance. The criticism was veiled, but it did not require 32-bit decryption. He ended with a memory from his time at Oxford, when he was up late one night with a friend, discussing life and death and Vietnam. Despite their other differences, both agreed that it all came down to the old adage: "If there is nothing worth fighting and dying for, then maybe there's nothing worth living for." Clark hammered it home: "Thirty-three years later, I still think there's a lot of truth in that. I happen to believe there's a lot worth living for, and there's a lot worth fighting for." As he left the podium for the reception at the officers club, I wondered if he had intentionally, or virtuously, deleted from his final observation the coda about dying.

Was Kosovo the first, the last, the future of virtuous war? The October 1999 After-Action Review, presented by Secretary of Defense Cohen and Chairman of the Joint Chiefs of Staff General Shelton before the Senate Armed Services Committee, left little doubt about it:

> For 50 years, NATO has given caution to our foes and comfort to our friends. As a watershed in NATO's long history, Operation Allied Force was an overwhelming success. NATO accomplished its mission and achieved all of its strategic, operational, and tactical goals in the face of an extremely complex set of challenges. We forced Milosevic to withdraw from Kosovo, degraded his ability to wage military operations, and rescued and resettled over one million refugees. We accomplished this by prosecuting the most precise and lowest-collateral-damage air campaign in history—with no U.S. or allied combat casualties in 78 days of around-the-clock operations and over 38,000 combat sorties.[6]

The *virtue* of the conflict could be measured by the low casualties, the discriminate use of violence, and the application of international norms (or at least those that coincided with American values). The *virtual* was operationally evident: the real-time, distant detection, targeting, and destruction of architecture that had been emptied of humans by advanced signaling (bridges were bombed only on week nights between 10 P.M. and 4 A.M.); the use of disinformation and information warfare, from denials and exaggerations of ethnic cleansing to going after the assets of Milosevic and his financial cohort; the widespread use of the Internet by all parties, civilian and military, to get out multiple and often conflicting versions of the "truth"; and finally, just as networked technologies closed strategic distances, so too did information networks collapse representational distinctions between fact and fiction.[7] Milosevic's skill at media dissembling is well known (less so was the skilful use of decoys—tanks, bridges, barracks—by the Yugoslavian army). But the allies contributed to the virtualization of the conflict by greatly overstating if not misrepresenting the technical successes of the war. For instance, before the Armed Forces Committee, General Clark testified that NATO warplanes had destroyed 110 Serb tanks, 210 armored personnel carriers, and 449 guns and mortars; subsequent press accounts have confirmed less than a dozen tanks destroyed.[8] The overselling of precision weaponry made the usual mistakes of warfare appear to be aberrations, if not war crimes. The NATO air campaign had bombed trains, schools, hospitals, embassies (China), and in one case, wrong countries (Bulgaria) with less-than-precise munitions. Indeed, Amnesty International requested (unsuccessfully) that the International Criminal Tribunal accept the collateral damage of the air campaign as proof that the laws of warfare had been violated by the Allied coalition.[9]

In short, technofetishism and casualty phobia in the military combined with feedback-loops in the media to give Kosovo a special virtuosity. Out of the faith in smart weapons and the fear of pilot casualties (and of a rescue effort going bad, as in Mogadishu), air ceilings of 13,000 feet were imposed on (but not always observed by) NATO warplanes, limiting how low they could fly. But when bombing accuracy suffered, the incidences of "collateral damage" increased, and the bombing campaign dragged on, public attitudes began to shift, to one of get it done, or get the hell out.

Kosovo shows us that virtuous war is much more than an

oxymoron. It is always double-edged: converting political issues into virtual imperatives that can be technologically enforced, the imposed solutions inevitably give rise to new political problems. When technological inertia trumps political constraint, it poses even greater dangers; as the political philosopher Jean Bethke Elshtain puts it, "Virtue without limits becomes terror."[10] Virtuous war presents a paradox: the more we resort to virtual means to resolve political problems, the more we undermine the very ground upon which our political virtues rest. All through the air campaign, whether one was television-viewing, web-surfing, or smart-bombing, "Kosovo" was always one click away from obliteration. All three virtual activities, collapsing distance and erasing epistemic distinctions, demonstrated a rare if not revolutionary talent for disappearing hard(ened) identities. To be sure, when something goes wrong, as inevitably does with new technologies, there is a vast difference between a broken link and a broken limb. But in all these cases, rightly or wrongly, something is lost in virtuality: not only the possibility but the very concept of political difference is hollowed out. It stops being a site of negotiation and becomes a screen for the display of dazzling virtual effects, from digital war games to national party conventions to video-camera bombing.

Virtuous war—indefinable, oxymoronic, and paradoxical, with good intentions and unintended consequences—might capture but cannot resolve the greatest challenge ahead: how to live in close proximity and high vulnerability with others? By virtuous war, from on high, we might attempt to technically fix and ethically justify our differences with others. However, as in the case of past global violence, especially those that target the vampire heart of the sovereign state, we can be sure these efforts will come back to haunt us. Alternatively, we can construct virtual political environments in which each difference represents a challenge of connectivity, creativity, and responsibility. In such a world, ambiguity, ambivalence, even uncertainty are no longer vices. As Nietzsche put it, "a bestowing virtue is the highest virtue." Might such a virtual world be even better than the real thing?

9 A virtual theory of the global event

Accidents will happen/We only hit and run.
(Elvis Costello, "Accidents Will Happen")

People got opinions
Where do they come from?
Each idea seems like a natural fact
But what we think changes how we act.
(Gang of Four, "Why Theory?")

What does it mean when the millennial turn, in the past marked by prophecy and hope, is reduced to a computer glitch? Most likely "Y2K" will be remembered as a virtual event that did not happen. But as a diagnostic and symptom of the pathologies operating in the complex system of the military-industrial-media-entertainment network, we best take the *accident* seriously. This is especially true after Y2K+1 looked to be the real thing. First there was the domestic accident of the United States presidential election, in which (voting) machines were injudicially deemed to be more competent than (counting) humans. Then the new Bush administration was almost immediately beset by a series of international military accidents. These accidents were distinguished by an accelerated shift from particular incidents into what we might call "global events," a virtualized state of affairs in which the rapid interaction of multiple players, complex systems, and networked information technologies produce a globalized security crisis.

Virtual reality in the airport.

Buddha and Yogi: "The future ain't what it used to be."

A short list of accidental global events would include a U.S. submarine executing an emergency surfacing drill off the coast of Hawaii, and a Japanese fishing trawler being sunk. A U.S. EP-3E Aries II aircraft on a routine reconnaissance flight is in a mid-air collision with a Chinese fighter plane; the Chinese pilot dies and the 24 U.S. crewmembers are detained for eleven days after an emergency landing on the Chinese island of Hainan. A CIA-contracted surveillance plane detects a suspicious plane flying over the Amazon and alerts the Peruvian Air Force, which shoots down a Cessna carrying not drugs but American Baptist missionaries and their two children. Fearing the outbreak of a hacking war on the anniversary of the accidental bombing of the Chinese embassy in Belgrade during the Kosovo conflict, the U.S. Joint Task Force for Computer Network Defense goes to its highest state of alert, "INFOCON ALPHA." In order to protect against future accidental as well as intentional attacks, President Bush announces in a major foreign policy speech at the National Defense University that the U.S. will proceed with a missile defense system.[1]

At the one-hundred day assessment of the Bush presidency, a major newspaper remarks: "[o]n an increasing number of occasions since he took office in January, Bush has antagonized foreign capitals not out of ideological differences but by accident."[2] What does this mean?

Accidents in world politics are hardly new phenomena. Edmund Burke, the eighteenth-century British philosopher and parliamentarian, noted that the "empire of circumstance" regularly trumps the rational and intentional actions of diplomats and generals.[3] In international relations, as in just about all other complex relations where antecedent and consequent are not preordained, accidents —perhaps the most destructive expression of circumstance—will happen and people will die.[4] There is significant, if not very extensive, literature on how accidents can precede and determine the outcome of some wars.[5] Yet the international accident per se rarely makes it past the front pages to become a research concern of the social sciences or think tanks. An even more glaring omission is how networked information technology plays such a critical role as both site and disseminator of the accidental global event.

There are, however, some exceptions, some critical theoretical "accidents" that inform my own analysis. Three keen observers of the accidental event provide a radically different perspective than the usual academic palaver. The first is sociologist Charles Perrow, whose now classic book on the subject, *Normal Accidents: Living with High Risk Technologies*, deploys the seemingly oxymoronic concept of the "normal accident" to make sense of how catastrophes are built into complex technologies, like Three Mile Island, petrochemical plants and exotic weapon systems.[6] He is particularly interested in how non-linear, tightly-coupled systems can produce a "negative synergy" that outstrips human decision-making capabilities.

From a more continental approach, French architect and social critic Paul Virilio assesses (some might say obsesses over) the value as well as danger of emergent technologies by the nature of their primary accidents (from train derailments and the sinking of the *Titanic* to the *Challenger* disaster and the 1987 stock market crash to the potential for a networked "integral accident").[7] Virilio is not merely a disaster junkie: he interprets the accident, the crash, the catastrophe as both diagnostic for an excessively accelerating technology and as spur for the re-establishment of human agency. Appearing as the destructive and constructive curves of scientific progress intersect, the accident in Virilio's apocalyptic terms represents an "inverted miracle" by which we might learn how to slow down the technological revolution from network speeds to human needs.

The third thinker is Gilles Deleuze, who assigns to theory the sole aim of being worthy of the event: a relatively easy task it would seem, until one begins to realize just how dependent the significance of the event is upon the interventions of the theorist, policymaker or media representative.[8] Indeed, Deleuze situates an ethical as well as aesthetic imperative to extract or "de-territorialize" an event from ideological positions set by media and political "first-responders" and others who trade in powerful emotions like fear, danger, and anxiety that define the edges of an accident. In such circumstances, theoretical intervention is not an abstraction or attenuation of reality; it becomes a necessary counter-strategy to officials who would wish opportunistically to transform local incidents into global events, real dangers into virtual threats, provisional accidents into a permanent state of insecurity.[9]

Together these thinkers help move the study of the accident from the margins to the center of international politics. They reveal how the accidentally-induced, virtually-constructed, deterritorialized global event is giving organized warfare a run for its money as the *ultima ratio* of the national security state. They point the way towards a "virtual theory" for understanding the increasingly fractal and imagistic nature of international relations.[10]

Semantically, it is understandable why the global event would be avoided, as one might skirt the scene of an accident. The *Oxford English Dictionary* definition—"an unusual event, which proceeds from some unknown cause, or an unusual effect of a known cause"—does not suggest an easy relationship with traditional concerns of the social sciences. As a precipitous, unforeseeable break from the usual, the accident as object of study does not render great returns for an academic discipline in pursuit of long-term rational explanation and prediction of normal behavior. In the conventional, more positivist study (if not in the actual practice) of international relations, events are neatly broken down into narrative accounts of cause/effect or rational models of independent/dependent variables. There is as well a fairly clear demarcation between what lies inside and outside theoretical purviews, with liberal theory focusing on domestic drivers and realist theory looking at external state-to-state interactions. Further boundaries are drawn between putatively discrete levels of analysis —the individual, the state, and the system—and left underexplored in the process is the increasingly significant and complex interplay of all three through global networks.[11] Moreover, positivist approaches—assuming that words transparently mirror objects, facts reside apart from values, and theory is independent of the reality that it represents—produce a fairly hermetic worldview with little room for the interpretation of accidents. Indeed, in the positivist world, the accident by definition exists only as spillover, an externality, an exception to the rule. Like the fall of the Berlin wall—an event that some positivist International Relations (IR) scholars notoriously dismissed as insignificant because it only represented a single data point—the accident fails to meet the criteria of an appropriate research topic.

To be sure, accidents might well be considered as *significant* externalities, taking the form of benefits (say, the invention of the Internet) or costs (like the subsequent appearance of viruses, worms, and trojan horses on the Internet); but they are nonetheless assumed to constitute a spill-over of the more important internal objectives and actions of decision-makers confronting the structures and exigencies of an international anarchy. Hence, according to the conventional social scientific approaches in general, and IR in particular, there are very good reasons for keeping accidents at the margins of research: that's where they happen, and that's why theorists can't pretend or bother to make much sense of them.[12] If anarchy, as the absence at the center, is the prerequisite of realist accounts of international relations, the accident is its kissing cousin, the peripheral disruption by which the liberal theorist affirms the normal flow of events.

Nor is this to say that conventional theoretical approaches, whether in the guise of positivist, realist, or liberal theories of international relations (or more commonly, some rationalist combination thereof), have *nothing* to offer for understanding the actual accident. For instance, take the role of information technology in the downing of the Cessna by the Peruvian Air Force: following procedure, the pilot of the Cessna faxed a flight plan to the Iquitos airport. At first the Peruvian authorities denied its existence; only after the World Baptist organization posted the fax on its website did the Peruvians undertake an investigation. At this point of analysis, a strong rationalist case could be made that both network externality and path dependence are working to the benefit of individuals and the system in question: a greater number of standardized fax machines produce a simultaneous decrease in price and increase in benefits to all involved, making it affordable to pilot and airport alike. And the same is true of the Internet, which made it possible to redress, or at least address, a human error. This is a plausible but not sufficient explanation. Had the network expanded one fax machine too many, shifting the feedback and synergy from positive to negative, making a "normal accident" more likely? Had the Cessna pilot operated under a false sense of security, placing too much faith in the beneficial technology of the fax (the authorities know who I am) and too little in empirical evidence (this jet interceptor outside my window has mistaken me for a drug runner)? Did the habituation to rules of engagement override the singularity of the event? What role did cultural identities, from the machismo of the Peruvian pilot to the vulnerability of a mother and child, play in the escalation of an accident into a global event? Rationalist approaches can provide some but not all the answers to these questions, especially the question of how and why this accident was transformed into a global event.

What is missing in international relations is a *supplemental* theory of the global event. The present need arises from technological as well as political questions that traditional social scientific theories have failed to address. First, as complexity and inter-penetration increases in military, industrial, and information technologies, does the margin of error decrease, thus heightening the likelihood as well as significance of accidental events? Second, taking into account the higher expectation of transparency that comes with globalized information technology, has our measurement of that margin, between stasis and accident, in fact become increasingly subjective, perceptually contingent, even virtual? Is a principle of uncertainty in operation, by which the method of representing the accident is influencing the momentum of the event itself? Third, as human interactions are increasingly represented as well as generated by high-speed, networked information technologies, are accidents more likely to have global, cascading effects? Fourth, do the sequence, scope, and impact of several recent international accidents suggest that accidents are fast becoming the norm in international relations? Underlying all these questions is the more fundamental suspicion, alluded to earlier, that the global event is challenging organized warfare as the means by which the national security state is constituted and legitimated, producing an even higher likelihood of irrational effects.

Positing the accident at the center rather than the margins of international relations raises many other questions, some methodological, but others more deeply ontological in character. Before going any further, let me preempt a few of the more important and potentially critical ones by returning to the definition of the accident. Judging from the authority of dictionary definitions, there are historical reasons for placing accidents at the center of international relations, as the absence that gives meaning to the presence of order. The first definition of the accident in the *Oxford English Dictionary* is straightforwardly simple: "1. Anything that happens"; which is followed by: "1.b. Anything that happens without foresight or expectation." We are back to Burke's "empire of circumstance," which just about covers every event of significance, small or big, local or global, that takes place without 'foresight or expectation."[13]

The definitions that follow further highlight the difficulty of developing a parsimonious theory of the accident. An accident is defined as "an unusual effect of a known cause; a casualty, a contingency." Further down the page, trauma is introduced into the meaning: "accident neurosis . . . a neurosis caused or precipitated by an accident, a disabling complaint of nervous origin: the symptoms are subjective, and there is usually no bodily sign of any emotional disturbance." Rationalist approaches are not well equipped to plumb the depths of such psychological effects, especially the paramnesia that almost always accompanies serious accidents. A case contemporary to these global events would be the inability of print and television pundits to understand the radical discrepancies in stories told by Navy SEAL team members Bob Kerry (a former U.S. senator) and Gerhard Kann of their Vietnam combat mission in 1969, during which more than 20 unarmed civilians, mostly women and children, were shot and killed.

Carrying on with dictionary definitions, it is the third meaning that reinforces the need for an alternative theoretical strategy: "3. Med. An occurring symptom; esp. an unfavourable symptom." Consider the narratives of ritual that embellish the global event. Subject to pre-negotiations of cultural differences, the dead are collectively mourned (if civilian) or celebrated (if military); investigations are launched and considered pending, until causes can be assessed, blame accepted, apologies articulated, and damages paid out. Scapegoats are sent into the desert (or not).[14] Fate, providence, or more secular teleological questions are raised, more as a rite of passage than with the expectation of resolution. The paramount question is why now, for the accident is before all else a disruption in the predictable flow of events, a breakdown of the present en route to the past, a rude awakening into the contingency of the future. After the questions of place and time comes the assessment of damage: what is the severity, scope, new consequences introduced by the accident?

These are vital questions, invoking deep concerns about what makes us feel at risk or secure. If one treats the accident as an ontological and psychological disruption (as suggested by the tertiary dictionary definitions), the symptoms of a disorder, even of a potentially disabling neurosis, can be found as well in the global event. To a social scientist, this might appear to be a strange tack; but it might just be the best means for understanding the cultural and semiotic conditions as well as the tolerances of disorder under which an accident unfolds and takes on meaning.[15] It might also help us to understand how psychological symptoms interact with political imperatives to re-establish order; that is, how the fear, insecurity, and paramnesia induced by the global event grants special prerogatives for the national security state to use its ultimate tool of coercion, virtuous war.

Such a suggestion might seem illogical if not perverse, unless one places it in the larger context of world order, or rather, in the stark contrast between the current international reality and past world orders. By now there should be no need to rehearse the fall-of-the-wall and rise-of-the-Internet story. However, taking into account both the devolution of the Soviet Union into Russia and of ARPANET into the Internet, it is important to note how the accidental elements in both of these synchronous events contributed to the end of a bipolar (dis)order. To be sure, the U.S. remains the dominant military power, with several state actors as potential "peer competitors"; but the story waiting to be told is the advent of a new *heteropolarity*, by which I mean the emergence of actors who are different in power and kind (state, corporate, group, individual) and connected nodally through networks rather than hierarchically through states. Sovereign states are still the most powerful actors, and one does not have to be, say, Chinese to recognize that a single state, the U.S., is definitely more equal than the rest. However, from the power of the powerless that emerged from the "velvet revolution" to the "global war on terror," new globalized identities and symmetries of power are reinscribing the map of world politics.

As the representations of new identities shift, so too has the nature of power in world politics. The global event, from the big bang of the original accident to the fizzled threat of the Y2K bug, has always played a critical role in the making as well as the unmaking of personal, national, and cosmopolitan identities. But as the complexity and extensivity of information technology networks increase, so too has the importance of a consumer identity based on the production, circulation, and acquisition of *images*. The tragic accident, from the *Titanic* to the *Hindenburg* to the *Challenger*, has always sold copy. But now the copy increasingly seems to sell the accident, in the sense of real-time, all-the-time, cable media and networked new media having the interest as well as the capability to elevate the particular accident to permanent global event. Look back to the images that took the U.S. in and then out of Somalia: the starving children, presented as an accident of nature, and the dead Rangers, as an accident of intervention. "Force-multiplied" by a networked media, adding further uncertainty to the mix, consumer identity takes on a power of its own in the global event.

States, particularly hegemonic ones like the U.S., usually have more of an interest than media conglomerates in normalizing the accident before it goes critical. Unfortunately, as Perrow presents in detail with Three Mile Island, particular incidents escalate into system accidents when contrived "solutions" interact to produce a negative synergy of increasingly complex problems. Is there a similar effect in operation within the interface of national security and information technology? Does the very effort of state to prepare for accidents and to reduce uncertainty—by war games, reconnaissance flights, missile shields, and media dissimulation—end up increasing the probability of normal accidents? Does the very effort of the global media to achieve total transparency of the accident shrink not only distance, but also the time in which deliberation can take place, making a crisis inevitable? Has national security become an accidental racket?

A scan of Y2K+1 provides incriminating evidence. Shortly after his inauguration, George W. Bush kicked off "National Security Week." A media blitz of Senate hearings, news of a top-to-bottom defense review, visits to military bases, and promises of new funds were accompanied by a burst of great power chest-beating, flag-waving patriotism, and sentimental testimonials for past and future sacrifices. Not everything, however, went according to script. Tragic accidents marred two separate war games in Hawaii: a U.S. submarine, playing theme park ride to a group of visiting civilians, executed an emergency surface maneuver that sunk a Japanese training ship, killing five sailors and four students; and in the "Lightning Thrust Warrior" exercise, two UH-60 Black Hawk helicopters collided, killing six soldiers. What was intended to be a precision-guided message to old enemies, potential foes, and the American public got a bit muddled in the process. However, when the week ended with twenty-four U.S. and British war-planes attacking five separate Iraqi air defense stations, no amount of background noise could drown out the signal emanating from the military-industrial-media-entertainment network: the national security state was back.

Into the first month of the new Bush administration, "National Security Week" took on the look of a trailer for "Virtuous War, the Video." Not that virtuous war had ever really disappeared; but with the new regime in place it was taking on an increasingly virtual character. We have seen how virtuous war evolved from the battlefield technologies of the Gulf War to the aerial campaigns of Bosnia and Kosovo, drawing on just war doctrine (when possible) as well as holy war (when necessary). We have seen how the infowar of global surveillance and networked simulation was cloned from the pure war of mutual assured destruction, producing a technical capability and ethical imperative to threaten and, if necessary, inflict discriminate violence from a distance. We have seen how the U.S. was leading a revolutionary transformation of military and diplomatic affairs long before George W. Bush became President. But Bush, Cheney, and Rumsfeld early on signaled their intention to fully operationalize virtuous war: using networked information, global surveillance, and virtual technologies to bring "there" here in near real-time and with near-verisimilitude, they viewed virtuous war as the ultimate means by which the U.S. would re-secure its borders, maintain its hegemony, and bring order and justice to international politics.

What was missing was an enemy. In the absence of a credible flesh-and-blood version, the virtual enemy of uncertainty, manifested by the global event, would have to do. National Security

Week provides a snapshot of how this was done. Head of the CIA, George Tenet kicked off the event, delivering to the Senate Select Committee on Intelligence his synopsis of the worldwide threats facing the U.S. today:

> As I reflect this year, Mr. Chairman, on the threats to American security, what strikes me most forcefully is the accelerating pace of change in so many arenas that affect our nation's interests. Numerous examples come to mind: new communications technology that enables the efforts of terrorists and narco-traffickers as surely as it aids law enforcement and intelligence, rapid global population growth that will create new strains in parts of the world least able to cope, the weakening internal bonds in a number of states whose cohesion can no longer be taken for granted, the breaking down of old barriers to change in places like the Koreas and Iran, the accelerating growth in missile capabilities in so many parts of the world—to name just a few. Never in my experience, Mr. Chairman, has American intelligence had to deal with such a dynamic set of concerns affecting such a broad range of U.S. interests. Never have we had to deal with such a high quotient of uncertainty. With so many things on our plate, it is important always to establish priorities. For me, the highest priority must invariably be on those things that threaten the lives of Americans or the physical security of the United States.[16]

A few days later, President Bush was on his way to Fort Stewart, Georgia, to make good on his campaign promise of a $5.7 billion boost in military pay as well as health and housing benefits. To a round of "hoo-ahs" (the infantry's version of applause) he announced:

> In a world of fast-changing threats, you give us stability. Because of you, America is secure. Because of you, the march of freedom continues. Our nation can never fully repay our debt to you, but we can give you our full support. And my administration will.[17]

The following day the President headed to the U.S. Joint Forces Command in Norfolk, Virginia to virtually participate in a battle simulation of a combined naval and land attack in Europe. The president was video-linked to the USS *Mount Whitney*, a command and control ship about 40 miles off Virginia Beach, so that he could watch and participate through three over-sized screens that used three-dimensional radar images to display every ship, missile, and aircraft in, under, and over the Atlantic. And then he gave one of his trademark speeches, short and to the point. He confined the poetry, as it were, to the opening lines:

> Eleven years after the Cold War, we are in a time of transition and testing, when it will be decided what dangers draw near or pass away, what tragedies are invited or averted. We must use this time well. We must seize this moment.

The bulk of the speech is a straightforward endorsement of virtuous war, explicitly linking the possibilities for peace and order to the military's ability to harness the technological revolution in information and surveillance, simulation and speed.

> We must extend our peace by advancing our technology. We are witnessing a revolution in the technology war. Power is increasingly defined not by size but by mobility and swiftness. Advantage increasingly comes from information, such as the three-dimensional images of simulated battle that I have just seen. Safety is gained in stealth and forces projected on the long arc of precision-guided weapons.[18]

And to punctuate his view that virtue and security are on the side of superior firepower, President Bush added to the written speech a personal benediction: "God Bless NATO."

That evening, Secretary of Defense Donald Rumsfeld went on PBS's "News Hour With Jim Lehrer" to declare that Moscow was "part of the problem," because "they are selling and assisting countries like Iran, North Korea and India with these technologies, which are threatening other people, including the U.S., Western Europe and several states in the Middle East." Senior Russian officials quickly responded, accusing Rumsfeld of using

Cold War rhetoric and of being a pawn of U.S. defense contractors.[19] The next day the President traveled to Charleston, West Virginia to participate in a mock disaster simulation with Reservists and National Guard personnel and to sympathize with the fact that the Clinton administration had previously sent them off to risky foreign adventures. After that he was off to Mexico to meet the new President, Vicente Fox, and, in the midst of informal talks about drugs, migration, and allowing Californians to tap into the Mexican electrical grid, U.S. and British war planes attacked the Iraqi air defense network. The two Presidents held an outdoor press conference, and President Bush declared that "it was a routine mission," taking care to let all know that it was one "about which I was informed and I authorized."[20]

In one of those media-enabled synchronicities, "National Security Week" enjoyed a double-billing with "UNITED STATES OF AMERICA v. U.S.AMA BIN LADEN, et al.," the New York-based trial of the alleged conspirators behind the bombing of the U.S. embassies in Tanzania and Kenya in 1998. The week's transcripts of the trial focused on the structure of bin Laden's organization, "Al Qaeda," linguistically translatable as "The Base," but structurally more closely resembling an information network. In one part of the testimony, Jamal Ahmed Al-Fadl, bin Laden's former paymaster turned informant, identifies the key players in an organization dedicated to asymmetrical forms of warfare. Take notice of the descending order of importance attached to the talents of individual members.

Q: During the time that you were in Khartoum and Al Qaeda, did you become familiar with a person by the name of Abu Muaz el Masry?

A: Yes.

Q: Can you tell us, is Abu Muaz el Masry a member of Al Qaeda?

A: Yes.

Q: Can you tell us what his specialty is?

A: He is member also with jihad group and he's very good with dreamer.

Q: Can you explain what it is that Abu Muaz el Masry did with dreams?

A: If any one of the Al Qaeda membership, he got dream after the fajr prayer.

Q: The fajr prayer, F-A-J-R?

A: Yes.

Q: When is that prayer?

A: Before the sunrise.

Q: Okay. Continue.

A: If anyone got dream and he believes that dream could become true, he go and he tell him, Abu Muaz, he got great experience to tell the people what the dream going to be and he's a scholar for that.

Q: Abu Anas al Liby, did he have any specialty within Al Qaeda?

A: Yes.

Q: What was that?

A: He's . . . he run our computers. He's a computer engineer.

Q: Are you familiar with the person by the name of Mohamed Shabana?

A: Yes.

Q: Is Mohamed Shabana part of Al Qaeda?

A: Yes.

Q: Did he have a specialty within Al Qaeda?

A: He's very good with the report, media report, and he got great experience with analysis about ballistics.

Q: You said he's very good with report. What kind of reports?

A: Media reports and he got good analysis about anything.

Q: Finally, are you familiar with a person by the name of Khalid el Masry?

A: Yes.

Q: Who is he?

A: Abu Khalid el Masry, he's a jihad group membership and he's also Al Qaeda membership.

Q: Did he have any specialty?

A: Yes. He's very good with tanks. He can fix tanks and run them during the war.

Q: Tanks, like army tanks?

A: Yes.[21]

Several journalists who were closely following the trial remarked on the unique nature of Al Qaeda, one going as far as to say: "[i]n his quest to wage jihad, or holy war, against the United States, bin Laden may have constructed something that is bigger than a guer-rilla group and more complex than a multinational corporation. Call it a virtual country—the Republic of Jihadistan."[22]

"National Security Week" showcased a major feature of virtu-ous war: representing, preparing, and, if necessary, eradicating the enemy threat. However, there was a problem in search of a solu-tion: finding a credible post-Cold War foe. In my earlier research I found there to be no shortage of "Blue," "Red," and "Brown" teams, or "opposing forces," "regional powers," even a "re-emergent global threat," which potentially match the U.S. in cap-ability and intentions.[23] But actual names and faces are hard to come by. We have seen how the Pentagon reached deep into its archive of historical film, comic-book, and free-floating enemies to come up with menacing, foreign names for its simulations, exercises, and war games, like the "Krasnovians," "Sumarians," and "Hamchuks" who roam the Mojave Desert in green jump suits and black berets; the unkempt "Sowenians," "Vilslakians," and "Juralandians" who clash in the hills of Hohenfels that bor-dered on the countries of "Fredonia" and "Ruritania"; and the grungy Boolean and Furzian refugees who stir up trouble in the "Country of Orange," located somewhere in the San Francisco Bay area during the extensive "Urban Warrior" exercises. But without fail, whenever I asked the military or civilian organizers for a real name, a real country, I got the party line: this is just a scenario, an exercise, an experiment. "We don't do countries," as one Air Force spokesman put it when queried during a recent space war game. In short, they now "do" uncertainty.

This is the conundrum of virtuous war and the crux of the global event: the more elusive the foe and the more virtuous the inten-tion, the more virtual the threat, until all that is left as the last enemy are a few rogue states, the demon state of uncertainty, and the demiurge of the accident.[24] The limited bombing of Iraq at the end of the week fit the bill. And while it garnered the most head-lines, the bombing will probably be of less consequence than the announcement made by Secretary of Defense Rumsfeld at the beginning of National Security Week, that he had chosen to head the top-to-bottom review of U.S. military strategy and struc-ture none other than Andrew Marshall, the forefather of the

"Revolution in Military Affairs."[25] We have seen how Marshall earlier in his career organized several task forces and instigated several scenarios based on an interwar analogy, in which the U.S. assumes the past hegemonic position of Britain, and is potentially facing yet unknown powers that will harness revolutionary technologies through asymmetrical warfare. Now Marshall's related concern began to show up in a series of newspaper articles: China was a clear, if not yet present, danger.

> Mr. Marshall is one of the unsung heroes of the Cold War . . . Few senior officials have better understood and done more to document the determination of the People's Republic of China to anticipate and prepare itself for conflict with the United States. He grasps the danger the Chinese might pose to U.S. interests in Asia and beyond—including outer space— and his recommendations about the sizing and equipping of America's military will surely reflect the need to be able to contend with the growing asymmetric and other threats from China.[26]

By the beginning of April, after the collision of the US EP-3E Aries II reconnaissance plane with the Chinese fighter plane, the U.S. had found an enemy, as if by accident.

The ephemera of the global event requires a de-territorialized theory, one that can travel quickly from one incident to the next, identifying and countering the official stories of a "National Security Week" that appear and disappear with celerity in the 24/7 global news cycle, yet leave behind the indelible watermark of a foreign policy based on fear and anxiety. Obviously more than one approach is needed for such complex global issues involving everything from geopolitical concerns about sea lanes to diplomatic issues of "saving face" to less frequently mentioned factors like racism. But no extant IR theory helps us to understand, let alone to preempt, the transformation of the accident by military planning, networked media and national security discourse into the global event.[27] It might be risky to extrapolate a theory from these shards of information, opinions, and concepts. But, as anthropologist Clifford Geertz notes, after the disintegration of

Cold War blocs and ideological certainties, there might not be much more on hand:

> If the general is to be grasped at all, and new unities uncovered, it must, it seems, be grasped not directly, all at once, but via instances, differences, variations, particulars—piecemeal, case by case. In a splintered world, we must address the splinters . . . And that is where theory, if there is to be any, comes in.[28]

Following Geertz's counsel, we might apply to the global event what I have called a *virtual theory*, in which the ambiguity of its name reflects the nature of its subject.[29] On my road trips I have traced how the rise of a military-industrial-media-entertainment network (MIME-NET) has increasingly virtualized international relations, setting the stage for virtuous wars in which history, experience, intuition, and other human traits are subordinated to scripted strategies and technological artifice, in which worst-case scenarios produce the future they claim only to anticipate, in which the tail wags the dog. In my research I discovered ample evidence that we have accelerated beyond a "post-modern condition," first identified as such by philosopher François Lyotard in 1979.[30] We have entered a digitally-enhanced "virtual immersion," in which instant scandals, catastrophic accidents, impending weather disasters, wishful foreign policies, constructive simulations, live-feed wars, and humanitarian interventions into still-born or moribund states are all available, not just primetime and realtime but 24/7, on the TV, PC, and PDA. Through a virtual theory I hope to provide the "red pill" for understanding and challenging the power of an all-too-real *Matrix*, the MIME-NET.

Virtual theory conveys the sense of an intellectual construct that seeks to interrogate and interpret rather than intervene or explain; as such it can be detached from partisan interests yet pose clear ethical questions. Using archival research, empirical techniques, and critical thinkers, a virtual theory endorses a policy of mix and match, plug and play, in the hope of creating a thick collage of insights into new dangers rather than an instruction manual for old problems. Seeking to negotiate the interplay of power and knowledge, modern and postmodern, empirical and critical, analogical and digital, virtual theory acts as both software and hardware for a densely networked global politics. A virtual theory, by the very ambiguity of its name, suggests both the creative potential of its gaze and the elusive nature of its object. Virtual theory repudiates the philosophical realism underlying most social science theory.[31] Virtual theory has the potential to make meaning and to produce presence, to create the actual through a theatrical differentiation and technical vision. Constructing a de-territorialized sense of being—neither here nor there as being but always as becoming different—virtual theory represents a reality in-the-making that does not fit the hard dyads of the social sciences, most notably between the real and the ideal.

In shorthand, a virtual theory is: thin on explanation and thick on description; instrumented for interpolation rather than framing; more concerned with shifting events and speculation than fixed structures, and double-blind proofs; more interested in consequences than causes; and not so much interested in how a problem is solved as why an event goes—or fails to go—critical and global. This makes virtual theory particularly sensitive to the accidental attributes of world politics, like paradoxes, synchronicities, accelerants, catalysts, feedback, white noise, negative synergy, phase shifts, bullet time, spatio-temporal rifts, and, not least, dreams.

In its potential for infinite reproducibility and by a capability to produce an effect at a distance, virtual theory itself is a technology—and like all technologies, virtual ones, it can make the worst as well as the best possibility actual. This puts a very high premium on reflexivity in virtual theory in the sense of a need to constantly question how, through acts of observation—and regardless of intention—virtual theory can influence or even actualize an event. Hence, as I have stated before (and shall persist so long as critics on both sides of the debate pretend there is no ethics to virtual as well as critical projects), virtual theory must out of necessity do what constructivist theory posits as a voluntaristic luxury: take responsibility, *as far as it can*, for its mapping of the world.[32]

To be sure, this open-ended, beta-version of virtual theory can elicit a kind of vertigo, but hopefully a productive one.[33] It opens up the simple, either/or questions that usually define the interface between politics and technology, like: Will new information technology bring prosperity and security, or accidents and anarchy? Are we entering a democratic peace or a new clash of cultures? A virtual theory encourages a different, more specific set of questions: What happens when violence can now travel by networks with such speed from object to subject, from one region to another, in one global feedback loop? When the most critical areas of defense and foreign policy become dependent upon virtual forms of military planning? When what one technologically *can* do comes to dominate what one legally, ethically, or even pragmatically *should* do? When defense simulations and public dissimulations make for a potentially permanent state of accidental global events?

These kinds of questions resist traditional responses. Whereas most theoretical approaches in the social sciences posit a bifurcation of intellect and will, theory and practice, of subjective mind and objective nature, virtual theory constructs an interaction among them all. Understandably, the social sciences (but interestingly enough, not the latest theories in the physical sciences) avoid the spatio-temporal rifts where simulacra reverses causality, being is simultaneously here and there, and identity is deterritorialized by interconnectivity. Virtual theory finds a home in this interzone, where critical ethical interventions routinely precede the retrieval of facts (empirical or social) and technical media constitute new virtual states of meaning and being. Both war and peace are still in need of approaches that study what actually happened (realism) and what needs to be changed (idealism). But world politics is also in need of a virtual theory that explores how reality is seen, framed, read, and generated in the conceptualization and actualization of the global event. Virtual theory does not, as vulgar realists would claim, deny the existence of "reality"; nor does it construct whole realities out of wishful thinking. In religious, political and technological theologies, reality has always been inflected by the virtual. Virtual theory seeks to understand how new technologies are also creating new virtual theologies, the most dangerous one being the belief that virtuous war can supernaturally solve the most intractable political problems.

At this point it should be obvious that there is no ready-made virtual theory. A virtual theory cannot be reduced to a fungible model, for, just as the virtual actualizes the real, the real—or at least any intended meaning of the real—always exceeds the reach of the virtual. And, just as surely as the powers of observation produce unpredictable and immeasurable effects, there can never be a unified field theory of virtuality. A virtual theory can, however, help us extend our intellectual as well as political grasp of the new. Against worse-case scenarios, especially the self-prophesying ones of realism that purport to reflect yet work to reproduce violence in global politics, a virtual theory offers strategies of interpretation that treat violence as a last-case option. Nonetheless, a virtual theory shares with realism the recognition that without a consensual center to world politics, violence—either in its organized form of "war" or in its disorganized state of "accident"—will not disappear, regardless of technological fixes or ethical claims to the contrary.

What does this preliminary conceptualization of virtual theory offer? First, it challenges the naive black/white, good/bad, doomed/saved binaries of techno-scientific discourse, and all the other contemporary statements, polemics, and manifestos about networked information technology that stand, by grace of a pure dialectical opposition, as authoritative.[34] Second, it provides a powerful search engine for the empirical and social data that can counter the daily, hourly, permanent media coup d'état of the global event. Third, it offers a counter-intervention to the political and strategic worst-case scenarios that daily revivify a moribund political realism. Fourth, it establishes a range of virtual environments for assessing the positive and negative qualities of reality. Finally, it challenges the producer of the most powerful virtual reality, the military-industrial-media-entertainment network, which captivates us with the image of a permanent state of violence.

The ultimate test for virtual theory is how well it "travels" across spatial, temporal, cultural, and most importantly, *existential* distances, to become worthy of the accident as the global event. This is not a blanket denial of purpose or responsibility behind such events. It is rather to recognize how dependent the national security state has become upon the complexity, uncertainty, and contingency engendered by networked global events for its own exceptional powers, or what political theorist Carl

Schmitt called the "political theology" of sovereignty.[35] Some, including the coterie of neo-conservatives in the newly elected Bush administration, might believe that the U.S. has become an empire by accident, or, as Robert Frost wrote in a poem by the title, "accidentally on purpose":

> Never believe it. At the very worst
> It must have had the purpose from the first
> To produce purpose as the fitter bred:
> We were just purpose coming to a head.[36]

But if we take Frost literally, when he writes of what we must believe when facing the very "worst"—the notion of a world without rhyme or reason—then a different interpretation emerges: we *need* to believe in the purpose of the American empire and the power òf virtuous war to keep that other, increasingly more powerful empire at bay, the "empire of circumstance."

10 After 9/11

Knowledge is limited. Imagination encircles the world.
(Albert Einstein)

Imagination is not a gift usually associated with bureaucracies.
(*The 9/11 Commission Report*, p. 344)

Before 9/11, the Florida Gulf Coast town of Venice was known as the "shark tooth capital" of the world, the winter home of the Ringling Brothers and Barnum & Bailey Circus, and having the second highest per capita number of retirees in America. After 9/11, Venice acquired a new notoriety: three of the Al Qaeda hijackers had learned to fly there. So when my cousin Steve volunteered to take me in a spin up the coast in his single-engine plane, I jumped at the chance.

I met him at the Venice Municipal Airport, which was built in the early 1940s to train the bomber pilots of the Second World War. Steve's plane wasn't much younger than the airport: a stick-controlled "tail dragger," the restored 1949 Piper Clipper looked like a red Tonka Toy on steroids. After a quick visual inspection, we took off and headed north towards Tampa. Over the noise of the engine we talked about flying, the hijackers, how difficult it might be to pilot a Boeing 767, and what turned out to be a shared obsession, UFOs.

As we taxied past the blue-and-white awning of Huffman Aviation, Steve filled me in about the flight schools in Florida. It was not uncommon for them to be full of foreign students

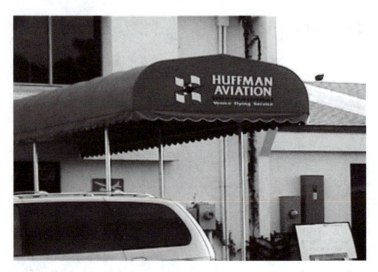

Huffman Aviation at the Venice Airport in Florida—where three of the Al Qaeda hijackers learned to fly.

Venice Airport—where U.S. Army airmen learned to fly during the Second World War.

attracted to their relative inexpensiveness and rapid certification. Always a marginal business, the schools weren't too fussy about paperwork or visas, so long as the checks cleared. My cousin knew of a German student who came over and was able to get his pilot certification in about two weeks. He would not be able to fly a jet, or multi-engine plane for that matter, but he did learn the fundamentals of aerodynamics: how to take-off, make turns, and, hopefully, land.

At one point my cousin asked if I wanted to try my hand at flying. Emboldened by his matter-of-fact attitude—he described it as just like driving a car but with one more spatial dimension—I gave it a go. After a few do's-and-don'ts, he handed over the stick while he worked the foot rudders. I made a couple of shallow turns and was starting to feel pretty comfortable. But one turn took us a bit too close to the controlled airspace of MacDill Air Force Base, which is just south of Tampa and more importantly home of U.S. Central Command and Special Operations Command. Thinking it best not to test their air defense systems, he took the stick and put us on a heading back to Venice.

We landed on one of the airport's long intersecting runways, and as we taxied back toward the hangars, my cousin pointed out the large concrete circles where the B-24s used to park. He pulled up close to Huffman Aviation and cut the engine. Dutch-born Rudi Dekkers, the owner when Atta came to town, had recently sold the place after being arrested on fraud charges. The new owners were known to be hostile to interviewers as well as sightseers, so we settled for a quick photo-op under Huffman awnings. Spotting a nearby bar and grill, bearing the odd name of "44th Aero Squadron," we went in for a beer.

The place was dark, musty, and decked out with Second World War memorabilia: sepia-tinted photos of aircrews, cracked leather flight jackets with squadron decals, camouflage nets haphazardly draped around the glass cases; it felt like we had stepped into a B-grade Hollywood movie set. But we had clearly come at the right time. It was "Two-for-One Air Raid Hour," with every delivery of drinks accompanied by a blinding searchlight and the wind-up wail of a siren. It did not seem like a very good place to work out any post-traumatic stress.

During one of the sonic lulls, I asked the beefy barman what was the local line on the hijackers. I got more than an earful. Mohamed Atta was "an arrogant S.O.B."; over the five months he attended the school he had hung out at the bar with a "girlfriend"—she evidently part-timed with an escort service—and he wasn't very nice to her, at all. The barman had less to say about Huffman Aviation, except that none of the instructors thought what they taught the hijackers could possibly have qualified them to pilot a Boeing 767 (skipping the fact that they did go on to a simulator school for large jets). With a wink and a nod he also told me that Huffman's wasn't just in the business of teaching students how to fly. The word "drugs" hung in the air—along with billowing clouds of CO_2 that now joined the wailing of the siren and the flashing of lights. I'm not sure if it was the flashing lights, deafening noise, or air-borne mold, but before I had finished my second draft I felt like I had skipped the buzz and gone straight to the hangover.

None of this, of course, jibed with the official accounts, so I decided to do some further investigations into the local scene. Papers like the Venice *Gondolier Sun* had made an effort to find and connect dots that eluded the national press, probably for good reason. Like the Internet, the local papers wove a web of conspiracy around Huffman Aviation.[1]

Huffman had rented out a hangar to Britannia Aviation, a company that listed assets of only $750 and one employee; yet Britannia had a multi-year contract to service aircraft from a variety of airlines, including Caribe Air, a Caribbean carrier whose aircraft were seized by federal officials at the Mena, Arkansas airport (yes, the same one that had become notorious during the Iran-Contra scandal for cocaine and gun trafficking). Other questions were raised in a series of articles and, following the rules of the conspiracy genre, never quite answered. Why were the Venice police told after 9/11 to keep their distance from Britannia? Was the company in fact a CIA front? Why were there no follow-up investigations after Atta and fellow hijacker pilot, Marwan al-Shehhi, abandoned a stalled airplane, rented from Huffman, on a runway at Miami International Airport?

When logic failed to connect the dots, juxtaposition of even stranger stories did the trick. What about the famous Ringling Brothers and Barnum & Bailey Circus that wintered in Venice? It turns out John Ringling North was an agent of the Second World War pre-cursor of the CIA, the OSS, and that his circus, "the Greatest Show on Earth," had provided perfect cover for agents gathering intelligence while traveling behind the Iron Curtain during the Cold War.[2] Not only that, the CIA sent operatives to Venice's Clown College to learn sleight of hand and the art of disguise. The curriculum included the study of classic clowns like Buster Keaton, Charlie Chaplin, and, my favorite, the Three Stooges; Bill Irwin and Penn Jillette are alumni.[3]

And then there were the UFOs. My cousin and I had exchanged stories about UFO sightings around Florida, many of them close to the Air Force bases that dot the area, like the famous Gulf Breeze incidents near Elgin Air Force Base in the 1990s. Ever since spotting one in my teen years, I had immersed myself in the lore and literature of UFOs. It could just have been triggered by our conversation but I did think there was something familiar about my cousin's plane. On my return I searched on the Internet for the Air Force Project Blue Book investigations into unidentified aerial objects, conducted from 1947–1969.[4] In one of the earliest and most famous cases, Harry F. Clark, owner of Clark's Flying Services in Nampa, Idaho was flying at 10,000 feet over Utah when he spotted seven delta-shaped objects. They traveled in perfect formation, seemed to oscillate, and followed his turn without any sign of banking or skidding typical of airplanes; after ten minutes, they flew off at high speed. Clark's engine ran rough throughout the encounter, and upon landing he discovered that his spark plugs had all shorted and burnt out. The Air Force Report of Investigation, dated July 28, 1949, stated that Clark was "reliable and sincere." The report also notes that the shorted-out spark plugs were sent to Wright-Patterson Air Force Base in Dayton, Ohio for analysis. The report notes the plane that Clark was flying: a 1949 Piper Clipper.

Some might dismiss this as a far-fetched coincidence. Others (and according to polls, the majority of Americans) would think otherwise. They understand, even live the Way of the Web: short on explanations, long on associations, it taxes credibility but enhances imagination. I have always found it shortsighted to dismiss the Web when it fails external litmus tests of "the truth." I am more interested in how not just new ways of thinking but new ways of being emerge from the virtual worlds of the Web. I think this is what Kevin Kelly, *Wired* magazine's founding editor, was getting at when he defined a network as "organic behavior in a techno-logical matrix."[5] Like a junkie chasing the dragon's tail, our synapses require more and more sensational information before they spark; soon our own neural networks start to mimic those of the Web. Rather than refute the Web, I wish to use and disabuse the Web as Nietzsche did of "History," to find within it the most dangerous symptoms of modernity, no matter where it might lead, from Venice Municipal Airport to the Air Force Blue Book to the dream world of bin Laden.[6] Once again I turned to Walter Benjamin, writing in an earlier interim of violence and uncertainty: "In times of terror, when everyone is something of a conspirator, everybody will be in a situation where he has to play detective."[7]

Before 9/11 and after 9/11: it is as if whole histories, critical ques-tions, and future hopes disappeared into this temporal rift, only to re-emerge as official stories and their carnival-mirror opposite, conspiracy theories. Lost in between was a credible story of what happened and why. Not only did the old rules of statecraft, diplo-macy, and warfare become victims of 9/11; in the interregnum a global *in terrorem* seemed to suspend all critical inquiry.[8]

Obviously, the sheer scale, scope, and shock of the event itself are partially to blame for the initial paucity as well as poverty of the critical response to 9/11. After terrorist hijackers transformed three commercial jetliners into highly explosive kinetic weapons, toppled the twin towers of the World Trade Center (WTC), substantially damaged the Pentagon, killed over three thousand people, and triggered a state of emergency—and before the dead could be fully grieved, Osama bin Laden's head brought on a platter, justice perceived as done, and information no longer con-sidered a subsidiary of war—there was very little about 9/11 that was *safe* to say. Unless one was firmly situated in a patriotic, ideological, or religious position (which at home and abroad drew uncomfortably close), it became intellectually difficult and even politically dangerous to assess the meaning of a conflict that phase-shifted with every news cycle, from "Terror Attack" to "America Fights Back"; from a "crusade" to a "counter-terror campaign"; from "the first war of the 21st century" to a familiar combination of humanitarian intervention and remote killing; from kinetic terror to bioterror; from the spectacle of war to a war of spectacles.

Detective work and some courage is needed because questions about the root causes or political intentions of the terrorist act have been either silenced by charges of "moral equivalency" or rendered moot by claims that the exceptional nature of the act placed it outside political discourse: explanation is identified as exoneration.[9] Reflecting the nature of the attack, as well as the chaos and confusion which followed, the conventional boundaries of the infosphere expanded during the first week to include political, historical, and ethical analysis by some voices not usually heard on primetime (I was shocked one evening by the sight of Noam Chomsky holding forth in primetime on ABC News). However, as the flow of information became practically entropic, there was a willingness (as judged by the unholy trinity of polls, pols, and programming) to accept as wisdom President Bush's early declaration that *evil*—which expanded from a person to a network to the now notorious "axis of evil"—was to blame. From that moment, policy debate and political action down-shifted to a simple declarative with an impossible performative: to eradicate all such evils. Binary narratives displaced any complex or critical analysis of what happened and why. Retribution required certainty, and certainty was produced as a salve for the actually as well as symbolically injured.

Even sophisticated analysts like Michael Ignatieff belittled the need for critical inquiry by declaiming the exceptionality of the act:

> What we are up against is apocalyptic nihilism. The nihilism of their means—the indifference to human costs—takes their actions not only out of the realm of politics, but even out of the realm of war itself. The apocalyptic nature of their goals makes it absurd to believe they are making political demands at all. They are seeking the violent transformation of an irremediably sinful and unjust world. Terror does not express a politics, but a metaphysics, a desire to give ultimate meaning to time and history through ever-escalating acts of violence which culminate in a final battle between good and evil.[10]

By funneling the experience through the image of American exceptionalism, 9/11 quickly took on an *exceptional ahistoricity*. For the most part, history was only invoked—mainly in the sepia tones of the Second World War —to prepare America for the sacrifice and suffering that lay ahead. The influential conservative George Will wrote that there were now only two time zones left for the United States:

> America, whose birth was mid-wived by a war and whose history has been punctuated by many more, is the bearer of great responsibilities and the focus of myriad resentments. Which is why for America, there are only two kinds of years, the war years and the interwar years.[11]

Under such forced circumstances, of being beyond experience, outside of history, and between wars, 9/11 does not easily yield to philosophical, political, or social inquiry. The best one can do is to thickly describe, robustly interrogate, and directly challenge the authorized truths and official actions of all parties who posit a world view of absolute differences in need of final solutions. I do so here and now by first challenging the common assumption that 9/11 is an exceptional event beyond history and theory, especially those theories tainted, as Edward Rothstein claimed in the *New York Times*, by "postmodernism" and "post-colonialism."[12] Second, I apply the insights of a virtual theory to examine the representations, technologies, and strategies of network wars that have eluded mainstream journalism and traditional social science. I conclude by uncovering what I consider to be the main dangers that emerged from the counter/terror of 9/11.

On the question of exceptionalism, consider a few testimonials, the first from an editorial in the *New York Times*:

> If the attack against the World Trade Center proves anything it is that our offices, factories, transportation and communication networks and infrastructures are relatively vulnerable to skilled terrorists ... Among the rewards for our attempts to provide the leadership needed in a fragmented, crisis-prone world will be as yet unimagined terrorists and other sociopaths determined to settle scores with us.[13]

Another from a cover story of *Newsweek*:

> The explosion shook more than the building: it rattled the smug illusion that Americans were immune, somehow, to the plague of terrorism that torments so many countries.[14]

And finally, one from the London *Sunday Times*:

> He began the day as a clerk working for the Dean Witter brokerage on the 74th floor of the World Trade Center in New York and ended it as an extra in a real-life sequel to *Towering Inferno . . .*[15]

It might surprise some to learn that these are all quotes taken from 1993, the first and much less deadly terrorist attack on the World Trade Center. They are presented here as a caution, against reading terrorism only in the light—the often-blinding light—of the events of September 11. Obviously the two WTC events differ in the scale of the devastation as well as the nature of the attack. 9/11 defied the public imagination of the real—not to mention, as just about every public official and media authority is loathe to admit, the official imagination and preemptive capacity of the intelligence community, federal law enforcement, airport security, military, and other governmental agencies. Shock and surprise produced an immediate and nearly uniform reading of the event that was limited in official discourse to condemnation, retribution, and counterterror. But there is a professional as well as a public responsibility to place 9/11 in an historical context and interpretive field that reaches beyond the immediacy of personal tragedy and official injury. Otherwise 9/11 will be remembered not for the attack itself but for the increasing cycles of violence that follow.

If 9/11 is not wholly new, what is it? As we have seen too well, the official response was a struggle of evil against good—of which, given the rhetorical excess deemed necessary by our leaders to mobilize the public to action, there have been more than a few cases in American history; the Cold War comes most readily to mind. As an actual practice of warfare we again received a better picture of what 9/11 is not than what it is: from the President and Secretary of Defense and down the food-chain of the national security hierarchy, we heard that this would not be the Gulf War or Kosovo, and it most definitely would not be Vietnam or Mogadishu. And they were partially right—certainly more so than commentators from the knee-jerk factions of both the Right and Left, who flooded the airwaves with a sloppy convergence of historical analogies from the Second World War (Pearl Harbor and the Reichstag being most prominent) and conspiracy theories (the Israeli Mossad and Big Oil pulling all the strings).

From my perspective, new and old forms of representation and violence synergized on 9/11. The neo-medieval rhetoric of holy war reverberated from the minaret to the television and, at an unprecedented level, to the Internet. A hyper-modern war of simulation and surveillance was played out at flight schools, airports, and in practically every nook, cranny, and cave of Afghanistan. Indeed it is noteworthy that many in the military thought the initial attack was part of a war game:

> Newly disclosed audiotapes provided to the [9/11] commission by Norad demonstrated widespread confusion within the military on the morning of the attacks, with many air-defense commanders uncertain whether the reports of the hijackings were part of an unannounced military exercise.[16]

In response, a remote aerial war over Afghanistan was directed from Central Command in Tampa, Florida, 7,750 miles away from targets that were surveyed by drone aircraft like the Predator and Global Hawk, and destroyed by smart GPS-guided JDAMs (Joint Direct Attack Munitions with a circular error probability of about ten feet), CBU-87 and CBU-103 "cluster bombs" (Combined Effects Munitions containing over 200 bomblets that have antitank, antipersonnel as well as an incendiary capability), and dumb bombs, topped by the 15,000 pound "Daisy Cutters" (BLU-82) that explode 3 feet above the ground and incinerate anything within 600 yards. And in a dirty war of blood and bluff, special operations forces led an anti-Taliban coalition in a limited and, by early reports, highly successful land campaign.

This strange new hybrid of conflict fully qualifies, perverse as it might sound, as another case of virtuous war. We have seen how a post-Vietnam, post-Cold War, post-modern, virtuous war emerged prior to 9/11, from the battlespace of the Gulf War and the aerial campaigns of Bosnia and Kosovo in which the killing was kept, as much as it was technologically and ethically possible, virtual and virtuous. Pre-9/11, virtuous war, relying on computer simulation, media manipulation, global surveillance, and networked warfare, was designed to deter and discipline any potential enemy. Post-9/11, it would be unleashed to destroy a very real (if overly magnified) enemy, one that came with a face (22 of which were prominently displayed on the FBI's new website of most-wanted terrorists[17]). The goal was the same: combine technical and ethical superiority to actualize violence from a distance with minimal casualties when possible.

This is not to claim that people do not die in virtuous wars, past or present, but rather that new technologies of killing skew the casualty rates, both off and on the battlefield. In the 9/11 attack, nineteen terrorist hijackers killed over 3,000 people in the United States. By the end of the major hostilities in Afghanistan in January 2002, twenty American military personnel had been killed overseas in the line of duty, the majority of whom died in accidents or by friendly fire: only one soldier, Sgt. First Class Nathan Chapman, was actually killed by hostile fire.[18] As was the case in the Kosovo campaign, more journalists *covering* the war were killed by hostile fire (ten by the end of January) than American military fighting in Afghanistan. The high incidence of friendly-fire deaths (as well as ratio to hostile fire deaths) reflects the increased lethality of precision munitions when they are mistargeted: three members of the U.S. Army 5th Special Forces Group team were killed and nineteen soldiers wounded after they mistakenly gave their own geo-coordinates for a satellite-guided JDAMs. It also reflects a "low risk, low yield" military strategy that some see as a lingering legacy of the "Vietnam Syndrome" (the erosion of public support if body-bags come home in high numbers)—which resurfaced at the beginning and then was declared "kicked" at the end of the Gulf War by the first President Bush in 1991.[19]

On the other side of virtuous war, enemy casualties were increasingly hard to come by. As the war was winding down in December, estimates of enemy combatant deaths ranged wildly, from 3,000–10,000. And when a lone economics professor, Marc

Herold at the University of New Hampshire, researched the number of Afghan non-combatant casualties at 3,767, a maelstrom of controversy erupted.[20]

From the start, it was apparent that 9/11 was and would continue to be a war of networks. Whether terrorist, internet, or primetime, most of the networks were linked by a push/pull propagation of violence, fear, and dis/mis/information. For a prolonged moment, in the first week of confusion and chaos where there was no detached point of observation, these networks seemed almost neurally attached, immersing viewers in a 24/7 cycle of tragic images of destruction and loss. A national state of emergency and trauma reached into all levels of society. It was as if the American political culture experienced a collective Freudian trauma, which could be re-enacted (endlessly on cable and the Internet) but not understood at the moment of shock. And in a state of emergency, as in war, the first images stick. There was an initial attempt by the media to transform these images of horror into responsible discourses of reflection and action, but the blame game kicked in with a fury. Moving at the speed of the news cycle and in the rush to judgment, there was little time for deliberation, for understanding the motivations of the attackers, or for assessing the potential consequences, intended as well as unintended, of a military response.

It quickly became apparent that the symbiotic networks of war and media were not merely nodes connected by wiring of one sort or another. They conveyed, mimicked, and in some cases generated human attributes and intentions; we are back to Kevin Kelly's definition of a network as "organic behavior in a technological matrix."[21] But 9/11 knocked akilter this always problematical relationship between meat and wire. Technologically driven events outpaced organic modes of comprehension, and human actions, whether out of trauma or information overload, seemed increasingly to resemble machinic reflexes. Indeed, the first reaction by most onlookers and television reporters was to deem the event an accident. The attack on the second tower destroyed the accidental thesis, and, as well, it seemed, our ability to cognitively map the devastating aftermath. Instead, into the void left by the collapse of the WTC towers and the absence of detached analysis rushed a host of metaphors, analogies, and metonyms, dominated by denial ("It's a movie"), history ("It's Pearl Harbor"), and non-specific horror ("It's the end of the world as we have known it").

In the contemporary public culture, the media networks rather than the family, the community, or the government provide the first, and, by their very speed and pervasiveness, most powerful response to a crisis. Questions of utility, responsibility, and accountability inevitably arose, and as one would expect, the media's pull-down menu was not mapped for the twin-towered collapse of American invulnerability. Primetime networks did their best (the late Peter Jennings of ABC better than the rest) to keep up with the realtime crises. But fear, white noise, and technical glitches kept intruding, creating a cognitive lag so profound between event and interpretation that I wondered at the time if superstring theory had not been proven right, that one of the ten other dimensions that make up the universe had suddenly intruded upon our own, formerly ordered one, exposing the chaos beneath.

Indeed, after the looped footage of the collapse of the towers began to take on the feeling of déjà vu, I seriously wondered if the reality principle had not taken a fatal blow. Like Ignatieff, I discerned a nihilism at work, but of a different kind, of the sort vividly on display when déjà vu shows up (all over again) in the movie *The Matrix*. The first déjà vu moment appears when some punky-looking customers in search of bootleg virtual reality software come to see Neo, the protagonist played by Keanu Reeves. He pulls from a shelf a green leather-bound book, the title of which is briefly identifiable as Jean Baudrillard's *Simulacra and Simulation*. When he opens the hollowed-out book to retrieve the software, the first page of the last chapter appears: "On Nihilism." Clearly a homage by the two directors, the Wachowski siblings, it all happens very quickly, too quickly to read the original words of Baudrillard, but here they are:

Nihilism no longer wears the dark, Wagnerian, Spenglerian, fuliginous colors of the end of the century. It no longer comes from a Weltanschauung of decadence nor from a metaphysical radicality born of the death of God and of all the consequences that must be taken from this death. Today's nihilism is one of transparency, this irresolution is indissolubly that of the system, and that of all the theory that still pretends to analyze it.[22]

With the toppling of the WTC a core belief was destroyed: it could not happen here. Into this void the networks rushed, to provide transparency without depth, a simulacrum of horror, a much purer form of nihilism than ever imagined by moralist commentators like Ignatieff or Rothstein. In official circles, there was a concerted effort to fence off the void: the critical use of language, imagination, even humor was tightly delimited by moral sanctions and government warnings. This first-strike against critical thought took the peculiar form of a semantic debate over the meaning of "coward." In the *New Yorker* and on *Politically Incorrect*, the question was raised whether it is more cowardly to commandeer a commercial airliner and pilot it into the World Trade Center, bomb Serbians from 15,000 feet, or direct a cruise missile attack against bin Laden from several thousand miles away. The official response was swift, with advertisements yanked, talk-show condemnations, and Ari Fleischer, White House press secretary, saying people like Bill Mahar of *Politically Incorrect* "should watch what they say, watch what they do."

Other protected zones of language began to take shape. When Reuters news agency questioned the abuse-into-meaningless of the term "terrorism," George Will on a Sunday morning news program retaliated by advocating a boycott of Reuters.[23] Irony and laughter were permitted in some places, not in others. At a Defense Department press conference Secretary of Defense Rumsfeld could ridicule, and effectively disarm, a reporter who dared to ask if anyone in the Department of Defense would be authorized to lie to the news media.[24] President Bush was given room to joke in a morale-boosting visit to the CIA, saying he was "spending a lot of quality time lately" with George Tenet, the director of the CIA.[25] And then there was *New York Times* reporter Edward Rothstein, taking his opportunistic shot at postmodernists and postcolonialists, claiming that their irony and relativism is "ethically perverse" and produces a "guilty passivity."[26] Some of us were left wondering where would that view place fervent truth-seekers and serious enemies of relativism and irony like Osama bin Laden? Terrorist foe but epistemological ally?

In terrorem ruled, and the road to Iraq would be paved with the dissembling, dissimulations, and manipulation of fear that followed on the heels of 9/11.

Like an auto-immune response, 9/11 triggered a virtuous war in which images clearly dominated words. It is important to recover from the mind's-eye how the air war started on October 7, 2001 with a split-screen war of images: in one box, a desolate Kabul seen through a nightscope camera lens, in grainy-green pixels except for the occasional white arc of anti-aircraft fire followed by the flash of an explosion; in the other, a rotating cast of characters surrounded by monitors, maps, and other graphics, beginning with President Bush, followed by Secretary of Defense Rumsfeld, Chairman of the Joint Chiefs General Meyers, and Attorney General John Ashcroft, then progressively down the media food-chain of war reporters, beltway pundits, and recently retired generals. On the one side we witnessed images of embodied resolve in high resolution; on the other, nighttime shadows with no-body in sight.

Strategic and narrative binaries also cropped up in President Bush's war statement, incongruously delivered from the Treaty Room of the White House: "as we strike military targets, we will also drop food"; the United States is "a friend to the Afghan people" and "an enemy of those who aid terrorists"; "the only way to pursue peace is to pursue those who threaten it." And once more, the ultimate either/or was issued: "Every nation has a choice to make. In this conflict there is no neutral ground."[27]

But the war programming was interrupted by the media-savvy bin Laden. Shortly after the air strikes began, he appeared on Qatar's al-Jazeera television network (still unknown enough to be billed as "the Arab world's CNN") in a pre-taped statement that was cannily delivered as a counter air-strike to the U.S. Kitted out in turban and battle fatigues, bin Laden presented his own bipolar view of the world: "these events have divided the world into two camps, the camp of the faithful and the camp of infidels." But if opposition constituted his worldview, a mirroring of history sanctioned the counter-violence: "America has been filled with horror from north to south and east to west, and thanks be to God what America is tasting now is only a copy of what we have tasted."[28]

Without falling into the trap of "moral equivalency," one can discern striking discursive similarities. Secretary of Defense Rumsfeld and others made much of the "asymmetrical" war being waged by the terrorists. And it is indeed a canny and even diabolical use of asymmetrical tactics as well as strategies when terrorists commandeer commercial aircraft and transform them into kinetic weapons of indiscriminate violence—and then deploy commercial media to counter the military strikes that follow. Yet, a fearful symmetry is also at work, at an unconscious, possibly pathological level, a war of escalating, competing, and imitative oppositions, a *mimetic war of images*.

A mimetic war is a battle of imitation and representation, in which the relationship of who we are and who they are is played out along a wide spectrum of familiarity and friendliness, indifference and tolerance, estrangement and hostility. It can result in appreciation or denigration, accommodation or separation, assimilation or extermination. It draws physical boundaries between peoples, as well as metaphysical boundaries between life and the most radical other of life, death. It separates human from god. It builds the fence that makes good neighbors; it builds the wall that confines a whole people. And it sanctions just about every kind of violence. President Bush announces that Iran is now part of the "axis of evil"; Iran complies by staging the first large-scale anti-American demonstration since the moderate Khatami regime came to power.

More than a rational calculation of interests takes us to war. People go to war because of how they see, perceive, picture, imagine, and speak of others: that is, how they construct the difference of others as well as the sameness of themselves through representations. From Greek tragedy and Roman gladiatorial spectacles to futurist art and fascist rallies, the mimetic mix of image and violence has proven to be more powerful than the most rational discourse. Indeed, the medical definition of mimesis is "the appearance, often caused by hysteria, of symptoms of a disease not actually present."[29] Before one can find a cure, one must study the symptoms—or, as it was once known in medical science, practice *semiology*.

It was not long before morbid symptoms began to surface from an array of terror and counter-terror networks. Al Qaeda members reportedly used encrypted e-mail to communicate; steganography to hide encoded messages in web images (including pornography); Kinko's and public library computers to send messages; underground banking networks called *hawala* to transfer untraceable funds; 24/7 cable networks like al-Jazeera and CNN to get the word out; and, in their preparations for 9/11, a host of other information technologies like rented cell phones, online travel agencies, and flight simulators.

In general, networks—from television primetime to Internet realtime—delivered events with an alacrity and celerity that left not only viewers but decision-makers racing to keep up. With information as the life-blood and speed as the killer variable of networks, getting inside the decision-making as well the image-making loop of the opponent became the central strategy of network warfare. This was not lost on the U.S. national security team as it struggled after the initial attack to get ahead of the network curve. Sluggish reactions were followed by quicker preemptive actions on multiple networks. Congress quickly passed the "Uniting and Strengthening America by Providing Appropriate Tools Required to Intercept and Obstruct Terrorism (U.S.A PATRIOT) Act," which allowed for "roving wiretaps" of multiple telephones, easier surveillance of e-mail and Internet traffic, more sharing between foreign and domestic intelligence, and the divulgence of grand jury and wiretap transcripts to intelligence agencies.[30] National Security adviser Condoleeza Rice made personal calls to the heads of the television networks, asking them to pre-screen and to consider editing Al Qaeda videos for possible coded messages.[31] Information about the air campaign as well as the unfolding ground interventions was heavily filtered by the Pentagon, which set up an "Office of Strategic Influence" to correct unfavorable news reports and, supposedly, to plant favorable ones in the foreign press. Open information flows slowed to a trickle from the White House and the Defense Department after tough restrictions were imposed against leaks. Psychological operations were piggy-backed onto humanitarian interventions by the dropping of propaganda leaflets and food packs. The "Voice of America" began broadcasting anti-Taliban messages in Pashto. After the twenty-two "Most Wanted Terrorists" were featured on the FBI's website, the popular TV program "America's Most Wanted" ran an extended program on their individual cases. The infowar was on.

Some of the most powerful networks are often the least visible, but it was hard to keep a secret when Hollywood was added to the mix. The entertainment industry journal *Variety* first broke the news about a meeting between White House officials and Hollywood executives. The stated intention was ominous enough, to "enlist Hollywood in the war effort":

> The White House is asking Hollywood to rally 'round the flag in a style reminiscent of the early days of World War II. Network heads and studio chiefs heard that message Wednesday in a closed-door meeting with emissaries from the Bush administration in Beverly Hills, and committed themselves to new initiatives in support of the war on terrorism. These initiatives would stress efforts to enhance the perception of America around the world, to "get out the message" on the fight against terrorism and to mobilize existing resources, such as satellites and cable, to foster better global understanding.[32]

Although some big media picked up this aspect of the story, none except for *Newsweek* took note of the how this alliance had been already staged by the military and, to no surprise for students of virtuous war, University of Southern California's Institute for Creative Technology.[33] We saw how in 1999 the Army ponied up $43 million to bring together the simulation talents of Hollywood, Silicon Valley, and the U.S. military.[34] Now it seemed that they were gathering top talent to fully coordinate a new virtuous war effort:

> In a reversal of roles, government intelligence specialists have been secretly soliciting terrorist scenarios from top Hollywood filmmakers and writers. A unique ad hoc working group convened at USC just last week at the behest of the U.S. Army. The goal was to brainstorm about possible terrorist targets and schemes in America and to offer solutions to those threats, in light of the twin assaults on the Pentagon and the World Trade Center. Among those in the working group based at USC's Institute for Creative Technology are those with obvious connections to the terrorist pic milieu, like "Die Hard" screenwriter Steven E. De Souza, TV writer David Engelbach ("MacGyver") and Joseph Zito, who directed the features "Delta Force One," "Missing in Action" and "The Abduction." But the list also includes more mainstream

suspense helmers like David Fincher ("Fight Club"), Spike Jonze ("Being John Malkovich"), Randal Kleiser ("Grease") and Mary Lambert ("The In Crowd") as well as feature screen-writers Paul De Meo and Danny Bilson ("The Rocketeer").[35]

It would appear that the response to 9/11 had been primed by the military-industrial-media-entertainment network. If Vietnam was a war waged in the living-rooms of America, the first and most likely the last battles of the counter/terror war are going to be waged on global networks that reach much more widely and deeply into our everyday lives.

On September 11, terror came to America not by rogue state or ballistic missile or high-tech biological, chemical, and nuclear weapons of mass destruction—as presaged by the intelligence and national security experts—but by an unholy network, hijacked airliners, and the terrorist's favorite "force-multiplier": primetime, cable, and Internet weapons of mass distraction and disruption. My greatest concern then and now is not so much the future but how past futures become reproduced; that is, how we seem unable to escape the feed-back loops of bad intelligence, bureaucratic thinking, and failed imagination. From my own experience, when confronted by the complexity and speed of networked conflicts, the fields of political science and international relations are too slow to respond when it matters most. This leaves another intel-lectual void into which policy-makers, military planners, and media pundits are always ready to rush. Among the advocates of the Revolution in Military Affairs, one concept became a mantra: "network-centric warfare." I had learned first-hand, during my interview with its forefather, Vice Admiral Arthur Cebrowski (formerly President of the Naval War College and hand-picked by Defense Secretary Rumsfeld to head-up the Pentagon's new Office of Force Transformation), how these techno-optimists believed network-centric war would get us inside the decision-making loop of the adversary's network, and disrupt or destroy it before it can do the same to ours.[36] The basic idea was that people make war as they make wealth, and, in the information age, networked technology had become the enabler of both (probably not a view widely shared by Enron stockholders). Information and speed were the key variables in warfare: whoever has the fastest network wins.

The shift from state-centric to network-centric modes of deterring and defeating new threats makes sense within a rational framework. However, diminishing the role of human decisions, *especially* ones in which emotion plays such a significant part, might not be the best way to anticipate and confront future threats of terrorism. Furthermore, after the Pentagon released the bin Laden home video in December, where dreams and theology mixed with strategies of destruction and slaughter, there was little evidence of any kind of rational purchase for a network-centric deterrence to work.[37] And after witnessing that same day the revival of missile defense as the *deus ex machina* cure for American vulnerability, the consignment of "lower-levels of decision-making" to networked technology seems practically (rather than as it had been in the past, mutually) suicidal.

It is clear that the allure of technological solutions reaches across cultures and often beyond rationality. Bandwidth as well as bombs might offer short-term fixes for the immediate threats posed by terrorism. But no matter how weak the flesh, neural networks, human spirit, and political will are still needed to make the future safe again. In the rush to extend, harden, and accelerate networks, all kinds of checks and balances were being left behind. Once again, there seemed to be little concern for what organizational theorists see as the negative synergy operating in tightly coupled systems, in which unintended consequences produce cascading effects and normal accidents, in which the very complexity and supposed redundancy of the network produce unforeseen but built-in disasters. Think Three Mile Island in a pre-1914 diplomatic-military milieu. Think Pentagon *and* Enron when Paul Virilio writes of the "integral accident":

> The proliferation of atomic weapons, freshly boosted by India, Pakistan and probably other destabilized countries on the Asian continent, is prompting the United States—the last great world power—to accelerate the famous "revolution in military affairs" by developing that emergent strategy known as "information war," which consists in using electronics as a hegemonic technology: a role it now takes over from nuclear

physics. . . . It is in this context of financial instability and military uncertainty, in which it is impossible to differentiate between information and disinformation, that the question of the integral accident arises once again. . . .[38]

Virilio, as usual, had the jump on traditional social scientists, who seemed congenitally unsuited for the kind of investigation demanded by the emergence of a military-industrial-media-entertainment network. We have moved far beyond the situation of which President Eisenhower warned in 1961, of the rise of a "military-industrial complex," and of what might happen should "public policy be captured by a scientific and technological elite." Once Silicon Valley, broadcast media, and Hollywood were added to the mix, the dangers morphed and multiplied. Think *Wag the Dog* meets *The Matrix*. Think of C. Wright Mill's power elite with much better gear to reproduce reality:

The media provide much information and news about what is happening in the world, but they do not often enable the listener or the viewer truly to connect his daily life with these larger realities. On the contrary, they distract him and obscure his chance to understand himself or his world, by fastening his attention upon artificial frenzies that are resolved within the program framework, usually by violent action or by what is called humor . . . There is almost always the general tone of animated distraction, of suspended agitation, but it is going nowhere and it has nowhere to go.[39]

Virtuous war was being played out by the military-industrial-media-entertainment network as our daily bread and nightly circus. Some in power (and wishing to stay so) would have us remain there, suspended perpetually, in between wars of terror and counterterror. How to break out of the distractive, often self-prophesying circles? Can a virtual theory respond without falling into the trap of the interwar? One that can escape the nullity of thought which equates the desire to comprehend with a willingness to condone terrorism? The use of sloppy analogies of resistance as well as petty infighting among critics does not give one much hope. We need to acknowledge that the majority of Americans—Republicans *and* Democrats—thought it best, whether out of patriotism, trauma, apathy, or sheer reasonableness, to leave matters in the hands of the Bush administration and the national security experts. That will not change, the cycle will not be broken, until a public rather than expert assessment is made of what distinguishes new from old dangers, real from virtual effects, terror from counterterror—and whether we are then ready to live with new levels of uncertainty about those very distinctions.

Otherwise, the last word might well come from the first words I heard over a decade ago, at the start of the last major war the U.S. had fought. It also happened in a plane: circling over Chicago O'Hare airport, the captain came on the PA to inform us that the bombing of Iraq had just begun. In the taxi on the way to my hotel, I heard the first radio reports of stealth aircraft, smart bombs, and incredibly low casualty rates. But what stuck with me from that evening were the last and only words of my cab driver. In the thickest Russian accent, in a terribly war-weary voice, without the benefit of any context but the over-excitement of the radio reports, he said: "They told us we would be in Afghanistan for ten weeks. We were there for ten years."

11 Global media in an Age of Infoterror

> Globes make my head spin. By the time I locate the place, they've changed the boundaries.
>
> (Marshal McLuhan, *War and Peace in the Global Village*)

Once in, it is hard to find one's way out from the military-industrial-media-entertainment labyrinth. Over the years I have collected a variety of objects—some found, some given, others taken on the sly—that act as bread crumbs for back-tracking my journey. They are scattered around my desk, hanging on the walls, perched on the shelves of the cubicle I constructed at the edge of my living room to write this book. The defense industry shows, filling enormous convention centers with the *Sturm und Drang* of the latest simulation technologies and killing machines, yielded the most plunder: promotional posters, branding luggage tags, videos, and mouse pads that would most likely fetch a fair price on eBay. I have a nice collection of match covers from hotels and motels, restaurants and bars, mostly from franchises like Holiday Inn, Ground Round, and The Olive Garden that ring America's military bases and training grounds, offset by a few exceptions, like the classical cherubs from Tabard Inn in D.C. (from the Pentagon trip to interview Andrew Marshall) and the cigar-chomping bulldog on the 44th Aero-Squadron Bar and Steakhouse in Venice, Florida (from my search for the "real" Mohammed Atta). There are a couple of 9 mm blue (good guys) and red (bad guys) sim-rounds that I pocketed as souvenirs after my cameraman took one to the earlobe during an exercise at

Nancy Burson's "Warhead 1."

Firefighter   *Freedomfighter*

A FIREFIGHTER FIGHTS FIRES.

A FREEDOMFIGHTER FIGHTS _____.

REFLECTIONS ON
TERRORISM

An Installation By
Les LeVeque
November 12-30, 1985
14 SCULPTORS GALLERY, 164 MERCER ST., NYC

Les Leveque's "Reflections on Terrorism."

29 Palms (some blood was spilt but the videocamera never dropped); coasters and cocktail napkins kept as mementos but also for their wine-stained scribblings of overheard conversations; business cards accepted as potlatch and reciprocated in kind that now invoke no recognizable faces; and most valuable of all, PX coffee mugs and T-shirts, of "Operation Desert Storm," "OPFOR," "All But War is Simulation," and "Bin Laden: Wanted Dead or Alive," brought back to appease the home front after long absences on the road.

This impromptu shrine is bracketed by two artifacts from an earlier project on espionage, terrorism, and war, that remind me daily, in the manner of J.L. Borges (the world's greatest guide to life's labyrinths) how much easier it is to get in than to get out of the MIME-NET. Both are images from 1985. The first is a simple black and white poster, most likely inspired by President Reagan's description of the Afghan *mujahideen* as "freedomfighters." Next to a photograph of Reagan is one of a New York City firefighter. The caption underneath asks: "A firefighter fights fires. A freedom-fighter fights _____?" The second one comes from the front page of *The Manipulator,* a short-lived, large-format art magazine. On the cover is a Nancy Burson photograph titled "Warhead 1," a digitized composite of world leaders proportioned according to their country's nuclear weapons, in which the facial features of Reagan (55% of the world's throw-weight) and Brezhnev (45%) dominate the fuzzier visages of Thatcher, Mitterand, and Deng (less than 1% each).[1]

After 9/11, these images took on an added significance, acting as a semiotic key for the corruption of politics and language that leapfrogged from the Cold War to the "Global War on Terror" (GWOT). When it comes to damage done to the English language, the Cold War was no slouch, creating a compendium of acronyms and euphemisms (from "MAD" to "terminate with extreme prejudice") that made it difficult to separate the theater of operations from the theater of the absurd. By mimesis but also *sui generis*, GWOT also oscillated from political tragedy to linguistic farce, producing the like of "unlawful enemy combatant," "total information awareness," "extraordinary rendition," as well as the various and increasingly heinous homilies of Rumsfeld.

What both global conflicts shared is a deep dependency upon

the word "terror" itself. And in both cases powerful new media abetted the production and circulation of highly politicized meanings of terror. Emerging from the shadowy playbooks of nuclear mass destruction in the Cold War, and re-surfacing from the political unconscious after the trauma of 9/11, terror's grammar and syntax began to shift, and its frequency of usage went into overdrive. Not all of this can be laid at the door of the Bush administration. As verb, code, and historical method, to terrorize has consistently been understood as an act of symbolically intimidating and, if deemed necessary, violently eradicating a personal, political, social, ethnic, religious, ideological or otherwise radically differentiated foe. Yet, as noun, message, and catch-all political signifier, the meaning of terror has always been murky. From Robespierre's endorsement to Burke's condemnation during the French revolution, from the Jewish Irgun blowing up the King David Hotel to the Palestinian Black September massacre at the Munich Olympics, from bin Laden the Good fighting the Soviet occupiers of Afghanistan to bin Laden the Bad toppling the Twin Towers of New York, terrorism, terrorists and terror itself have already morphed into the political pornography of modernity: in our image-soaked environment one knows "terrorism" with certainty only when one sees it. Now, on the nightly news and jihadist websites, the terrorist in the blink of an eye and the flash of an explosion becomes the freedom fighter *and* vice versa: at one time or another nearly everyone, from righteous statesmen who terrorbomb cities to virtuous jihadists who suicide-bomb women and children, seems to have a taste for terror.

Inscribing new borders of inclusion and exclusion, the most powerful model of terror mutated at the end of the Cold War. With the decline (if not the total) demise of a logic of deterrence based on a nuclear balance of terror, so too eroded the willingness and capacity to inflict mutually unacceptable harm that had provided a semblance of order if not an actual state of peace or justice to the bipolar system. A new model has emerged, an *imbalance of terror*, based on a mimetic fear and hatred coupled with an asymmetrical willingness and capacity to destroy the other without the formalities of war.

Again, this cannot be reduced, as much as leaders on both sides of the conflict have tried, to merely a post-9/11 phenomenon. Its origins can be traced at least as far back to 1992, with the Pentagon's secret effort authored by Paul Wolfowitz to model seven post-Cold War "war scenarios," including the rise by the year 2001 of an "REGT" (Resurgent/Emergent Global Threat).[2] It was publicly established in the 1998 U.S. Defense Policy Guidance, which shifted from a strategy of *deterring* to *destroying* the enemy (reiterated in the subsequent Quadrennial Defense Review). Mirroring this shift, bin Laden issued his pseudo-*fatwa*, which decreed Christian and Jewish civilians legitimate targets of jihad.

As in the older, tidier, nuclear balance of terror, the doctrine of taking civilians hostage and if necessary killing them still held for both sides of the conflict, but it now operated as a contingent factor of an asymmetrical relationship. Regardless of nomenclature— "terror" or "counter-terror"—high numbers of civilians would (and continue to) be killed in the process. It might be small solace to the victims whether they were primary targets as opposed to "accidental" or "collateral" victims, especially with casualty rates being terribly skewed in both cases. When one takes into account how over the last one hundred years the civilian–military ratio of war-related fatalities has been reversed, and compares the combatant-to-non-combatant casualty figures of 9/11, the Afghan War, and the Iraq War, the terror/counter-terror distinction begins to fade even further.[3] Perhaps it is time for a new Burson composite, using the faces of the leaders behind these three events proportionally to represent the number of civilian casualties.

In the Global War on Terror, a war of images not just sporadically but continuously undermines the historical meaning of words. In no small way this is because of the alacrity and rapidity by which the codes of the Cold War and the Information Age have morphed into a seamless "Age of Infoterror," in which information becomes the tool and force-multiplier of anxiety, fear, and hatred. Historic moments as well as the transition between them all too often appear to speak for themselves. Think of the "Middle Ages," the "American Century," the "1960s." Consider 2001, a year, thanks to Stanley Kubrick's film, that signified awe (and some dread) for an extraterrestrial future; that is, until kamikaze airplanes piloted by Al Qaeda terrorists brought the year, and the World Trade Center (WTC), crashing back to earth. Abetted by a global media, powerful representatives on both side of the conflict created an era of "Infoterror." On a series of video- and audio-tapes, bin Laden invoked jihad for a global caliphate, while Bush, Cheney, Rumsfeld, and others re-packaged the "long wars" against Nazism and Communism as ruling metaphors and justifications for the most controversial aspects of the GWOT, like the detention and rendition of unlawful combatants, the expansion of wiretapping and surveillance programs, and the sanctioning of torture techniques.

Although the religious and political fundamentalism of the major combatants have deservedly drawn the most attention, we need also examine how a *techno-fundamentalism* facilitated the convergence of information and terror after 9/11. Fueled by a revolution in the digitization and networking of information, the early forces driving the Information Age were primarily techno-scientific. From its embryonic moments in the 1940s (when Claude Shannon wrote the first paper on information theory, transistors were invented, and ENIAC, the first computer, was built) to its accelerated take-off in the 1990s (when packet-switching, personal computers, html, and the Internet produced a world wide web), the information revolution outpaced, outlasted, and outperformed all commensurable comers. However, the Information Age, especially in its characterization as a politically neutral, culturally anodyne movement, never really earned the status of a *longue durée*. Although the Information Age stretched in the United States from Silicon Valley to Alley and globally from Bangalore to Singapore, the distinguishing characteristic of the Information Age is a spatio-temporal *intensivity* rather than a geopolitical *extensivity*; that is, a capacity to intensify global effects through a collapse of time and distance. Developing unevenly within and across nation-states, and beset by rapid cycles of dot-com booms and busts, the Information Age is short on universality and long on instability. When a revolution stops auguring change and begins signifying an age, it usually means that a regime has been stabilized, a cultural shift codified, predictability restored. Not so with the Information Age, which is why Paul Virilio prefers to call this array of effects not an age (suggesting duration) but a "bomb" (suggesting intensity).[4]

The only constant of the Information Age is fast, repetitious, and highly reproducible change: a kind of hyper-speed Nietzschean "eternal recurrence" that defies—in spite of efforts by democratic peace theorists (with Thomas Friedman leading the pundit's charge)—the pre-determined logic of progressivist teleologies. With the Information Age, it is difficult to discern a linear path of development defined by an all-powerful actor. The closest contender, enabled by a globalized economy and the convergence of multiple networked platforms (radio, television, computers, and cell phones), would be a *new global media*. The most visible and perplexing manifestations of the Information Age—the oscillations of message and medium (signal-to-noise ratio), regressive repetitions of images (feed-back loops), and rapid phase-shifts between order and disorder (complexity)—are produced by global media and not state actors.

Global media plus global terror has tarnished the early promise of the Information Age. To get back to the future, we need to have a better picture of how media contributed to the realignments of power and knowledge that followed 9/11.

First, and most obviously, new global media attracts but ultimately defies national control. Enabled by the rapid spread of new information technologies, global media is producing a multitude of platforms and networks of power (creating what Kelly described as "organic behavior in a technological matrix") that must be, can only be, developed, managed, and regulated through global institutions.[5] Yet sovereign powers have responded to this new challenge by resisting all but the most functional and technical fixes.[6] Obviously, the United States emerged from the end of the Cold War as the dominant military and economic power, and even in the worst-case nightmares of the wargamers, it is difficult to identify a potential "peer competitor" on the horizon. However, post-Cold War, post-9/11, we have witnessed the emergence of competing sources and mediations of power: what I call a *global heteropolar matrix*, in which different actors are able to produce profound global effects through interconnectivity. Varying in identity, interests, and strength, ranging from fundamentalist terrorists to peace activists, new global actors gain advantage through the broad bandwidth of information technology rather than through the narrow stovepipe of territorially based sovereign governments. Enhanced by global media, non-state actors have become super-empowered players in international politics. Traditional forms of statecraft have become transformed and in some cases undermined by infowar, cyberwar, and netwar.

Second, global media, increasingly, repetitively, unavoidably, acts not only as trigger and transmitter of the global event, but also as a catalyst for how we respond to the event.[7] From the actual moment to the eventual interpretation—for better or worse—global media records, relays, represents, and informs our response to global events. It also shapes how we remember or forget their significance: linear narratives and cause/effect chronologies are short-circuited by the global media. We are all familiar with the contemporary production and transformation of multimedia by networked information technologies, from increased CPU speeds and broadband access, to realtime cable news and CNN—and al-Jazeera—effects, to embedded journalists and network-centric warfare. The global networking of multi-media has become unstoppable, producing an information flow that may well have accelerated beyond not only national control but our theoretical grasp. Evidence of this can be found in a public attention deficit disorder that leaves little time for critical inquiry or political action by a permanently distracted audience.

Third, we need to recognize that the impact of global media is now largely measured by its capacity to produce a *moving* image of the world. In both senses of the word, global media is *e*-motive, *a transient electronic affect conveyed at speed*. At the emotional level, this means image-based sentiments of fear, hate, and empathy come to dominate word-based discourses of ideas, interests, and power. At the electronic level, the speed of the transmission—with realtime currently the gold standard of media—matters as much as the content of the message. Paul Virilio, urban architect and social critic, has spent a lifetime demonstrating how this media-driven acceleration has produced what he calls an "aesthetics of disappearance," in which the political subject—be it the accountable leader, participatory citizen, the deliberative process itself—is diminished and quickly engulfed by a growing "infosphere."[8] This is not to say that images speak for themselves: there is a continuous political and rhetorical struggle to anchor the free-floating meanings of images with captions of one kind or another.

There is some cause to hope that this process might become more democratized with the development of newer media, from guerrilla video to political blogging.[9]

Fourth, as networked multiple media provide new global actors the means to traverse political, economic, religious, and cultural boundaries, how war is fought and peace is made are rapidly changing. Indeed, the rise of global media makes it ever more difficult to maintain the very distinction of war and peace. For the moment, the "West" might enjoy an advantage in surveillance, broadcast media, and military technologies; but the "Rest," including fundamentalist terrorist groups, non-governmental organizations, and anti-globalization activists, have tapped the political potential of networked technologies of information collection, transmission, and storage. Global political actors daily force-multiply their influence in war and diplomacy through networked multiple media. When the global war on terror began, there was one Al Qaeda website; within a few years they numbered in the hundreds (with jihadist websites now in the thousands); and with the production values of their videos vastly improving, so too (arguably) has their impact.[10]

Fifth, the informational, technological as well as political networks of global media require new modes of comprehension and instruction, and scholars have not been very quick to take up the challenge. The virtual nature and accelerating pace of global media is partly responsible: actualizing global events in realtime across traditional political, social, and cultural boundaries, global media resists the social-scientific emphasis on discerning rational behavior, applying static models, and conducting incremental research projects. Moreover, the study of global media requires the kind of deep dialogue among technological, scientific, military and other non-academic circles that has been notably lacking in discipline-bounded university programs and politically oriented think tanks. Taking into account the heteropolar and increasingly virtualized nature of global politics, we need *virtual strategies* that combine theoretical and conceptual as well as multicultural and multidisciplinary approaches.

Easier said than done: just what might such strategies look like? More importantly, what might they yield in the way of collective thought and action? Against the infoterror we currently face, critique is not enough—or it might even be too much: fear feeds on starkly and forcefully put oppositions. Adapting Foucault's distinction of "anti-justice" and "counter-justice,"[11] in which the former simply engages in critique while the latter enables emergent alternatives to challenge a dominant reality, I wish to explore five virtual strategies against infoterror that are counter-theoretical, counter-conceptual, counter-factual, counter-historical, and counter-media.

First, dismantling the effects of infoterror takes more than the realists' narrow focus on national interests or liberals' wishful thinking for a democratic peace; it requires getting up close to the war machine and full immersion into the global media matrix. I have already argued that a "virtual theory" is one way to get there. It allows us to examine the tragedy of global politics without the amorality of realism or the virtuous condemnations of liberalism, instead offering a truly agnostic and openly pluralist approach towards the world's most pressing dangers. It taps into the dual power of virtuality, which is defined by its potential for infinite reproducibility and capability to produce an effect—creative or destructive—at a distance. In this sense virtuality is the *pharmakon* of the military-industrial-media-entertainment network, going back to the Greek concept to locate both the poison and the potential cure for the worst excesses of infoterror. This places a very high premium on reflexivity in virtual theory, in the sense of a critical awareness of how acts of observation and analysis might help or hinder the actual implementation of alternatives.[12] Virtual theory seeks to leverage technology—especially multiple media—that can make the best possibility actual; that also means constructing a better world within the limits of the possible, i.e., not *ex nihilio* but *ex machina*. Neither realist or idealist, utopian or nihilist, virtual theory pragmatically posits a future forged by the encounter between theoretical imagination and technological determinism.

Second, we need to develop robust counter-concepts to the war machine: the paramount task is to counter the representation and continuation of violence through *infowar* with a new concept for the prevention and resolution of conflict; or what I refer to as *infopeace*.[13]

To understand the power of infowar, we need to know its origins and the source of its persistence. Recently information warfare, or infowar, has become the umbrella concept for cyberwar, hacker-war, netwar, virtual war, and other network-centric conflicts. However, it has a history that goes back at least as far as Sun Tzu, who considered defeating an enemy without violence to be the "acme of skill" in warfare. From its earliest application in the beating of gongs and drums, to more sophisticated uses of propa-ganda and psychological operations, infowar has traditionally been deployed by the military as a "force-multiplier" of other, more conventional forms of violence. In this sense, infowar is an adjunct of conventional war, in which command and control of the battlefield is augmented by computers, communications, and intelligence. However, with the development of mass and multiple media, infowar has taken on new forms and greater significance. As the infosphere engulfs the biosphere, as the global struggle for "full spectrum dominance" supplants discrete battlefields, as transnational business, criminal, and terrorist networks challenge the supremacy and sovereignty of the territorial state, informa-tion warfare has ascended as a significant site for the struggle of power and knowledge. Infowar now is the major supplier of materiel for an epistemic battle in which opinions, beliefs, and realities are created and destroyed through networked information and communication systems.

The power of infowar resides in its capacity to couple sign-systems and weapons-systems. Command and control, simulation and dissimulation, deception and destruction, virtual reality and hyperreality: these are the binary functions—sometimes sym-biotic, other times antagonistic—which enable infowar. Networks of remote sensing and iconic representation enable the targeting, demonization, and, if necessary, killing of the enemy. In its "hard" form, infowar provides "battlespace domination" by vio-lent (GPS-guided missiles and bombs) as well as non-lethal (pulse weapons and psychological operations) applications of technol-ogy. In its "soft" form, infowar includes a virus attack on a com-puter network or the wiping out of terrorist organizations' bank accounts. In its most virtualized form, infowar can generate simu-lated battlefields or even create *Wag the Dog* versions of a terror-ist event. In any of these three forms, information warfare can be offensive (network-centric war, Trojan horse virus, or intelligence dissimulations) or defensive (ballistic missile defense, network firewall, or preventive media). In spite of the official spin, infowar is not a precision munition. It might seek to discriminate in its targeting of enemies, but it is as broadcast forms of media that it is likely to produce all kinds of collateral damage, blowback, as well as newly resentful enemies.

At the other end of the information (and power) spectrum lies *infopeace*, by which I mean the production, application, and analysis of information by peaceful means for peaceful ends. Starting with Gregory Bateson's definition of information as "a difference that makes a difference"[14]—this is war, that is peace, this war is here, that war is over there, this war is now, that war was then—infopeace seeks to make a difference through a difference in the quality of thinking about the global contest of will, goods, and might. Measuring information in terms of quality rather than quantity, and assessing quality by the difference it makes in the reduction of personal and structural violence, infopeace opens up possibilities of alternative thought and action in global politics. Unabashedly utopian yet virtually pragmatic, it counters a "natural" state of war with a historicized account of past and future possibilities of peace.

Infopeace also relates to internal states of being. It seeks to prevent, mediate, and resolve states of war by the actualization of a mindful state of peace. Positing the eventual abolition of violence as a global political option, peace-mindedness ranges from the prevention, admonition, and mediation of violence, to the outright disavowal of violence to resolve problems in the international arena. It draws on a long tradition of peace-thinking, exemplified in early Christian pacifism and Eastern philosophies, in which the need for peace begins internally and proceeds outwardly. It starts by embracing a wholeness of the individual, and expands to families, communities, countries, and beyond. The notion of Gaia as a self-regulating biosphere contributes to the rhetoric of peace thinking, but it is the networked reality of an expanding infosphere that makes peace an attainable and ever more vital necessity.

Infopeace stresses the actualization of peace through the creative and pragmatic application of information technology. As a form of critical imagination, infopeace counters a technological determinism that increasingly circumscribes human choices. It does not seek to deny the reality of violence. Rather, infopeace integrates a strategy in which difference, conflict, and antagonism are recognized as essential aspects of human relations. It aims to develop an awareness of how these aspects can be addressed by non-violent means.

Third, we need to develop counter-factual narratives. Obviously, we cannot reverse history; but to get beyond 9/11 we might attempt a counter-factual experiment by reversing dates. How might we re-envision 9/11 in the dying light of 11/9, the date that marks the opening of the Berlin Wall and the beginning of the end of the Soviet Union? Vaclav Havel, the Czech playwright and dissident, remarked (he was actually quoting the Oxford historian Timothy Garton Ash) that what took years in Poland, months in Hungary, weeks in Germany, would probably take days in Czechoslovakia.[15] This compression of time has many causes, but as many have suggested, and as I discovered firsthand, the media played a key role. In the spring of 1990, with the assistance of a small grant, I traveled to Central and Eastern Europe to explore the impact of the media on the transformation of the Soviet bloc. After stops in Berlin and Budapest, I arrived in Prague to cover the first free elections in over fifty years. I had already learned that the best place to find the media was in the hotel bars; over drinks at the Palace Hotel, Claude Adams, foreign correspondent for the Canadian Broadcast Corporation (CBC), told me the most remarkable story of my journey.

On October 7, 1989 protest demonstrations in Berlin on the fortieth anniversary of the GDR were violently broken up by the police. However, two days later, 100,000 in Leipzig staged a peaceful demonstration. Some might remember the grainy images of the incredible night-time, candle-lit procession. That video was taken by Claude Adams. While all other western camera crews were detained at the border, Adams traveled by train, alone, as a tourist, with a new Sony mini-camcorder under his coat. Those same images spilled over the borders into Czechoslovakia at a key moment, the November 17 anniversary demonstration for the Czech student martyr Jan Opletal, who died at the hands of the country's Nazi occupiers fifty years earlier. Bolstered by smuggled images of the Leipzig demonstrations, 15,000 showed up that day, followed by a march of 2000,000 a week later and the resignation of the Communist party leadership in December 1989.

Now jump forward to 9/11, and remember the critical role of multiple media: the use of the internet, cell phones, flight simulators, hawalas, and other technologies which made it possible to convert three commercial airliners into kinetic weapons of mass destruction. Remember the second strike on the WTC, which not only transformed an accident into an intentional attack but because of the 17 minute gap between attacks, produced a rare televisual simultaneity that became a global feedback loop of trauma, terror, and heroism. Review bin Laden's use of videotape, especially the November tape in which he recounted the need to stop the sharing of dreams before 9/11 because they were threatening operational secrecy within Al Qaeda. Remember the "information operations" that preceded the U.S. decision to go to war in Iraq, and the counter-terror wars that have followed, in which informational, technological, and ethical superiority have produced few victories and many casualties.

9/11 and 11/9. One date speaks of toppling towers, terror, and trauma; the other a falling wall, joy, and hope. Both subsequently suffered from a political reduction of possible meanings. One version—that the end of the Cold War was not the result of anti-political mass movements but Reagan's beggaring of the Soviet Union through an arms race—effectively became the master narrative *after* 9/11, when the rich complexity and cosmopolitan promise of 11/9 was trumped by the fundamentalist and patriotic narratives of 9/11. This is the narrative produced and sustained by the U.S. media, from feedback loops of terror and counter-terror to the freeze-frame of trauma, fear, and hate. We cannot reverse the video of 9/11, watch the two towers climb back out of the rubble, two planes emerge intact from the buildings, nineteen terrorists return to Hamburg, Saudi Arabia, Yemen. We cannot rewind what followed 9/11. But if we are to reclaim the dream of 11/9, we must use counter-factuals to awake from the nightmare of 9/11 and to imagine plausible alternatives to the dominant narrative of terror.

Fourth, we need to establish *counter-histories* to ones currently being circulated at the highest levels of the national security state. At the pinnacle would be the *National Security Strategy of the United States of America*, a powerful discourse full of virtuous statements through which material interests are instantiated. I provided here one counter-history among others as an alternative to what became the *ur*-document of the "global war on terror."[16] My reading follows in chapter-and-verse the structure of the original and seeks to decode the inconsistencies, contradictions, and outright mythologizing of U.S. history and foreign policy into justification for infoterror.

I. Overview of America's International Strategy

> Our Nation's cause has always been larger than our Nation's defense.[17]

From President Bush's opening lines to the 2002 *The National Security Strategy of the United States of America* (*NSS*), the gap between rhetoric and reality takes on mythic proportions:

> Our Nation's cause has always been larger than our Nation's defense. We fight, as we always fight, for a just peace—a peace that favors liberty. We will defend the peace against the threats from terrorists and tyrants. We will preserve the peace by building good relations among the great powers. And we will extend the peace by encouraging free and open societies on every continent.[18]

Regardless of authorial (or good) intentions, the *NSS* reads more like a Kiplingesque folk tale of the nineteenth century than a strategic doctrine for the twenty-first. The rhetoric of the White House favors and clearly intends to mobilize the moral clarity, nostalgic sentimentality, and uncontested dominance reminiscent of the last great empires against the ambiguities, complexities, and messiness of the current world disorder. However, the gulf between the Nation's stated cause ("to help make the world not just safer but better," p. 1) and defensive needs ("to fight a war against terrorists of global reach," p. 5) is so vast that one detects what Nietzsche referred to as the "breath of empty space," that void between the world as it is and as we would wish to be which produces all kinds of metaphysical concoctions.

In short shrift (thirty pages), the White House articulation of U.S. global objectives to Congress elevates strategic discourse from a traditional, temporal calculation of means and ends, to the theological realm of monotheistic faith and monolithic truth. Relying more on aspiration than analysis, revelation than reason, the *NSS* is not grand but grandiose strategy. In pursuit of an impossible state of national security against terrorist evil, soldiers will need to be sacrificed, civil liberties curtailed, civilians collaterally damaged, and regimes destroyed.

Were this not an official White House doctrine, the contradictions of the *NSS* could only be interpreted as poetic irony. How else to comprehend the opening paragraph which begins with: "The United States possesses unprecedented—and unequaled—strength and influence in the world"; and ends: "The great strength of the nation must be used to promote a balance of power that favors freedom"? Perhaps the cabalistic Straussians that make up the defense intellectual brain trust of the Bush administration (among them, Paul Wolfowitz, Richard Perle, William Kristol, and other advocates of the "New American Century") have come up with a nuanced, indeed, anti-Machiavellian reading of Machiavelli that escapes the uninitiated. But so fixed is the *NSS* on the creation of a world in America's image, that concepts like balance of power and imminent threat, once rooted in historical, juridical as well as reciprocal traditions, become free-floating signifiers. Few Europeans, "Old" or "New" (to use Rumsfeld's less than diplomatic distinction), would recognize the balance of power principle deployed by the *NSS* to justify pre-emptive, unilateral, military action against not actual but "emerging" imminent threats (p. 15). Defined by the 18th century jurist Vattel as a state of affairs in which no one preponderant power can lay down the law to others, the classical sense of "balance of power" is effectively inverted in principle by the *NSS* document and in practice by the go-it-alone statecraft of the U.S. Balance of power is global suzerainty, and war is peace.

II. Champion Aspirations for Human Dignity

> Some worry that it is somehow undiplomatic or impolite to
> speak the language of right and wrong. I disagree. Different
> circumstances require different methods, but not different
> moralities.[19]

What significance should we make of the fact that the shortest
section of the *NSS* (barely a page-and-a-half) is on the "non-
negotiable demands" of "human dignity and rights, including free
speech, freedom of worship, equal justice, respect for women,
religious and ethnic tolerance, and respect for private property."[20]
Are these rights so self-evident and inalienable that they do not
warrant further clarification or justification? It would seem so:
"History has not been kind to those nations which ignored or
flouted the rights and aspirations of their people." And yet this
universalist avowal of rights requires a selective if not outright
denial of history. Where was the U.S. support of freedom, justice,
and religious and ethnic tolerance when it supported the "second
Hitler" in his earlier war against Iran? When it provided intelligence, arms, and the precursors for chemical weapons of mass
destruction? When it abandoned the Shiites in the south and the
Kurds in the north of Iraq after the Gulf War?

Most significant is that these rights are considered "non-
negotiable," making war, if not the first, certainly more of a viable
option when these rights are violated. In this regard, President
Bush's *NSS* is a continuation rather than a repudiation of President Clinton's *National Security Strategy of the United States
1994–1995: Engagement and Enlargement*.[21] To be sure, it places
greater emphasis on "preventive diplomacy" (p. 17) and multilateral intervention (p. 18) than Bush's preference for pre-emptive
war and unilateralist predispositions. But the virtuous imperatives
are in full evidence in the Clinton *NSS*: "All of America's strategic interests—from promoting prosperity at home to checking
global threats abroad before they threaten our territory—are
served by enlarging the community of democratic and free market
nations to help preserve them as democracies committed to free
markets and respect for human rights, is a key part of our
national security strategy" (p. 76).

Hardly surprising, then, that many liberals, both within the government and the university, supported the war against Iraq; and it is hardly unfair to question the extent to which Clinton and other moral interventionists prepared the high ground for this war. As a microcosm, consider again that one of the most visible splits in the ranks at top American universities, when "moral" liberals like Joseph Nye, Michael Ignatieff, and Samantha Power came out in support of the war, whereas "amoral" realists like Stanley Hoffmann, Steve Walt, and John Mearsheimer publicly opposed it. It is useful to return to Nietzsche, who always detected the smell of the swamp in all talk of virtue and found a "bestowing virtue" in the realist's "courage in the face of reality."[22]

III. Strengthen Alliances to Defeat Global Terrorism and Work to Prevent Attacks Against Us and Our Friends

> Just three days removed from these events, Americans do not yet have the distance of history. But our responsibility to history is already clear: to answer these attacks and rid the world of evil. War has been waged against us by stealth and deceit and murder. This nation is peaceful, but fierce when stirred to anger. The conflict was begun on timing and terms of others. It will end in a way, and at an hour, of our choosing.[23]

A war to rid the world of evil, and ending it on the hour, even one so chosen by the most powerful nation in the world, is yet another tall order set by the *NSS*. The war is to be fought simultaneously on multiple fronts, aiming, when possible, "to disrupt the financing of terrorism" and "to enlist the support of the international community"; and, when necessary, to "not hesitate to act alone . . . to exercise our right of self-defense by acting preemptively."[24] The strategy for defense might start but it does not stop at our border. States that support terrorism will be "compelled to accept their sovereign responsibilities"; "terrorism will be viewed in the same light as slavery, piracy, or genocide"; and public diplomacy will be used "to promote the free flow of information and ideas." And should the ghost of Vince Lombardi prove insufficient ("While we recognize that our best defense is a good offense . . ."), then the war must be waged at home as well (". . . we are also strengthening America's homeland security to protect against and deter attack").[25]

In most of the sections that follow, after all the early fist-waving at terrorism and its supporters, the hand of the U.S. is opened to the international community that must be constituted in "a war of freedom against fear," one that has "no quick or easy end."[26] In these sections the *NSS* seeks to "Work with Others to Defuse Regional Conflicts" (Section IV); "Ignite a New Era of Global Economic Growth through Free Markets and Free Trade" (Section VI); "Expand the Circle of Development by Opening Societies and Building the Infrastructure of Democracy" (Section VII); and "Develop Agendas for Cooperative Action With the Other Main Centers of Global Power" (Section VIII). But the document seems schizoid: after a prologue in which lines are drawn and ultimatums issued, the call for international dialogue rings hollow.

The *NSS* might aim for peace but it amounts to a blueprint for a permanent war. Gone is any trace of the humility that presidential candidate Bush invoked in his foreign policy addresses. In its place, hubris of an epic size obviates any historical- or self-consciousness about the costs of empire. What ends are not predestined by America's righteousness are to be pre-empted by the sanctity of virtuous war. The *NSS* leaves the world with two options: peace on U.S. terms, or the perpetual peace of the grave. The evangelical seeps through the prose of global realpolitik, and mitigates its harshest pronouncements with the solace of a better life to come. We all shall be—as played by the band as the *Titanic* sank—"Nearer My God to Thee."

V. Prevent Our Enemies from Threatening Us, Our Allies, and Our Friends with Weapons of Mass Destruction

The gravest danger to freedom lies at the crossroads of radicalism and technology. When the spread of chemical and biological and nuclear weapons, along with ballistic missile technology—when that occurs, even weak states and small groups could attain a catastrophic power to strike great nations. Our enemies have declared this very intention, and have been

caught seeking these terrible weapons. They want the capability to blackmail us, or to harm us, or to harm our friends—
and we shall oppose them with all our power.[27]

It is clear from the *NSS* that the end of the Cold War was the
harbinger of a new world disorder rather than order. "New
deadly challenges have emerged rogue states and terrorists"; and
while they might not possess the might of the Soviet Union, they
have the asymmetrical advantages garnered by weapons of mass
destruction and the will to use them.[28] Positing that traditional
deterrence no longer works, the *NSS* presents axiomatically
the right to pre-emptively strike against these new enemies: "The
greater the threat, the greater is the risk of inaction—and the
more compelling the case for taking anticipatory action to defend
ourselves, even if uncertainty remains as to the time and place
of the enemy's attack."[29] This is a not grand strategy; this is a
blank check, to take whatever actions whenever deemed necessary
against whomever fits the terrorist profile.

Facing an "age where the enemies of civilization openly and
actively seek the world's most destructive technologies," the *NSS*
sanctions a counter-strategy based on superior intelligence, ethics,
and technological capability: "The reasons for our actions will be
clear, the force measured, and the cause just."[30] In short, war will
be virtuous. First auditioned in the Balkans, and dress-rehearsed
in Afghanistan, virtuous war took center stage in the invasion of
Iraq. Virtuous war projects a technological and ethical superiority
in which computer simulation, media dissimulation, global surveillance, and networked warfare combine to deter, discipline, and
if need be, destroy the enemy. Ethically intentioned and virtually
applied, drawing on the doctrines of just war when possible and
holy war when necessary, virtuous war is more than a felicitous
oxymoron. After September 11, as the United States chose
coercion over diplomacy in its foreign policy and deployed a rhetoric of total victory over absolute evil, virtuous war became the
ultimate means by which the United States intended to re-secure
its borders, assert its suzerainty, and secure the holy trinity of
international order: global capitalism (Section VI. IGNITE A NEW
ERA OF GLOBAL ECONOMIC GROWTH THROUGH FREE MARKETS
AND FREE TRADE, p. 17); western models of democracy (Section

VII. EXPAND THE CIRCLE OF DEVELOPMENT BY OPENING SOCIETIES AND BUILDING THE INFRASTRUCTURE OF DEMOCRACY, p. 21); a hegemonic "balance of power" (Section VII. DEVELOP AGENDAS FOR COOPERATIVE ACTION WITH THE OTHER MAIN CENTERS OF GLOBAL POWER, p. 25); and preventive interventions. . . .

IX. Transform America's National Security Institutions to Meet the Challenges and Opportunities of the Twenty-first Century

> Terrorists attacked a symbol of American prosperity. They did not touch its source. America is successful because of the hard work, creativity, and enterprise of our people.[31]

The *NSS* calls for nothing less than a transformation of the "major institutions of American national security," in which the military and the intelligence community are to lead the way.[32] The various tenets of the "RMA"—the revolution in military affairs—were fully evident in the Iraq war, not only in the unfolding of the war plan, OPLAN 1003 VICTOR, but also by the high values placed on flexibility, speed, and information. The opening decapitation strike, the infowar of "shock and awe," the reliance on light ground forces and precision munitions for a "rolling start," all reflect Secretary of Defense Rumsfeld's efforts to implement a radical transformation in how the United States fights and defends itself.

Ultimately, however, real-world transformations exceed the grasp of the *NSS*. What falls outside the engineering and imaginary of the plan, what Edmund Burke called the "empire of circumstance," is in the driver's seat and beyond the cybernetic machinations of the *NSS*. Many scholars saw the end of the Cold War as an occasion to wax nostalgic over the stability of a bipolar balance of power and to debate the merits of a new unipolar order. These debates continued to be state-centric as well as materialist in their interpretation of how power works. By such criteria, there was little doubt that the United States would emerge as the dominant military, economic, and indeed, civilizational power. Even in Paul Wolfowitz's worst-case nightmares, it was difficult to identify a potential "peer competitor" on the horizon.

But then came 9/11, and the shock of the unexpected rippled through the dreams of a steady-state hegemony. Asymmetrical power and fundamentalist resentment, force-multiplied by the mass media, prompted a permanent state of emergency. After the first responders came a semiotic fix with a kick, the *National Security Strategy of the United States of America*. The *NSS* draws lessons from the tragedy of 9/11 that can only lead to new follies. It might be small solace, but out of this nihilistic moment might yet come a real balance of power *and* truth, in which the imperial reach of the *National Security Strategy* is foreshortened by a new secular grasp of global reality.

Finally, and probably most critically in age of infoterror, we must develop counter-media. Without access to the modes of information, all other alternative efforts will fail. We have seen how global media has become essential for the global circulation of power, the waging of war, and the imagining of peace. It is now an unparalleled force in the organization, execution, justification, and representation of global violence, as witnessed in the first Gulf War, the Kosovo air campaign, and the terrorist attacks on September 11.[33] Global media continues, in spite of concentrated efforts, to evade national management.[34] Networked terror, network-centric warfare, and network attacks continue to have an intense if intermittent transnational impact. Networked technologies merge issues of national, corporate, and personal security (and liberty) into an interconnected global problem. Global media is systemically disposed towards rapid responses rather than deliberative processes. Information, to paraphrase William Burroughs, has become a virus, and the auto-immune response is often worse than the original contagion, as we saw with the towers toppling, the bin Laden tapes, and the Abu Ghraib photos. Moreover, densely networked systems of image production often produce negative as well as positive synergies with cascading effects; and everywhere global institutions of governance are failing to keep up with the new global risks of interconnectivity. Counter-media must adopt new strategies, concepts, and policies for the new dangers and opportunities of world politics.

But how? Rather than invest too much time or hope in some imaginary, pre-media state of nature, in which sweet reason wins out over the prefabrications and white noise of the infosphere, we are better off embracing global media, and fighting fire with fire, media with media. The conceit, stretching from Descartes through Marx to Chomsky—that there exists a universal truth waiting to be discovered once the veil of superstition, religion, media, or false consciousness of one sort or another is lifted by the right technology of knowledge—might well be an enlightened one. It might even be true; but in our current multicultural, multimedia, heteropolar world, it is one more truth competing among a host of much more powerful other ones. To counter the ubiquitous surveillance, information overload, and fundamentalist thinking that has transformed global media into weapons of mass distraction, deception, and destruction, we need not to just consume but to produce counter-media *now*. It will not happen by primetime broadcast or even on public television: whatever independence they once enjoyed has been eroded by corporate interests, partisan politics, and the need to meet the lowest common denominator of public culture. As the last quasi-independent institutions, I believe it falls upon universities and non-governmental organizations to develop the content as well as techniques for counter-media.

It will, of course, take more than these five strategies to reverse the effects of 9/11 and end an era of infoterror. I have sought to make the case for how 9/11 was not the cause but the occasion for a radical transformation in global politics, one that had its beginnings in an earlier series of changes in the art of warfare, the politics of identity, and the information revolution. A *post*-9/11 world will continue to exceed our grasp if we cannot understand how virtuous wars emerged from a *pre*-9/11 convergence of information technology and discourses of terror. That said, we should be less concerned about pinpointing the date and immediate cause of this transformation and more about our lack of intellectual capacity and political will to now comprehend and manage the after-effects of 9/11.

We have the essential information. We know how terrorists used e-mail, cell phones, flight simulators, and the Internet to amass the knowledge and to coordinate the machinery that killed 3,000 people and caused billions of dollars worth of damage. We know how the U.S. military used global surveillance, networked communication, smart weapons, robotic aircraft, realtime simulation, and rapid deployment of special forces to conduct a virtuous war (i.e., low-casualty, long-distance, good visuals) in Afghanistan. We know in the aftermath of Afghanistan how the Internet itself became a battlefield, with blogs posting conspiratorial accounts of 9/11, "digihadists" creating hip-hop videos against the "Dirty Kuffar," and organizers mustering millions of antiwar demonstrators in several cities—while the U.S. government developed new techniques of surveillance and data-mining for the war against terror. We are in a technologically-enabled, mythologically-informed war of terror and counter-terror.

But there lurks an added danger, one also abetted by global media, one that further confounds any effort to leave the age of infoterror behind: the increasing banalization of terror *and* virtue. In her study of the "thought-defying" nature of evil that earmarked the killing machine of Nazi Germany, Hannah Arendt identified the political effects of one form of banalization. Her response to an interview from late in her life leaves us with a sense of what radical measures are needed when not only terror but virtue itself, in the service of virtuous war, achieves a state of banality:

> It is indeed my opinion now that evil is never "radical," that it is only extreme, and that it possesses neither depth nor any demonic dimension. It can overgrow and lay waste the whole world precisely because it spreads like a fungus on the surface. It is "thought-defying," as I said, because thought tries to reach some depth, to go to roots, and the moment it concerns itself with evil, it is frustrated because there is nothing. That is its "banality." Only the good has depth and can be radical.[35]

12   The desert of the real and the simulacra of war

Such a perfect democracy constructs its own inconceivable foe, terrorism. Its wish is *to be judged by its enemies rather than by its results*. The story of terrorism is written by the state and it is therefore highly instructive. The spectators must certainly never know everything about terrorism, but they must always know enough to convince them that, compared with terrorism, everything else must be acceptable, or in any case more rational and democratic.

(Guy Debord, *Comments on the Society of the Spectacle*)

I was heading back to the Mojave Desert, where my journey into the military-industrial-media-entertainment network first began. Since I traveled in 1994 to observe the Advanced Warfighting Exercise at Fort Irwin, much had changed; and yet, much had stayed the same. Back then, the global situation appeared to be on the upward swing: the end of the Cold War left the United States without a peer rival, and the Gulf War had been deemed a military (if not entirely a political) success. Then came 9/11, a body blow to American exceptionalism, but one that nonetheless lead to a relatively successful intervention into Afghanistan and the routing of Al Qaeda and the Taliban. The invasion of Iraq that followed, although controversial, toppled Saddam Hussein and enjoyed congressional as well as popular support. To mark the end of combat operations, President Bush made a tail-hook landing aboard the USS *Abraham Lincoln* on May 1, 2003 to declare, under a large "Mission Accomplished" banner, that victory had

David Udris, Michael Udris, and James Der Derian with Major General Douglas O'Dell, Commanding General of 4th Marine Division.

Marines negotiate with Iraqi role-players at "Mojave Viper" counter-insurgency training exercise.

been won in Iraq and that terrorists were on the run. Inside the beltway, the revolution in military affairs (RMA) was heralded as the key to both successes. "Shock and awe" was hailed as a new war-fighting doctrine. The U.S. military had won both wars speedily, with remarkably few casualties.

But almost as quickly, the U.S. began to lose the peace in Iraq, Al Qaeda remerged as a global franchise, and the Taliban enjoyed a resurgence in Pakistan and Afghanistan. Over 98 percent of the Iraq war casualties occurred after "Mission Accomplished." What happened? In short, the first full-fledged virtuous war proved to be a perfect disaster. It is obvious—even to those who now hide their complicity behind the official mantra, "if we only knew then what we know now"—that this was a war of choice, not necessity. It was motivated by an evangelical foreign policy, rationalized by faulty intelligence, and supported by a fear-filled public. But virtuous war was the "x-factor," the magical element—evoking Arthur C. Clarke's predictive law that advanced forms of technology are indistinguishable from magic—incanted by the inner order to transform the indeterminacies and complexities of policy, intelligence, and war into the "sure thing" (Cheney), a "slam-dunk" (Tenet), a "cake-walk" (Wolfowitz). The Bush foreign policy team brought to the table a new-found faith, untroubled by doubt, that superior force backed by superior morality would transform the Middle East into a region of peaceful and democratic regimes, and, not incidently, secure the supply and transportation of oil fields. A virtuous war would right decades, even centuries, of wrongs. Virtuous war would make short work of the devil that lurked in the details. The 500,000 troops called for in the original invasion strategy, OPLAN 1003-98, were whittled down to half that by Rumsfeld; dissenting voices like General Shinseki, who as Army Chief of Staff testified that several hundred thousand troops would be needed in post-war Iraq, were publicly pilloried by Wolfowitz. The State Department's "Future of Iraq Study," an amateur effort but the closest thing to an actual plan for post-war reconstruction, was scrapped by the Pentagon.

In December, Central Command was forward-deployed to Qatar to play "Internal Look 2002."[1] The media was invited along, and they willingly played the role of force-multiplier in the Bush administration's game of coercive diplomacy. The various tenets of the RMA were fully evident in the lead-up to the Iraq war, not only in the unfolding of OPLAN 1003 but by the high values placed on flexibility, speed, and information. The opening decapitation strike, the infowar of "shock and awe," the reliance on light ground forces and precision munitions for a "rolling start," all reflect Secretary of Defense Rumsfeld's efforts to implement a radical transformation in how the United States fights.

This proved to be a recipe for disaster. But it was a recipe long in the making, going back to the transformations promoted by Andrew Marshall, Arthur Cebrowski, and other advocates of the RMA, individuals who filled Rumsfeld's inner Pentagon think tank.[2] Ethical high-mindedness cloaked a deep cultural ignorance; an overwhelming military superiority fueled an imperial arrogance. The costs were high: over 4,000 American and at least 90,000 Iraqi dead (and counting); close to two million refugees; a conflict longer than the Second World War; and a total price-tag approaching the trillion dollar mark. A virtuous dream to transform the Middle East turned into a mass nightmare, from which many seemed unwilling or incapable of awakening.

The faith in virtuous war would be shaken but never quite defeated by events on the ground. Probably the most virtuoso display came when a Predator drone armed with Hellfire missiles first found an Al Qaeda "target of opportunity" in the Yemen desert and, ordered from 6,000 miles away, shot to kill. From Bosnia to Kosovo, from Afghanistan to Iraq, virtuous war had taken on the properties of a game, with high production values, mythic narratives, easy victories, and few bodies. From the decision to deploy troops to the daily order of battle, from the highest reaches of policy-making to the lowest levels of field tactics and logistics, war games, computer simulations, and command post exercises, virtuous war came of age in Iraq. Then, from the 2004 battle for Fallujah to the 2006 bombing of the Golden Mosque in Samara, this faith was shaken by a rising insurgency. Controversy would continue over the causes, whether it was an indigenous civil war in the making or whether "foreign elements" were to blame; but the need for a new strategy became apparent. The political goal of an outright victory and installation of a unified democratic regime remained, but on the ground, there was an immediate need to stabilize a rapidly deteriorating situation. The debate over what to do next opened a long-brewing inter- and intra-service struggle going back to the 1990s, spilling over the already weakened firewalls between military strategy and civilian policy. Facing increased bloodshed in the streets of Iraq and declining support at home, the ideologues of the Bush administration had no choice but to defer to heretical military thinkers who were seeking to substitute lessons on the ground for the failed doctrines of virtuous war. Influential officers like General David Petraeus, Colonel H. R. McMaster, and Lieutenant Colonel John Nagl challenged the Pentagon's desk-jockey faith in high-tech strategies and minimal forces. The change was slow in coming but by year five, "shock and awe," "RMA," and "victory in Iraq" had been replaced by the "Surge," "COIN," and "stabilization operation."

As was the case with the RMA, there is a longer and more complex history to the COIN (counter-insurgency) strategy than suggested by press accounts. The Iraq war was as much the consequence as the catalyst of a long-brewing contest within and between the armed services. However, over the course of the occupation two opposing camps began to coalesce in the Pentagon, the War Colleges, and most critically, the Army's Training and Doctrine Command (TRADOC). We can call them the "transformationists" and the "neotraditionalists."[3] The transformationists continued to put their faith in network-centric warfare and superior firepower to stabilize if not wholly solve the political, civil, and religious conflicts gripping Iraq and—to the extent anyone in the U.S. was still paying attention—Afghanistan. The neotraditionalists, in contrast, were going back to the future for new strategies, to the "low-intensity conflicts" of Malaya and Vietnam, the "small wars" that Marines fought in Central America in the interwar period, and even the lessons learned (and not) by the British in Iraq in the First and Second World Wars.[4] Eventually lumped together under the rubric of "Irregular Warfare," a new concept emerged from the neotraditionalist camp to underwrite the counter-insurgency strategy: "cultural sensitivity," which quickly morphed into the less touchie-feelie term, "cultural awareness."

I had learned from my earlier research and travels that paper revolutions are fairly easy to generate: operationalizing doctrinal change is not, even when a powerful constituency is behind it. Rather, acceptance, adaptation, and implementation comes at that vaunted point where the "rubber hits the road"—and it is always better, to the extent possible, that the process, which is accident-prone and mistake-filled, takes place on the training ground rather than on the battlefield. This is why I was now heading back to the Mojave Desert, and why I had decided to go not to the army's Fort Irwin, home of the Army's National Training Center (NTC), but to the vast desert expanse south of the Interstate 40, home of the Marine Corps Air Ground Combat Center at Twentynine Palms, California. The Marines have a long history of fighting contingency operations and low-intensity conflicts. After the battles for Fallujah and deployment to vulnerable forward operating bases across the Al Anbar Province, they had plenty of incentives to plan, train, and implement a new counter-insurgency strategy for Iraq. While the army could boast of its billion-dollar, mock-Iraqi city of Medina Wasi at Fort Irwin, the Marines were doing what they do best, more with less at Twentynine Palms. So I was heading out to "the Stumps," the Marines less-than-affectionate name for the desert outpost of pawn, barber, and tattoo shops surrounded by sand, mountains, and blighted palm trees. Tucked away in nearby towns and backroads were displaced Californian artists (installation artist Noah Purifoy started the desert migration decades earlier), aging rock and rollers and old L.A. punk bands (Robert Plant and Concrete Blond hang out here), and my favorite oasis of oddness, the Integratron (an acoustically perfect geodesic dome built in the 1950s by U.F.O. abductee George Van Tassel to communicate with aliens). Adding considerable edge to the whole mix were the "tweakers," methamphetamine users and producers who; on a monthly basis; would provide local fireworks when one of their trailer-park labs would explode, lighting up the desert landscape for miles.

Twentynine Palms was now the staging area for "Mojave Viper," a counter-insurgency urban warfare exercise that provided final training for Marines before they depart for Iraq. The mock-town was made up of sand-colored single and stacked containers with punched-out windows, Iraqi flags fluttering atop the police station and the mayor's home, a golden onion-dome signifying the local mosque, and in the central square of the simulated town, a broken-down M-60 Patton tank. I had been invited to embed with New England reservists from Charlie Company, First Battalion, 25th Marines, as they mixed conventional live-fire kinetic operations with the new programs of counter-insurgency and cultural sensitivity training.

The trip got off to a bad start. My flight into Palm Springs had been delayed, and running late for my first meeting with the base Public Affairs Officer I decided to take a shortcut. I spotted on my map a "Berdoo Canyon Road" cutting across Joshua Tree National Park; it looked like it could save me a half-hour, maybe even forty-five minutes. The hash marks on the map did not inspire confidence but they looked safer than the parallel lines that simply disappeared into the blank whiteness of the park. Besides, I had a rental SUV, which had been required by the Visitors Agreement that I had signed and faxed back to the PAO (along with a Hold Harmless Agreement spelling out all kinds of possible accidents and dangers, including bodily harm by "large carnivorous animals"). But barely fifteen minutes after I had left the two-lane blacktop, the "road" became a wadi; a few more miles and I could not tell road from desert. When my tires started to spin in soft sand, I decided it was time to do what I had learned in the Boy Scouts, to stop and assess my situation.

After popping a warm beer and admiring the desert landscape, I examined the map again. On closer inspection I realized that it was the same one I had picked up in 1994 for my first trip to the Mojave to observe the "Desert Hammer" exercise at Fort Irwin.[5] On my way from LAX, I had stopped at the Triple-A headquarters in southern California, housed in an ersatz castle in South Central L.A. The highlighted route brought back the memory of a guy with a short ponytail in a faded Hawaiian shirt. With yellow marker he had traced a route from L.A. to Barstow—"the armpit of America"—to the turn-off for the forty-mile access road to Fort Irwin. Changing markers to a florescent orange, he had also marked some essential side trips. Calico Mountains was circled as were the Mitchell Caverns: with a wink and a nod he told me that Jim Morrison and the Doors used to "trip" there and check out the petroglyphs. There was one last big circle around Lake Havasu City, where the "real" London Bridge, taken apart and reassembled, now sits astride the Colorado River. Looking at the map, then up at the landscape, and back down again, I weighed the possibility of saving forty-five-minutes against a wide variety of worst-case scenarios offered by the desert sands ahead. I decided to backtrack, reversing most of the way back to the two-lane.

I did what many—or at least the male half of the automobile kingdom—do when lost: I blamed the map. Historically, map-makers have left out important details, misrepresented the relative size of continents, even omitted a country or two. Consider the past millennial turn, which produced a particularly bad spate of map "errors." The Mars Climate Orbiter was lost because NASA was mapping in metric while Lockheed Martin was using imperial units of measurement: a $125 million "oops." NATO blamed an out-of-date map, which turned out to be perfectly accurate, for three cruise missiles striking the Chinese Embassy in Belgrade, killing three.[6] But topping off the millennial hysteria was "Y2K," a case of faulty computer mapping that was going to cause a global meltdown that never came. But on the other side of the representational divide there lurks a much larger model of errors, the universe of bad map-readers, mistaking the goat path for a road, a church spire for a missile silo, a pharmaceutical plant for a chemical warfare factory. When such mistakes happen, regardless of cause, we prefer to finger the cartographer rather than blame our own mistaken eyes.

Maps, per se, do not lie. However, as assemblages of signs, maps are like other texts, open to interpretation, contestation, refutation, exculpation; they are also simulations in search of a particular and sometimes false reality. They reflect multiple interests even when presented as accurate (like the techno-scientific map that identified WMDs in Iraq) or universal (the liberal economic map that was to create a new Middle East of democracy and free markets). It might be convenient to blame the author of the map for this sorry state of affairs; but the end of new worlds to "discover" was attended by the death of the author-mapper. After Amerigo Vespucci, when was another country, let alone an entire continent, named after a cartographer? Do we even know, let alone remember, the names of authors-producers of modern maps? Interpretive responsibilities have shifted from author to reader.

Of course, the White House and the Pentagon had key allies within the MIME-NET in their efforts to pre-empt the future through superior mapping. As simulations (wargames, training exercises, scenario planning, modeling) and dissimulations (propaganda, disinformation, deceit, and lies) ratcheted up, the vaunted firewall between the military and the media became as formidable as an Iraqi border berm. The wild card in this new infowar was the embedded journalist. After the protests by the press of being excluded from the U.S. invasions of Grenada, Panama, and the first Gulf War, the Defense Department came up with the idea of selectively placing journalists in the various armed services, aboard ships at sea as well as on the frontlines of the battlefield. It was, given the new technological capabilities of the media as well as the uncertainties of the outcome, a fairly courageous decision by the Pentagon. Yet, as a war long-billed as virtuous and rapid failed to achieve success according to the plan – that is, after unexpected resistance, widespread looting, and creeping rises in casualty rates – the Pentagon might have viewed it as a regrettable decision.

A full-fledged infowar was also launched off the battlefield and in the home studios. After decapitation strikes by cruise missiles and F-117s, breathless reports by journalists traversing the desert with the troops, and Defense Department briefings of "shock and awe" over Baghdad, the fighting and the reporting of the second Gulf War effectively blurred into a combined information operation. Surfing the channels and scanning the pages of the U.S. media exposed information consumers to repetitive doses of hi-tech exhibitionism and media voyeurism. Infowar, deployed after September 11 as the discontinuation of diplomacy by other means, became a force-multiplier in Iraq, a weapon of destruction as well as persuasion and distraction.

Lost in the hoopla over the stories and images streaming in from the desert was the fact that the military had taken over the television studios. Retired general and flag officers exercised full spectrum dominance on cable and network TV as well as on commercial and public radio. The new public affairs officers of the military-industrial-media-entertainment network included Clark and Sheppard on CNN, Nash and Hawley on ABC, Kernan and Ralston on CBS, McCaffrey and Meigs on NBC, and Olstrom and Scales on NPR. Fox News alone had enough ex-military to stage their own Veteran's Day parade. A relationship that had always been intimate in times of crisis now appeared incestuous.

Color commentary and shades of opinion were reduced to the nightscope-green of videophone verité in the desert, and red, white, and blue in the studios.

In addition to the content bias created by a pre-selection of what can be said by whom, a martial aesthetic kicked in with visual vengeance. When the invasion premiered, the television studios introduced new sets that mimicked the command and control centers of the military. Fox News actually referred to its own, without a trace of Strangelovian irony, as the "War Room." Computer-generated graphics of the Iraq battlespace were created by the same defense industries (like Evans and Sutherland, Digital Globe, and Analytical Graphics) and commercial satellite imaging firms (like Space Imaging and Earthviewer.com) that supply the U.S. military. The networks showcased a veritable Jane's Defense Review of weapon-systems, providing "virtual views" of Iraq and military hardware that are practically indistinguishable from target acquisition displays.

Once again, the image won out over the word. When pictures proved hard to get, celebrity anchors were reduced to googling their reporters for substitute realities: in the course of one day, Peter Jennings and Ted Koppel, both from ABC, asked reporters in the field to "give us a word-picture of that." Supporting the troops became the method and mantra of avoiding any analysis or value judgments on whether force was justified, under what circumstances, and with what potential consequences, intended or not. Describing the lead-up to a much more destructive war (that was nevertheless shorter in duration), Walter Benjamin wrote: "All efforts to aestheticize politics culminate in one point. That one point is war."[7] Indeed, it would seem that we had gone full circle, out of Borges's labyrinth and once more back into Baudrillard's simulacrum:

> Today abstraction is no longer that of the map, the double, the mirror, or the concept. Simulation is no longer that of a territory, a referential being, or a substance. It is the generation by models of a real without origin or reality: a hyperreal. The territory no longer precedes the map, nor does it survive it. It is nevertheless the map that precedes the territory—*precession of simulacra*—that engenders the territory, and if one must

return to the fable, today it is the territory whose shreds slowly rot across the extent of the map. It is the real, and not the map, whose vestiges persist here and there in the deserts and that are not longer those of the Empire, but ours. *The desert of the real itself.*[8]

Out in a real desert, this rather abstract thought would take on a concrete character, usually after a GPS would go down, at which point my driver would reach for a paper map and magnetic compass (if available) and try to figure where he was. He'd usually get it wrong—and he too would blame the map. I take some pride in my Boy Scout orienteering merit badge, and during my annual off-the-grid canoe trips in northern Canada, I will not bring along (nor, dictatorially, allow others) any GPS gear. And yet, during my research travels I also repeatedly "misread" maps at critical points. I have come to realize finding one's way is not simply a matter of better maps or skill-sets. There are probably deeper para-psychological forces at work, that, paradoxically, spike as our maps increase in verisimilitude. One does not need to read French theory to pick up clear signals that the MIME-NET was playing a key role in this development. Stuck in the middle of the wilderness or desert or enemy territory, with anxiety-levels already amped up, as rifts between the representation and reality of war begin to tear open, a form of cognitive dissonance peculiar to war is often produced. We might seek to adjust our mental maps, as we might for magnetic deviation in our compass, but war is complex, contingent upon multiple factors, full of fog and friction.

Such moments can produce a multitude of dysfunctional effects, ranging from misinterpretation of aluminum tubes as nuclear bomb-making components to getting coordinates wrong and calling in artillery on our own troops. However, if one is not tied to the map reality, it can produce a wholly different effect, a moment of inspiration or ecstasy, as Kant described the sublime as a blissful sense of well-being that comes from the acceptance of the fact we are all, in the long run, lost. As I went deeper into the MIME-NET, the more often I felt the need to leave the map behind, not because it was flawed but because it was taking me to the wrong place, in which the illusion of command and control squeezed out the rich contingencies of life. In short, I'd rather get lost, at some subliminal level, than end up where the map was taking me. I harbor a suspicion that this sentiment was probably shared by some of the original designers of wargames as well as the first generation of videogames. There is no mistaking the avatar for the real thing when small iconic figures are being moved around in sandboxes or pixilated in low-res on a screen. Games then clearly sought to model rather than to replicate or anticipate the deviations of war. This is why it will be, must always be, called the art rather than the science of war.

Looking back on my efforts to map the military-industrial-media-entertainment network, I realize that getting lost produced some of the most important insights. Maybe the very destiny of modernity is to be lost, as Borges wrote, because of the modern imperative to superannuate old maps before new ones can be created. Getting lost forced me to reconsider the interdependent relationship between map-making and map-reading; it illuminated the shadow space between the landscape and the map, revealing why and how the modern map-reader would come to prefer the inaccurate map to a recalcitrant landscape. In my travels I often found the most interesting perspective—and interesting people— at the edge of the map, where the monsters lurk, where the distinction between the representation and the real thing begins to break down but is not yet overwhelming, what I would call, for lack of a better term and *pace* Borges, Burroughs, and Baudrillard, a *simulacral interzone*. In this spatio-temporal rift I found remarkable individuals inside, outside as well as at the edges of the military, who were seeking to understand what happens when the Empire enters its Last Days, when the Emperor strives to create his own reality, and, in bewildering numbers, the inhabitants are all-too-happy to join the mass migration from the landscape to the map.

Getting lost in a real desert on my way to a simulated military exercise, perched between the inchoate nature around me and the war machine that was seeking to tame it, I began to feel comfortable in that liminal state. From my trip to the AWE at Fort Irwin to "Mojave Viper" at Twentynine Palms, with Borges along with Benjamin and Baudrillard as critical guides, I came to understand the shortcomings of maps that define who we are by where we have been, as well as those that would pretend to inscribe where we are heading and becoming before we ever arrive. "Natural" frontiers might inscribe paper differences between "us" and "them," but demarcations set by circumstances, coincidences, and even identifiable consequences exceed the boundaries and capabilities of the maps we keep, whether they are tucked away in the glovebox or stuck in the prefrontal cortex.

Metaphorically or just literally, the Prussian General and strategist Moltke put it best: no battle plan survives first contact with the enemy. If one is overly reliant upon the plan and not one's own compass for not just ascertaining east and west but right and wrong, panic shock—a kind of cue conflict gone mad—can result. One might think that as the fidelity of the map to reality increases and our map-making/reading skills improve—think GPS, Google Earth, the iPhone (which can provide a satellite image of wherever I might be)—that this moment might be postponed by superior technology, even pre-empted. But herein lies the double irony: our dependency on a variety of technological prostheses has managed to atrophy our natural senses, gut intuitions, and historical reasoning without a commensurate increase in predicting what lies ahead.

This is why I had decided, at a critical juncture in the Iraq war, to embed with the Marines rather than the Army. At Fort Irwin, with observer/controllers around every corner, lasers attached to every player and weapon, hill-top video cameras tracking every action, little was left to chance: every action was surveilled and thus disciplined into narrower and narrower parameters of choices, giving it all the feel of one very big but fairly predictable video game. Soldiers seemed to know that getting to the next level of expertise (and acceptance by superiors) was a matter of learning what *not* to do to. The prime directive, also known as the rules of engagement, was to avoid the equivalent of the pinball "tilt" function, which would bring observer/controllers running from behind the Potemkin-village walls to reprimand the wayward soldier. Lost in the process was the unanticipated moment where the soldier might be able to transform an "error" into insight, rote behavior into innovative action. Without the latitude to make big mistakes in wargames, and to mother invention through failure, the military was bound to have trouble when the real thing broke with the given plan. One such moment came only five days into the Iraq invasion, after relentless sandstorms and attacks by irregular forces, when General William Wallace, Commander of V Corps publicly remarked (and was subsequently rebuked), "The enemy we're fighting is a bit different than the one we war-gamed against."[9]

Obviously there is a difference between war and games, a statement I must often repeat to avoid easy misinterpretation: unlike most games, people die in wars. We have seen how the technological properties and political imperatives of virtuous war can skew or simply disappear the whole issue of casualty rates, both off and on the battlefield.[10] Early in the Afghanistan intervention, General Tommy Franks openly declared, "You know, we don't do body counts." This was a policy that he would publicly continue as commander of the U.S. forces in Iraq—even though the military had been counting civilian casualties but just not publicizing them.[11] One year after the "Tommy Franks Doctrine" was announced, and two weeks into the Iraq war, U.S. Central Command's chief spokesman, Captain Frank Thorp, provided a figure of seventy-three American and British troops killed. When asked by a reporter from the *New York Times* about Iraqi dead, he stated that "the numbers are not knowable, and besides, that number may not be an indication of anything."[12] One week later, after Baghdad was taken, a total of 138 Americans and British were listed as killed. At that point, the pattern of casualty rates resembled earlier virtuous wars: ratios of around 30–40 percent for troops killed by accident and friendly fire; eleven journalists killed; and the number of Iraqis killed ranged from 2,000–10,000 for troops and 1,000–3,000 for civilians.

Although represented by the military and the media as "accidental" or "incidental," friendly-fire ("blue-on-blue") deaths as well as the increased ratio of friendly-fire deaths to hostile fire deaths are built into the system of virtuous war. This partially reflects the increased complexity of networked warfare, in which precision munitions play a significant part. In the first Gulf War—and in spite of the images produced by the military briefings—less than 10 percent of the weapons used were smart; by the second Gulf War, the figure was just under 70 per cent (the figures seem to remain less precise than the weapons themselves). And with increased precision comes an increase in lethality. This was evident in Afghanistan when three members of the U.S. Army 5th Special Forces Group team were killed and nineteen soldiers wounded after they mistakenly gave their own geo-coordinates for a satellite-guided JDAMS; and when two U.S. F-16 pilots (allegedly amped-up on "go-pills") dropped a 500-pound smart bomb on Canadian troops engaged in a training exercise, killing four and wounding eight.

The precision munitions of virtuous war have other targets as well, most notably the ever-lingering legacy of the "Vietnam Syndrome" (the erosion of public support if body-bags come home in high numbers). The Vietnam Syndrome resurfaced at the beginning of the first Gulf War, and was countered by the Powell doctrine of overwhelming force, which meant sending 550,000 troops to the Gulf and mounting a six-week air campaign. At the end of the war, the Vietnam Syndrome was officially declared "kicked" by the first President Bush during a speech at the Raytheon plant that made the Patriot missiles (which, according to Congressional Report 102-1086, destroyed 100 percent of Scuds during the war, 96 percent in testimony to Congress after the war, 25 percent after a review by the army, and less than 9 percent after an independent review).

The Marines were now being asked, or rather, ordered to get lost, not as Chet Baker sings, but to lose their hard-won identity as virtuous killers and to become, in effect, cultural warriors. As I waited by the Twentynine Palms base gate for my Marine escort, the radio offered what I thought was a perfect sound-track for the week ahead. I had learned from previous trips just how bad local radio could be around far-flung military outposts (Fort Hood, located in the belly of the Texas Christian belt, was easily the worst), so this time I had paid the extra buck for a rental with Sirius satellite radio. Morrisey of the Smiths was singing "Girl-friend's in a Coma" ("Girlfriend in a coma, I know/I know—it's serious"), followed by Midnight Oil, "Dead Heart" ("We don't serve your country/Don't serve your king/Know your custom/ Don't speak your tongue/White man came took everyone"). I was in the desert again, and whether it was because of a disastrous effort to re-map the Middle East in the image of the U.S., or to keep the oil flowing, or both, the situation was definitely serious: the Marines were ready to innovate.

In my experience, the Marines, out of expediency as much as out of principle, seemed to play faster, looser as well as harder in their training exercises, best exemplified by the preference for the kinetic and often painful whack of the 9mm simulation rounds (as my camera man, who caught one on an unprotected ear, found out) to the annoying beeping and flashing of the MILES laser tag. This is also evident at the level of the big macro-games, most notoriously "Millennium Challenge 2002," at the time the largest joint wargame ever conducted, with over 13,500 military members and civilians involved in live exercises networked to command-post computer simulations.[13] The Red Team, lead by Marine General Van Riper, creatively (and virtually) used motorcycle messengers to avoid electronic detection, fired cruise missiles from hidden on-shore locations, and deployed a swarm of speedboats against a far superior Blue Team naval force in the Persian Gulf, effectively defeating it. At the Blue Team's insistence, the controllers agreed to a "do-over," re-starting the wargame because Van Riper had broken from script. I suspect Van Riper felt vindicated when news broke in January 2008 of an incident at practically the same location of "Millennium Challenge," the Straits of Hormuz and choke-point for much of the world's oil: five small Islamic Revolutionary Guard patrol boats swarmed a three-ship Navy convoy, nearly leading to a shooting war. It seems that the Iranians learned more from "Millennium Challenge" than the Americans had.

Maps assume a fixity of territory and identity; this was the way of geopolitics and organized violence in the past. In regular war-fare Marines and soldiers receive maps (and ROEs) of a world demarcated between "good guys" and "bad guys," making it eas-ier, when called upon, to use lethal force. Now, in the middle of the Mojave, they were being asked to adopt a new kind of map for encounters of the third kind, for an imaginary world at the edge of the map where the boundaries between friend and foe were in constant flux; in one big feedback loop, largely determined by the Marine's reactions, they could shift loyalties and locations with shocking ease. If Marines were "culturally sensitive," the Iraqis might be less inclined to treat the Marines as occupiers, and all the friendlier for it. But if the Marines became too helpful, friendly, courteous, and kind (back to Scouting), they risked losing their lethal edge, and with it, the ability to deter and if necessary destroy the bad guys who were still out in force. I have seen, and attempted to show how at the level of doctrine, virtuous war operated as a felicitous oxymoron. However, at ground-level it could easily become an equal-opportunity killer, a Marine trying to decide in a split-second who was the bad guy, who was the good guy, and realizing that if he made the wrong decision he might be dead—or slightly better, alive and possibly up on war crime charges. This was not going to be an easy exercise.

At the end of one short week of embedding with the 1/25th, after following Marines through countless "lane" exercises ranging from knock or knock-down-the-door entry drills to mock-IEDs putting everyone into permanent flinch-mode, weathering a wind storm that brought down platoon-sized tents and got our sleeping cots airborne, scrounging MREs for anything resembling real food, trying to raise the communication level with bussed-in Iraqi-Americans above sign-language, all of this happening through the thick fog of too little sleep (and the reek of too little hygiene), and I had a better understanding of why, when I asked a lance corporal what he made of the new training exercises in cultural awareness, he leaned in close, possibly in case a PAO was within earshot but probably just to get in my face, and said: "One big mind-fuck."

The Marines were right in the middle of the controversial effort to transform the American way of war—again. I had been following the Marines' efforts since 2004, when I had gone out to an old Air Force base on the edge of Riverside, California, to observe Marines apply lessons learned the hard way (after the 82nd Airborne had left them with a highly volatile situation in Fallujah). It was a ramshackle exercise. For local color there were female Marines wearing white bed sheets to mimic the full-bodied abaya. The few Iraqi role-players, bussed in from L.A., seemed to spend most of the time hanging out at the rough facsimile of a Baghdad café. Probably the highest level of authenticity came from the rent-a-wrecks the Marines had begged, borrowed, and some said stole for setting up a variety of roadblock scenarios; that, along with the ubiquitous noise of small gas-powered generators (the base had no electricity, and judging from the flooded-out trailer serving as headquarters, it was not likely to be upgraded anytime soon).

The Marines had launched a tenacious effort to convert an embryonic doctrine of cultural sensitivity into a tactical level of cultural competence, in spite of a lack of funding or general support from the Pentagon. It was hard not to be impressed by the up-tempo, improved nature of the exercise, with troops running through upwards of forty different scenarios a day. And after a long interview with the soft-spoken but intense officer who was running the show, Major Patrick Kline, I came away convinced that the program had a future. That said, much of the early effort had a cartoon-character to it, featuring a mono-cultural version of the "other" that more closely resembled the essentialist portrayal of the "Arab Mind" written by Ralph Petai in the 1970s (that allegedly informed the shaming tactics used at Abu Ghraib) than anything modern anthropologists would recognize as ethnographically correct. To be sure, not many soldiers or Marines were too interested in the subtleties that postcolonial studies might bring to the fight. They needed culture reduced to a story that could be carried in a cargo pocket—which is what they got: a folded up, laminated "smart card," jammed with colorful graphics of stereotypical Iraqis with typical weapons, behaving in predictable fashion, running roadblocks, planting IEDs, wearing sly smiles. The cards did contain some helpful Arabic phrases, and a list of do's (accept hospitality, show respect to men but not too much attention to women, use your essential Arabic) and don't's (put a boot on someone, inappropriately use the left hand, misinterpret two males holding hands). But this was culture as a fixed code, not as an changing process of interaction. Knowing oneself, and how others might understand your own peculiar customs, beliefs, and behaviors, did not figure in this version of culture.

During my research I was told by several individuals that I must talk to Dr. Barak Salmoni from the Marine Corps Training Education Command, who had taken on the task of upgrading cultural awareness into a more sophisticated training operation. Judging from my inability to schedule an interview, I'd say he was a vital and perpetually moving part of the program. After many e-mails and phone calls, I finally caught up with him at Quantico, Virginia, where freshly-minted second lieutenants were being put through the paces of urban warfare and cultural awareness training at the FBI's mock town, "Hogan's Alley." In an interview in the base library, full of memorabilia from past Marine campaigns, he traced the origins of the program for me back to late 2003, when Major General Magnus, the Marine division commander who led the assault into Afghanistan as well as Iraq, first recognized a pressing need for a new kind of training that focused on rapid shifts from rural to urban cultural terrains—what Salmoni called "rurban." Instead of regular forces in uniform, there was what British General Rupert Smith referred to as "war amongst the people"—but with people who speak languages and come from cultures radically different than your own. In this complex environment, with more civilians than soldiers on the battlefield, you have to understand, as much as you can, the people, their motivations, their ways of acting. Salmoni recognized the need for authenticity, and he provided the kind of details that helps bring a high level of verisimilitude to the exercise.

"We brought in Arabic-speaking, mostly Iraqi role-players with heritage capabilities that reflected, in broad terms, what Marines would face in certain scenarios in country. And we also heightened the realism by forcing them to deal with scenarios in real-time decision processes, so during a soft search of a house or a raid, the young Marine wouldn't simply worry about the kinetic aspects of how to attack a house—how to have ranges of fire, how not to interdict, how not to use the wrong caliber of munitions for example—but would also have to be concerned about the father of the house on the other side of that door, with the first and second son, a grandmother, women in the house, food on the table, graffiti, books that are in Arabic, that could just be books or could be insurgent propaganda. How do you deal with the implications of your decisions?"

After the early, rather primitive efforts at urban operations training exercises that I had first observed at the Riverside March Air Reserve Base, the cultural awareness operation moved in 2005 to Twentynine Palms, where a series of small Iraqi villages were created for the "Mojave Viper" exercises. Salmoni was clearly proud of what they had achieved in such a short period of time, and sincerely believed that the program had reduced both military and civilian casualties in Afghanistan and Iraq. They intended to create more buildings, more of an Iraqi environment, with more and more role-players. But the key piece, said Salmoni, was the "theater dynamics"—meaning how quickly and effectively the Marine Corps could feed what's happening in Anbar province back to the tactical training and exercise control group so new scenarios could be created for the Marines at "Mojave Viper."

Salmoni projected an upbeat, energetic attitude, but by the end of the interview I sensed that he was trying to convince himself as much as me. The controversies over cultural awareness training, both within and outside the Corps, were growing: was it "weaponizing culture," "feminizing" the fighter, or "militarizing" the academic? There was some concern that a program built to understand the cultural "other" might well fall victim to the military's inability to understand its own culture, and what impact it might be having on the conduct of the war. Salmoni was fully aware of these issues, but reluctant to directly discuss them.[14]

I found Salmoni's concerns shared, both on and off the record, by many of the officers I interviewed during the "Mojave Viper" exercise. In fact, once the recording devices were off, many put it much more bluntly. I had one high-ranking officer tell me in a candid moment just how far up a lower part of the human anatomy he would like to shove the "bleep-bleep" neo-conservatives who got us into the Iraq war. There clearly was a gap between the civilian and military leadership on what it would take to achieve a level of stability (few Marines I spoke to used the language of victory) that would allow the U.S. to withdraw. Indeed, I got the distinct impression during my time embedded at Twentynine Palms that the primary purpose of the cultural awareness training wasn't to win hearts and minds, but to find the best way to draw the "Get-out-of-Iraq" card from the bottom of the deck.

In general, as I worked my way down the ranks in a series of interviews, I observed more of a pragmatic imperative than a virtuous attitude behind the cultural awareness training at Twentynine Palms. Major General Douglas O'Dell, Commanding General of the 4th Marine Division had flown in for the exercise, and in a walk-and-talk interview he provided the best sound-bite of the exercise: "We are in a very complex and long strong struggle that demands subtlety and where in the case of this sort of training, not only is the senior leadership need to put on the mantle of diplomacy but so does the young lance corporal. We're in a different war."

The next day Lt. Colonel Kline—promoted since I had first interviewed him at Riverside—addressed the assembled officers of the 1/25th in one of the double-trailers that Marines like to call a headquarters. He simplified the task at "Mojave Viper" down to getting "the Marines familiar, proficient, and confident in urban operations." They would face a population that might be friendly, neutral, or unfriendly—or some combination of all three. Working their way through complex environments, they needed to operationalize the Marine motto of "No better friend, no worse enemy." Who can they trust? Who can they negotiate with? How do they deal with the population? How would they train Marines in counterinsurgency, where tactical cultural awareness is mission essential? Kline also got down to the nitty-gritty. Never make promises you can't keep; don't be vague in your questions; never pay money for information. He acknowledged that practicing cultural sensitivity was not the easiest thing to ask of the troops: "It might get a little bit edgy out there."

I also had an opportunity to interview Kline's predecessor, the outgoing Urban Warfare Director, Lt. Col. Andrew Kennedy. If Kline cut against the grain, in his mild manner and managerial style, Kennedy was from central casting: blunt, buzz-cut, cigar-chomping. He got right to the point.

"Someone sticks their head up and tries to kill us, whether with an IED, or AK-47, or a PKC (machine gun) or whatever it may be, he tries to kill us. The Marine needs the immediate ability to kill that person discreetly. In a counter insurgency fight you can't afford to shoot the wrong person. You must—*you must*—shoot the right person immediately. You must protect yourself. You must protect your buddy. And you must demonstrate to your population that you will not kill without discretion. That ethical use of force is critical to our success. That same Marine who was facing death five minutes before needs to be able to put a smile on his face, take off his sunglasses, and look at those kids and smile at 'em and make sure they get the firm, fair consistent treatment that they deserve. This is hard for a 19-year-old guy to get. And it takes a lot of training. This place is about a couple of things. First, giving them the opportunity to see all the challenges in a realistic environment. But it's also time for them to gain confidence because a confident guy is much more likely to be able to dial it back. A guy who doesn't have confidence in himself and his unit might have a problem with that. And so this sort of training, this sort of challenging preparation is designed to give guys a level of confidence they're going to require in order to go from one spectrum of operations immediately to another spectrum of operations and to be able to feel a level of comfort with that, that you can't get with untrained units."

Following Kline, Captain Alex Wright, a civil affairs officer and an enthusiastic advocate of the program, opened his brief with the question he heard most often from the troops: "Sir, why the hell do I care?" His response was to recognize that Marines already do "kinetic ops" all too well; if they want fewer problems on the battlefield they had better develop a new talent at spotting who is supportive, non-hostile, or hostile. He offered that most Iraqis fall in the middle ground; moving others into that or the supportive category was the primary purpose of the exercise. Sure, the Marines could achieve their mission by superior fire-power, but sometimes a "wave and a smile" was much easier. His punchline? "Train like you fight."

We had been promised a live-fire exercise, but a new base commander was reluctant to allow outsiders on the range. So we got shunted off to simulation training. At first it looked to be something out of nineteenth century *kriegspiel*; a squad of Marines and a trainer clustered around a waist-high sand table, filled with multi-colored icons of people, houses, and vehicles. But then I noticed the small metal ID attached to the two nondescript, sand-colored container trailers that flanked the table: "Virtual Combat Simulator." Ducking inside, we entered the twenty-first century. The outer room was jammed with banks of computer monitors and civilian technicians working keyboards and joystick. From the inner room we could hear the sounds of combat: lots of shouting of orders, a humvee engine revving up, a turret swiveling, then the heavy bark of a .50 caliber machine gun. We entered the room, and hugging the wall we became bit-players in a 360-degree panorama of an Iraqi desert scene, with roads, a checkpoint, houses, palm trees and what looked to be a speeding car heading our way. In the center of the room was the cab of a Humvee topped by a fully operational turret. The operator of the machine gun was shouting directions to the driver, who in turn was calling in for close air support. An Apache roared overhead; we ducked. The level of versimilitude was spectacular, amped up by the hi-res projection, multiple movement sensors, and surround-sound that got the heart beating.

The simulation trainer who was running this sound-and-light show, Sgt. Frank Tramano, had a bulldozer build, wraparounds, and a take-no-prisoners attitude. He had been around, starting with a couple of combat tours in Vietnam. He walked us through the simulation.

"What we're giving them here is muscle memory. Here I can go through ten scenarios, one right after the other, where out in that field I only would have time to do one. Anything they see in here is the beginnings of a plan, and if the plan goes wrong you can adjust. You're never going to see the same fight twice. What you have is basic elements of each fight. You're still going to have to suppress. You're still gonna' have to create, you're still going to have to assess the casualties and get them out of the kill zone. Those things are never going to change. It's just your way to approach it that's going to change. I can go through escalations of force on vehicles where a gunner—you're talking a 18-, 19-, 20-year-old Marine or serviceman, whoever he be—and he's got his hands on the butterfly trigger. He has life and death in his hands. He's the one who has to decide, 'Is that a vehicle-born IED, or is that a momma' and five kids, just scared and driving erratically?' If I show it to him enough in here—which is the difference between the two—then when he gets in country we have less chance of killing the innocent. We're not killers. We're professional killers. We don't kill women and children. We kill those people who are trying to kill us. And this technology helps that."

My initial view of the exercise had come from Gunnery Sergeant Peter Walz, our affable Public Affairs Officer from the 1/25th New England Reservists. It was his task to sell the Corps and the program, and, leading us with unflagging enthusiasm through Mounted Patrols, Cordon Searches, Urban Patrolling, and Live Sniper Fire, he did a pretty good job of it. He maintained his good nature even when we approached a Vehicle Check Point in our rental SUV and a bunch of Marines opened up on us in a burst of (simulated) friendly fire. He made sure we got our grub before he did. But he could not help showing us the worst of it along with the best. Indeed, probably the greatest revelation of the trip came the second night, after I shared with him some of the bourbon I had smuggled in. The Udris brothers (the film crew) and I had crawled exhausted and cold into our sleeping bags (there would be a freak snowstorm that week). Gunny dug into an MRE, the only illumination coming from his head-mounted LED. I asked him what he did before this, and after some hesitation he told us in a low monotone about his previous gig: the door knock. He was the first to notify families of the death of their sons or daughters, fathers, or mothers. He thought it was the toughest job in the Marine Corps. He'd seen whole families break down weeping, he'd had mothers throw stuff at him, fathers throw him out of their houses. Being a father himself with two boys, it was something he could not imagine having his own kids face. He went through the visits in considerable detail, giving us just about every stage of denial and anger and grief that he had personally witnessed. We listened in silence as he chewed his way through the MRE and told the stories, unable to respond.

At the bottom of the Twentynine Palms pecking order were the Iraqi role-players. Marines were cordial towards them during the exercises—that was the purpose after all—but on more than one occasion I overheard Marines perform some classic in-group, out-group behavior. Curiously, it was expressed in economic rather than in cultural terms, usually something along the lines, "fuck, if I was getting paid $300 a day, I'd be an Iraqi too." (I wasn't able to confirm that figure, but I did know that the Iraqis in the exercises had no benefits, including health, which was a problem given the injuries that inevitably occurred during the exercises.) The Iraqi role-players were called "Titans," which at first I thought had some mythical significance, until I met one of the civilian contractors who was willing to talk about their employees. "Titan" was the name of the company originally contracted to select, transport, and train the Iraqis who played the mayor, police chief, wife, family member, insurgent, or, most numerously, the idle wanderer. Titan subsequently got bought by one of the largest defense firms, L3, which was now running much of the "Mojave Viper" show. Many of its American employees were ex-military, some Special Forces; almost all of them were reluctant to talk, much more so than the active-duty Marines. I eventually found a site manager who was willing to provide some background to the program, but nothing much was revealed. The overall goal, he said, was to reduce the number of Marines playing Iraqis (usually "short-enders" on their way out of the Corps for one reason or another, transferred to Twentynine Palms for the remaining months left on their contracts, and usually none too happy about it), and to increase the number of L3/Titan linguists and role players. It was also difficult to get information from the "Titans," many of whom still had family back in Iraq and feared possible reprisals (testimony to the power, at least perceived, of the insurgency). However, I eventually did get permission to interview one of the "Titans." As a PAO hovered nearby, he kept it short and to the point.

"My name is Gabriel Durait. I am Iraqi. I live in the United States, San Diego. The idea, we are role-playing Iraqis as back in Iraq. We give the idea how does life look like over in Iraq, so we are doing the same thing here. To get the Marines trained good so when they go back in Iraq, we make sure they know what they are doing how to deal with the people. We do culture class for them, teach them how is the Iraqis way, what religion they have, what they respect and disrespect."

My final interview of the exercise was with a medic. "Gunny" Walz had kept asking me if I wanted to meet the guy "who saved the pig." I had begged off—it didn't really sound that interesting—but he insisted. I met Corpsman Cleveland, whose job was to treat the wounded on the battlefield. To better the survival odds, the Marine Corps had developed a new two-week program in which an anesthetized pig is wounded with increasing severity, beginning with a knife, then a 9 mm handgun, followed by an AK-47, and finally subject to smoke and fire. The task of the Corpsman is to keep the pig alive as long as possible. Corpsman Cleveland was good: he kept his pig breathing for twelve hours. No one wanted to talk about the possibility of their own deaths on the battlefield, but it seemed like every Marine had a story about the pig. And every squad wanted a Corpsman who had gone to "pig school."

Gunny was right: it was an amazing story. But it registered in a different way than Gunny had intended. At the time I was simply stunned, stupefied by the matter-of-fact story told by the "pig man." But after the exercise ended and I returned to the wonderful oasis of the Twentynine Palms Inn for some real food and lots of drink, the battlefield convergence of the military and medical arts took on a new meaning. It reminded me of an historical moment, some time in the seventeenth century, when the advent of gunpowder and the need to maneuver at greater distances changed the nature of battle and, in response, armies developed a new visual system of signaling. At roughly the same time the incipient practice of modern medicine was applying novel instruments and methods (as well as painterly representations) for the scientific study of symptoms of disease. In their respective theaters of operations, the medical and the military fields coined a new term to describe the study of symptoms and signs: *semiology*, or as we know it today, semiotics. In this originating moment, the professional arts of healing and killing shared a common imperative: survival of the body as well as the body politic meant getting the signs right. Facing the multiple pathologies of the global war on terror, having spent a decade deciphering the mixed signals of virtuous wars, and after the sacrifice of so many humans, I no longer doubt that the cure has proven worse than the disease. I'm not even sure the pig was worth it.

Notes

Preface

1   I am referring to the media mavens, think-tank courtiers, and cash-iered government officials—often rapidly rotating through all three identities with ethical nonchalance—who flooded the marketplace of public opinion with policy papers, short-order books, and quickie documentaries. Their work might have varied in tone, ranging from celebratory to condemnatory, but their descriptive accounts as well as prescriptive recommendations display a remarkable similitude in historical shallowness, cultural myopia and theoretical thinness. Feeding on public fear, anger, and revenge, knowledge-brokers coming from the conservative right and the liberal left helped produce a post-9/11 discourse that oscillated between triumphalism and defeatism, leaving very little room for reasoned argument.

   I think three books stand out as exceptional accounts of the military, political, and religious factors leading to 9/11 and the response to it, best read in sequence: Steve Coll, *Ghost Wars: The Secret History of the CIA, Afghanistan, and Bin Laden, from the Soviet Invasion to September 10, 2001* (London and New York: Penguin, 2004); Lawrence Wright, *The Looming Tower: Al-Qaeda and the Road to 9/11* (New York: Knopf, 2006); and Thomas Ricks, *Fiasco: The American Military Adventure in Iraq* (London and New York: Penguin, 2006).

2   See James Der Derian, *Critical Practices in International Theory* (New York and Oxford: Routledge, 2008), in particular: "Mediating Estrangement: A Theory for Diplomacy" (1987); "Arms, Hostages and the Importance of Shredding in Earnest: Reading the National Security Culture" (1989); "The (S)pace of International Relations: Simulation, Surveillance and Speed" (1990); "The Terrorist Discourse: Signs, States, and Systems of Global Political Violence" (1991); "Cyberwar, Videogames, and the Gulf War Syndrome" (1992); and "The C.I.A., Hollywood, and Sovereign Conspiracies" (1993).

3   My different perspective and reaction should not and cannot be reduced to intellectual background or political belief. To this day, I strongly believe that how one first *received* the news of 9/11 greatly shaped one's response. I first heard of the initial plane strike from a reporter who called in the morning and wanted a reaction to a "Cessna hitting the World Trade Center." I said I knew nothing about it but would get back to him. I then got immediately in my car for a two-hour drive to Brown University, during which time I scanned multiple news stories on the radio, ranging from NPR and BBC to Howard Stern and local stations. By the time I arrived at the Watson Institute I was pretty sure it was Al Qaeda, having closely followed and written about the first WTC bombing as well as having read the court transcripts of the February 2001 trial of the Al Qaeda conspirators behind the bombing of the U.S. embassies in Tanzania and Kenya in 1998. I had also been closely following the assassination two days earlier (by a bomb hidden in a television camera) of Ahmed Massoud, Afghan leader of the Northern Alliance, which had all the earmarks of an Al Qaeda operation (see Chapter 9, pp. 214–16; Chapter 10, pp. 223–39; and "A Reinterpreation of Realism: Genealogy, Semiology, Dromology," *International Theory: Critical Investigations*, London: Macmillan, 1995, pp. 363–367). But probably my greatest shock came when I arrived at the Watson Institute to find all my colleagues staring at the TV, seemingly numbed by the loop viewing of the second strike and then collapse of the towers. My attempts to distract them, with comments about possible culprits, the need to quickly organize some kind of campus-wide event, etc., received a singular response, a kind of silent shock, tinged by a reproach for not sharing their collective state of mind. I am convinced that the visual, as opposed to audio, reception of the 9/11 event, even if televisual, produced a profoundly traumatic effect; and as Freud and psychologists have noted, it is as if such event gets lodged in the optical nerve, unable to reach the prefrontal cortex where they can be processed into insights and action (or not). It is also worth noting that it usually takes a second trauma, comparable in effect but not necessarily similar in content, to dislodge such profound trauma and allow it to be neurally, intellectually and affectively processed.

4   See Ron Suskind, quoted in Chapter 11, n.12, p. 316.

5   This gap is overlaid by the controversy that has been engendered by the Defense Department's effort to enlist academics in the war on terror, especially through the Human Terrain System and Minerva programs. See Chapter 12, n.14, p. 319.

6   I am happy to say the day ended on a more hopeful note. That evening I stumbled upon an impromptu peace vigil on Franklin Street in Durham, North Carolina, organized by a remarkable group of high school students and their mothers. For the next three hours the drumming, dancing, and honking by passing cars provided a

fine antidote to the hate and fear I had witnessed in that seminar room.

7 See "War as Game," *Brown Journal of World Affairs* (Summer/Fall, 2003, vol. x, issue 1), pp. 37–50. I am grateful to Andrew Horesh and Keith Stanski, the student editors-in-chief of the *BJWA*, who published an essay that probably otherwise would not have seen the light of day.

8 Walter Benjamin, *The Arcades Project*, trans. and ed. Howard Eilan and Kevin McLaughlin (Cambridge, MA: Belknap Press, 1999), p. 463.

Prologue

1 The London *Daily Telegraph*, May 23, 2000 (online).

2 Walter Benjamin, *The Arcades Project* (Cambridge, MA: Belknap Press, 1999), p. 461.

3 In March 1999, Air Force Major General John Campbell, then vice-director of the Defense Information Systems Agency (DISA), which is in charge of cybersecurity and provides worldwide communication and network and software support to the Department of Defense, told Congress that there were a total of 22,144 "attacks" detected on Defense Department networks, up from 5,844 in 1998. From January to August 2000, there have been a total of 13,998 reported "events," according to Betsy Flood, a spokeswoman at DISA (she defined "events" as "probes, scans, virus incidents and intrusions"). However, according to Richard Thieme, a technology consultant and one of the chairs of the annual computer hackers convention "DEF CON" (a play on the Department of Defense's levels of alert, or "Defense Conditions"), all but 1,000 of last year's reported attacks were attributed to recreational hackers. See Jim Wolf, "Hacking Of Pentagon Computers Persists," *Washington Post*, August 9, 2000, p. 23.

4 See Tony Perry, "Navy Takes a Scene Out of Hollywood: Command Center Designed by Former Disney Exec Boasts Zen-Like Serenity," *Los Angeles Times*, November 27, 2000, online.

5 See Martin Walker, *American Reborn* (New York: Knopf, 2000).

6 See Manuel De Landa, *War in the Age of Intelligent Machines* (New York: Zone, 1991); Paul Edwards, *Closed Worlds: Computers and the Politics of Discourse in Cold War America* (Cambridge, MA: MIT Press, 1996); and Friedrich Kittler, *Literature, Media, Information Systems* (Amsterdam: OPA, 1997).

1 The tank and the tortoise

1 Carl von Clausewitz, *On War*, ed. and trans. Michael Howard and Peter Paret (Princeton, NJ: Princeton University Press, 1976), p. 140.

2 Ibid., p. 168.

3   Michael Herr, *Dispatches* (New York: Avon Books, 1978), p. 20.
4   *ABC Nightline*, transcript, September 26, 1990.
5   News Release, United States Central Command, July 23, 1990. Most accounts of the Gulf War fail to take note of this exercise, and those that do, like Michael Gordon and General Bernard Trainor's *The Generals War* (Boston: Back Bay Books, 1995, p. 29), give the impression that Internal Look was a response to Saddam Hussein's preparations for war in July. But according to a Freedom of Information Act request made by Michael Klare, planning for Internal Look began at least a year earlier and a secret Planning Directive was distributed through Central Command as early as January 1990 (FOIA response, Central Command, January 17, 1992).
6   See Bruce Sterling, "War is Virtual Hell," *Wired*, 1.0.
7   Lewis Mumford, *The Pentagon of Power: The Myth of the Machine* (New York: Harcourt Brace Jovanovich, 1964), p. 342, illustrations 18–19.
8   Donna Haraway, "A Cyborg Manifesto," *Simians, Cyborgs and Women: The Reinvention of Nature* (New York: Routledge, 1991), p. 154.

2 Between wars

 1   In a footnote—the *only* footnote—in his most popular book, *Strategy*, Hart's contribution to the Salisbury Plain exercises is acknowledged: "The strategy and tactics of the Mongols are dealt with more fully in the author's earlier book *Great Captains Unveiled*—which was chosen for the first experimental Mechanized Force in 1927." See *Strategy*, 2nd rev. ed. (New York: Signet, 1974), p. 62.
 2   See B. H. Liddell Hart, *Paris, or the Future of War* (New York: 1925); and "Liddell Hart and De Gaulle: The Doctrines of Limited Liability and Mobile Defense," Brian Bond and Martin Alexander, *Makers of Modern Strategy from Machiavelli to the Nuclear Age*, eds. Gordon Craig and Felix Gilbert (Oxford: Clarendon Press, 1986), pp. 598–623. For a more critical view of Hart's contributions, see John Mearsheimer, *Liddell Hart and the Weight of History* (Ithaca and London: Cornell University Press, 1988).
 3   This convergence of weapon and image in the Gulf War was anticipated by Paul Virilio in the preface to the English edition of *War and Cinema: The Logistics of Perception*, trans. Patrick Camiller (New York: Verso, 1989), p. 4: "A war of pictures and sounds is replacing the war of objects (projectiles and missiles). In a technician's version of an all-seeing Divinity, ever ruling out accident and surprise, the drive is on for a general system of illumination that will allow everything to be seen and known, at every moment and in every place."
 4   For instance, the *Wall Street Journal* claimed that Marshall's ideas on the revolution in military affairs influenced the decision by

Northrop to merge with Grumman in 1994. See Thomas Ricks and Roy Harris, "Marshall's Ideas Help to Change Defense Industry," *Wall Street Journal*, July 15, 1994, p. 3.

5 Interview, Andrew Marshall, June 21, 1996. "With the arrival of the new Bush administration, Andrew Marshall's star was to rise yet again: In February 2001 he was appointed by Secretary of Defense Donald Rumsfeld to head a complete "'top-to-bottom review' of U.S. military strategy and force structure." See Frank J. Gaffney Jr., "The Marshall Plan," *Washington Times*, February 13, 2001, p. 15.

6 See Friedrich Nietzsche, *Genealogy of Morals*, II, #19, ed. and trans. Walter Kaufmann (New York: Random House, 1967), pp. 88–89.

7 See Friedrich Nietzsche, *Twilight of the Idols*, trans. R. J. Hollingdale (Harmondsworth: Penguin, 1968), p. 35: "You ask me about the idiosyncrasies of philosophers? . . . There is their lack of historical sense, their hatred of even the idea of becoming, their Egyptianism. They think they are doing a thing *honour*, they dehistoricize it, *su specie aeterni*—when they make a mummy of it. . . . What is, does not *become*; what becomes, *is* not. . . . Now even they all believe, even to the point of despair, in that which is."

8 "Everywhere that a culture *posits* evil, it gives expression to a relationship of *fear*, thus a weakness." Friedrich Nietzsche, *The Will to Power*, #1025, trans. Walter Kaufmann and R. J. Hollingdale (New York: Vintage Books, 1968), p. 530.

9 See Friedrich Niezsche, *Daybreak: Thoughts on the Prejudices of Morality*, #174, trans. R. J. Hollingdale and Michael Tanner (Cambridge, UK: Cambridge University Press, 1982) pp. 105–106. "*Moral fashion of a commercial society*—Behind the basic principle of the current moral fashion: 'moral actions are performed out of sympathy for others,' I see the social effect of timidity hiding behind an intellectual mask: it desires, first and foremost, that *all the dangers* which life once had should be removed from it, and that only those actions which tend towards the common security and society's sense of security are to be accorded the predicate 'good.'"

10 Ibid., #5. See also Nietsche, *Gay Science*, #355, trans. Walter Kaufmann (New York: Random House), pp. 300–302. "Look, isn't our need for knowledge precisely this need for the familiar, the will to uncover under everything strange, unusual, and questionable something that no longer disturbs us? Is it not the *instinct of fear* that bids us to know? And is the jubilation of those who obtain knowledge not the jubilation over the restoration of a sense of security?"

11 *Genealogy of Morals*, II, #11.

12 *Will to Power*, #53 and #576.

13 *Genealogy of Morals*, II, #19.

14 See Nietzsche, *Twilight of the Idols*, pp. 106–107.

15 For an excellent introduction of the concept, see Gunter Gebauer and Christoph Wulf, eds., *Mimesis: Culture, Art and Society*, trans. Don

Reneau (Berkeley, CA: University of California Press, 1995). There is a wide range of literature on the subject, but my own interpretation of the history and persistent power of mimesis relies on the allusive work of Walter Benjamin on the mimetic faculty; René Girard on mimetic desire (*Violence and the Sacred*, trans. Patrick Gregory, Baltimore: Johns Hopkins University Press, 1977), and the more analytical interpretation of mimesis and poeisis by Philippe Lacoue-Labarthe (*Typography: Mimesis, Philosophy, Politics*, Cambridge, MA: Harvard University Press, 1989).

16 Gebauer and Wulf, pp. 1–8.

17 It has, however, reappeared in the interface of culture and biology, most prolifically in the secondary literature on "memes," a concept first coined in 1976 by Oxford zoologist Richard Dawkins in his book, *The Selfish Gene* (New York: Oxford University Press, 1990), to convey how cultural elements are transmitted historically and horizontally by imitative, viral-like means.

18 Walter Benjamin, "Das Kustwek im Zeitalter seiner technischen Reproduzierbarkeit," in *Gesammelte Schriften* I.2, ed. Rolf Teidemann and Hermann Schweppenhauser (Frankfurt: Suhrkam, 1974–89). I rely here on Jeneen Hobby's translation and interpretation of the "second version" of the essay (discovered by Gary Smith in the Max Horkheimer Archive in the 1980s and included in the collected works) since it includes the epilogue as well as material on mimetic theory that is missing from other versions. See Jeneen Hobby, "Raising Consciousness in the Writings of Walter Benjamin," Ph.D. dissertation (University of Massachusetts at Amherst, 1996), p. 254, fn. 1.

19 Walter Benjamin, "On the Mimetic Faculty," *Reflections*, ed. Edmund Jephcott (New York: Schocken, 1978), p. 333.

20 Ibid.

21 Ibid., p. 335.

22 Ibid., p. 336.

23 *Gesammelte Schriften*, VI, p. 127, quoted by Jeneen Hobby, p. 270. Compare to an earlier, more general statement by Benjamin: "The gift to see similarities which we possess, is nothing else but a weak rudiment of that violent compulsion in former times to become similar and to behave similarly" (II, p. 210).

24 See, for example, "Theories of German Fascism: On the Collection of Essays *War and Warrior*, edited by Ernst Junger (1930), *Gesammelte Schriften*, III, pp. 238–250.

25 "Berliner Spielzeugwanderung II," in *Aufklärung für Kinder*, p. 49, quoted in Jeffrey Mehlman, *Walter Benjamin for Children: An Essay on His Radio Years* (Chicago: University of Chicago Press, 1993), p 4.

26 "Spielzeug un Spielen," p. 71, quoted in Mehlman, p. 5.

27 Ibid., p. 67, quoted in Mehlman, p. 4.

28 Theodor Adorno, although critical of Benjamin's interpretation of mimesis, does acknowledge that "Art that seeks to redeem itself from

semblance through play becomes sport"—opening another important link to practices of war. See *Aesthetic Theory* (Minneapolis, Minn.: University of Minnesota Press, 1997), p. 100; and in *Dialectics of Enlightenment* (New York: Herder and Herder, 1972), Adorno and Max Horkheimer also link a "false mimesis" to the violence of fascism and anti-Semitism (pp. 4–9 and 182–186).

29 See Girard, *Violence and the Sacred*; and also "System as Delirium," *To Double Business Bound* (Baltimore: Johns Hopkins University Press, 1978), in which Girard goes further, to claim the origin of desire is a mimesis in which the death of the original source of desire is in turn desired, where "*mimesis* meets violence and violence redoubles *mimesis*" (p. 93).

30 Walter Benjamin, *The Arcades Project* (Cambridge, Mass.: Belknap Press, 1999), pp. 456 and 173.

31 Nietzsche's definition is worth quoting at length, since it foreshadows the power behind Benjamin's "mimetic faculty": "Insofar as the individual wants to preserve himself against other individuals, in a natural state of affairs he employs the intellect mostly for simulation alone. But because man, out of need and boredom, wants to exist socially, herd-fashion, he requires a peace pact and he endeavors to banish at least the very crudest *bellum omnium contra omnes* from his world. This peace pact brings with it something that looks like the first step toward the attainment of this enigmatic urge for truth. . . . What, then, is truth? A mobile army of metaphors, metonyms, and anthropomorphisms—in short, a sum of human relations, which have been enhanced, transposed, and embellished poetically and theoretically, and which after long use seem firm, canonical, and obligatory to a people: truths are illusions about which one has forgotten that this is what they are; metaphors which are worn out and without sensuous power; coins which have lost their pictures and now matter only as metal, no longer as coins." See Friedrich Nietzsche, "On Truth and Lie in an Extra-Moral Sense," in *The Portable Nietzsche*, ed. and trans. Walter Kaufmann (New York: Penguin, 1976), p. 44.

32 *Briefe* (425), Benjamin's letters, quoted in John McCole, *Walter Benjamin and the Antimonies of Tradition* (Ithaca, N.Y.: Cornell University Press, 1993), p. 12.

33 Zygmunt Bauman, *Life in Fragments: Essays in Postmodern Morality* (Oxford: Basil Blackwell, 1995), p. 193.

34 Benjamin, "Dream Kitsch," *Walter Benjamin: Selected Writings, Volume 2, 1927–1934* (Cambridge, Mass.: Belknap Press, 1999), p. 3.

35 Ibid.

3 Global swarming and the Bosnia question

1   Leon Trotsky, *The Balkan wars, 1912–13: The war correspondence of Leon Trotsky* (New York: Pathfinder Press, 1980), p. 148.

2   Jean Baudrillard, *The Gulf War Did Not Take Place*, trans. Paul Patton (Bloomington, Ind.: Indiana University Press, 1995), pp. 61–87.

3   Slovoj Zizek, ed., *Mapping Ideology* (London: Verso, 1994), p. 5.

4   "Mission Training Plan for Military Operations Other than War," Seventh Army Training Command White Paper, Coordinating Draft for Peace-keeping Operations (December 1994).

5   Ibid., p. I–2.

6   Timothy Garton Ash, *The Magic Lantern: The Revolution of '89* (New York: Vintage Books, 1993).

4 The simulation triangle

1   B. H. Liddell Hart, *Strategy* (New York: Signet, 1967), p. 5.

2   Guy Debord, *Society of the Spectacle* (Detroit: Black and Red, 1983), #1.

3   Jean Baudrillard, *Simulations* (New York: Semiotext(e), 1983), p. 43.

4   Paul Virilio, *Block 14* (Autumn 1988), p. 7.

5   Paul Virilio, *The Vision Machine* (Bloomington: Indiana University Press, 1994), p. 70.

6   Guy Debord, *Society of the Spectacle*, #31.

7   Jean Baudrillard, *Fatal Strategies* (New York: Semiotext(e), 1990), p. 37.

8   Jean Baudrillard, *Simulations* (New York: Semiotext(e), 1983), p. 2.

9   Paul Virilio, "Afterword," *Bunker Archeology* (New York: Princeton Architectural Press, 1994), p. 202.

10 Baudrillard, *Simulations*, p. 25.

11 Guy Debord, *In girum imus nocte et consumimur* (*We go around in circles in the night and are consumed by fire*, 1978 film), cited in *On the Passage of a few people through a rather brief moment in time: The Situationist International* (Cambridge, Mass.: MIT Press, 1989), p. 104.

5 The virtual enemy

1   Steven Mufson, "What's In A Name? U.S. Drops Term 'Rogue State,'" *Washington Post*, June 20, 2000, p. 16; "Updating Diplomacy's Language," *New York Times*, June 23, 2000. However, "rogues" made something of a comeback on the 2000 presidential campaign trail. Amidst all the malapropisms, George W. Bush gave a revivifying speech to Iowa fund-raisers, including lines like: "We cannot let terrorists and rogue nations hold this nation hostile or hold our allies hostile." Gail Collins, "A Reality-Television Campaign," *New York Times*, August 25, 2000, p. A25. The final word on the matter went to "C.J.," President Barlet's press secretary on the television program *West Wing*, who shortly afterward informed the press that the White House no longer used the term "rogue."

2 U.S. Department of State, Daily Press Briefing, June 19, 2000, Richard Boucher, Spokesman, http://secretary.state.gov/www/briefings/0006/000619db.html.

3 See U.S. Department of State, Diplomatic Security Service, at http://www.heroes.net/warcrimes/warcriminals.html.

4 DARPA Welcome, http://www.darpa.mil/.

5 DARPA News Releases, http://www.darpa.mil/.

6 DARPA ATO, http://www.darpa.mil/ato/.

7 Although Katz falls on the other side of this argument, he does raise the important pros and cons (with much more eloquence) at *Wired-News*: http://www.wired.com/news/topstories/0,1287,6191,00.html. He does confess that the column was "my most universally rejected, condemned, and disagreed-with Internet opinion ever" and that "of the hundreds of responses, two or three agreed with my position, and the nearly unanimous, articulate, eloquent majority thought I was nuts."

8 Clifford Geertz, "Thinking as a Moral Act: Ethical Dimensions of Anthropological Fieldwork In the New States," *Available Light: Anthropological Reflections on Philosophical Topics* (Princeton, N.J.: Princeton University Press, 2000), p. 39.

9 Ryan Henry, Interview at DARPA, June 21, 1996.

10 J. Michael Brower, "QDR for dummies," *Army News Service*, May 16, 1997, http://www.dtic.mil/armylink/news/May1997/a19970516 qdr2.html; Brower is a program analyst in the Office of the Assistant Secretary of the Army for Financial Management and Comptroller.

11 Robert Holzer, "Report: Allies No Substitute For U.S. Troops," *Defense News*, August 28, 2000, p. 1.

12 For a good history of the QDR, see Brower, and the website of the Commonwealth Project on Defense Alternatives, http://www.comw.org/qdr/.

13 The full text of the QDR can be found at: http://www.fas.org/man/docs/qdr/.

14 Secretary of Defense Cohen, Press briefing after the EXFOR war game at the National Training Center, Fort Irwin, March 18, 1997, DOD website. My thanks to Neta Crawford for flagging the quote.

15 *The American Heritage Dictionary of the English Language*, 3rd ed. (Boston: Houghton Mifflin Company, 1992). Electronic version licensed from InfoSoft International, Inc.

16 Francis Bacon, *Works of Lord Bacon* (London: Henry Bohn, 1864), book VII, ch. ii, p. 281.

17 Francis bacon, "Of the True Greatness of Kingdoms," *Essays* (London: Dent and Sons, 1939), p. 95, quoted by Martin Wight, *International Theory: The Three Traditions* (Leicester: Leicester University Press, 1991), p. 208. Wight also takes note of the switch from "just and honorable" in the first sentence to "foreign" in the second.

18 Francis Bacon, "Of Simulation and Dissimulation," *Essays*.
19 See Chapter 4; and Jean Baudrillard, *Simulations* (New York: Semiotext(e), 1983), p. 5.
20 Baudrillard, p. 5.
21 Ibid.
22 Ibid., p. 12.
23 Ibid., p. 13.
24 See Der Derian, "Cyberwar, Videogames, and the Gulf War Syndrome," *Antidiplomacy: Spies, Terror, Speed, and War* (Oxford: Blackwell Publishers, 1992).
25 Ibid.
26 *Airpower Journal* 8 (January 1, 1994), p. 35.
27 Ibid.
28 Paul Virilio, interview from *Art and Philosophy* (Milan: Giancoarlo Politi Editore, 1991), p. 140.
29 Paul Virilio, *Art and Philosophy*, pp. 143–144.

6 Virtuous war comes home

1 Unless one counts Francisco "Pancho" Villa's March 1916 raid with 500 men as an "invasion" and Columbus, New Mexico, as a "city." President Woodrow Wilson did think it enough of an insult to American sovereignty to eventually dispatch over 150,000 troops to the border, and order General Pershing's "Punitive Expedition" of 10,000 cavalrymen into Mexico. Perhaps a more apt analogue would be the 1938 Halloween invasion of New Jersey and New York, in which both Orson Welles (the genius behind the radio broadcast of *The War of the Worlds*) and the Martian invaders (who left cities intact but destroyed the networks of the time, bridges, railroads, telephone and power lines) put into practice a kind of proto-infowar.
2 "'Peaceful' protesters called out of control," *The Oakland Tribune*, March 18, 1999, p. 1.
3 "Marines/CEOs Team Up for IT War Game," Joint Information Bureau, March 1, 1999, http://208.198.7/mcwl-hot/uw/media/pressr.html.
4 Interview, Vice Admiral Arthur K. Cebrowski, U.S. Navy, May 25, 1999.
5 Kevin Kelly, former executive editor of *Wired* magazine, and author of *New Rules for the New Economy: 10 Radical Strategies for a Connected World* (New York: Viking, 1998).
6 For the most objective account and a compilation of key documents, see the *PBS Frontline* website for its documentary, "Waco: the Inside Story," http://www.pbs.org/wgbh/pages/frontline/waco/.
7 See interview with General Wesley Clark, Chapter 8.
8 *Christian Science Monitor*, "Launching A 'Homeland Defense': To protect itself from terrorism, United States embarks on protection

program reminiscent of early Cold War," January 29, 1999. To hammer the point home, two years later a congressionally mandated commission on national security recommended the creation of a "National Homeland Security Agency," calling for institutional reforms in the national security apparatus, higher spending in the sciences and on technology, and on the National Guard to protect the U.S. homeland: "A catastrophic attack is likely to hit U.S. soil in the next 25 years, and the National Guard should be retrained as America's main protector against such an assault, an advisory commission on national security said yesterday." Pauline Jelinek, *Philadelphia Inquirer*, February 1, 2001.

7 Virtuous war goes to Hollywood

1 Peter Marks, "Republicans Seeking Parity in TV Convention Coverage," *New York Times*, August 11, 2000, p. A13.
2 Bob Herbert, "Gore's Crucial Week," *New York Times*, August 14, 2000, p. A21.
3 Paul Virilio, *Bunker Archeology* (New York: Princeton Architectural Press, 1994), p. 46. In a 1991 Afterword to the book (p. 202), Virilio returns to the question of the bunker, to ask whether we have now rendered it invisible in a kind of "nonwar": "in which nuclear deterrence founded upon ruling out surprise attacks thanks to capabilities for scanning and controlling, point by point and second by second, not only enemy territory but the entire planet from outer space, as announced in Reagan's strategic defense initiative as early as 1983? An Orwellian vision of a divine eye, a *deus ex machina* powerful enough to rule out mankind's potential for mutual destruction? An ideal technique, a utopia? An idol capable of realizing exactly what men's faith has been unable to accomplish. ... A utopia of *technical fundamentalism* that has nothing at all to do with the religious variety that still requires virtues of men instead of advantages to 'machines'?"
4 Jean Baudrillard, *Simulacra and Simulation*, trans. Sheila Glaser (Ann Arbor, Mich.: University of Michigan Press, 1994), p. 6.
5 Coincidentally, the army released for the first time its recommended reading list for generals; among the books was Paul Kennedy's *Rise and Fall of the Great Powers*, an epic historical study of what happens when powerful states spend too much on the military. See Thomas E. Ricks, "Up In Arms: The Defense Department," *Washington Post*, August 1, 2000, p. 21. And military readiness would go on to dominate the foreign policy questions in the October presidential and vice-presidential debates.
6 Baudrillard, *Simulacra*, p. 7.
7 Steven Lee Myers, *New York Times*, July 28, 2000, p. A15.
8 See http://www.r2kphilly.org/ and http://www.d2kla.org/.

9 Jeffrey Rabin and Beth Shuster, "Judge Voids Convention Security Zone," *Los Angeles Times* (July 20, 2000), http://www.latimes.com/news/politics/elect2000/pres/demconven/lat_dnc000720.htm.

10 Ludwig Feuerbach, *The Essence of Christinaity*, trans. George Eliot (New York: Harper and Row, 1957).

11 Sara Miles, "The Nasdaq-ing of Capitol Hill," *New York Times Magazine*, August 13, 2000, pp. 48–40.

12 John Markoff, "Oracle Leader Calls Microsoft Spying 'Civic Duty,'" *New York Times*, June 29, 2000, p. 1.

13 James Stewart, "Mousetrap: What Time Warner didn't consider when it unplugged Disney," *The New Yorker*, July 31, 2000, p. 28. Time Warner later apologized (to its customers) with a full-page ad in the *New York Times* (May 8, 2000, p. A13), offering two days of credit for Basic Cable service, and promising to go back to the negotiating table with Disney-ABC. On the same day, demonstrating the full spectral reach of virtuous war, an Internet storage and backup company, Xdrive, ran a full-page ad (p. C11) in response to the "Love Bug" virus unleashed by a Filipino hacker (causing an estimated $10 billion in lost data and productivity). In bold letters it read: "On May 4, 2000, a virus spread through the world, cleverly disguised as a love note. In a matter of hours, it began to wipe out attachments, documents and files on e-mail servers everywhere. It destroyed vital information. It shut down multinational corporations. It ruined futures. Perhaps careers. In the midst of all this destruction, there were a significant number of people who found their files totally unaffected. And their businesses and lives intact."

14 *Fortune*, August 14, 2000, pp. 34–35.

15 Paul Virilio, *War and Cinema: The logistics of perception*, trans. Patrick Camiller (London: Verso, 1989).

16 See Paul Virilio, "The Strategy of the Beyond," "The Vision Machine," and "Desert Screen" in *The Virilio Reader*, ed. James Der Derian (Oxford: Blackwell Publishers, 1998).

17 See Siegfried Kracauer, *From Caligari to Hitler*, and *The Mass Ornament: Weimar Essays*, trans. and ed. Thomas Y. Levin (Cambridge, Mass.: Harvard University Press, 1995); and Friedrich Kittler, *Gramophone, Film, Typewriter*, trans. Geoffrey Winthrop-Young and Michael Wutz (Stanford, Calif.: Stanford University Press, 1999).

18 Kracauer, *From Caligari to Hitler*, p. 299.

19 Ibid., p. 303.

20 Walter Benjamin, "The Work of Art in the Age of Mechanical Reproduction," *Illuminations*, ed. Hannah Arendt, trans. Harry Zohn (New York: Schocken Books, 1969), p. 251.

21 Rick Lyman, "Building Rome by Computer," *New York Times*, April 28, 2000, p. C3.

22 Reinhold Niebuhr, "The Revival of Feudalism," *Harper's* Magazine (March 1935), quoted in David Little, "The Recovery of Liberalism:

Moral Man and Immoral Society Sixty Years Later," *Ethics and International Affairs* 7 (1993), pp. 171–202.

23 Triangle Institute for Security Studies, *Project on the Gap Between the Military and Civilian Society*, http://www.unc.edu/depts/tiss/CIVMIL.htm.

24 Ibid.

25 USC News Service, http://uncnews.usc.edu, August 17, 1999.

26 According to Oleg Gordievsky, former KGB station chief in London, the Soviet leadership became convinced in November 1983 that a NATO command-post simulation called Able Archer '83 was in fact the first step towards a nuclear surprise attack. Relations were already tense after the September shoot-down of the KAL 007—a flight that the Soviets considered part of an intelligence-gathering mission—and since the Warsaw Pact had their own war game that used a training exercise as cover for a surprise attack, the Soviets assumed the West to have one as well. No NATO nuclear forces went on actual alert, yet the KGB reported the opposite to Moscow. On November 8 or 9, flash messages were sent to all Soviet embassies in Europe, warning them of NATO preparations for a nuclear first strike. Things calmed down when the Able Archer exercise ended without the feared nuclear strike, but Gordievsky still maintains that only the Cuban Missile Crisis brought the world closer to the brink of nuclear war. This is based on a conversation I had with Gordievsky after he defected, on November 8, 1991, in Toronto, Ontario; and on Christopher Andrews and Oleg Gordievsky, *KGB: The Inside Story* (New York: HarperCollins, 1991), pp. 583–605.

27 *Opportunities for Collaboration Between the Defense and Entertainment Research Communities*, http://books.nap.edu/catalog/5830.html.

28 I received a tongue-in-check e-mail from Mike Macedonia shortly after the ICT officially opened—and the Yugoslavs gave Milosevic the boot: "We opened the ICT building last week. Milosevic subsequently caved to the pressure of America's latest high tech achievement." A newspaper article covering the opening calls it "Fort Dix meets Paul Verhoeven . . . an eye-popping mix of voice recognition, artificial intelligence, and gee-whiz hardware that makes computer-generated humans look and act like the real thing." But the reporter also introduces a "moral question": "Does this sophisticated new technology used to train soldiers in any way make a statement about the impact simulated violence can have on human behavior—notably kids?" See Gloria Goodale, "Simulated violence and human behavior: Army enlists Hollywood to help harden its soldiers," *Christian Science Monitor*, October 2, 2000, http://www.csmonitor.com/durable/2000/10/02/fp2s2-csm.shtml. See also the website of the Institute for Creative Technology at www.ict.usc.edu.

8 Kosovo and the virtuous thereafter

1 "Individual Protective Measures for Personal Security," GTA-19–4–3, July 1997.

2 Dana Priest, "Russia Jets Flew Within U.S. Range in Exercise," *International Herald Tribune*, July 2, 1999, p. 1.

3 Two that stand above the crowd, and should be read in tandem, are: Michael Ignatieff's *Virtual War: Kosovo and Beyond* (New York: Metropolitan Books, 2000); and Thomas Keenan, "'Looking like flames and falling like stars': Kosovo, the first Internet war," http://www.bard.edu/hrp/keenan/kosovo.htm.

4 Richard Holbrooke, *To End a War: From Sarajevo to Dayton and Beyond* (Random House, 1998).

5 Milosevic is reported as saying at the time that details in diplomacy were mere "technology." See Roger Cohen, "After the Lost Wars and the Ruined Economy, 'the Greater Slobo' Falls Silent," *New York Times*, October 6, 2000, p. A14.

6 *DefenseLink*, Department of Defense, http://www.defenselink.mil:80/news/Oct1999/b10141999_bt478-99.html.

7 "The bombing of Serbia has become the first Internet war, with e-mail missives from local people providing day-by-day accounts of the conflict from the front lines in Belgrade and Pristina." See Robert Uhlig, "Front-line news now travels by e-mail," The London *Daily Telegraph*, March 27, 1999, p.4.

8 "Most RAF Kosovo bombs 'off-target,'" *Guardian*, August 14, 2000.

9 See "'Collateral Damage' or Unlawful Killings? Violations of the Laws of War by NATO during Operation Allied Force," *Amnesty International Report*, June 2000, http://www.amnesty.org/ailib/aipub/2000/SUM/47001800.htm.

10 Jean Bethke Elshtain, *Democracy on Trial* (New York: Basic Books, 1995), p. 123.

9 A virtual theory of the global event

1 "'We will deploy defenses as soon as possible,' Lucas Fischer, the deputy assistant secretary of state for strategic affairs, told the Danish Parliament. 'Therefore, we believe that the ABM treaty will have to be replaced, eliminated or changed in a fundamental way' . . . In addressing the Danish Parliament, Mr Fischer said the aim of the missile defenses is to defend not only against attacks from rogue states like Iran or Iraq but also against accidental or unauthorized launches. That means the defense system needs to have some capacity to counter the launching of Russian and Chinese missiles." See Michael R. Gordon and Steven Lee Myers, "Bush Team Vows To Speed Up Work On Missile Shield," *New York Times*, April 30, 2001, p. 1.

2 Bob Kemper, "Bush Team Adjusts To World Realities," *Chicago Tribune*, May 15, 2001, p. 1.

3 See Christopher Hill, "World Opinion and the Empire of Circumstance," *International Affairs* 72, 1 (1996), pp. 109–113.

4 Bad luck is often confused with or disguised as accidental circumstance rather than as the product of bad policy choices. This was most clearly demonstrated several years later by Secretary of Defense Rumsfeld, who, when criticized for the massive looting taking place in Iraq after the U.S. "victory," responded, "Stuff happens." Luck then and now is knowing how much to leave to circumstance, like being sure to have enough troops on hand to win the peace that follows the war.

5 In international relations, most of this literature focuses more on irrational civilian policy or a series of military mistakes—"follies" in the language of Barbara Tuchman—than on single precipitous events that can be more narrowly categorized as accidents. See, for example, Barbara Tuchman, *The March of Folly: From Troy to Vietnam* (New York: Ballantine, 1992) and *The Guns of August* (New York: Ballantine, 1994).

6 Charles Perrow, *Normal Accidents: Living with High-Risk Technologies* (Princeton, NJ: Princeton University Press, 1999). Perrow's work does not focus specifically on information technology, but there is a lengthy postscript to the new edition that applies the concept of normal accident to the Y2K problem. For an excellent account of some more recent "normal accidents" (such as the faulty network card on a desktop computer that led to U.S. Customs and Border Protection shutting down all entry and exit into the U.S. through LAX one day in August 2007), see Jonathan Schwartz, "Who Needs Hackers?" *The New York Times* (September 12, 2007), p. H1.

7 See Paul Virilio, *The Virilio Reader*, ed. James Der Derian (Oxford: Blackwell Press); "Cybermonde, la politique du pire", *Libération* (Mai 10, 1996); *The Information Bomb*, trans. Chris Turner (London: Verso, 2000); and *Strategy of Deception*, trans. Chris Turner (London: Verso, 2000).

8 "Philosophy's sole aim is to become worthy of the event." See Gilles Deleuze and Felix Guattari, *What is Philosophy?*, trans. Hugh Tomlinson and Graham Burchell (New York: Columbia University Press, 1994), p. 160 and Paul Patton, "Introduction," in Paul Patton ed., *Deleuze: A Critical Reader* (London: Blackwell Publishers, 1996).

9 See Deleuze and Guattari, *What is Philosophy?*, p. 33 and Gilles Deleuze and Felix Guattari, *Difference and Repetition*, trans. Paul Patton (London: Athlone Press, 1994), p. 189.

10 Deleuze and Guattari, *What is Philosophy?*, p. 160.

11 For a more visual and interactive representation of this effort to open up IR to new categories of threats and vulnerabilities as well as levels of analysis, see www.globalsecuritymatrix.org.

12 See James Der Derian, "A Reinterpretation of Realism: Genealogy, Semiology, and Dromology," in James Der Derian ed., *International*

Theory: Critical Investigations (New York: New York University Press, 1995), pp. 363–396.

13 See Christopher Hill, op. cit.

14 See James Dao, "Senators Question Handling of Cole Case: Suggestions That Navy Has Eased Accountability for Commanders," *New York Times*, May 4, 2001, p. A17.

15 It might seem less strange to acknowledge the political and cultural construction of the accident-based global event knowing that the authoritative *Diagnostic and Statistical Manual of Mental Disorders* ("D.S.M.-I.V.") came out in 1994 with a new category of psychiatric illnesses known as "culture-bound syndromes," meaning culturally rather than bodily induced mental disorders, like *latah*, the hyper-startle syndrome in Malaysia. See Lawrence Osborne, "Regional Disturbances," *New York Times Sunday Magazine*, May 6, 2001, pp. 98–102.

16 George J. Tenet, Statement on the "Worldwide Threat 2001: National Security in a Changing World" before the Senate Select Committee on Intelligence, February 7, 2001 (http://www.cia.gov/cia/public_affairs/ speeches/ UNCLASWWT_02072001.html).

17 Mike Allen and Edward Walsh, "A 'Hoo-Ah!' And Some Numbers," *Washington Post*, February 13, 2001, p. 6.

18 "Excerpts From Bush's Remarks on the Military," *New York Times*, February 14, 2001, p. A26.

19 See Deborah Seward, "Russia Angered By U.S. Charges Of Spreading Missile Technologies," *Fort Worth Star-Telegram*, February 16, 2001, p. 1 and Toby Harnden and Marcus Warren, "Russia Selling Atomic Know-How, Says U.S.," *London Daily Telegraph*, February 16, 2001, p. 1.

20 "In the President's Words on the Bombing: 'It's a Routine Mission,'" *New York Times*, February 17, 2001, p. A4.

21 Trial transcripts, *United States of America v. Usama bin Laden, et al.*, February 6, 2001, online (http://cryptome.org/usa-v-ubl-01.htm). It should be noted that this chapter was written before 9/11.

22 Peter Grier, "A Terrorist Version Of NATO?," *The Christian Science Monitor*, February 16, 2001, p. 1; see also Alan Feuer, "Terror Exports Are The Business Of Jihad Inc," *New York Times*, February 13, 2001. It should be noted that this chapter was written before 9/11: another accident?

23 See Chapter 5.

24 On June 19, 2000, "rogue state" was officially, if only semantically, retired by the Clinton administration. After being asked on a public radio news program if Kim Jong of North Korea, who had just summitted with South Korean leader Kim Dae Jung, was still a "rogue leader," Secretary of State Madeline Albright let it be known that "we are now calling these states 'states of concern' because we are concerned about their support for terrorist activity, their development

of missiles, their desire to disrupt the international system." The final word on the matter went to "C.J.," President Bartlett's press secretary on *West Wing*, who shortly afterwards informed the press that the White House no longer used the term "rogue." See Steven Mufson, "What's In A Name? U.S. Drops Term 'Rogue State,'" *Washington Post*, June 20, 2000, p. 16; "Updating Diplomacy's Language," *New York Times*, June 23, 2000, A13. However, "rogues" made a comeback on the 2000 Presidential campaign trail, and it is now back in the political discourse, in spite or perhaps because of George W. Bush reintroducing the term in a malapropism-laden speech to Iowa fund-raisers, which included lines like: "[w]e cannot let terrorists and rogue nations hold this nation hostile or hold our allies hostile." Gail Collins, "A Reality-Television Campaign," *New York Times*, August 25, 2000, p. A25.

25 See Chapter 5, pp. 28–33.

26 Frank J. Gaffney Jr., "The Marshall Plan," *Washington Times*, February 13, 2001, p. 15. See also John Dillin, "Pentagon Braces For A Makeover," *Christian Science Monitor*, February 12, 2001, p. 1.

27 In assessing the balance of power between government and media— never an easy proposition—it is worth noting the battle over terms, in particular, the semantic slide during from "accident" to "event" to "incident" to "crisis." For example, during the recent confrontation with China over the EP-3E Aries II surveillance plane, Bush was singularly intent (by most accounts) on the incident not becoming a crisis. "'Let's avoid making this a crisis,' Bush said all week long" (Johanna McGeary, "Safe Landing A Carefully Engineered Game Plan Helped Bush Bring the U.S. Flight Crew Home," *Time*, April 23, 2001). Yet, by my unscientific month-long survey of 160 front page and editorial articles in six major newspapers (*New York Times*, *Washington Post*, *Washington Times*, *Los Angeles Times*, *U.S.A Today*, *Wall Street Journal*) and two major news magazines (*Time* and *Newsweek*), "crisis" was used at least 98 times to describe the event. For purpose of illustration, compare just one newspaper's reportage at the beginning and the end of the coverage. Two days after the collision, *U.S.A Today* reports: "Several White House officials insisted that there was no crisis with China. Their sensitivity to the use of the word 'crisis,' however, underscored the tense nature of the situation" (Laurence McQuillan, "Bush Intent On Averting Crisis," *U.S.A Today*, April 3, 2001, p. 10). One month later the newspaper uses the term "crisis" in a headline, "Taiwan: Spy Plane Crisis Proves China Is Threat," without any equivocation in the article (Paul Wiseman, *U.S.A Today*, May 3, 2001, p. 2). In this period there were also two serious accidents during U.S. war games, including the "Lightning Thrust Warrior" exercise in Hawaii, in which two UH-60 Black Hawk helicopters collided, killing six soldiers; and the training bombing of an observation post in the Kuwaiti desert by a Navy F-18 pilot, killing

six U.S. and allied troops. See also Neil King Jr., Michael Phillips, Greg Jaffe, and Charles Hutzler, "Crisis Forces Bush To Balance Clashing China-Policy Camps," *Wall Street Journal*, April 4, 2001, p. 1; Jim Mann, "Crisis Forces Bush Team To Speed Up Decisions On China Policy," *Los Angeles Times*, April 3, 2001, p. 1; and Jane Perlez, "Powell Warns Of Damage To Ties As Crisis Drags On," *New York Times*, April 9, 2001, p. 1.

28 Clifford Geertz, "The World in Pieces: Culture and Politics at the End of the Century," in *Available Light: Anthropological Reflections on Philosophical Topics* (Princeton, NJ: Princeton University Press), p. 221.

29 Here I am heeding as well as inverting Raymond Aron, who states in his magisterial work, *Peace and War*, that the "ambiguity in 'international relations' is not to be imputed to the inadequacy of our concepts: it is an integral part of reality itself." See *Peace and War: A Theory of International Relations*, trans. Richard Howard and A. B. Fox (London: Weidenfeld and Nicolson, 1966), p. 7.

30 François Lyotard, *The Postmodern Condition* (Minneapolis: University of Minnesota Press, 1984).

31 See Der Derian, "A Reinterpretation of Realism," pp. 363–396. For a more rigorous treatment of the ideas behind my virtual theory, see Deleuze and Guattari, *What is Philosophy?*; *Bergsonism, A Thousand Plateaus: Capitalism and Schizophrenia*; and *Difference and Repetition*; Jean Baudrillard, *Simulacra and Simulation*, trans. Sheila Faria Glaser (Ann Arbor: University of Michigan Press, 1994); and "Speed Pollution," interview of Paul Virilio, *Wired* (May 1996), p. 120.

32 This definition and the description of the virtual which follows is a shorthand, highly condensed interpretation drawn from the work of Martin Heidegger, Gilles Deleuze, Félix Guattari, Jacques Derrida, Pierre Lévy, and Paul Virilio. I have found the best synoptic article on the topic to be Wolfgang Welsch, "Virtual Anyway?," in Candido Mendes and Enrique Larreta eds., *Media and Social Perception* (Rio de Janeiro: UNESCO), 1999, pp. 242–285.

33 Or as William Connolly once told me, "a little vertigo is a good thing but a lot can turn you into a zombie." See also Der Derian, *Project Z* (forthcoming).

34 See, for example, the debate between the so-called techno-realists (http://www.technorealism.org) clustered around Harvard University Law School's Berkman Center for the Internet and Society (http://cyber.law.harvard.edu), and what I refer to as the techno-irenists, clustered around *Wired* magazine (http://www.wired.com/wired/ and http://www.hotwired.com/).

35 Carl Schmitt, *Political Theology: Four Chapters on the Concept of Sovereignty* (Cambridge, MA: MIT Press, 1988).

36 Robert Frost, "Accidentally on Purpose," *The Poetry of Robert Frost* (New York: Henry Holt, 1969).

10 After 9/11

1 See, for example, "The Secret History of Mohamed Atta," http://www.madcowprod.com/02212006.html.

2 This tidbit triggered a flashback for me. At the height of the first détente of the early 1960s with the Soviets, the famous Moscow Circus toured the U.S.; performers would stay with American families to promote peace and understanding. I'm not sure whether it was due to his Armenian heritage or rudimentary Russian language skills, but my father was chosen to host three of them; for a couple of nights we shared our Pittsburgh home with two "Cossack" trick horse riders and a strongman who threw cannonballs in the air and caught them in the massive nape of his neck. Language was an issue, so I doubt whether much espionage was going on; my abiding memory was of the strongman holding my new-born sister in his enormous arms and singing her to sleep with a lullaby in Russian.

3 See http://en.wikipedia.org/wiki/Ringling_Brothers_and_Barnum_&_Bailey_Clown_College.

4 http://www.af.mil/factsheets/factsheet.asp?id=188; http://www.nicap.org/mthome490724dir.htm.

5 Kevin Kelly, *New Rules for the New Economy* (London: Fourth Estate, 1999), p. 31.

6 Friedrich Nietzsche, *The Use and Abuse of History* (http://www.geocities.com/thenietzschechannel/history.htm).

7 Walter Benjamin, *A Lyric Poet in the Era of High Capitalism* (London: Verso, 1997).

8 "*in terrorem*, as a warning, in order to terrify or deter others," *OED*.

9 For an earlier discussion of the ideological, epistemological, and ontological obstacles facing any inquiry into terrorism, see James Der Derian, "The Terrorist Discourse: Signs, States, and Systems of Global Political Violence," *Antidiplomacy: Spies, Terror, Speed, and War* (Cambridge, MA and Oxford, UK: Blackwell, 1992), pp. 92–126.

10 Michael Ignatieff, "It's war—but it doesn't have to be dirty," *Guardian*, October 1, 2001. Ignatieff would go on to become a controversial apologist for the Iraq War.

11 George Will, "On the Health of the State," *Newsweek*, October 1, 2001, p. 70.

12 Edward Rothstein, "Attacks on U.S. Challenge the Perspectives of Postmodern True Believers," September 22, 2001, p. A17.

13 Mark Edington, *New York Times*, March 2, 1993.

14 *Newsweek*, March 8, 1993, p. 22.

15 *Sunday Times*, February 28, 1993, p. 10.

16 Phil Shenon and Jim Dwyer, "Agency Says Military Did Not Lie to 9/11," *New York Times*, August 5, 2006.

17 See http://www.fbi.gov/mostwant/terrorists/fugitives.htm.

18 See http://abcnews.go.com/sections/us/DailyNews/STRIKE_Casualties.html; and *New York Times*, February 9, 2002, p. A7.

19 By comparison, 35 of 148 U.S. troops killed in action in the Gulf War were hit by U.S. fire, with 11 killed by accidental U.S air strikes; and of 467 U.S military personnel wounded, 72 were hit by friendly fire.

20 See   http://www.media-alliance.org/mediafile/20-5/dossier/herold12-6.html. On the difficulty of assessing civilian casualties in Afghanistan, see http://www.washingtonpost.com/ac2/wp-dyn?pagename=article&node=&contentId=A59457-2002Jan3   and   http://www.arizonarepublic.com/news/articles/0125attacks-civilian25.html. More recently, the Project on Defense Alternatives, using mainly media sources, has put the number of Afghanistan civilian casualties between 1,000 and 1,300. See "Uncertain Toll in the Fog of War: Civilian Deaths in Afghanistan," *New York Times*, February 10, 2002, p. A1.

21 Kelly, p. 31.

22 Jean Baudrillard, *Simulacra and Simulation*, trans. Sheila Glaser (Ann Arbor, MI: 1994), p. 159.

23 *ABC Sunday News*, September 30, 2001.

24 See   http://www.defenselink.mil/news/Sep2001/t09252001_t0925sd.html.

25 See   http://www.washingtonpost.com/wp-srv/nation/specials/attacked/transcripts/bushtext_092601.html.

26 See *New York Times*, September 22, 2001 (http://query.nytimes.com/search/abstract?res=FA091FF6355F0C718EDDA00894D9404482).

27 See   http://www.whitehouse.gov/news/releases/2001/10/20011007-8.html.

28 See   http://www.cnn.com/2002/U.S./01/31/gen.binladen.interview/index.html.

29 *OED*.

30 See   http://www.eff.org/Privacy/Surveillance/Terrorism_militias/20011025_hr3162_usa_patriot_bill.html.

31 In a videotape interview with the Arabic cable network, al-Jazeera (which they never aired but was partially seen January 31 on CNN), bin Laden displayed his affinity for information technology while scoffing at the White House "request" that American television networks not broadcast his statements:

> They made hilarious claims. They said that Osama's messages have codes in them to the terrorists. It's as if we were living in the time of mail by carrier pigeon, when there are no phones, no travelers, no Internet, no regular mail, no express mail and no electronic mail.

See   http://www.washingtonpost.com/wp-dyn/articles/A5371-2002Jan31.html.

32 See *Washington Post*, September 26, 2001 (http://www.variety.com/index.asp?layout=story&articleid=VR1117854476&categoryid=10&query=H%27wood+enlists+in+war).

33 Disclaimer: I provided the information to them. See http://www.msnbc.com/news/642434.asp.
34 See my account of the opening of the Institute of Creative Technologies in Chapter 7.
35 See http://www.variety.com/index.asp?layout=story&articleid=VR1117853841&categoryid=10&query=Institute+for+Creative+Technology).
36 See my interview with Cebrowski in Chapter 6.
37 See http://www.defenselink.mil/news/Dec2001/b12132001_bt630-01.html.
38 Paul Virilio, *The Information Bomb*, trans. Chris Turner (London and New York: Verso, 2000), p. 132.
39 C. Wright Mills, *The Power Elite* (New York: Oxford University Press, 1957), pp. 314–315.

11 Global media in an age of InfoTerror

1 Based on techniques first developed in the 1870s by the founder of eugenics, Francis Galton, in which photographs of criminals were superimposed into a "natural kind," Burson's digitalized images of the 1980s subverted the notion of ideal and racial types, including "Beauty" (a composite of Hollywood starlets Jane Fonda, Brooke Shields, Meryl Streep, Diane Keaton, and Jacqueline Bisset) and "Mankind" (a proportional composite of Asian, African, Caucasian, and other races).
2 See Patrick Tyler, *New York Times*, February 17, 1992, p. A8.
3 The actual numbers in both cases are controversial. The most commonly accepted shift over the last 100 years in the killing ratio is of one civilian killed per eight soldiers, to a current ratio of eight civilians per soldier killed (see Mary Kaldor, *New Wars*). Rather than suggest a single authoritative figure, I would recommend the Project on Defense Alternatives as being the most credible source and collator of debates on civilian casualty counts in the Afghanistan and Iraq conflicts (http://www.comw.org/pda/index.html).
4 See Paul Virilio, *The Information Bomb* (London and New York: Verso, 2000).
5 Kevin Kelly, *New Rules for the New Economy* (London: Fourth Estate, 1999), p. 31.
6 One need only go back to the debates of the early 1980s over a New World Information and Communication Order, which lead to the UNESCO MacBride Commission for a more equitable global media —and to the U.S. pulling out of UNESCO in 1985. There has not been any serious multilateral effort since to redress this ongoing problem.
7 See *Philosophy in a Time of Terror: Dialogues with Jurgen Habermas and Jacques Derrida*, ed. Giovanna Borradori (Chicago, IL and London: University of Chicago Press, 2003), pp. 85–90.

8　See Paul Virilio, *The Aesthetics of Disappearance*, trans. Philip Beitchman (New York: Semiotext(e), 1991), and James Der Derian, "Introduction," *The Paul Virilio Reader* (Oxford: Blackwell Publishers, 1998), pp. 1–15.

9　However, this hope must be tempered by the fact that information only truly and globally registers when picked up by a major cable or primetime network; and as ownership of those networks shrinks to a handful of large conglomerates, the catalytic power of blogs and other independent news outlets diminishes.

10　A more recent and even more remarkable example was Ayatollah Nasrallah's video appearances on Al-Manar, the Hezbollah-owned satellite TV channel. Early during the Israeli intervention into Lebanon he gave a long speech, punctuated by the announcement of a successful missile strike on an Israeli destroyer: images of the burning ship followed. Americans could watch it all, uninterrupted, on CSPANN.

11　Michel Foucault, "On Popular Justice: A Discussion with Maoists," *Power/Knowledge: Selected Interviews and other Writings 1972–1977*, ed. Colin Gordon (Brighton, Sussex: Harvester Press, 1980), pp. 1–36. His Maoist interlocutors found his concept of counter-justice "completely idealist," a charge that could well be leveled against my four counter-strategies. I would also adhere to Foucault's response: obviously counter-powers are needed to implement the strategies, but one must be aware of how those very powers are enabled by the performative, even if highly idealistic and ritualized, function of the concepts.

12　This was acutely confirmed two years later when a senior advisor in the Bush administration came clean to Ron Suskind, writing in a *New York Times Sunday Magazine* feature:

> The aide said that guys like me were "in what we call the reality-based community," which he defined as people who "believe that solutions emerge from your judicious study of discernible reality." I nodded and murmured something about enlightenment principles and empiricism. He cut me off. "That's not the way the world really works anymore," he continued. "We're an empire now, and when we act, we create our own reality. And while you're studying that reality—judiciously, as you will—we'll act again, creating other new realities, which you can study too, and that's how things will sort out. We're history's actors . . . and you, all of you, will be left to just study what we do."

Perhaps it *is* time to be an *in*judicious student of the new virtual realities of world politics. See Ron Suskind, "Without a Doubt," *New York Times Sunday Magazine*, October 17, 2004, http://www.nytimes.com/2004/10/17/magazine/17BU.S.H.html?adxnnl=1&adxnnlx=1110053172-nwfUWTatdh70umpUzIod5Q.

13 I wish to thank Annick Wibben and Solon Barocas for their early assistance in formulating the concept of "infopeace" for the Info-TechWarPeace Project (see www.infopeace.org).

14 Gregory Bateson, *Steps to an Ecology of Mind* (Chicago: University of Chicago Press, 2000), p. 459.

15 Timothy Garton Ash, "The Revolution of the Magic Lantern," *New York Review of Books*, January 18, 1990, p. 42.

16 It also served as the ideological blueprint for the Iraq War that soon followed.

17 *The National Security Strategy of the United States of America* (September, 2002), p. 1, www.whitehouse.gov/nsc/nss.html.

18 Ibid.

19 *NSS*, p. 3.

20 Ibid.

21 *National Security Strategy of the United States 1994–1995: Engagement and Enlargement* (Washington and London: Brassy's, 1995).

22 See pp. ix and 37 [original edition].

23 *NSS*, p. 5.

24 Ibid.

25 Ibid.

26 *NSS*., p. 7.

27 *NSS*, p. 13.

28 Ibid.

29 *NSS*, p. 15.

30 *NSS*, p. 16.

31 *NSS*, p. 29.

32 Ibid.

33 With the war in Iraq, the global effects of media became inescapable. We witnessed how anti-war organizers used the Internet globally to muster millions of protesters in large metropolitan areas; U.S. military commanders leveraged technological superiority to wage network-centric warfare; and embedded journalists provided influential battlefield reports by satellite videophones in realtime. A glut of information (if a dearth of knowledge) drew viewers by the millions, not only to primetime TV and cable news, but also to instantly updated online press sites and unofficial war blogs. We witnessed the first, but certainly not the last, networked war.

34 This was born out at the December 2003 World Summit on the Information Society recently held in Geneva, at which the techno-optimists, vamping the political, cultural, and developmental promise of technological interconnectivity, had center stage while critics—especially American ones—were marginalized and kept out of the main planning sessions.

35 Hannah Arendt, interview http://www.radioopensource.org/hannah-arendt-and-the-banality-of-evil.

12 The desert of the real and the simulacra of war

1 The first "Internal Look" exercise was developed after it was learned that Iraq was using a software program supplied by an American engineering company to run computer simulations and war games for the invasion of Kuwait. General Schwarzkopf responded by preparing his own war game, and in July 1990 at U.S. Central Command in Tampa, Florida, command post exercise "Internal Look '90" was run. According to a Central Command news release issued at the time, "command and control elements from all branches of the military will be responding to real-world scenarios similar to those they might be expected to confront within the Central Command AOR." Iraq invaded Kuwait while the exercise was still running, and Schwarzkopf recounts in his memoirs how Central Command often confused communications from the real invasion with the simulated event.

2 See Chapter 2, "Between Wars" for the views and influence of Andrew Marshall; see Chapter 6, "Virtuous Wars" for an interview with then Vice Admiral Cebrowski, President of the Naval War College, who would go on to be picked by Rumsfeld in November 2001 to head the Pentagon's new Office of Force Transformation (which was pretty much closed down after Cebrowski's death in 2005 and Rumsfeld's departure from the DOD in 2006).

3 Some experts neatly map these differences along lines dividing the missions of the armed services, with the stand-off, high-tech Air Force and Navy naturally filling the transformationist camp, and the boots-on-the-ground Army and the Marines in the neotraditionalist. However, if one takes a longer view the dichotomy is not quite so hard and fast, as I witnessed from the very start of my investigations at the Advanced Warfighting Exercises in 1994, after which the Army put a considerable amount of eggs into the RMA basket for the Future Combat Systems (to the tune of $200 million and now up to $3 billion)—a program that had as an early advocate, General Shinseki. Also, in the discrete interests of the various armed services the RMA were often trumped by the elevated status of "Jointness" in the Pentagon, as demonstrated by Joint Vision 2010 and other early attempt to transform all the military services as a top-down, doctrinal imperative.

4 See John A. Nagl, *Learning to Eat Soup with a Knife: Counterinsurgency Lessons from Malaya and Vietnam* (2005); *The U.S. Army and Marine Corps Counterinsurgency Field Manual* (2007); *A Short Guide to Iraq* (1943); and *Small Wars Manual* (1940).

5 Ibid.

6 A subsequent investigation revealed that NATO forces had in fact a "non-target" map on which the embassy was correctly located, and clearly marked as "don't hit." Less well-known is that after alliance fighter planes took out Milosevic's own transmitters, the Chinese

embassy became a rebroadcast station for the Yugoslav army, making it fair-game for those who were mapping electro-magnetic as opposed to geo-spatial terrain.

7 Walter Benjamin, "The Work of Art in the Age of Its Technological Reproducibility," Second Version, *The Work of Art in the Age of Its Technological Reproducibility and Other Writings on Media*, eds. Michael W. Jennins, Bridgid Doherty, and Thomas Y. Levin (Cambridge, MA: Belknap Press, 2008), p. 41.

8 Jean Baudrillard, *Simulacra and Simulation* (Ann Arbor, MI: University of Michigan Press, 1994), p. 1.

9 See Jim Dwyer, "A Nation at War: A Gulf Commander Sees a Longer Road", *New York Times*, March 23, 2003, p. A1.

10 See Chapter 10.

11 General Franks' original statement was from a March 2002 news conference held at Bagram Air Base in Afghanistan. On the controversy over the "Tommy Franks doctrine" of civilian casualty statistics, see http://blog.washingtonpost.com/fact-checker/2007/10/counting_civilian_deaths_in_ir.html.

12 See John C. Broder, "A Nation at War: The Casualties; U.S. Military Has No Count Of Iraqi Dead In Fighting," *New York Times*, April 2, 2003.

13 See http://en.wikipedia.org/wiki/Millennium_Challenge_2002.

14 In its various evolutions, from training cultural sensitivity to cultural awareness to cultural competence, the program came under criticism within and outside the military. Most of the early criticism focused on the primitive, "orientalist" versions of culture being promulgated by the program. Ironically, the army and Marine response—to reach out to academics for assistance, especially to anthropologists, sociologists and political science—engendered an even greater furor. The centerpiece of these programs, the Human Terrain System, was created in 2006 with an initial budget of $40 million. To fulfill its mission statement, "to provide commanders in the field with relevant socio-cultural understanding necessary to meet their operational requirements," nine-person teams composed of social scientists, regional experts, and research analysts were formed and assigned to Iraq and Afghanistan. Within a year the HTS program would be at the center of an ongoing controversy between the military and the academy, as to whether it was appropriate, for moral or practical reasons, for social scientists to contribute their expertise to the counterinsurgency effort. With my colleagues Keith Brown and Catherine Lutz, two Anthropology professors at the Watson Institute, we co-founded the Cultural Awareness in the Military Project, to research and engage the issues raised by the new military programs. For more information see http://www.watsoninstitute.org/project_detail.cfm?id=71. Professors Brown and Lutz have written extensively on the topic in a various anthropology journals; and, in association with

the Global Media Project and Udris Productions, I have completed a documentary on the topic, *Cultural Warriors*. For a comprehensive and balanced account of the controversy, see the article written by David Glenn in the *Chronicle of Higher Education* (http://chronicle.com).

Index

In this index published works appear in italics. Notes are indicated by n.; illustrations by ill.